CALL OF DUTY GHOSTS

SPECIALIZED TRAINING

You've answered the call; now it's time to get you ready. This chapter is specifically designed for novice first-person shooter and *Call of Duty* players. However, it also covers some of the differences between *Call of Duty: Ghosts* and prior installments in the franchise, as well as the types of weapons that you can find in the campaign. It's worth a skim even for veterans.

THE BASICS

DISCHARGING YOUR WEAPON

Call of Duty: Ghosts is called a first-person shooter for a reason: most of the action takes place from the protagonist's perspective while firing a weapon. There are two different ways you can fire your weapon:

Aim Down Sight (ADS): Refers to when you press and hold a button to look down your weapon's sights. Aim Down Sight increases the accuracy of your weapon and makes it easier to aim at your enemy, but it dramatically slows down how quickly you can move. Additionally, bigger, heavier weapons take longer to enter and exit ADS mode.

Hipfire: Refers to firing a weapon without using Aim Down Sight. Hipfire is dramatically less accurate than using ADS, but it does not restrict movement. Use Hipfire when an enemy is at point-blank range.

Aim Assist: A menu option that makes Aim Down Sight more accurate. When Aim Assist is on, activating ADS causes the weapon to snap to a nearby enemy. Many advanced players prefer to play without Aim Assist enabled.

THE INTERACT BUTTON

Throughout the game, one of the most useful buttons is the **Interact** button. You can use this button to complete a variety of actions, including hacking computers, cutting a hole in glass, or setting an explosive.

Whenever you see a yellow glowing object, this usually means you must hit the **Interact** button to advance the story. If you aren't sure what to do next, try checking your Objectives in the Pause menu and looking around for a glowing object.

STANCES

In the field, there are three stances a player can adopt: standing, crouching, or prone. You can cycle through these stances by using the **Jump** and **Crouch** buttons (on PC, there is an additional **Prone** button that takes you straight to that position).

Crouching and prone both increase your firing accuracy, but they restrict how quickly you can move. Crouched players move at about half speed, and prone players move along at a crawl.

Additionally, you need room in the surrounding environment to go prone. If the game tells you that you can't go prone where you are standing, that means you should find a more open area.

Besides making your shots more accurate, going prone and crouching also makes you harder to hit. Whenever you take some damage, you should go prone behind cover to regenerate your health before returning to battle.

MELEE

There are two uses for melee attacks. If an enemy accidentally gets too close to you, the quickest way to down him is to use a melee attack. Melee attacks are always one-hit kills.

Melee attacks are also silent kills, so there are a few stealth sequences in the game where you can use your knife to execute a perfectly silent kill.

Be aware that if you melee an enemy while in view of other opponents, it opens you to attack for as long as the melee animation is playing. As such, it's a good idea to avoid melee attacks outside of emergencies or stealth scenarios.

GRENADES

The *Call of Duty: Ghosts* campaign has two kinds of grenades: Tactical and Frag.

Tactical grenades include Flashbangs, Tear Gas, and Smoke Bombs that you can use to stun your enemies or provide cover. These are particularly useful against adversaries behind cover, as these grenades let you advance on your foes, or pick them off when they come stumbling out.

Frag grenades are explosive grenades that can kill an enemy outright. They are also useful for forcing an opponent out from cover. Enemies in Call of Duty: Ghosts are smart, and they won't just stand on top of a ticking grenade. Instead, they run in an attempt to find different cover. This gives you an opportunity to pick them off safely.

Additionally, Frag grenades can be "cooked." To cook a grenade, hold down the Frag Grenade button. A red set of dots appears in the middle of the screen. This is a counter for your grenade, and when the four red dots fill up, the grenade detonates. Cook the grenade until there are three red dots, then release it to have a better chance of killing an enemy outright with the explosive.

If an enemy throws a grenade at you, an indicator on-screen illustrates in which direction the grenade is rolling. When you see this indicator, you have two choices: run, or throw it back.

If you think you have enough time to throw a grenade back, run toward the grenade. When you are close enough, you will see a grenade throwback indicator. Press the **Frag Grenade** button to toss it back at the enemy.

TAKING STOCK — YOUR INVENTORY

In the single-player campaign, you can always carry two weapons. The **Switch Weapons** button allows you to toggle between your two active weapons. When you first pull a weapon out, its name appears on the bottom-right corner of the screen. The weapon's current clip level and the ammo stock you have for the weapon are displayed next to the name.

Just above the weapon ammunition indicator is your grenade count. You can see both your Tactical and Frag grenade supply. There's also an indicator that shows your current stance in the same area.

After you kill an enemy, they drop the weapon they were holding. You can pick up the weapon by walking over to it and pressing the **Interact** button.

SPECIALIZED TRAINING THE CAMPAIGN MP INTRO & BASIC TRAINING SQUADS MP ARMORY PERKS KILLSTREAKS MP MAPS MP GAME MODES SAFEGUARD EXTINCTION CLASSIFIED ACHIEVEMENTS & TROPHIES

3

BREACHING

When your team knows there's a large group of enemies on the other side of a door, they usually set up a Breach. When a Breach is set, your character must either place a charge with the **Interact** button, or move toward a door. When the Breach blows, the game enters slow motion.

While in slow motion, you need to take down any enemies you see before they start firing at you and your team. If you miss a shot, you may get killed instantly.

It's very important to make sure your weapon is reloaded before you start a Breach. Additionally, use a lightweight weapon so that you can enter ADS quicker and start firing accurately at your foes.

TACTICAL EQUIPMENT

In several levels in the campaign, you gain access to special Tactical equipment that you can use to activate a laptop, detonate an explosive, or even take the controls of your air support.

Each type of Tactical equipment operates differently. Luckily, there are in-game tutorials whenever you operate equipment for the first time. Additionally, this guide provides specific hints on the best way to utilize the equipment in the campaign walkthrough.

MEDIC! TAKING DAMAGE

Even the best *Call of Duty* players are going to get shot once in a while. Unlike real life, if you are shot in the game, it has no lasting repercussions. Even on the hardest difficulty, you can still take two or three shots before getting killed.

When you are shot, your screen becomes bloodied. However, you start regenerating health shortly, as long as you are not hit again by another bullet. If you are shot too many times, your character dies, and you must restart from the last automatically saved checkpoint.

In addition to your health indicator, you also see a bloody smear whenever you are shot in the game. This smear indicates the direction you were shot from, making it easier to find where an opponent is targeting you. Learn to interpret these smears, and quickly react by turning toward your enemy. Even blind firing in their direction may force them into cover.

CHECKPOINTS

The game automatically saves your progress whenever you clear a significant hurdle in the single-player campaign.

If you quit the game and then come back to play later, be sure to hit "Resume Game." If you select the last mission played with the Chapter Select option, you lose your checkpoint progress and must start the chapter from the beginning.

The game also features a "Last Checkpoint" option in the Pause menu. Use this to immediately restart from the last saved checkpoint. This is useful if you are going for a particularly hard Achievement, or if you missed something and want to try again.

GAME DIFFICULTY

There are four game difficulties in all *Call of Duty* games. The harder the game is, the more accurate and deadly your enemies are. Additionally, you can take less damage before dying, and some of the mini-games are more difficult.

Recruit is for players who want to focus more on the story than the action. Though you rarely get killed in normal gun combat, you still need to watch out for enemy melee attacks and grenades (both of which can kill you instantly).

Normal is for novice players who want a challenge. You need to employ good tactics to survive some of the bigger gunfights, but you won't get too frustrated from constantly dying.

Hardened is designed to challenge veterans of first-person shooters, but even the best players will run into a few combat actions that give them pause. If you've played more than a couple of *Call of Duty* games before, you should choose this difficulty.

Veteran is the ultimate challenge. Enemies can cut you down with one or two shots and have insane accuracy. Veteran is for players who crave achievements, or those who just want to experience the toughest Infinity Ward has got.

If you find a difficulty to be too hard, you can lower it in the Pause menu at any time. For this reason, you should challenge yourself with the hardest difficulty you think you're up to. If you get too frustrated, you can always lower it later.

FIELD STRATEGY

This guide covers strategy for dozens of specific scenarios in the campaign walkthrough. However, you should utilize the following advice throughout the campaign in every firefight. It can help you succeed in even the most difficult combat scenarios.

USE COVER

Always, always, always find cover when engaging enemies. Use crouch and prone stances to get behind short cover, or lean out from the side while standing in large cover. Cover can be blown-out cars, rubble, or concrete barriers. Whatever it is, it's better than standing out in the open.

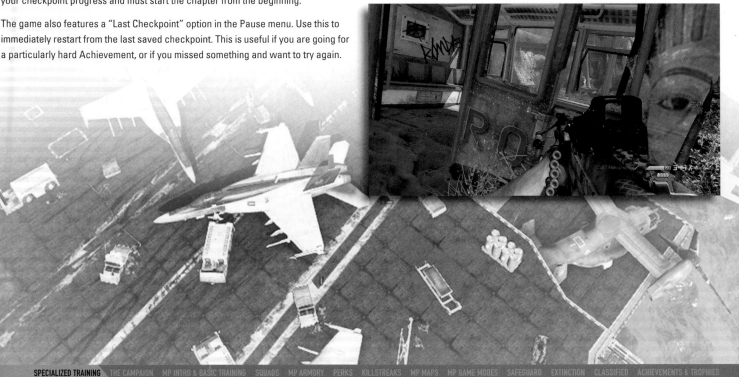

SPECIALIZED TRAINING   THE CAMPAIGN   MP INTRO & BASIC TRAINING   SQUADS   MP ARMORY   PERKS   KILLSTREAKS   MP MAPS   MP GAME MODES   SAFEGUARD   EXTINCTION   CLASSIFIED   ACHIEVEMENTS & TROPHIES

5

WEAPON PENETRATION

One warning about cover: wood and thin metal won't stop bullets. Your enemies rarely take advantage of this fact, but you should capitalize on it. Whenever an adversary takes cover behind a flimsy item, just shoot them directly through the cover. Provided you have a powerful enough weapon (light machine guns or assault rifles both have good penetration), you can kill them even from behind cover.

WATCH YOUR AMMO

The sound of a dry-click on your current ammo clip can spell out a quick death. As such, it's always a good idea to keep an eye on your ammo level. Eventually, you'll be able to keep track of how much ammo you have left in your clip by memorization.

Whenever you are at less than half a clip, think about reloading. Look for some safe cover and a good opening before you start the reload. Depending on the weapon, reloading can take quite a bit of time.

STAY CROUCHED IN COMBAT

Crouching doesn't restrict your movement too much in combat, but it dramatically increases your accuracy and ability to avoid incoming fire from cover. It's good to get into a habit of always crouching when you enter combat.

FIRE IN BURSTS

Just because a weapon is fully automatic does not mean you should just hold down the trigger when attacking an enemy. Firing in bursts extends the time between reload and also increases your accuracy, making your shots more deadly.

GO FOR CRITICAL SHOTS

Always aim for the upper half of your enemies' bodies. Headshots are best, but they can be difficult to nail in combat. Instead, just focus on hitting your opponents' torsos. Adversaries who are hit above the belt take significantly more damage and go down fast.

COOK YOUR GRENADES!

To actually score a kill on an enemy with a grenade, it's imperative that you cook your Frag grenades before you toss them. Your challengers are good at evading a tossed grenade, so don't give them the opportunity. Try to time your cooks so that the grenade explodes exactly when it hits the ground.

SUBTITLES

Consider turning in-game subtitles on in the Options menu. This can help you hear your teammates' instructions in the middle of a heated firefight.

CAMPAIGN WEAPONS ARSENAL

There are several classes of weaponry in *Call of Duty: Ghosts*. Everyone has a favorite weapon, but in the campaign, the weapons you can use are limited by what's available. As such, it's a good idea to familiarize yourself with the strengths and weakness of all the weapon classes.

HANDGUNS

Handguns are generally not as effective as the other weapon types. They are good at short to medium range, but they're somewhat ineffective at long range. The advantage of a pistol is that you can switch to it and run with it faster than other weapon types.

You start a few campaign missions with a handgun, but it's best to immediately switch it out for one of the weapons you find on enemy bodies or in arsenals.

M9A1

This is the standard U.S. pistol issue, and you begin many missions with it.

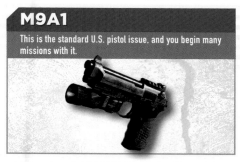

MP-443

Fast fire rate, decent damage.

P226

Decent damage, and better range than the M9A1.

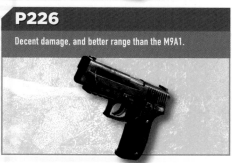

.44 MAGNUM

You only get access to this in special sequences. The Magnum is an extremely powerful pistol that can cut through multiple enemies.

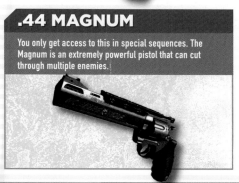

ASSAULT RIFLES

Assault rifles (or ARs) are the primary weapons in the campaign. Assault weapons are good at medium and long range, and you can even hipfire them at short range in a pinch. They also have excellent damage when balanced with their rate of fire and accuracy. Even if you miss an enemy's head, two or three shots to their upper torso almost always kills them. Generally, you always want to have an assault rifle as one of your two weapons.

SC-2010

A Ghost favorite, the SC-2010 is an excellent long-range assault rifle. Coupled with a good scope, it's ideal for picking off enemies before they're even aware of your presence.

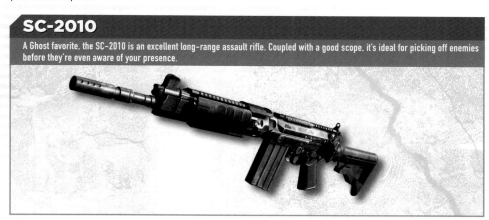

SA-805

The SA-805 has moderate damage, but good range and accuracy.

AK-12

A Federation assault rifle, the AK-12 has good damage and high accuracy. A good pickup if found on an enemy.

SPECIALIZED TRAINING   THE CAMPAIGN   MP INTRO & BASIC TRAINING   SQUADS   MP ARMORY   PERKS   KILLSTREAKS   MP MAPS   MP GAME MODES   SAFEGUARD   EXTINCTION   CLASSIFIED   ACHIEVEMENTS & TROPHIES

7

ASSAULT RIFLES (CONTINUED)

FAD

Commonly found on Federation troops. The FAD is an average assault rifle with moderate damage, accuracy, and range, but a good fire rate.

ARX-160

This is the weapon you use in zero gravity during the campaign.

REMINGTON R5

Slow fire rate, but high damage and excellent range.

MSBS

The MSBS fires three-round bursts that make it very accurate, but it has relatively low damage.

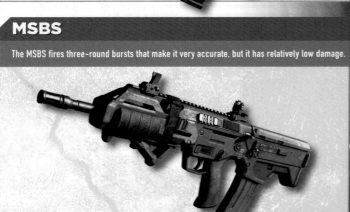

HONEY BADGER

The Ghosts' default assault rifle. Quick fire rate, good silencer, good damage, poor range.

SUBMACHINE GUNS

Submachine guns (or SMGs) are designed for close-combat fighting. In a pinch, you can use them at medium to long range with a decent scope, but generally, you should use them at short range with either hipfire or ADS.

You find more SMGs than shotguns in the campaign, and they are a good choice for a short-range weapon when coupled with a longer-range rifle.

BIZON

The Bizon is the preferred Federation SMG. It can feel weak compared to the assault rifles, but if you fire it in targeted bursts, it can be extremely deadly.

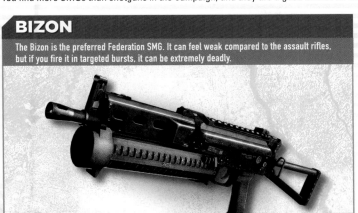

VEPR

The Vepr has low recoil and high ammo capacity, but it has low damage and performs slightly below average in combat.

CBJ-MS

A good hipfire weapon, the CBJ has the highest rate of fire of the SMGs. Can be useful as a "spray and pray" weapon, but you need a lot of ammo because the gun blows through it.

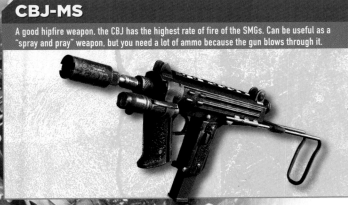

K7

The K7 is a typical "spray and pray" type of SMG. Fire it in short bursts to cut through enemies, but don't count on using it beyond short range.

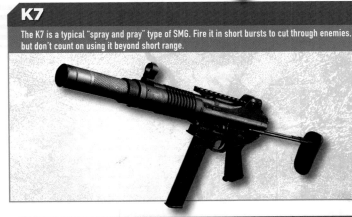

VECTOR CRB

The Vector is a high-damage SMG that has a slower rate of fire. It's good with a red dot scope for tackling enemies at medium range.

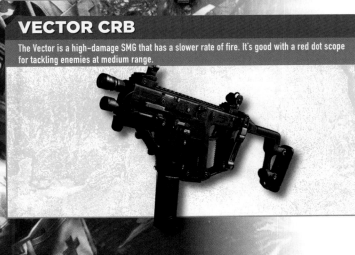

MTAR-X

The MTAR-X has excellent range for an SMG and performs like an assault rifle. Commonly used by Federation forces, it's a good pickup if you loot one from a corpse.

LIGHT MACHINE GUNS

Don't let the word "light" fool you: light machine guns (or LMGs) are heavy weapons that are designed for stationary combat. LMGs have large clip sizes and inflict very heavy damage.

You can use LMGs at all ranges, but because of how long it takes to reload them and their slow speed, they are not recommended at short range.

AMELI

A slow-firing LMG, the slower rate of fire means fewer ammo clips to burn through and more rounds on target. Classed as an LMG, but performs more like an assault rifle.

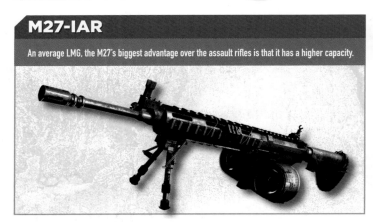

LSAT

This is the Federation standard-issue LMG, so you will find many in the campaign. You should always grab this gun if you find it, as it has superior range and extremely high damage. Hundred-round clips don't hurt, either.

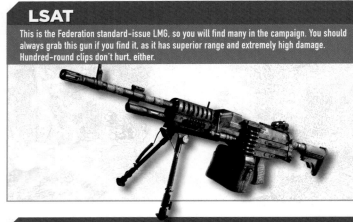

M27-IAR

An average LMG, the M27's biggest advantage over the assault rifles is that it has a higher capacity.

CHAIN SAW

The Chain SAW is the U.S. LMG. It has very high accuracy and beats the LSAT in most performance metrics. However, it's much more rare.

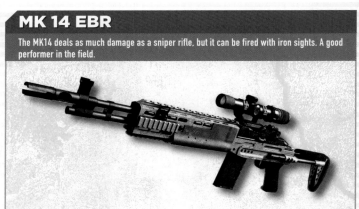

MARKSMAN RIFLES

Marksman rifles are unscoped semi-automatic (meaning one shot per trigger pull) weapons. Even without the sniper scope, marksman rifles have excellent range and are very good at scoring critical hits.

MR-28

The M28 couples extreme range with extreme accuracy. It works best when equipped with a long-range scope like the ACOG or Holographic types.

MK 14 EBR

The MK14 deals as much damage as a sniper rifle, but it can be fired with iron sights. A good performer in the field.

SNIPER RIFLES

Sniper rifles are the longest-range weapons in the game. You can pick enemies off from complete safety. The disadvantage is that they are slow to fire and completely useless at short range.

LYNX

The Lynx is a powerful sniper rifle that can kill most enemies, even if you don't nail a headshot.

L115

The lower damage L115 is a decent pick if you are a fan of sniper rifles, but otherwise, it's better to stick with the other long-range weapons like ARs and LMGs.

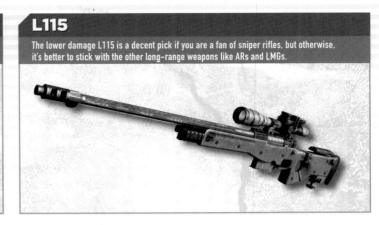

SHOTGUNS

Like SMGs, shotguns are designed for close-quarters combat. Unlike SMGs, shotguns are only effective at short range. Their damage falls off quickly as an enemy approaches middle range. However, shotguns compensate for that by being incredibly easy to aim. As long as you are facing directly toward an opponent, you can hit them with a shotgun blast. You should generally not use ADS while firing a shotgun.

BULLDOG

The Bulldog has a funny reload method, but don't let that deter you from using it in close quarters. It's a one-hit kill in range, but unfortunately, the range is extremely short.

MTS-225

The MTS also has a really interesting reload animation. It outputs even more damage than the Bulldog and has slightly better range.

ABOUT THE WALKTHROUGH

The walkthrough was written while playing the game on Hardened difficulty. This means that if you are playing the game on another difficulty setting, you may see different numbers of enemies or have a slightly varied strategy experience.

In addition to in-depth combat strategy, each chapter of the walkthrough outlines how to earn the Achievements and where the level's Rorke File is located.

While experienced players may not need the play-by-play combat strategy, it's not a bad idea to read through the chapter to prepare for what you have ahead of you. The guide avoids explicit story spoilers, but it does discuss the events that occur on each mission.

SPECIALIZED TRAINING   THE CAMPAIGN   MP INTRO & BASIC TRAINING   SQUADS   MP ARMORY   PERKS   KILLSTREAKS   MP MAPS   MP GAME MODES   SAFEGUARD   EXTINCTION   CLASSIFIED   ACHIEVEMENTS & TROPHIES

11

WALKER HOUSE

START

LOGAN WALKER

"Oh, a Little Tremor There."

Through most of *Call of Duty: Ghosts*, you play as Logan Walker. The game starts with you controlling Logan during a conversation with his brother, Hesh, and his father, Elias.

After the talk, follow Hesh up the forest trail. Take some time to get your bearings on the basic controls. If you need to invert the camera or adjust the movement and look sensitivity, now is the time to do it.

HESH WALKER   ELIAS WALKER

"Odin, It's Odin!"

When the second tremor hits, Elias realizes the heavy rumblings are more serious. Follow Hesh over the log (the **Jump** button allows you to climb over obstacles) and up the trail. When you emerge on the street, follow Hesh closely. Avoid walking into the street as several out-of-control cars barrel down from the hill.

Press the **Sprint** button to keep up with Elias. This definitely isn't an earthquake!

"What the Hell is Going On?!"

Elias takes a separate route from Hesh. Follow Hesh on the second mountain trail and charge up the back of the house. Hesh pulls you inside. After another tremor knocks you down, push forward to help Hesh burst through the door.

What's Odin? You're about to find out.

SPECIALIZED TRAINING   THE CAMPAIGN   MP INTRO & BASIC TRAINING   SQUADS   MP ARMORY   PERKS   KILLSTREAKS   MP MAPS   MP GAME MODES   SAFEGUARD   EXTINCTION   CLASSIFIED   ACHIEVEMENTS & TROPHIES

13

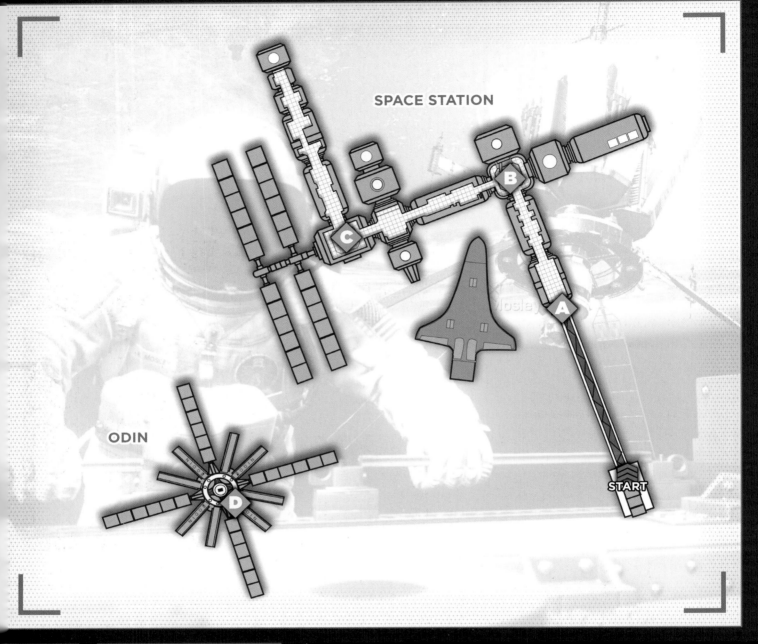

SPACE STATION

ODIN

START

A

B

C

D

OBJECTIVES

A Return to Odin control.

B Reach the Odin shutdown controls.

C Escape from the Space Station.

D Destroy the Odin Satellite.

A OBJECTIVE

RETURN TO ODIN CONTROL

Flashing back 15 minutes, you now control Specialist Baker, a U.S. Air Force operative at the top secret Odin station.

Space controls are slightly different than on Earth. Use the **Jump** or **Tactical Grenade** button to move your astronaut up, and use the **Crouch** or **Frag Grenade** button to move your astronaut down. While moving around, be careful not to move too far from the station—you fail the mission if you do.

Keep SPC Mosely in your view and follow her up to the Odin control airlock. Push forward into the airlock

"I'm Really Looking Forward to Going Home."

Follow Mosely through Airlock C. Inside, move toward the crew. There's nothing you can do to stop the surprise attack.

B OBJECTIVE

REACH THE ODIN SHUTDOWN CONTROLS

In moments, everything goes to hell. Somehow, the friendly shuttle contains enemy operatives with nefarious purposes. You must shut down Odin before they can use it.

Follow Mosely through the control station. When Mosely is attacked, the enemy operative's weapon is sent toward you. When you get the gun, aim the weapon at the attacker's face with the Look analog. When the gun is targeted, press the **Fire** button to finish the attacker.

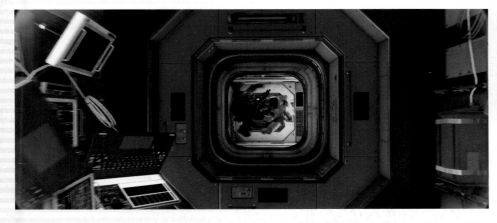

 SPATIAL AWARENESS

You earn this Achievement/Trophy once you kill the first enemy astronaut.

ACHIEVEMENT/TROPHY

"Houston, They're Federation. They've Broken the Truce."

Mosely IDs the attackers as members of the Federation.

KNOW YOUR ENEMY

In this section, you fight Federation astronauts. You can ID them by their distinctive tan suits. Your allies wear white or blue astronaut suits.

Their objective is likely to use Odin on U.S. cities. Shutting down Odin is now vital to the survival of the United States!

Follow Mosely through the passages. You now have a rifle equipped. Shoot the three Federation agents in the next chamber. Note that you don't need to get headshots to take down the agents—a shot anywhere on their suits is enough to kill them.

SPECIALIZED TRAINING **THE CAMPAIGN** MP INTRO & BASIC TRAINING   SQUADS   MP ARMORY   PERKS   KILLSTREAKS   MP MAPS   MP GAME MODES   SAFEGUARD   EXTINCTION   CLASSIFIED   ACHIEVEMENTS & TROPHIES

15

"Estimated Casualties, Over 27 Million."

Follow Mosely past the dead Federation soldiers. Odin unloads its first payload before you can disable the controls. Ground control is forced to destroy the station.

C OBJECTIVE

ESCAPE FROM THE SPACE STATION

Follow Mosely. You are both sucked out of the station into space near Odin.

D OBJECTIVE

DESTROY THE ODIN SATELLITE

Ignore the struggling Federation soldiers; your job now is to bring down Odin before it can hit more U.S. cities.

"I Don't Think We're Making It Home, Baker."

Follow Mosely up to Odin. You need to set it off 23 degrees left or right to stop its second payload from finding its target.

When you reach the satellite, hold the **Interact** button to open the RCS panel. Once the RCS is open, fire with your rifle. Keep firing even after you are blasted from the satellite.

Baker's last mission is a success. But sadly, there's no way for him to make it home.

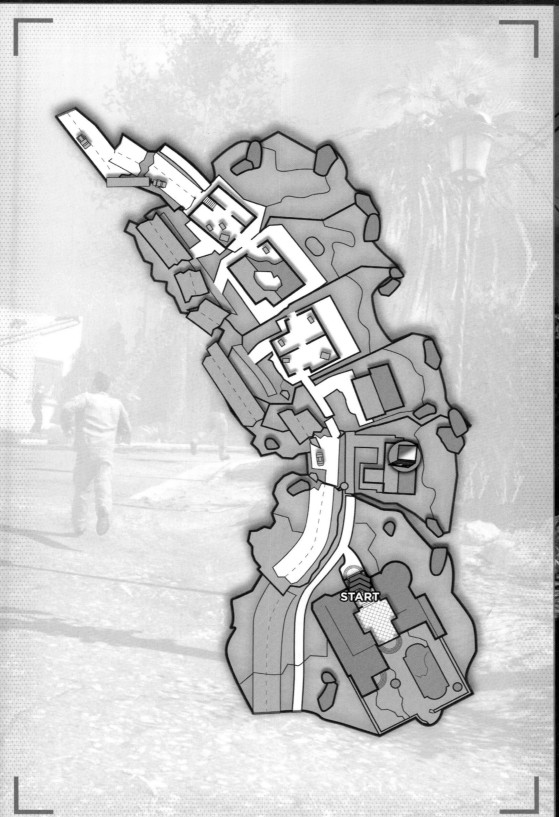

START

LANDSLIDE

Back on Earth, Logan and Hesh are in the middle of the Odin strike. The key to surviving the attack is to follow Hesh closely. Be careful of fissures as they open, and jump to clear them safely. Watch when Hesh jumps; it means you must follow with a jump of your own.

"Ghost Stories" Rorke File

Rorke Files are special computer collectibles that can be found on every level. This mission has one of the most difficult Rorke files to snag. When you regain control of Logan back on Earth, sprint after Hesh as normal.

When you pass the first house on the right, look for a dusty car in a driveway. Instead of following Hesh here, jump on top of the car, then jump through the open door. The briefcase is on the ground inside this second house.

If you get hit by a tremor, you may be forced to crouching position. When this happens, hit the **Jump** button to get back to standing so you can more easily move and jump.

HOUSE HUNTING

Carefully navigate through the sliding house. When you reach the other side, wait for Hesh to jump. Then follow him down. Avoid the obstacles and follow Hesh closely to escape safely.

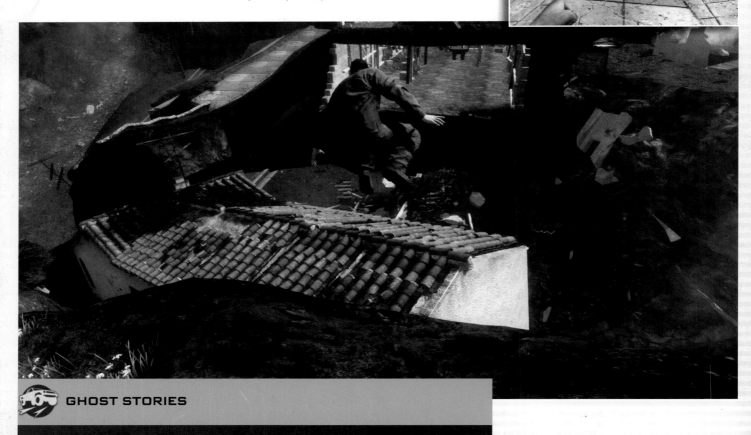

GHOST STORIES

Complete this mission on any difficulty to earn the Achievement/Trophy "Ghost Stories."

ACHIEVEMENT/TROPHY

02 BRAVE NEW WORLD

LOS ANGELES, CA | MISSION DETAILS: 10 YEARS LATER.

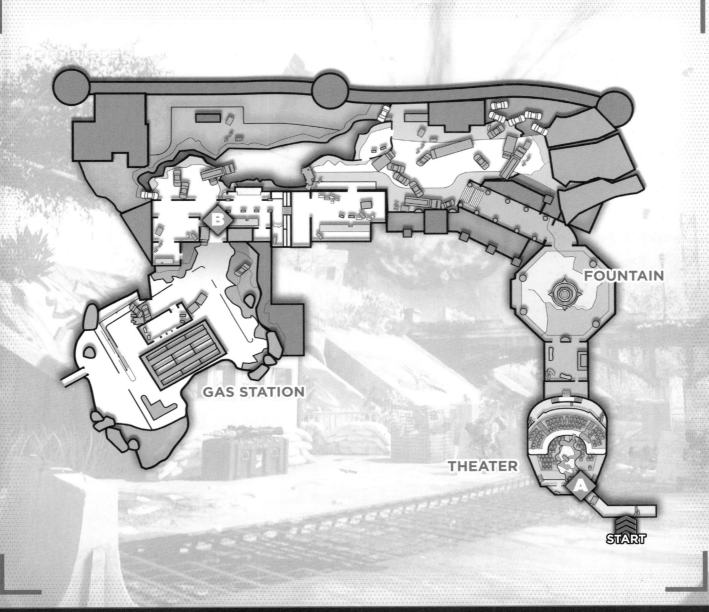

FOUNTAIN

GAS STATION

THEATER

A

START

OPERATIVE

LOGAN WALKER

SUPPORT

HESH WALKER

RILEY

OBJECTIVES

- **A** Finish security sweep with Hesh and Riley.
- **B** Meet with Team 2 at the wall.
- **C** Back up team at LA River checkpoint.
- **D** Take out enemy choppers with the MAAWS rocket launcher.
- **E** Get in the back of the MATV.
- **F** Report to Fort Santa Monica for mission briefing.
- **G** Report to Elias with Hesh.

LOADOUT

PRIMARY	SECONDARY
	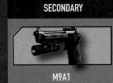
HONEY BADGER ACOG SIGHT	M9A1

GRENADES & EQUIPMENT

FRAG GRENADES

OBJECTIVE

FINISH SECURITY SWEEP WITH HESH AND RILEY

The second mission begins 10 years after the events of the first. You still control Logan, but now both Hesh and Logan are members of the military.

This is your first time meeting Riley, the brothers' faithful trained military dog. Riley smells something, and it's time for you to pick up your patrol. Follow Hesh and crouch through the debris to explore the building corridor.

"Through Here."

Hesh opens the way into an abandoned theater. Follow Hesh up the rubble heap into the theater lobby. Then move to the door on the right to spot what has Riley so excited.

"Guess Riley was Getting Hungry."

Exit the front of the theater and follow Hesh down the street.

OBJECTIVE

MEET WITH TEAM 2 AT THE WALL

Just ahead, you meet with Team 2—Private Moore and Corporal Davis.

Continue your patrol with Riley and Hesh by crossing the destroyed interstate. On the other side, Riley gets the scent of a real threat: Federation troops.

Enter the building on the left. Wait for Riley to attack. When he does, shoot the other troops nearby. Riley can take care of his target on his own.

The Federation troops in this mission wear gray camo and maroon berets or black helmets. It's easy to distinguish them from the beige uniforms your allies wear.

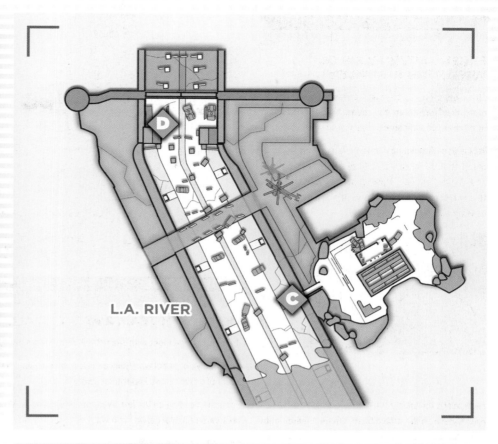

L.A. RIVER

Stay behind cover and wait for the Federation troops to appear and attack your position. About five soldiers are in this recon team. After you've killed them all, search the bodies to replace your pistol with one of the enemy SMGs.

Follow Hesh after he smashes the brick wall, and come to a building hole overlooking the area. This is Overwatch position; Team 2 will join you shortly.

The Federation is killing civilians! Crouch next to the ambulance, and open fire on the troops. There are several Federation soldiers in the gas station. A small group of reinforcements also arrives when you move down toward the gas station.

OBJECTIVE

BACK UP TEAM AT LA RIVER CHECKPOINT

When you've safely cleared the gas station, another team radios that they've encountered the Federation at the LA River. Follow Riley and Hesh through the tunnel into the dried-up river.

Battle of the LA River — **E** ENEMY

ROCKET LAUNCHER

FRIENDLIES (GREEN SMOKE)

SNIPER RIFLE

START

SPECIALIZED TRAINING **THE CAMPAIGN** MP INTRO & BASIC TRAINING SQUADS MP ARMORY PERKS KILLSTREAKS MP MAPS MP GAME MODES SAFEGUARD EXTINCTION CLASSIFIED ACHIEVEMENTS & TROPHIES

21

The Federation is assaulting the LA River checkpoint. The enemy is attacking from the bridge overhead as well as from the lower river basin. Before charging into the area, stay in cover and unload on the helicopter flying overhead. It takes several clips to shoot it down, but if you are successful, you can prevent a wave of reinforcements from landing.

With the bird down, stay crouched and move to the center Jersey barrier. There you can find a long-range rifle, the MK14 EBR. Focus on the troops in the basin. Hang back and pick off any troops that pop their heads out.

With the nearby troops clear, move to the smashed car where Hesh and Riley are positioned. Stay crouched behind the car and use your Honey Badger to pick off the Federation resistance.

Let your team move up while you hang back. Use the extended range of the ACOG scope to safely pick off the enemy from behind the smashed cars.

"Logan, Grab a Launcher, Take Care of the Birds. We'll Cover You!"

When you've cleared the basin, your allies pop green smoke on an overlook ahead. You now need to grab the rocket launcher and take down quickly-approaching helicopters.

The rocket launchers are available on both the left and right side of the river. One is in front of the small building at the river's left side. This launcher is the MAAWS guided rocket system.

TAKE OUT ENEMY CHOPPERS WITH THE MAAWS ROCKET LAUNCHER

When firing a rocket with the MAAWS, you must keep its laser sight on your target in order for the rockets to hit. The rockets are bound by physics, so they don't go directly to your target. They may need to loop around a few times to get close enough for a hit.

There are a few tricks to using the MAAWS successfully:

> Always fire two rockets at a time. This doubles your chances of hitting your target. There is unlimited rocket ammunition in front of the small building.

> Never point the laser at the ground or at something in front of you. This results in a danger-close missile that could very well kill you.

> Aim your rockets well above your intended target. This gives your rocket enough leeway to circle back and nail your target. If you aim directly at your target, it will likely require the missile to make too sharp of a turn, resulting in a miss.

When you get the MAAWS, your first target is a helicopter at the bridge you just crossed under. Turn around and immediately fire on the helicopter to down it before it can unload its troops.

Shortly after, an attack chopper arrives. The attack chopper has a deadly MG as well as rocket attacks. Stay in cover behind the MATV and the Jersey barrier until the attack chopper passes by. After its first pass, fire two rockets and try to guide them into the helicopter.

LIBERTY WALL
x2

You automatically earn this Achievement/Trophy if you take down both choppers with the MAAWS.

ACHIEVEMENT/TROPHY

If you miss, don't worry. Go back in cover and wait for it to circle around again. Never attempt to take down the chopper while it is facing you; it will kill you very quickly.

GET IN THE BACK OF THE MATV

With the chopper down, it's time to load up and move out. Press the **Interact** button to enter the back of the MATV.

REPORT TO FORT SANTA MONICA FOR MISSION BRIEFING

After a short trip through the LA River, you arrive at Fort Santa Monica.

REPORT TO ELIAS WITH HESH

When you unload, follow Hesh into the base to reunite with Elias. Elias leads the brothers to a briefing that ends the mission.

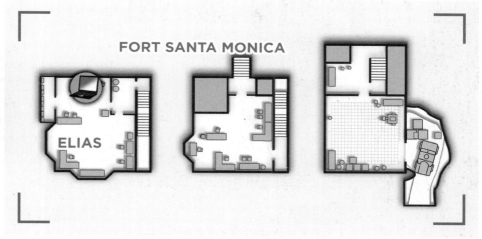

FORT SANTA MONICA

ELIAS

"Brave New World" Rorke File

The file is on a desk on the third floor of the building you meet Elias in. When Elias leads you upstairs, the briefcase is out in the open just to the right of Hesh.

BRAVE NEW WORLD

Complete this mission on any difficulty to earn the Achievement/Trophy "Brave New World."

ACHIEVEMENT/TROPHY

SPECIALIZED TRAINING **THE CAMPAIGN** MP INTRO & BASIC TRAINING SQUADS MP ARMORY PERKS KILLSTREAKS MP MAPS MP GAME MODES SAFEGUARD EXTINCTION CLASSIFIED ACHIEVEMENTS & TROPHIES

23

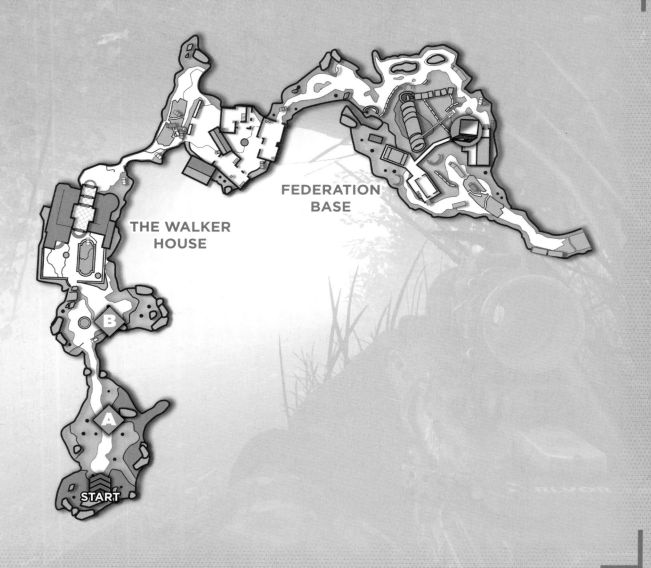

FEDERATION
BASE

THE WALKER
HOUSE

B

A

START

OPERATIVE

LOGAN WALKER

SUPPORT

HESH WALKER   RILEY

OBJECTIVE

A Gather intel
on Federation
activity in

MERRICK   KEEGAN

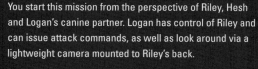

A **OBJECTIVE**

GATHER INTEL ON FEDERATION
ACTIVITY IN THE AREA

You start this mission from the perspective of Riley, Hesh
and Logan's canine partner. Logan has control of Riley and
can issue attack commands, as well as look around via a
lightweight camera mounted to Riley's back.

Wait for Hesh to issue the command, then hit the **Tactical
Equipment** button to tell Riley to attack. After issuing the command, control switches back to Logan. Help Riley

OPERATIVE

LOGAN WALKER

SUPPORT

HESH WALKER

RILEY

OBJECTIVES

B Meet up with the recon team.

C Reach Firebase Charlie.

LOADOUT

PRIMARY	SECONDARY

HONEY BADGER ACOG SIGHT	P226

B OBJECTIVE

MEET UP WITH THE RECON TEAM

With the recon group handled, your new objective is to locate the nearby recon team. Follow Hesh and Riley up the trail to the angelic statue fountain.

KNOW YOUR ENEMY

The Federation soldiers wear dark green camo in this mission.

"Welcome Home. What's Left of It, Anyway."

Hesh and Logan's pre-war home is just past the angel statue. This is the house that you saw during the Odin strike in the first mission.

Continue past the house and along the ledge overlooking the remains of San Diego. When Riley starts barking, stay in cover and approach him. Press **Use** near Riley to sync up with him again.

"Wherever You Want Him to Go, He'll Follow."

Now that you're back in control of Riley, look to the left for the Federation soldier in the orange hazmat suit. Approach the enemy with Riley and hit the **Tactical Equipment** button for a silent kill.

Move Riley into the main courtyard and press the **Use** button to command Riley to bark. Wait for Hesh to snipe the second soldier, then move Riley past him into the destroyed house.

SPECIALIZED TRAINING **THE CAMPAIGN** MP INTRO & BASIC TRAINING SQUADS MP ARMORY PERKS KILLSTREAKS MP MAPS MP GAME MODES SAFEGUARD EXTINCTION CLASSIFIED ACHIEVEMENTS & TROPHIES

25

"Hang On, I've Got a Sniper on the Balcony."

On the other side of the house, Riley approaches a group of three soldiers. Hesh will kill the sniper above; the other two are for Riley. Sprint to the armed guard (the one in the camo) first. Now, have Riley attack the hazmat suit on the left.

With the Federation group down, control returns to Logan.

"Riley. Search."

Move to the door opposite Hesh, and you automatically prepare for a breach. Riley charges inside. Moments later, Federation enemies tumble out. Dispatch the two enemies leading the charge; Riley and Hesh have the rest.

In the next house, replace your pistol with the L115 sniper rifle. The rifle is leaning on a vertical support beam in the middle of the house.

There's another small group of Federation behind the metal debris. Use the sniper rifle to pick them off from inside the house.

Riley, Attack!

You can now issue attack orders to Riley by hitting the **Tactical Equipment** button. You have this ability throughout the mission. Just be careful not to send Riley too far ahead, or he may get shot.

Switch back to your Honey Badger and eliminate the next group of enemies on the forest trail. The trail leads to a large, destroyed structure. There are several Federation troops in the area. They are too far away to send Riley, so instead use nearby cover and your sniper rifle to pick the enemies off.

When the initial resistance is dispatched, move forward and look down the trail on your left to spot another group of Federation. Use Riley to distract them, then shoot them with your rifle. Hesh moves up when the area is safe.

"Targets at Three O' Clock."

Follow Hesh. Another group of defenders is camped on the right. Use Riley to kill any enemies behind cover, and use your ACOG Honey Badger to pick off any soldiers dumb enough to pop their heads out.

More soldiers are inside the work facility. Use the concrete walls for cover, and shoot at them through the windows. When the building is quiet, approach it.

"No Man's Land" Rorke File

This Rorke file is inside the large work facility. It's on the desk in the main area.

"Stalker, There's Nothing Here. They Must Have Moved It All."

The work facility leads to a corrugated walkway. Keep your scope trained on the doorway at the opposite end of the area. Fire at the Federation troops that emerge.

When you've cleared that group, follow Hesh down a fire trail full of semis and heavy-duty construction equipment. Charge ahead and slide down the hill to the paved road.

"Tracks are Fresh. Looks Like They Went This Way."

Hesh picks up the Federation trail and proceeds down the road. Follow him into the tunnel.

Stealth is Imperative

Throughout the stealth area, stay crouched when moving around. If you stand up in the open or sprint, you alert the enemy and automatically fail the mission.

Hit the **Crouch** button to stay low and hide on the right side of the cars in the tunnel. A Federation convoy approaches. Stay in cover and wait for it to pass.

The tunnel exits into an open area. On the left, a second convoy is slowly proceeding ahead. Use Riley to silently down the guard on the right. Crouch behind Hesh and follow him through the tall grass.

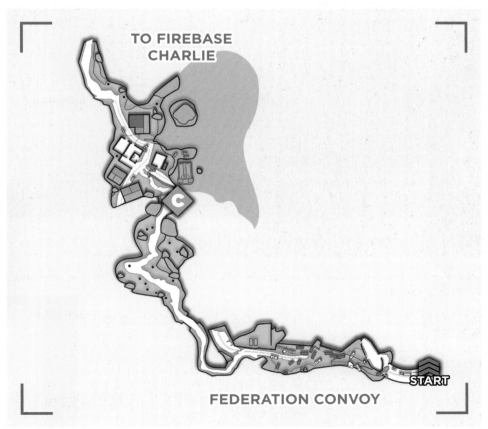

TO FIREBASE CHARLIE

C

START

FEDERATION CONVOY

SPECIALIZED TRAINING **THE CAMPAIGN** MP INTRO & BASIC TRAINING SQUADS MP ARMORY PERKS KILLSTREAKS MP MAPS MP GAME MODES SAFEGUARD EXTINCTION CLASSIFIED ACHIEVEMENTS & TROPHIES

27

"Jackpot. Stalker, We're Seeing a Massive Enemy Camp Ahead."

As you proceed, notice a large number of troops slowly moving forward to a Federation base. Move up and sync with Riley. He is your key to getting through this area undetected. To prevent Riley from being spotted, keep him in the tall grass.

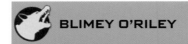

BLIMEY O'RILEY

To earn this Achievement/Trophy, you need to kill ten enemies while controlling Riley. You get at least three at the beginning of the mission. To earn this, you'll have to stray a bit from the following Step-by-Step Breakdown. Kill at least one of the pairs of patrolling guards. To do this, wait until the pairs are somewhat separated, then hit the rear guard. The front guard will see Riley, but if you're quick, you can down him before he fires at Riley, alerting the other guards. The Achievement/Trophy triggers immediately when you bite the tenth guard. Because of this, you don't need to worry about surviving if the guards are alerted on your tenth attack.

ACHIEVEMENT/TROPHY

STEP-BY-STEP BREAKDOWN

1 Move forward, then up the small hill on the left.

2 At the top of the hill, move through the large pipe on the right.

3 Sneak behind the guard and press the Tactical Equipment button to kill him.

4 Crawl through the abandoned bus to the tall grass on the other side.

5 Kill the second solo guard while staying hidden in the grass.

6 A third guard is loitering on the right. Stealth kill him as well.

7 Wait for the two patrolling guards to pass, then walk around them through the grass on the left.

"The Guy on the Trailer, You See Him?"

When Riley has made it safely through the field, use the camera to spy on the Federation. Hit the **Zoom** button and focus on the orange-highlighted enemy slightly above Riley's position.

After recording the mysterious confrontation, steer Riley to the exit point. The exit is a straight shot through the grassy field. Have Riley sprint ahead to return control to Logan. Chase Riley along the forest path, sliding down the hill ahead.

"Something isn't Right."

Riley is barking furiously in the clearing. Wolf pack incoming!

Switch to your Honey Badger, and start firing at the wolves. When the wolf jumps on Logan, follow the onscreen prompts to survive the attack long enough for Riley to save you. When you recover, grab the pistol and shoot the wolf before it can do serious damage to Riley.

"You Look Lost."

After an abrupt introduction to the No Man's Land recon team leader, Captain Merrick, Hesh hands over the intel you retrieved from the Federation base. Merrick is in charge now. Follow him up the trail.

OBJECTIVE

REACH FIREBASE CHARLIE

Past the iron gate, your team encounters more Federation patrolling the flooded road. Wait for Keegan to open fire, and then charge across the street to use the large transformer box for cover. Your sniper rifle comes in handy here. Fire at the soldiers in the buildings across the road. When the gunfire dies down, switch to your Honey Badger and follow Hesh through the building on the right. Use Riley to distract the arriving soldiers, and mow them down with your AR.

Move to the second floor of the next building to find more sniper rifle ammunition. Use the hole in the side of the building to fire on the enemy holding the hill ahead.

"Move Up. Top of the Hill, Let's Go!"

Once you've cleared the Federation defending the hill, Merrick leads a charge up the side. Follow him to successfully complete the mission.

NO MAN'S LAND

Complete this mission on any difficulty to earn the Achievement/Trophy "No Man's Land."

ACHIEVEMENT/TROPHY

SPECIALIZED TRAINING **THE CAMPAIGN** MP INTRO & BASIC TRAINING SQUADS MP ARMORY PERKS KILLSTREAKS MP MAPS MP GAME MODES SAFEGUARD EXTINCTION CLASSIFIED ACHIEVEMENTS & TROPHIES

29

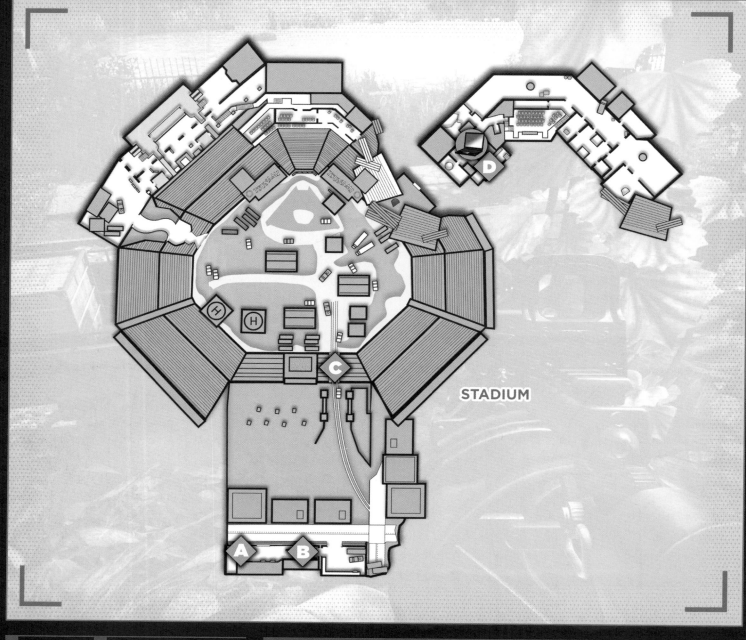

STADIUM

OPERATIVE

LOGAN WALKER

SUPPORT

HESH WALKER

MERRICK

KEEGAN

AJAX

OBJECTIVES

A Locate Ajax using the remote sniper rifle.

B Mark the convoy with explosives.

C Rescue Ajax.

D Escape from the enemy base.

LOCATE AJAX USING THE REMOTE SNIPER RIFLE

You start this mission looking through a sniper scope. Your team needs to ascertain Ajax's location. Use the **Movement** controls to zoom in and out. Ajax is located in the press box ahead and just to the left of where you're looking when the mission starts (261 horizontal, -2 vertical incline).

Wait for your orders to stop using the rifle.

MARK THE CONVOY WITH EXPLOSIVES

After deactivating the sniper rifle, grab the MK32 holographic grenade launcher. Load the weapon and look out the window ahead.

The convoy you need to tag with the grenades approaches from the left. Fire the launcher into each truck as it passes. You have six shots, so fire one or two at each vehicle. Aim carefully—there's not enough time to reload.

After the convoy passes, head to the lower area and board the convoy truck by hitting the **Use** button near the door.

"Watch and Learn, Kid."

Keegan is driving the truck; you are in charge of detonating the planted grenades.

RESCUE AJAX

Wait until the truck is just outside the guard checkpoint, then press the **Fire** button to set off the chain of explosions. Keegan keeps the truck on the road as you blast through the enemy defenses. Use your rifle to blast enemies through the smashed-out windshield.

"Ajax is through this Atrium. Move! Move!"

When the truck stops, find some cover—the enemies are dense in this area. Move to the concrete barrier and switch to the MK32 grenade launcher. Fire at the Federation defenses from the safety of the wall. Send Riley after any enemies that are hiding behind cover.

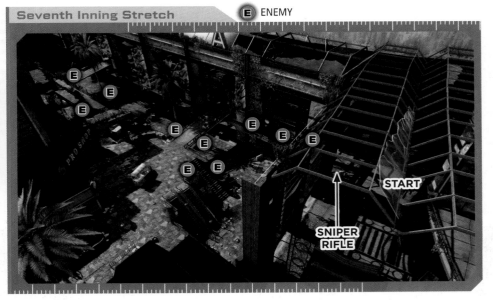

SPECIALIZED TRAINING THE CAMPAIGN MP INTRO & BASIC TRAINING SQUADS MP ARMORY PERKS KILLSTREAKS MP MAPS MP GAME MODES SAFEGUARD EXTINCTION CLASSIFIED ACHIEVEMENTS & TROPHIES

31

When you've cleared the enemies at near and mid-range, switch your grenade launcher for the L115 sniper rifle located on the top of the concrete barrier. Use the rifle to finish the long-range enemies.

Now strafe to the area's left side and pick off any visible enemies. When the area is clear, inch to the next concrete barrier. This causes more enemies to advance to your position. Stay safe, behind cover, and fire at the enemies with your sniper.

If you run out of ammo, feel free to move ahead and hit enemies with your SC2010 assault rifle. There's more sniper ammo at the ammo crates near the outdoor bar. The enemies like to flank from the right. Keep your eye there to ensure you don't get surprised while moving.

You can use the upper walkways here to get some leverage on your enemies, but you probably won't need to. Just keep in cover, and keep pushing forward.

"This Must Be Where They're Holding Ajax."

Follow your squad up two flights of stairs until you reach the large double-door. Muffled shouting is audible from the other side. Use the **Inventory** button assigned to the remote sniper to get a better look.

WASTE NOT

You need to hit with every shot of your sniper rifle to earn this Achievement/Trophy. Just take your time and line up your shots perfectly beforehand. This is the first of four remote sniper sequences: VIP box, rocket launchers, protecting Keegan and Merrick, and protecting Player and Hesh. You have to obtain 100% accuracy in all four for the Achievement/Trophy. If you mess up, pause the game and hit "Last Checkpoint."

ACHIEVEMENT/TROPHY

Six soldiers are visible on the other side of the door. Wait for the two guards shouting near the door to line up so you can take two down with one shot. Your squad will charge in to finish off the remaining troops. Keep firing to clear the room.

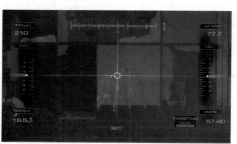

"He's Not Here!"

In the press box, Riley picks up Ajax's scent.

Slide down the collapsed walkway, then take cover behind the debris. Open up the remote sniper again to pick off the RPG soldiers in the bleachers.

"Stick with Riley, He'll Lead Us to Ajax."

When you get the all clear, continue following Riley through the stadium. Riley leads you into a flooded basement below the stadium. After your team dons the gas masks, hit the **Grenade** button to toss a gas grenade under the garage door.

Wait for the stunned soldiers to come out on the left. Mow them down with your rifle, then move in to the under-stadium area.

Under Stadium

Like the outer-stadium upstairs, this underground corridor is heavily defended by Federation. Use the same strategy. Stay at range, behind cover, and pick off the enemies as they attempt to charge your team. Don't forget to use Riley for any enemies hidden in cover.

"Riley's Picked Up the Scent Again."

When you've made it to the end of the corridor, Riley resumes tracking Ajax's scent.

Stay behind Keegan as he uses a flare to find an alternate route to Ajax. When he finds the locked door, use the **Interact** button to pop a gas grenade into the locker rooms. When the breach starts, you have about a dozen enemies to contend with. Hesh and Merrick attack from the door opposite. Focus on the enemies directly ahead.

Equip the remote sniper again. You need to clear a path for the evac. Use the rifle to shoot any soldiers you see, and the Ghosts will make their way to the first evac chopper.

When the view returns to Logan, Riley takes down the Federation chopper.

With the chopper ready for takeoff, follow Hesh closely as he moves from crate to crate to the chopper. When you get to the last crate, sprint to the chopper to automatically board.

Once inside the chopper, Logan switches back to the remote sniper. Use the powerful .50 caliber rounds to explode the approaching machine trucks and clear the evac route.

"Struck Down" Rorke File

This Rorke File is in the locker room. Look to one of the lockers on the left as you enter the room.

"Rorke's Targeting Ghosts."

With the room clear, Riley quickly finds Ajax in the next room. Follow him, and Merrick leads a search that uncovers the name of the Federation leader you saw on the trailer at the previous level's end.

D OBJECTIVE

ESCAPE FROM THE ENEMY BASE

When you head back to the locker room area, the doors to the stadium burst open. A heavily fortified group of enemy soldiers opens fire on your team.

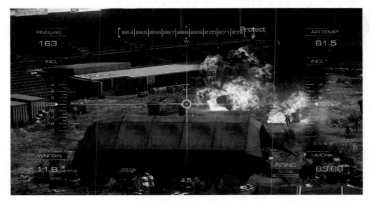

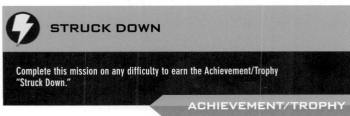

⚡ STRUCK DOWN

Complete this mission on any difficulty to earn the Achievement/Trophy "Struck Down."

ACHIEVEMENT/TROPHY

SPECIALIZED TRAINING   **THE CAMPAIGN**   MP INTRO & BASIC TRAINING   SQUADS   MP ARMORY   PERKS   KILLSTREAKS   MP MAPS   MP GAME MODES   SAFEGUARD   EXTINCTION   CLASSIFIED   ACHIEVEMENTS & TROPHIES

33

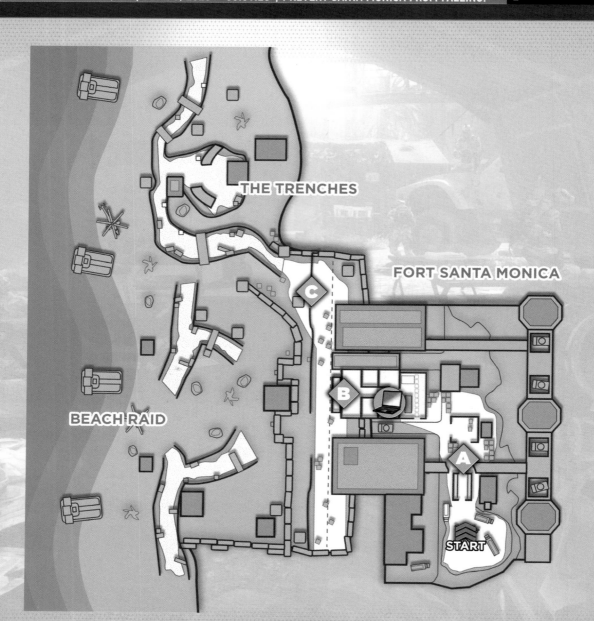

THE TRENCHES

FORT SANTA MONICA

C

BEACH RAID

B

A

START

OPERATIVE

LOGAN WALKER

SUPPORT

HESH WALKER

OBJECTIVES

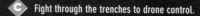

A   Get to the front lines.

B   Defend the beach from the Federation invasion.

C   Fight through the trenches to drone control.

D   Retreat!

LOADOUT

PRIMARY

SA-805 ACOG SIGHT

SECONDARY

M9A1

GRENADES & EQUIPMENT

FRAG GRENADES, FLASHBANGS

"Just Get Here Fast, We Need Every Available Shooter on the Line!"

This mission picks up where the previous one left off. You are still in the captured Federation helicopter and about to land at Fort Santa Monica, which is currently getting hammered by a Federation invasion.

A OBJECTIVE

GET TO THE FRONT LINES

After the helicopter lands, follow Hesh through the camps.

Follow Hesh indoors to the base where you first reunited with Elias at the end of "Brave New World."

. . . .

"Homecoming" Rorke File

Find this Rorke File in a side room before going upstairs in the command HQ. Before following Hesh up the stairs, explore the room to the left. Inside, the Rorke laptop is on a sandbag table.

. . . .

B OBJECTIVE

DEFEND THE BEACH FROM THE FEDERATION INVASION

Sprint up the stairs after Hesh, and get on the mounted MG (use the **Interact** button). Immediately fire on the helicopter ahead. With the first chopper down, fire at the black helicopters arriving to drop troops on the beach.

This sequence can be tricky on the harder difficulties. By the time you get the warning to take cover because you've taken damage, it's too late. Make sure to keep track of the damage you take, and dismount well before your vision starts to turn red.

Stay low behind the sandbags to recover your health. When your vision is clear again, remount the MG.

"Enemy Smoke, They're Marking Our Position!"

After you've blunted the initial Federation attack, they pop red smoke on the beach and call in mortar strikes. Dismount from the MG, and take cover further into the building, away from the beach.

When the next wave of attack choppers arrives, stay in cover and wait for your A10 reinforcements to get in position. Use the **Inventory** button to switch to the A10 when it's ready.

GO UGLY EARLY

You earn this Achievement/Trophy if you manage to kill 50 enemies with your A10. The best way to achieve this is to avoid hitting the big vehicles, and focus the drone fire on the many soldiers on the beach. If you do it well, you should earn the Achievement/Trophy during the second strafe.

ACHIEVEMENT/TROPHY

The A10 is far overhead, and you only get a few seconds to strike. Prioritize the tanks and helicopters highlighted with the orange circles.

After your first successful strike, stay in cover and wait for the A10 to ready a second time. Destroy the helicopter, and you are blasted out of the bunker onto the beach.

SPECIALIZED TRAINING   THE CAMPAIGN   MP INTRO & BASIC TRAINING   SQUADS   MP ARMORY   PERKS   KILLSTREAKS   MP MAPS   MP GAME MODES   SAFEGUARD   EXTINCTION   CLASSIFIED   ACHIEVEMENTS & TROPHIES

35

OBJECTIVE

FIGHT THROUGH THE TRENCHES TO DRONE CONTROL

KNOW YOUR ENEMY

In this mission, the Federation invasion forces are wearing welder-mask-like head protection and black uniforms. Your allies are wearing beige camo.

Move down the trenches, keeping the beach on your left. As the trench turns left toward the beach, be ready to fight some Federation invaders. Stand with your allies, and when the enemies are eliminated, push forward toward the trenches.

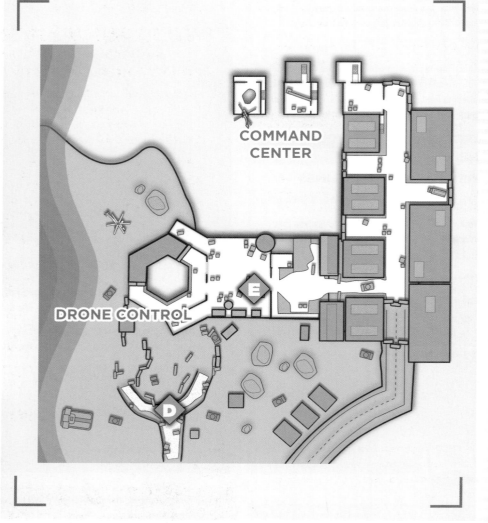

COMMAND CENTER

DRONE CONTROL

E

D

Stay behind your allies and use the barrels and sandbags for cover. Use a long-range weapon (there are some available in the trenches) to pick off the enemies from safety.

There's no reason to move too quickly through this area. Take your time, and don't move forward until the incoming gunfire subsides.

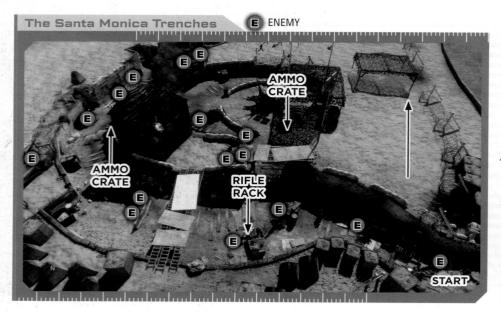

The Santa Monica Trenches E ENEMY

AMMO CRATE

AMMO CRATE

RIFLE RACK

START

N

"Command, We Have an Enemy Hovercraft Approaching Our Position."

As you push into the trenches, a hovercraft arrives with armor. Once again, you gain access to the A10 controls. Use it to destroy the tank before it can do serious damage to your squad.

Ammo Crates

Throughout this section, you can find ammo crates. Using one of these crates takes a moment, but it completely refills your ammo supplies.

Continue pushing through the trenches, and a hovercraft flies over. Stay in cover and wait for the A10 to activate again. Use the A10 to destroy the attack chopper.

With the first chopper down, wait in cover a few more seconds for the A10 to reactivate so you can destroy a second attack chopper. Unfortunately, the Federation is ready this time, and your A10 is shot down.

D **OBJECTIVE**

RETREAT

With the drone control down, fight with your team to the building so you can evac the injured soldiers inside. The front of the area is defended by about a dozen Federation. Stay in cover and pick them off. When the area is safe, Hesh moves to the building. Follow him inside.

"There's Riley!"

Continue through the building. The U.S. Army is in full retreat mode now. Keep up with your squad as they move to the main streets of Santa Monica, away from the beach.

When you reunite with Riley, turn your focus down the street on the left. Federation reinforcements rappel from the helicopters above. Shoot them from cover and wait for Hesh and Riley to join you.

E **OBJECTIVE**

GET TO THE COMMAND CENTER AND FIND YOUR FATHER

Hesh and Logan now need to find Elias back in the command center. Hesh opens the door to the command HQ, which is now in flames. Follow Riley up the stairs and wait for Hesh to lift the support beam. Hold down the **Crouch** button to go prone and crawl under the beam. Now head upstairs, and be ready for a quick time event to complete the level. Hit the displayed button as fast as possible to prevent Logan from getting stabbed to death.

HOMECOMING

Complete this mission on any difficulty to earn the Achievement/Trophy "Homecoming."

ACHIEVEMENT/TROPHY

CARACAS, FEDERATION CAPITAL | JULY 8, 2016 — 12:46:15

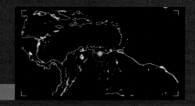

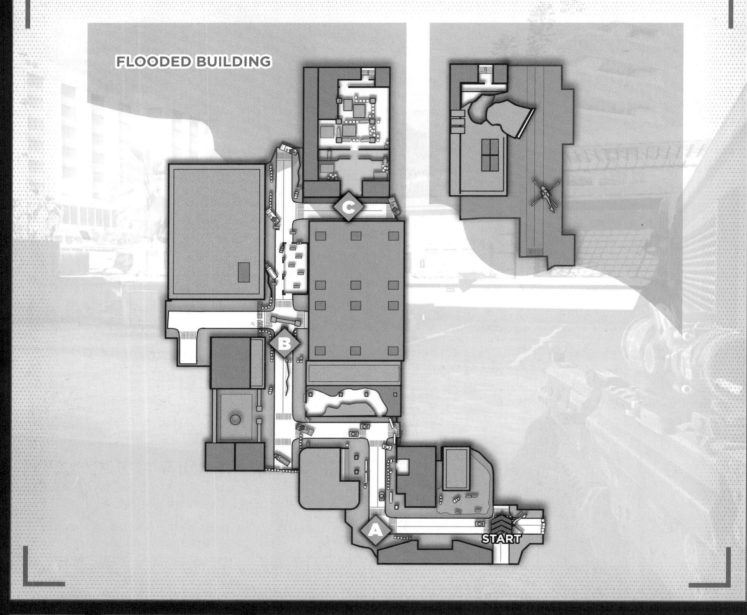

FLOODED BUILDING

C

B

A

START

OPERATIVE

ELIAS WALKER

SUPPORT

GABRIEL RORKE

AJAX

MERRICK

MISSION DETAILS

12 years ago, the Ghosts, led by Gabriel Rorke, invaded Caracas, Venezuela to take out Federation General Diego Almagro.

OBJECTIVES

A Locate Almagro.

B Disable the mobile rocket launcher.

C Get to higher ground.

D Regroup with Merrick.

E Get to the Hotel.

F Stop Almagro.

PRIMARY

REMINGTON R5 RED DOT SIGHT

SECONDARY

P226

LOADOUT

GRENADES & EQUIPMENT

FRAG GRENADES, FLASHBANGS

OBJECTIVE

LOCATE ALMAGRO

This flashback mission takes place 12 years in the past, when Rorke was leading the Ghosts. You now play as Elias, Logan's father.

The leader of your squad in this mission is Rorke, but note that another Ghost—Merrick—is with your team. After landing, follow Rorke and Merrick up the street.

Use the tank for cover; the Federation is attacking from the opposite side of the street. When your tank blows, stay in cover and wait for Iron Horse to reinforce your position.

When the tank blasts through the wall, charge across the street into the parking garage. Move fast to avoid taking shots from the Federation tank parked at the junction.

KNOW YOUR ENEMY

The Federation troops are wearing standard green camo during this mission.

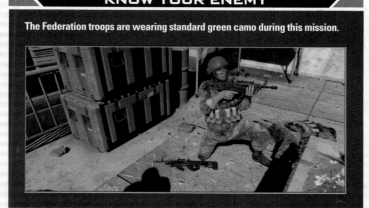

"Keep It Tight. Follow Me."

Move up through the destroyed parking garage and take cover at the edge overlooking the street. Open fire on the rocket launcher soldiers on the balcony across the street. Once they are eliminated, rain hell on the soldiers in the street.

B
OBJECTIVE

DISABLE THE MOBILE ROCKET LAUNCHER

You need to approach the stuck missile truck and hijack it. Clear the street first, and when you have an opening, sprint down the building's side and charge to the right door. Move toward the door, and Elias automatically scales the truck's side. Use a melee attack to stab the truck operator.

SPECIALIZED TRAINING **THE CAMPAIGN** MP INTRO & BASIC TRAINING   SQUADS   MP ARMORY   PERKS   KILLSTREAKS   MP MAPS   MP GAME MODES   SAFEGUARD   EXTINCTION   CLASSIFIED   ACHIEVEMENTS & TROPHIES

39

When you're clear of the missile truck, immediately find cover. The area on the wall's other side is reinforced by at least a dozen Federation soldiers. Use grenades and flashbangs to flush the enemies out from behind the defensive barriers. Rorke and Merrick help you clear out the soldiers. When the street is quiet, charge to the second missile truck.

"We've Got to Get Off the Street. Move!"

C OBJECTIVE

GET TO HIGHER GROUND

No time to waste; follow Rorke closely to avoid the rushing waters. If you delay, you'll get swept away!

When you make it inside the warehouse, keep sprinting until you find the stairs. The stairs give your team a moment to rest before continuing the mission.

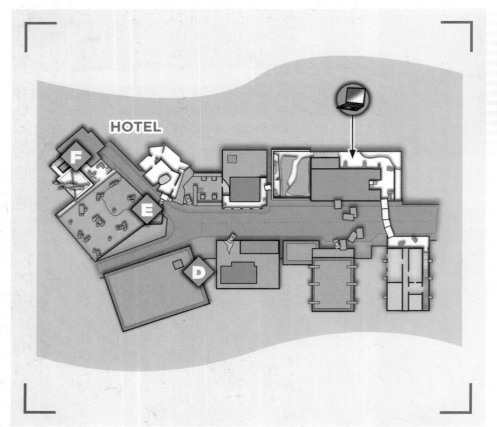

"We're Ghosts, Merrick. We Finish the Mission."

Follow your team outside and take cover behind one of the metal air ducts. Line up the Feds on the roof and open fire. Some reinforcements arrive from the area's right side. Unfortunately, the floodwaters prove too strong for the roof you're standing on, and the Ghosts get swept downstream.

"Looks Like It's Just You and Me Now, Brother."

After Rorke pulls you up, use the **Crouch** button to get low in the water and stay out of sight of the patrolling Federation soldiers. Stay down, and wait for Rorke to kill the trailing soldier.

Go back underwater and move to the left. There are two soldiers to deal with here. Approach the closest one and use a **Melee** attack to kill him; Rorke takes care of the far guy.

Search the area for a Bizon SMG.

"Just Like Old Times. Eh, Elias?"

When you emerge outside, sprint after Rorke across the glass bridge. Two soldiers are in the office area ahead. Rorke waits for you to open fire.

"Legends Never Die"
Rorke File

Find this laptop on the desk in the sunny office area.

When you've downed the two soldiers, search the crates for a Bizon Holographic, which makes your Bizon a bit more accurate.

Proceed up the stairs. A half dozen soldiers are guarding an attack chopper. Find some cover, and dispatch all of the enemies.

D OBJECTIVE

REGROUP WITH MERRICK

When you've cleared the roof, Merrick radios in. You and Rorke must get to Merrick's position. Follow Rorke down to the lower flooded rooftop. Use the water for cover, and unload on a platoon of Federation enemies.

IT CAME FROM BELOW!

You earn this Achievement/Trophy by knifing five enemies while crouched underwater. This is a good spot to score a few bonus kills meeting this requirement. Wait for the enemies to step into the water, then crouch under the water and knife them. If you have trouble getting spotted and killed before you get to the enemy, try playing on Recruit difficulty.

ACHIEVEMENT/TROPHY

If you get injured here, crouch down and wait for your wounds to heal before popping back out and resuming the fight.

When you make it to the end of the flooded area, watch for the extra Federation reinforcements that arrive on the right. These enemies have better weapons than the Bizon, so search their corpses to upgrade to an LMG like the Ameli or an assault rifle like the FAD.

E OBJECTIVE

GET TO THE HOTEL

Through the next section, you can hear Merrick in a gun battle. He's engaged with forces on the opposite side of the newly-formed river going through the middle of the city. Take cover behind some rubble and fire on the soldiers across the street.

SPECIALIZED TRAINING **THE CAMPAIGN** MP INTRO & BASIC TRAINING SQUADS MP ARMORY PERKS KILLSTREAKS MP MAPS MP GAME MODES SAFEGUARD EXTINCTION CLASSIFIED ACHIEVEMENTS & TROPHIES

41

Rorke leads your team across the river via a capsized bus. More Federation troops are defending the other side. You can use the water for cover in this section as well.

To make it through this area, move left and right between cover. Stay above the water when you're safe, and duck down if you take a shot. There are a lot of enemies in this area, so be patient and don't proceed too quickly.

When you make it about halfway through the parking lot, the hotel maintenance entrance is visible. This is Almagro's last line of defense, and they aggressively combat your advance.

After struggling with and killing Almagro, you awake with the helicopter teetering over the floodwaters. Follow the onscreen instructions to grab the rope as you slip past it. This requires some timing. Try to hit the buttons when you are just about to slide past the overhanging rope.

To complete the level, you must release Rorke.

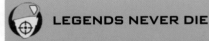

OBJECTIVE

STOP ALMAGRO

When you've cleared the hotel entrance, Rorke sees Almagro's helicopter taking off. Sprint after Rorke and jump into the back of the helicopter. Be ready to fire when prompted.

LEGENDS NEVER DIE

Complete this mission on any difficulty to earn the Achievement/Trophy "Legends Never Die."

ACHIEVEMENT/TROPHY

07 FEDERATION DAY

CARACAS, FEDERATION CAPITAL | MISSION TIME: JUNE 15, 2028 — 00:41:17

OPERATIVE
LOGAN WALKER

SUPPORT
KEEGAN

HESH WALKER

OBJECTIVES

A Confirm target's identity.

B Fire the zipline launcher.

C Capture the HVT.

D Upload virus to the power system.

E Escape the building.

MISSION DETAILS

Find and interrogate Victor Ramos.

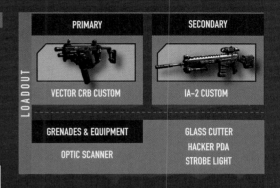

LOADOUT

PRIMARY	SECONDARY
VECTOR CRB CUSTOM	IA-2 CUSTOM
GRENADES & EQUIPMENT	GLASS CUTTER
OPTIC SCANNER	HACKER PDA
	STROBE LIGHT

"Target Confirmed, Mission is a Go."

Deactivate the Optic Scanner, and follow Keegan to the building's edge. Hesh is waiting below.

A OBJECTIVE

CONFIRM TARGET'S IDENTITY

Back in the present day, the mission starts on the rooftops of Caracas, in the middle of Federation territory. Logan and Keegan are waiting for Victor Ramos to arrive in the capital via helicopter.

When the helicopter lands, press the appropriate **Inventory** button to activate the Optic Scanner. Zoom in on the helicopters and wait for the passengers to exit.

> ### High Value Target
> During this mission, you may hear your team refer to a "HVT." This is short for "High Value Target" and refers to Victor Ramos.

You can spot your target easily; he's wearing a white suit, which makes him stand out from the gray jackets surrounding him. Track the target's face to confirm his identity by holding down the **Fire** button while the target is facing the screen. The Optic Scanner automatically tracks the target until released, so keep the button held down until confirmation is received over your radio.

B OBJECTIVE

FIRE THE ZIPLINE LAUNCHER

The middle crate is yours. **Interact** with the crate to reveal the massive zipline launcher. It's used to get to the target's skyscraper.

Fire your line in the general direction of the skyscraper. Then move in front of the launcher to hook up.

SPECIALIZED TRAINING | THE CAMPAIGN | MP INTRO & BASIC TRAINING | SQUADS | MP ARMORY | PERKS | KILLSTREAKS | MP MAPS | MP GAME MODES | SAFEGUARD | EXTINCTION | CLASSIFIED | ACHIEVEMENTS & TROPHIES

43

OBJECTIVE

CAPTURE THE HVT

Outside the skyscraper, you can walk around as you normally would, except that pushing Up on the movement controls causes Walker to scale the skyscraper's side, and pushing Down causes Walker to slide down the side.

KNOW YOUR ENEMY

This mission's enemies are all dressed in gray jackets with flak jacket vests. As in previous missions, they wear a variety of head gear.

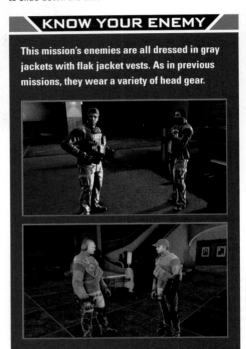

Move down two floors. A Federation soldier is working at a desk on your left. Shoot the soldier in the head. Walk to the right to see the next room. There, two soldiers are talking to each other. You are responsible for taking both of these guys out.

Unless you are particularly good with the sniper rifle, the Vector is the safer bet to quickly down both targets. Take your time and use **ADS** to line up your shot on the left guy. When you've killed him, continue firing short bursts to eliminate the second guy before he can fire on your team.

"Targets Down, We're Clear."

Move down another floor. Directly ahead, three soldiers are in an elevator, and three are at a poker table. Hold your fire and move to the left. Notice an enemy digging through the fridge on the left. Quickly kill this soldier before he can turn around.

Now, focus on the kitchen entrance. Drop this next guy once he is out of view of the poker table. When he stops moving, shoot him.

Swing back to the right and wait for the poker table to return to normal (one soldier gets talked back to the table). When Keegan gives you a go order, work your way around the table, killing the other two before they can get to their weapons.

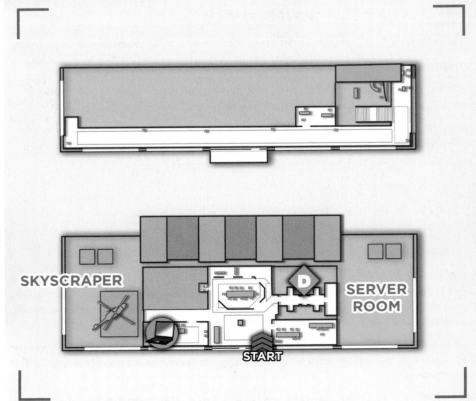

"Control Center is on This Floor."

Move down one more floor. Then hit the **Interact** button to cut a hole in the glass and slip through.

"Federation Day" Rorke File

Before following Keegan to the Control Center, take a left at the first hallway in the dark office. If you see Hesh hanging on outside, you are in the correct room. Search a cubicle to find this Rorke File. The screen is facing the wall, so it's hard to see until you walk around the side of it.

▷ OBJECTIVE

UPLOAD VIRUS TO THE POWER SYSTEM

Follow Keegan through the door on the back-right wall into a server room. A glowing computer panel is on the left. Interact with the panel to pull out the hacking device. Now, hold down **Fire** until the device reads 100.

If you're quick, you can upload the virus before the wandering guards arrive. However, you can cancel the process early and hide in the shadows if need be. There are a lot of guards, so you don't want to fire on these guys. Just wait until they've passed.

With the virus uploaded, it's time to head back outside the skyscraper. Move to the glass hole you cut and use the **Interact** button to hook back up.

"Kill the Lights."

When Keegan gives the order, press the **Fire** button to activate the hacking device and kill the building's power. Two soldiers step outside on the left balcony. Shoot them, and then continue forward.

SLEEPING BEAUTY

A sleeping guard is in a folding chair near the window two floors down from the pair of guards you first encounter in the face-down rappel section. Kill this secret guard for the Achievement/Trophy.

ACHIEVEMENT/TROPHY

Straight ahead is another balcony. Continue moving down the building's side, and Logan automatically takes out a knife. Keep the enemy in your crosshairs and hit the **Melee** button when close enough.

After landing on the soldier, two of his buddies arrive. Quickly press the **Fire** button to kill the leader with a thrown knife. Keegan finishes the second guy.

SPECIALIZED TRAINING **THE CAMPAIGN** MP INTRO & BASIC TRAINING SQUADS MP ARMORY PERKS KILLSTREAKS MP MAPS MP GAME MODES SAFEGUARD EXTINCTION CLASSIFIED ACHIEVEMENTS & TROPHIES

45

ATRIUM

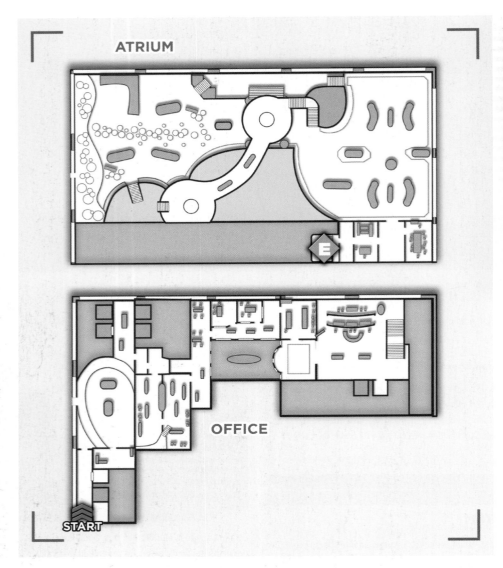

OFFICE

START

Follow Keegan to the next office area. Five soldiers are inside. Find a good spot for cover and open fire. Keegan helps clear out any survivors.

"Looks Like Elias's Training is Paying Off."

Keegan leads you to a banquet room filled with soldiers. Take out the TV on the left to darken the room. With the room completely dark, use your weapon's strobe attachment (activated with the **Inventory** button).

The strobes can be somewhat difficult to use. Stay in cover and move to the right side of the divider Keegan is using. Peek out and pick off any troops stumbling around in the banquet area. Some reinforcements arrive from the bar's opposite side.

When Keegan gives the all clear, turn your strobe off and follow him to the other side of the room.

"Go Give Hesh a Hand, I'll Hook Up the Ropes."

Follow Keegan until you exit into a large area with a balcony. Hesh arrives through a door on your left. Move to him.

A cache of SA-805 guns and some elevator controls are inside this small room. Press the **Interact** button to disable the elevators, then grab a gun and join the firefight outside.

"We'll Rendezvous at the Junction to Cut the Secondaries."

Follow Keegan down the hall on the right. Descend the stairs, and have your weapon ready. Two enemies stand in front of the elevator. Wait for the elevator's light to reveal their position, and then quickly drop them with your rifle.

"Go Hook Up, I'm Right Behind You."

About eight enemies are in the large area. Take cover behind one of the ammo crates and open fire. When the enemies are dead, Keegan issues another all clear. Move to the balcony and **Interact** with the glowing rope on the ground.

"Here They Come!"

As soon as you start rappelling, a group of Federation arrives to reignite the attack. Fire at any troops that lean over the edge. Be ready to move to the left when the giant printer falls from the top floor.

Hold the **Jump** button to rappel to the next floor. Watch out for more troops firing at you from the other side. Use the edges of the building for cover.

CARBON FACEPRINT

Earn this Achievement/Trophy by getting hit in the face by the photocopier. Don't worry; it won't kill you!

ACHIEVEMENT/TROPHY

Camper

Instead of using the Step-By-Step run-and-gun strategy, you can find a high-powered sniper rifle near the atrium entrance. Hang back and pick off the soldiers, letting Keegan push the attack forward.

"We Need to Get Inside, Now!"

Rappel down a second time, and you enter a large atrium area. The enemies are thick here, but you need to charge ahead to reach your target before he can evac.

1 Sprint up the stairs on the right.

2 If you're hit, take cover and heal before charging up the second set of stairs.

3 Stay crouched and move up the stairs. Two soldiers are at the top.

4 Now use the planters for cover, and fire at the enemies defending the walkway on the left.

5 Reload your gun, and then move down the walkway. Be ready for the pair of soldiers climbing the stairs on the right.

6 Use the superior vantage point and cover of the walkway to kill the enemies down on the main atrium floor.

7 Now move down to the main floor. Proceed all the way to the right of the atrium and use the shrubbery for cover to flank the last group of enemies defending the rear exit.

"In Position."

Your target is on the other side of the atrium. Follow Keegan as he pushes through the corridors and into Ramos' office.

The mission is successful, but it's all been a setup! Time to leave.

When you get thrown out of the building, hit the **Interact** button to quickly deploy your chute.

E OBJECTIVE

ESCAPE THE BUILDING

Sprint after Hesh and Keegan as they rush down the building's stairs. The building is coming down. Keep up with Keegan and press forward. When you start sliding, move left or right to avoid the debris.

 FEDERATION DAY

Complete this mission on any difficulty to earn the Achievement/Trophy "Federation Day."

ACHIEVEMENT/TROPHY

08.1 BIRDS OF PREY

CAMPECHE OIL FIELDS, GULF OF MEXICO | JUNE 16, 2028 — 19:42:20

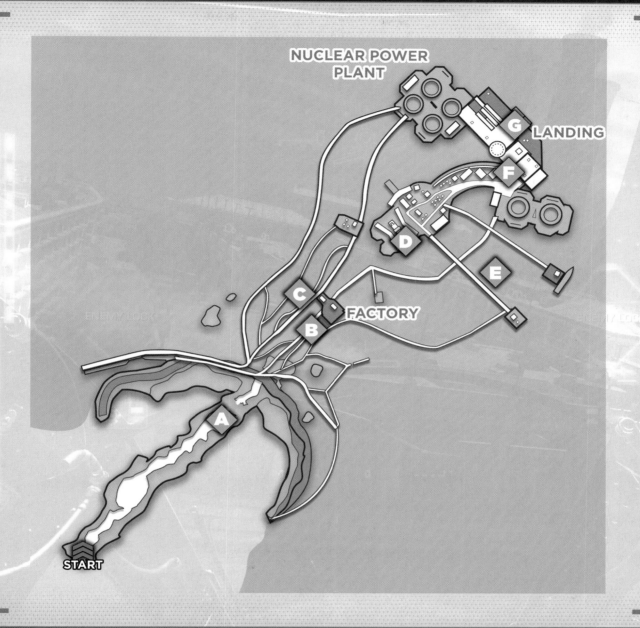

NUCLEAR POWER PLANT

G LANDING

F

D

E

C

B FACTORY

A

START

OPERATIVE

APACHE GROUP,
25 S.O.W.

MISSION DETAILS

Capture Gabriel Rorke.

OBJECTIVES

- A Fly with team.
- B Assault factory.
- C Clear the anti-air targets.
- D Clear the main island anti-air targets.

- E Control the air.
- F Protect the Blackhawk.
- G Clear the landing.

SPECIALIZED TRAINING   **THE CAMPAIGN**   MP INTRO & BASIC TRAINING   SQUADS   MP ARMORY   PERKS   KILLSTREAKS   MP MAPS   MP GAME MODES   SAFEGUARD   EXTINCTION   CLASSIFIED   ACHIEVEMENTS & TROPHIES

49

A OBJECTIVE

FLY WITH TEAM

In the first part of this mission, you fly with a team of Apache helicopters that are providing air support for the Ghosts.

The helicopter controls are a modified version of the normal first-person controls. You can move your helicopter around, and it automatically rises and lowers to avoid obstacles. Additionally, it's impossible to crash your helicopter by steering it into a wall.

You also have three types of weapons at your disposal in the chopper. The **Fire** button unleashes a mounted machine gun. The **Aim Down Sight** button zooms in. The **Frag Grenade** button fires a set of dummy rockets. Holding down the **Frag Grenade** button fires locked missiles that track enemies. Finally, the **Tactical Grenade** button fires flares, which help your chopper evade enemy missile locks.

At the start of the mission, feel free to familiarize yourself with the controls and helicopter HUD indicators. All of the Apache's ammunition automatically replenishes (slowly).

KNOW YOUR ENEMY

While you fly the Apache, your allies are highlighted blue, and your enemies are highlighted orange. This makes it easy to distinguish enemy choppers from friendly ones, even in the heat of battle.

When you're comfortable with the helicopter controls, push forward and follow your flight team through the canyon.

B OBJECTIVE

ASSAULT FACTORY

The canyon exits onto a large, open factory area. Enemies are everywhere. Your initial focus should be the factory at the base of the smoke stacks directly ahead. Use your weapons to demolish the troops on the roads below, but keep moving toward the factory.

BURN BABY BURN

For this Achievement/Trophy, you must destroy 80 oil containers. The containers in question are mostly vertical (but sometimes horizontal) gold cylinders. You'll see these scattered throughout the mission's helicopter portion. There are some on the elevated highways, but the building areas have the highest concentration. If you are thorough, you should get this Achievement/Trophy after destroying the factory and moving to the next section.

ACHIEVEMENT/TROPHY

If an enemy gets a missile lock on you, fire your flares (**Tactical Grenade** button) and steer your helicopter to the left or right.

Circle the factory, destroying the anti-air crews, helicopters, and gun trucks. Use the explosive gas containers to more easily destroy the fortifications.

C OBJECTIVE

CLEAR THE ANTI-AIR TARGETS

When the factory is clear, break from the factory and proceed to find anti-air enemies positioned on the roads around the factory. In addition to the enemies on the roads and buildings near the factory, there are also some gun boats floating in the water. When the area is completely clear, you get the green light to move ahead to the main island.

D OBJECTIVE

CLEAR THE MAIN ISLAND ANTI-AIR TARGETS

The majority of the Federation anti-air defenses are in the buildings to the right of the gigantic smoke stacks. Search the long rows of buildings for rocket launcher soldiers and more giant guns.

When you've destroyed the majority of the ground enemies, enemy choppers arrive.

CONTROL THE AIR

The initial air attack is three helicopters to your right. These attack choppers aren't much of a threat, as long as you use your locked-on rockets and keep your flares ready for incoming seekers. If you get in close to an enemy, feel free to engage with the MG; however, the locked rockets are the quickest way to down them.

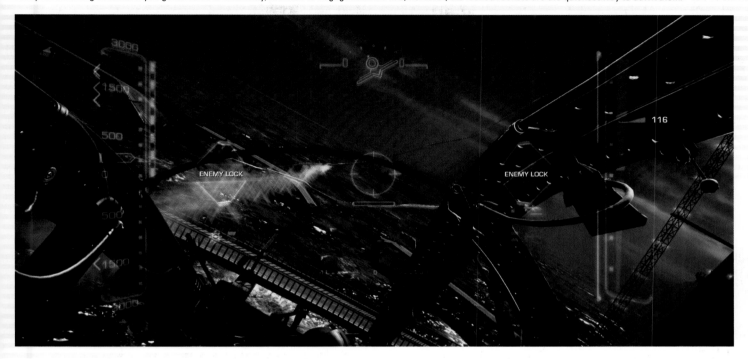

With the first three down, three more helicopters arrive in the western part of the city. Fly toward them, kicking out flares and veering left or right whenever they get a lock on your Apache. You can use the giant smoke stacks for cover. When you're close enough to get a lock of your own, begin firing pairs of locked rockets until all three choppers are down.

PROTECT THE BLACKHAWK

After eliminating the last helicopter, the Ghosts' Blackhawk chopper flies onto the scene. A large number of enemy machine gun trucks arrive to defend the ground. You must clear out these trucks to give the Ghosts a chance at landing.

CLEAR THE LANDING

To make matters more difficult, the buildings in the area have Federation soldiers armed with rocket launchers firing at your helicopters. Kill the soldiers before engaging with the less deadly MG trucks.

When the area is clear, the Blackhawk can finally move in and drop off the Ghosts.

SPECIALIZED TRAINING **THE CAMPAIGN** MP INTRO & BASIC TRAINING SQUADS MP ARMORY PERKS KILLSTREAKS MP MAPS MP GAME MODES SAFEGUARD EXTINCTION CLASSIFIED ACHIEVEMENTS & TROPHIES

51

OPERATIVE

LOGAN WALKER

SUPPORT

HESH WALKER

KEEGAN

MERRICK

OBJECTIVES

H Find Rorke.

LOADOUT

PRIMARY

SC2010 ACOG SIGHT

SECONDARY

M9A1

GRENADES & EQUIPMENT

FRAG GRENADES, FLASHBANGS

RORKE'S OFFICE

H

H

START

FIND RORKE

After the helicopter section of the mission, you regain control of Logan Walker as his Ghost team is deployed from the Blackhawk. Once on the ground, move to the crates with your team. The Federation is well aware of your presence and has mounted a serious defense.

Stay behind cover and fire into the MG truck until it explodes. This should soften some of the enemy resistance. Move behind your team and cautiously scale the raised platform to the left. Peek through the doorway and shoot any Federation that charge.

LOADING BAY

When you reach the garage, use the area indicated in the Air Intel for cover.

E ENEMY   **R** ROCKET LAUNCHER ENEMY

Enemy HQ Loading Bay

GOOD COVER AREA

A lot of enemies are spaced throughout this area. To survive, be patient. Wait for the enemies to pop out from cover to get a clear shot.

After clearing the area, lead your team through the opposite building. Watch out for a pair of defenders near the red vending machine.

The doorway near the vending machine leads into a second outside area. This section is also heavily defended. Use the large window for cover and wait for the enemies to reveal themselves from behind their cover in the open yard.

YARD

Secondary reinforcements arrive from the back of the main area once you step through the glass window. Use the large ammo crate on the right for cover.

SPECIALIZED TRAINING   **THE CAMPAIGN**   MP INTRO & BASIC TRAINING   SQUADS   MP ARMORY   PERKS   KILLSTREAKS   MP MAPS   MP GAME MODES   SAFEGUARD   EXTINCTION   CLASSIFIED   ACHIEVEMENTS & TROPHIES

53

After you've killed some of the initial reinforcements, climb the ammo crate to reach the building's second floor and access a nice vantage point for this battle. Kill the remaining enemies and your team proceeds through the building on the right.

FACTORY EXTERIOR

The building leads to another tough battle in an outdoor factory area. Initially, the defenses are light, but as you progress, many more Federation arrive to reinforce their positions.

Enemy HQ Factory Exterior   **E** ENEMY   **R** ROCKET LAUNCHER ENEMY

The primary concern here is the rocket launcher troops. These enemies hang back and pop out from cover to deliver an explosive payload. Stay in cover near the stairs and wait for the enemies to present themselves—there's no rush here. A run-and-gun strategy is not smart with this many enemies.

When the fire dies down, stay low and move from cover to cover. There are likely more enemies hiding in alcoves. If you're having trouble getting a bead on a defender, use a flashbang to flush him out.

When you've cleared the factory exterior, cautiously climb the stairs on the opposite side of the area. When near the top of the stairs, drop a flashbang to stun the nearby soldiers. Then mow them down with a SMG.

FACTORY INTERIOR

Follow your squad into the factory. There are more Federation defending the right room area. Stay in cover at the end of the hall, and toss frag grenades at the other end. Keep your gun ready to mow down troops running from the grenades.

At the end of the hall, control temporarily switches back to the Apaches. Fire missiles into the guns blocking the side of the building, and use your machine gun on the soldiers. When the area is clear, control reverts to Logan.

"Ordinance Destroyed, You're Good to Go."

As Logan, move with your team to the factory roof. About eight more Federation soldiers are fighting from the rooftops. Use the air conditioners for cover. When your team has cleared the roof, it's time to head inside and retrieve Rorke.

"You Boys Sure Know How to Make an Entrance."

Follow Merrick through the corridors into Rorke's control room. Merrick captures Rorke. Mission successful!

"Birds of Prey" Rorke File

As soon as you enter Rorke's room, look for this computer in the middle of the desk. Retrieve the file before the level automatically ends; otherwise, you have to restart from the beginning!

BIRDS OF PREY

Complete this mission on any difficulty to earn the Achievement/Trophy "Birds Of Prey."

ACHIEVEMENT/TROPHY

SPECIALIZED TRAINING   **THE CAMPAIGN**   MP INTRO & BASIC TRAINING   SQUADS   MP ARMORY   PERKS   KILLSTREAKS   MP MAPS   MP GAME MODES   SAFEGUARD   EXTINCTION   CLASSIFIED   ACHIEVEMENTS & TROPHIES

55

"You Haven't Beaten Me, Elias; You've Just Made My Job a Hell of a Lot Easier."

This mission starts in the back of a cargo plane. All the Ghosts are here, and Rorke's interrogation is just getting started.

When Elias prompts you, move to Rorke's chair and hit the **Interact** button to grab hold. Then, push Rorke to the back of the plane. There's nothing you can do to change what happens next.

Luckily, Logan is wearing a parachute. Unluckily, the plane debris makes the landing anything but safe.

"If You Make it Outta This, Kid, Come Find Me! There's Always Room For One More!"

When you awake hanging from the tree, press the **Melee** button to cut yourself down. Crawl forward through the jungle.

"Saw Him Get Snagged on Some Trees before We Landed."

GRASS
FIELD

WATERFALL

C

B

EXFIL

PLANE
WRECKAGE

JUNGLE

A

START

OBJECTIVES

OPERATIVE

LOGAN WALKER

 Regroup with Ghosts.

 Prevent teammates' execution.

 Evac to the river for exfil.

LOADOUT

PRIMARY

P226

SECONDARY

COMBAT KNIFE

GRENADES & EQUIPMENT

MOTION DETECTOR

REGROUP WITH GHOSTS

Throughout this early part of the mission, you use silenced weapons to keep your stealth. You won't fail if you alert a guard, but he may alert nearby guards to rush your position.

In addition to the silenced arsenal, you also have access to a motion detector. This tells you where the enemies are relative to the direction you're facing. The motion detector has a slow refresh rate, so when using it to track enemies, take your time and err on the side of caution. Luckily, the Federation patrolling this area are all carrying silenced weapons. This makes it easy to upgrade your weapon early on. Since you can only use your pistol with the motion detector, only use the silenced automatic weapons when the enemy is in plain sight.

Use Stealth

This Step-By-Step breakdown avoids alerting the enemy. That means staying crouched or prone, moving slowly, and using the foliage for cover.

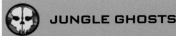

JUNGLE GHOSTS

For the Achievement/Trophy, you must make it all the way through the enemies without being detected. This means no alarms set off throughout. If you make a mistake, just select "Last Checkpoint" in the Pause menu and try again.

ACHIEVEMENT/TROPHY

STEP-BY-STEP BREAKDOWN

1 When you emerge from the forest, an enemy is straight ahead. Use your pistol to down him from a distance. Approach and grab his weapon as your secondary.

2 Switch back to your pistol so your motion detector is onscreen. Follow the center path up the hill.

3 At the top of the hill, find a lone patrolling guard. Take him down with a melee attack.

4 Walk down the hill toward the smoking wreckage. Here, two or three guards are talking. Keep these guards on your right (be sure to give them plenty of space).

5 Keep pushing forward through the shrubbery until you reach the side of the mountain and can't move any further.

6 Turn to your left, and see the bulk of the crashed cargo plane through the foliage.

7 Keep the mountain wall on your right and slowly approach the plane wreckage. A large group of soldiers is on your left, but they will clear out quickly.

8 When you make it to the wreckage, take the left path. You'll be going around the wreckage.

9

As you move forward, the wreckage is on your right. When you make it past the wreckage, keep the wreckage on your right side, and look down the path in the new direction.

10

A guard patrols this section of the path. Keep in cover and wait to get a bead on the guard with your motion detector. When you see him, quickly down him with your pistol.

11

Continue to push north toward the waterfall. Use your motion detector to track patrolling enemies. When they are clear, continue to push forward until you arrive at the waterfall.

12

Elias and Keegan are waiting near the small waterfall.

B **OBJECTIVE**

PREVENT TEAMMATES' EXECUTION

"The Hunted" Rorke File

When you rendezvous with Elias, follow the stream to the left. The laptop is in plain sight at the end of the stream.

Follow Elias through the woods and find Merrick and Hesh being held at gunpoint. When Elias gives the go ahead, open fire with your automatic weapon.

SPECIALIZED TRAINING **THE CAMPAIGN** MP INTRO & BASIC TRAINING SQUADS MP ARMORY PERKS KILLSTREAKS MP MAPS MP GAME MODES SAFEGUARD EXTINCTION CLASSIFIED ACHIEVEMENTS & TROPHIES

59

C OBJECTIVE

EVAC TO THE RIVER FOR EXFIL

Follow the Ghosts up the watery path. Federation troops are helicoptering a crate out of the area. Wait behind a boulder for the troops to clear out.

Continue moving up the stream bed. Another large group of Federation appears. Sprint to the waterfall and hide underneath until the group passes.

"Keep It Up. We're Almost to the River, Just a Little Further."

Sprint to stay with Elias as he runs up the stream. The stream leads to the jungle. Crouch behind Elias and wait for the team orders to advance. If you follow his orders precisely, you can make it through this section without getting spotted at all. Just crouch alongside Hesh and move when he moves.

When you are through the grass, sprint after the squad.

After the rocket blasts off, sprint to the left to avoid the attack chopper. Slide down the hill and keep sprinting through the forest, chasing Merrick.

The jungle leads to tall grass. A number of ghillie-suited Federation arrive via helicopter.

"Move Quiet, and Keep Low. Meet Up at the Ridge on the Other Side."

For this section, move with the Ghosts single-file through the grass. Keegan is an excellent leader, and he gets you through undetected—provided you stay low and keep close.

When you make it to the waterfall, the level is complete.

THE HUNTED

Complete this mission on any difficulty to earn the Achievement/Trophy "The Hunted."

ACHIEVEMENT/TROPHY

10 CLOCKWORK

THE ANDES, PATAGONIA | JUNE 20, 2028 — 22:35:42

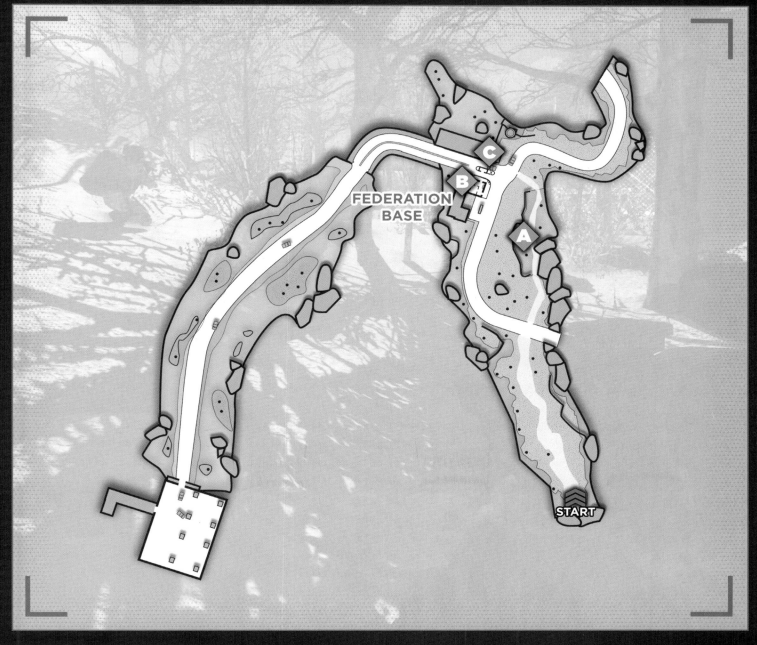

FEDERATION BASE

C

B

A

START

OPERATIVE

LOGAN WALKER

SUPPORT

HESH WALKER KEEGAN MERRICK

MISSION DETAILS

Infiltrate a Federation facility and retrieve data on their missile program.

OBJECTIVES

A Get into base undetected.

B Clean up Checkpoint.

C Take out the vehicle's driver.

D Disable the security door before power is restored.

E Advance to the data center.

F Defend Hesh as he retrieves the data.

G Escape through the vault door.

H Exit the Facility.

I Get to the Extraction Point.

LOADOUT

PRIMARY	SECONDARY
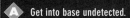	
LYNX SILENCED	SA-805 CUSTOM

GRENADES & EQUIPMENT	
	NIGHT VISION GOGGLES
	TEAR GAS
	PROXIMITY MINES
	SHOCK CLAYMORES
FRAG GRENADES, FLASHBANGS	AUTOMATED TURRET

GET INTO BASE UNDETECTED

This mission starts moments after your team has neutralized and exchanged uniforms with a group of Federation soldiers. Follow your team to the snowy path.

"…and the Guard on the Tower Makes Nine."

When you reach the Federation HQ's checkpoint, Merrick counts the soldiers. He gives you the order to kill the tower guard. The target enemy is standing at the top of a very tall circular tower—look up, and to the right. You must use your silenced Lynx to take him down.

Take your time to line up the perfect shot, and down the defender. Don't forget, you can hold your breath to steady your shot.

Now Merrick changes focus to the three soldiers in front of the second floor of the building on the left. Line up the middle soldier, and down him when ready. Your team eliminates the other two.

Now pick any of the lower targets, and open fire when ready. When the checkpoint is clear, Merrick instructs your team to move up.

CLEAN UP CHECKPOINT

Move down into the base and press the **Interact** button on the soldier slumped over the front concrete barrier. Now, wait for the convoy to arrive. Stand near the body you just cleared.

TAKE OUT THE VEHICLE'S DRIVER

After a few moments, the mechanical patrol arrives. Approach the driver of the jeep and use a **Melee** attack to kill him. Press the **Interact** button to board the back of the jeep.

"Everyone In, Let's Go."

Keegan drives the team into the base. Your disguises are solid, so you won't initially attract any enemy attention.

Get out of the vehicle and keep your weapon down. Follow your team through the security doors. When the countdown completes, the lights go out in the base. Press your **Inventory** button to equip your Night Vision Goggles. Time to clean house.

The uniforms on this level are Federation snow camo. The Ghosts are disguised as Federation on this mission, so distinguishing them from your enemies can be tricky. The easiest way to tell them apart is by the backpacks they are carrying. In the last part of the level, you must distinguish them by their headgear.

Open fire with your SA-805 on the blind enemies.

Keep up with your team as they move to a computer room.

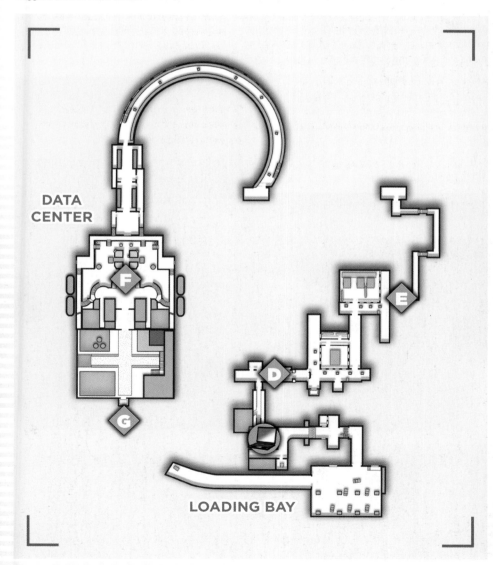

DATA CENTER

F

G

E

D

LOADING BAY

SPECIALIZED TRAINING   **THE CAMPAIGN**   MP INTRO & BASIC TRAINING   SQUADS   MP ARMORY   PERKS   KILLSTREAKS   MP MAPS   MP GAME MODES   SAFEGUARD   EXTINCTION   CLASSIFIED   ACHIEVEMENTS & TROPHIES

63

"Clockwork" Rorke File

Find this level's Rorke File in the same room that Hesh plants the bug on the Federation server. Look on a desk to the right of where Hesh and the rest of the group are standing.

Wait for Hesh to run the computer program. When he's done, follow your team down the hall. The Federation troops have found some flashlights, but they are still pretty much helpless against your night vision. Mow down any resistance while proceeding to the blast door.

D OBJECTIVE

DISABLE THE SECURITY DOOR BEFORE POWER IS RESTORED

When you reach the blast door, you automatically remove your Night Vision Goggles. Wait for Hesh to mark the door. Then pick up the drill with the **Interact** button and press **Fire** to begin drilling on the X.

When drilling, watch the screen above the drill. You don't want to drill into the "Fault Line" point in the x-ray diagram.

E OBJECTIVE

ADVANCE TO THE DATA CENTER

When the door blows, push through to the secure laboratory. Initially, the guards are very confused and won't attack your team, but that quickly changes. Find cover and pick off the defenders in the main hallway.

Some enemy reinforcements arrive from the left. Keep firing until Merrick issues an order to go. Move with the team down the corridor and through a doorway on the left. When you see two soldiers run past through the double doors, open fire. About a half dozen more defenders are past the double doors on the right. Stay in cover and work with your team to clear out the area.

"I'm Seeing Minimal Activity on the High Road."

When you've defeated the resistance, Keegan leads the team to an outside walkway. Follow him until you see the large rotunda area. You have the drop on these troops. Move to the end of the walkway, and use the square structure for cover. Fire through the glass at the enemies inside. Your team charges ahead, but you should hang back and provide cover.

YOU'RE THE GOOD GUYS HERE...

Once you enter the lab area, several scientists are running around. Be careful not to shoot them—killing civilians results in an immediate mission failure.

When you've cleared most of the enemies, it's time to move through the rotunda. Advance cautiously and use the pillars for cover. Some stragglers arrive toward the end of the area. Keep a cautious eye to the walkway above; one or two guards may still be alive there.

When you reach the end of the rotunda, you've cleared the data center's defenses. Only unarmed scientists remain. Fire your weapon to clear the scientists, and then move to the raised platform in the data center's middle. At the top of the platform, notice a hot spot to drop your bag off. Quickly hit the **Interact** button to deposit the bag.

"I'll Need 2 Minutes 30 to Complete the Download."

DEFEND HESH AS HE RETRIEVES THE DATA

Your job now is to set up defenses to protect Hesh while he hacks into the data center. You have claymores, mines, and an automated turret at your disposal.

A large amount of enemies are about to arrive. There's no perfect strategy for this section. You also don't have enough time to place all the mines and claymores. We recommend you prioritize planting the claymores, then the mines. Save the turret for when the enemies start arriving.

Plant your mines and claymores on the indicated chokepoints. Make sure to space any mines you put down outside of the chokepoints far enough apart so they don't cause a chain explosion.

When the enemies start arriving, quickly plant the turret in the main window. Then grab either the Lynx sniper rifle or the M27-IAR LMG resting on the main platform's edges. Finally, grab the Tear Gas Grenades out of the bag. This keeps the enemies at bay once they've destroyed your traps.

When the enemy charges your position, your traps won't be enough to stop them. You need to use cover to kill the troops before they can get close to Hesh. Initially, fire at the troops as they advance from the entranceways. Later, take cover behind the control panel to shoot the enemies as they make it onto the raised platform near Hesh. When the enemy starts making it to your position, flip the auto gun around so it defends Hesh directly.

When the enemy starts charging the platform en masse (Hesh will have his progress at around 90%), start using your flashbangs or tear gas to slow down the enemies. You need to keep the enemies off Hesh for a few more seconds to complete the objective.

ESCAPE THROUGH THE VAULT DOOR

When Hesh is done, sprint to the back of the area to the open door. Once through, turn toward your team and provide cover as everyone fights through to the door. Take the freight elevator up to exit the area.

EXIT THE FACILITY

Keep your gun down and follow your team through the destroyed facility. Your team makes it all the way to the jeep area where you first arrived at the base.

Avoid firing or meleeing once in the jeep. When the alarm goes off, you automatically get on the jeep's missile turret.

GHOSTS ARSENAL

HESH

H I

☐ CHOKE POINT

SPECIALIZED TRAINING **THE CAMPAIGN** MP INTRO & BASIC TRAINING SQUADS MP ARMORY PERKS KILLSTREAKS MP MAPS MP GAME MODES SAFEGUARD EXTINCTION CLASSIFIED ACHIEVEMENTS & TROPHIES

65

GET TO THE EXTRACTION POINT

During this driving section, focus on attacking the ice. Blowing a hole in the ice can not only destroy the jeep you are aiming at, but it also blocks the path for any enemies traveling behind it. You have unlimited grenades that reload in about a second.

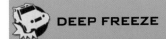

DEEP FREEZE

To score this Achievement/Trophy, you have to drop eight of the vehicles into holes. Follow the preceding strategy outlines, and this should be no problem.

ACHIEVEMENT/TROPHY

STEP-BY-STEP BREAKDOWN

1 Keep the gun aimed forward as you exit the base. Fire on the road block.

2 As you exit the base, turn the turret behind your jeep. Destroy the jeeps that come into view.

3 When your jeep falls to the ice, start making holes in the ice to stall your pursuers.

4 Keep firing into the ice to destroy the snowmobiles.

5 When you exit the tunnel, you are attacked by jeeps on the left and right. Destroy them quickly by blowing holes in the ice. If you get it right, you can prevent reinforcements from arriving.

6 After crossing under the bridge, change your focus to the jeep's left side.

7 After the right jeeps are down, turn to the front of your vehicle. More jeeps will assault from ahead.

8 You are clear when the sun comes out.

CLOCKWORK

Complete this mission on any difficulty to earn the Achievement/Trophy "Clockwork."

ACHIEVEMENT/TROPHY

FEDRATION ANTARCTIC BASE

C

B

A

ICE

START

OPERATIVE

LOGAN WALKER

SUPPORT

HESH WALKER

MERRICK

KEEGAN

KICK

MISSION DETAILS

Sabotage the Atlas oil platform as a diversionary tactic.

OBJECTIVES

A — Detonate charges.

B — Clear the base camp.

C — Ascend to catwalks using Ascender Gun.

D — Fight to the pressure regulators.

E — Shut off the pressure regulators.

F — Fight to the command center.

G — Disable the water suppression and destroy the oil rig.

H — Escape the oil rig.

LOADOUT

PRIMARY

REMINGTON R5 RED DOT SIGHT

SECONDARY

P226

GRENADES & EQUIPMENT

FRAG GRENADES, FLASHBANGS, ASCENDER GUN

"Eyes Coming Up."

You start this mission staring through a tactical periscope; a Federation base is in view with several soldiers walking around. After getting an eyeful, you return under the ice where your Ghost team has planted charges.

A OBJECTIVE

DETONATE CHARGES

When Merrick gives the order, press the **Fire** button to detonate the ice charges, sending a swathe of Federation soldiers into the icy waters. Use your machine guns to finish them, then follow Hesh and Merrick as they head to the ice break above. Push into the ice break to automatically exit the waters.

B OBJECTIVE

CLEAR THE BASE CAMP

Keegan helps you to your feet. The Federation defenses are in shambles. Take cover on a nearby wooden crate and pick off the remaining defenses.

A helicopter brings in reinforcements. Stick to cover and continue picking off the enemies from long range.

When you've killed most of the nearby enemies, search the downed troops for a second assault rifle to replace your pistol.

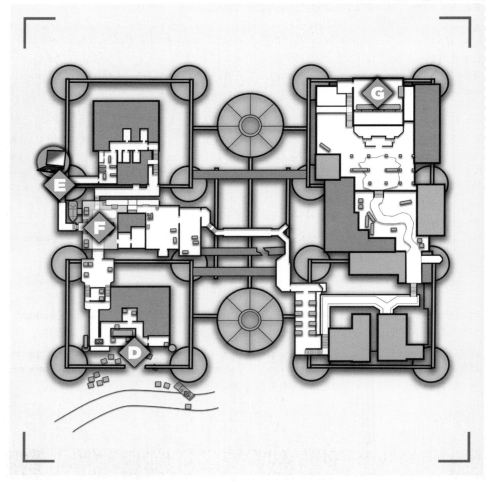

C OBJECTIVE

ASCEND TO CATWALKS USING ASCENDER GUN

Once the Federation reinforcements are defeated, Merrick orders you to the area below the oil rig. Move close to your team, then press and hold the **Interact** button to pull out the Ascender Gun. Press **Fire** to release a grappling hook. Hold down the **Fire** button to climb to the catwalks.

FIGHT TO THE PRESSURE REGULATORS

A significant enemy force guards the catwalks. Immediately move to cover, and then start firing on the closest enemies to soften the incoming fire. If you're getting some trouble from this force, use a flashbang to soften them up.

When the lower area is clear, crouch and proceed up the steep stairs. These stairs provide excellent cover while crouching. Creep up and look for enemies perched on an upper walkway. Kill both the enemies above, and then turn your focus to the defenders on your level.

"Pressure Regulators are Up Ahead, Let's Move."

Follow Merrick and Hesh into the crew quarters. They do the job of clearing the rooms, so just hang back and wait. Replace one of your guns with the MTS-255 shotgun from the enemy Hesh kills.

When Merrick gives the order, press the **Interact** button to place a charge on the door. A serious contingent of about 10 enemies is on the opposite side of the door. Press the **Tactical Grenade** button to toss flashbangs into the room, and fire on the enemies with your newly acquired shotgun.

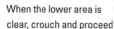

PIECE OF CAKE

For this Achievement/Trophy, you have to clear this room without taking damage on Veteran difficulty. The title of this Achievement/Trophy is a hint that this isn't as hard as it sounds. After the door breach, hang back to the left of the door. Fire at the door—a couple of enemies pop out there. They'll have a hard time getting a bead on you. Eventually, Merrick and Keegan move up through the door. Just hang back, and do not enter the room. Toss cooked Frag grenades into the room, but don't enter the doorway, or you risk getting shot. If you're patient and kill a few enemies, you can let Merrick and Keegan do most of the work for you, avoiding damage and earning the Achievement/Trophy!

ACHIEVEMENT/TROPHY

The flashbangs have limited range, so be cautious of the enemies at the back of the room; they may not be affected by the stunning blast.

SHUT OFF THE PRESSURE REGULATORS

When you've cleared the room, your team now has access to the oil rig's pressure regulators. Proceed with Merrick and press and hold the **Interact** button to blow the pressure regulators.

"Atlas Falls" Rorke File

Before hitting the pressure regulator button, check the room on the right. The Rorke File is on a file cabinet.

"It's about to Get Nasty Out There."

FIGHT TO THE COMMAND CENTER

Follow Merrick topside and wait for the pressure containers to blow. When they do, open fire on the enemies running through the area.

Oil Rig Workers are Fair Game

The oil rig workers in the area are considered enemy combatants since they are armed. You may fire on them with impunity throughout this area.

When you've cleared the initial group of Federation enemies, move to the building on your right. Use the windows inside for cover while firing on the remaining defenders at the back of this area. Pay special caution of the soldier on the catwalk above; he has a rocket launcher.

SPECIALIZED TRAINING   THE CAMPAIGN   MP INTRO & BASIC TRAINING   SQUADS   MP ARMORY   PERKS   KILLSTREAKS   MP MAPS   MP GAME MODES   SAFEGUARD   EXTINCTION   CLASSIFIED   ACHIEVEMENTS & TROPHIES

69

Smoke Fight

When the area is safe, Merrick runs forward to lead the charge along the catwalk to the rig's next section. Follow Merrick into the smoky corridors, but keep crouched to avoid taking damage from the smoke.

Push through the smoke and use your shotgun to mow down the enemies before they can muster a defense. Climb the staircase at the back of the area to get above the smoke.

"Merrick, We're on Station. Ready for Targets."

When you make it up top, air support hovers nearby. Climb one more set of stairs, and your gunship opens fire on the enemies trying to contain the fire. Time to make your final assault to the command center.

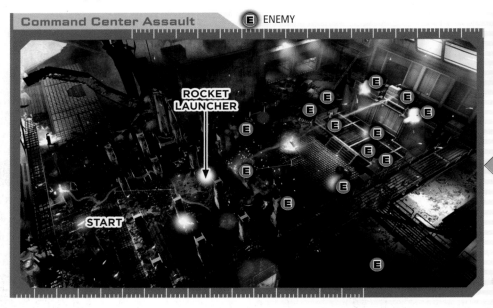

Command Center Assault   ENEMY

The command center is well defended by many Federation troops. Stay behind the nearby barrels to pick off any white uniforms popping out from cover. Pay attention to the catwalk above; one rocket launcher troop is up there.

As you push forward, some enemies move to use the machine gun at the back of the area. When this happens, move to the rocket launcher marked on the Air Intel. Use the rocket to take out one of the machine guns. Then use your long-range weapon from the good cover there to take out the second.

When the balcony is secure, your helicopter arrives to eliminate the remaining troops. Follow Merrick up the staircases into the fire suppression command center.

G **OBJECTIVE**

DISABLE THE WATER SUPPRESSION AND DESTROY THE OIL RIG

Once inside the command center, press the **Interact** button to remove the corpse from the console. This starts a mini-game where you must keep the three bars in the middle green zone long enough for Merrick to overload each of the pumps.

 GRINDIN'

This Achievement/Trophy is a reference to another Activision title: Tony Hawk's Pro Skater. In Tony Hawk, you have to balance a meter to successfully grind along a rail, similar to how you have to blow the pressure valves here. Simply pass the mini-game on your first attempt.

ACHIEVEMENT/TROPHY

Keeping it in the yellow is fine, but if the dial is in the red for too long, you fail.

H **OBJECTIVE**

ESCAPE THE OIL RIG

Once the rig blows, it's time to go. Sprint after Merrick as he runs outside to the catwalk. Run to the catwalk's end and jump to complete the mission.

ATLAS FALLS

Complete this mission on any difficulty to earn the Achievement/Trophy "Atlas Falls."

ACHIEVEMENT/TROPHY

LIGHTHOUSE

A

START

OPERATIVE

SUPPORT

LOGAN WALKER

KEEGAN

OBJECTIVES

◆ A Neutralize AEGIS class combat ship.

◆ B Regroup at the rally point.

MISSION DETAILS

Take out the remaining Federation ship to
infiltrate the factory.

LOADOUT

PRIMARY	GRENADES & EQUIPMENT
APS UNDERWATER RIFLE	PROTEUS MISSILE

OBJECTIVE

NEUTRALIZE AEGIS CLASS COMBAT SHIP

This mission takes place entirely underwater. You and Keegan are in charge of destroying a Federation ship. You're equipped with an APS Underwater Rifle. The rifle does low damage and has a slow rate of fire, but it's more effective and reliable than a normal weapon underwater.

Press the **Jump** or **Tactical Grenade** button to move up in the water; press the **Crouch** or **Frag Grenade** button to dive. Follow Keegan through the underwater passage.

Feeling Disoriented?

If you lose track of Keegan, his location is always indicated by a white arrow at the edge of the screen. To find him, turn toward the arrow.

"Keep Away from Open Water. We're Not the Only Hunters Out Here."

DON'T ENGAGE THE SHARKS!

It may be tempting, but trying to kill a shark on this level is always a bad idea. The shark almost always wins.

Throughout this intro section, follow Keegan's path very closely. If you stray too far, you may get eaten by a shark.

Swim to the shipwreck, and stay in cover as the submersible floats by.

Follow Keegan as he swims out of the shipwreck and to the next section. When you spot a group of four swimmers, get some good cover on the debris, and then open fire. The divers take cover behind the balloon submersible; keep firing at any body parts poking out from behind the cover.

Eventually, you encounter a boat patrol overhead. The boats deposit some Federation divers. Wait for Keegan's order, then slowly approach the divers. At the next rocky outcropping, line up the right diver with your sights. Open fire when Keegan gives the go ahead.

"We're Going Down through the Cave."

When you've finished off the diver troops, Keegan gives the order to swim through the cave at the other end of the area. As you move through the cave, sonic blasts rip through the water. These blasts cause damage if you're caught out in the open when one goes off.

Depth Charges

The sonic "ping" happens a few seconds before the blast rips through the water. When you hear the ping, do your best to get inside or underneath a structure to avoid taking damage from the water pressure.

At the end of the tunnel, hit the **Interact** button to help Keegan weld through the sealed ship door. When you're outside, swim to the shipping crate to avoid taking damage from the sonic blast. Immediately after the blast, hold the **Sprint** button to quickly move to the second container.

UNDERWATER KNIFE COMBAT

Getting too close to an enemy causes a "sudden death" quick time event. You must time a melee attack correctly in order to fight back and kill the enemy diver.

"The Target is on the Move. You Boys Need to Double-Time It..."

Keegan leads you to a larger group of enemies working in an underwater field. Swim up the large rock on the right to get a good flanking position above the divers. Fire at the closer divers first, then start working your way to the enemies at the back.

Now swim to the metal overhang. Wait there while Keegan swims ahead to the lighthouse. Wait for the "ping" to sound, and then quickly swim to the lighthouse.

Move to Keegan and hold the **Interact** button to deploy the Proteus missile. Press **Fire** to release the missile, and you automatically switch to the missile's infrared camera. You must steer the missile into the ship's red "hot zone" to destroy it. Be careful to avoid the netting in front of the ship. If your missile gets caught in it, you fail the mission.

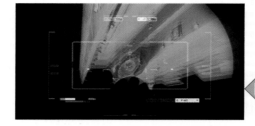

DAVID & GOLIATH

Destroy the ship on your first attempt to earn this Achievement/Trophy.

ACHIEVEMENT/TROPHY

WARNING: SHARKS!

B

"Talk to Me, Logan. You Okay?"

After the lighthouse collapses, follow the onscreen prompts to escape from the debris.

B **OBJECTIVE**

REGROUP AT THE RALLY POINT

When you've escaped, hold down the **Sprint** button to keep up with Keegan as he swims to a safe area. As long as you stay directly behind Keegan, you can avoid the incoming wreckage.

When you see the submersibles pass overhead, use the nearby metal piece for cover: enemies incoming! Keep in cover; it frustrates the divers, causing them to charge you. This makes them easy targets.

"Into the Deep" Rorke File

This Rorke File is hard to see due to the depth-of-field effect while you're swimming. Look to your right when exiting the top of the first ship you attacked the enemies from. The ship is positioned vertically and has some rusty cars inside.

The Rorke File is on a rock, facing away from the ship. Swim around the right area after you've cleared the enemies to find it. If you reach the natural arch, you went too far.

When the waters are clear, inch forward. A second submersible arrives with six more enemies on board. Use the coral for cover and pick them off before they release from the vessel.

"They're Dropping Depth Charges!"

Through the natural underwater arch, more soldiers defend an area near another shipwreck. As you move towards the arch, the Federation ships start dropping depth charges on your position. Ignore the underwater defenders and swim after Keegan as he travels to the shipwreck.

SHARK WATERS

Inside the wreck, Keegan slows down. Keep behind him until you see the great white shark pass. The sharks are full on Federation, so they aren't very aggressive. Just keep your distance to avoid getting eaten.

Follow Keegan's orders closely to make it through the patrolling sharks. In the overhead shark room, wait patiently for an opening between the patrolling sharks.

When you've cleared the shark room, follow Keegan through the ship's ballroom and down the hatch to the lower deck. The other side leads to safety and the end of the mission.

 INTO THE DEEP

Complete this mission on any difficulty to earn the Achievement/Trophy "Into the Deep."

ACHIEVEMENT/TROPHY

SPECIALIZED TRAINING   THE CAMPAIGN   MP INTRO & BASIC TRAINING   SQUADS   MP ARMORY   PERKS   KILLSTREAKS   MP MAPS   MP GAME MODES   SAFEGUARD   EXTINCTION   CLASSIFIED   ACHIEVEMENTS & TROPHIES

75

13 END OF THE LINE

NORTH RIO DE JANEIRO, FEDERATION TERRITORY | JUNE 27, 2028 — 22:17:22

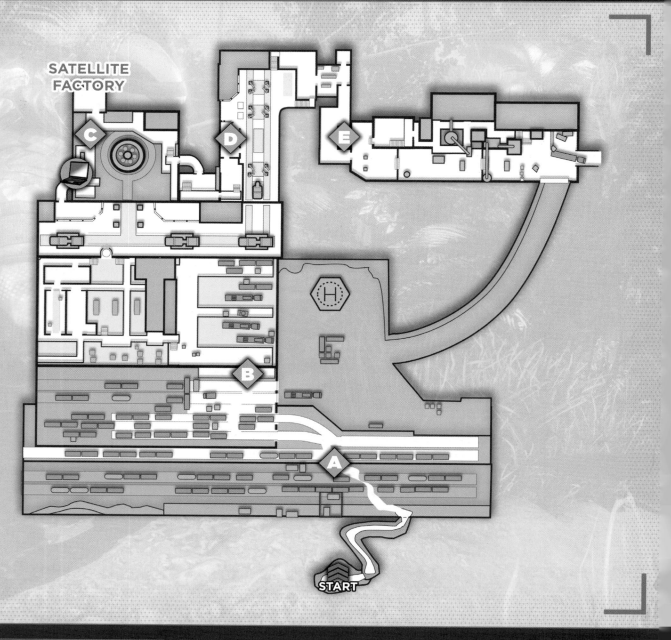

SATELLITE FACTORY

C

D

E

B

H

A

START

OPERATIVE

LOGAN WALKER

SUPPORT

MERRICK

KEEGAN

HESH WALKER

KICK

MISSION DETAILS

Learn what the Federation is hiding.

OBJECTIVES

A — Infiltrate the factory.

B — Access Black Zone.

C — Upload visual scans of the weaponized rods.

D — Investigate the factory computer records.

E — Escape the factory.

LOADOUT

PRIMARY

HONEY BADGER CUSTOM

SECONDARY

P226 CUSTOM

GRENADES & EQUIPMENT

FRAG GRENADES, FLASHBANGS
CAMERA
THERMAL GOGGLES

"There Was Something in That Factory, Something the Federation Never Wanted Us to See…"

This mission starts just outside a Federation factory. This top-secret facility contains whatever weapon the Federation has been constructing in secret.

Start the mission with a drop-kill. Press the **Melee** button to drop down with Merrick and dispatch the pair of guards.

Follow Merrick to Entry A. When you see the solo guard move, finish him silently with a melee attack.

OBJECTIVE

A

INFILTRATE THE FACTORY

Kick heads off on his own to prepare your evac and get eyes on the base. Follow the bulk of your squad to the left.

Around the corner, a large truck arrives. When your squad is in position, use your silenced weapon to down a guard; your team finishes the rest.

OBJECTIVE

B

ACCESS BLACK ZONE

🐇 COG IN THE MACHINE

You must kill five enemies stealthily to earn this Achievement/Trophy. Before the large bay door opens, you should have three stealth kills. The two guards just on the other side are numbers four and five. Down them quickly to earn the Achievement/Trophy.

ACHIEVEMENT/TROPHY

Hesh secures an access card and opens the bay door. Merrick and Keegan kill the two guards near the door. Grab an assault rifle to replace your pistol from one of these guards.

Inside the facility, follow Hesh to a computer room. A lone guard blocks the corridor. Kill him with your silenced weapon. Around the next doorway, use a **Melee** attack to finish the guard sitting at the computer. Then regroup with your team at the south vault door.

"Whatever's in There, They Want to Keep It Safe."

A half dozen Federation guards are inside the Black Zone. Your team has the jump on them. Stay in the doorway and down any enemies out from cover. More reinforcements arrive from the room to the left and back of the area.

OBJECTIVE

C

UPLOAD VISUAL SCANS OF THE WEAPONIZED RODS

When the area is clear, move to the room where the reinforcements came from.

SPECIALIZED TRAINING **THE CAMPAIGN** MP INTRO & BASIC TRAINING   SQUADS   MP ARMORY   PERKS   KILLSTREAKS   MP MAPS   MP GAME MODES   SAFEGUARD   EXTINCTION   CLASSIFIED   ACHIEVEMENTS & TROPHIES

77

"End of the Line" Rorke File

Before taking pictures of the kinetic rods, find the Rorke File on the crate behind the stairs leading into the room.

Hit your **Inventory** button to take out the camera. With the camera engaged, look up at the satellite until the kinetic rods are highlighted (Elias instructs you where to look).

D OBJECTIVE

INVESTIGATE THE FACTORY COMPUTER RECORDS

Follow your team out of the area. When your team stops, **Interact** with the computer to search the records.

When the lights go dim, back away from the door.

E OBJECTIVE

ESCAPE THE FACTORY

After the blast, use your gun to eliminate enemies breaching from the right side. When they're clear, crawl to the desk and shoot over it to kill the enemies attacking from the left side. Defend from the desk area until the team pops the smoke.

KNOW YOUR ENEMY

With your thermal up, enemies are highlighted in red hues, while your allies are highlighted in blue hues.

1 Activate thermal and move into the smoke.

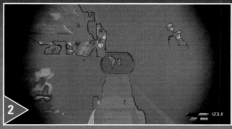

2 Shoot any enemies in front of you. They won't be able to see you.

3 To get the shield enemies, toss a flashbang to stun them and force them to move their shield.

4 Move to where the riot shield guards were and deactivate your thermal when the flashbang goes off.

5 Grab one of the guard's riot shields.

6 Hang back behind cover and fire on the enemies attacking from the corner of the room. Clear out the entire area.

7 Use your riot shield and head up the stairs. With the riot shield out, charge the enemies, leading your team through the armory.

8 Follow Merrick down the hallway.

9 Use your riot shield for cover. When the guy on the left goes down, replace your shield with the guard's LMG (M27-IAR).

10 Wait for an enemy to emerge from the doorway above. Kill him, reload the LMG, then head upstairs.

11 Stay crouched and move along the walkway, using the LMG to mow down any enemies that get in your way.

12 When you reach the end of the walkway, use the vantage point to kill the remaining Federation resistance blocking your exit.

Now that you've survived the initial counterattack, follow your team to the lower area. Find cover behind a dumpster, and wait for Kick to arrive with your evac.

Don't bother shooting the main force of enemies here, just focus on the ones that try to flank your right side. When Kick arrives, sprint to the back of the flatbed semi.

For this last section, go prone to avoid taking damage. Fire on the trucks as they approach, but the air strike does most of the work to secure your exit.

END OF THE LINE

Complete this mission on any difficulty to earn the Achievement/Trophy "End of the Line."

ACHIEVEMENT/TROPHY

SPECIALIZED TRAINING **THE CAMPAIGN** MP INTRO & BASIC TRAINING SQUADS MP ARMORY PERKS KILLSTREAKS MP MAPS MP GAME MODES SAFEGUARD EXTINCTION CLASSIFIED ACHIEVEMENTS & TROPHIES

79

14 SIN CITY

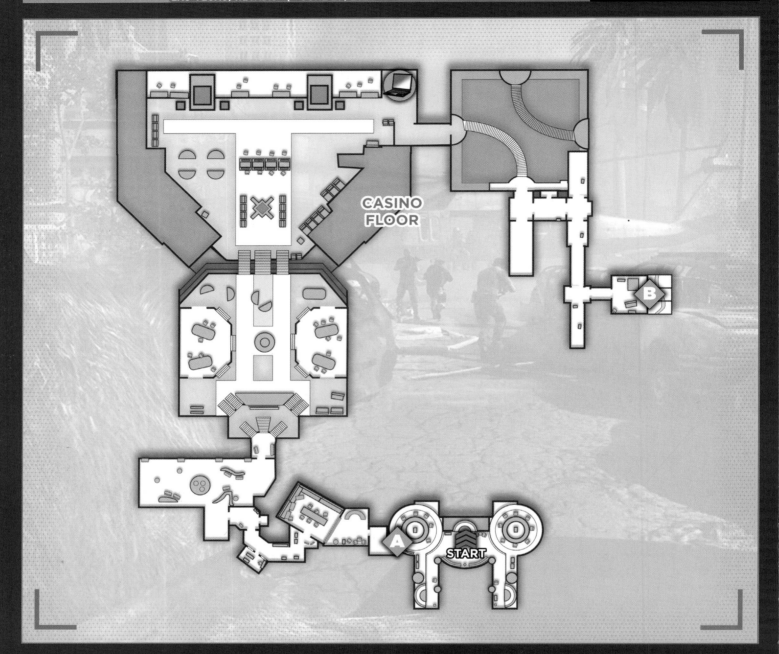

CASINO FLOOR

B

A

START

OPERATIVE

LOGAN WALKER

SUPPORT

ELIAS WALKER

MERRICK

HESH WALKER

RILEY

LOADOUT

PRIMARY

REMINGTON R5, ACOG SCOPE

SECONDARY

P226 PISTOL

OBJECTIVES

 A Escape.

 B Carry Riley to the extraction point.

MISSION DETAILS

Return to the safehouse and wait for Keegan.

"Hold Up, Something Feel Off to You?"

The Ghosts return to their Vegas safehouse and are ambushed by Rorke. Upon waking to find yourself tied to a chair, you must wait for an opportunity to escape. When Rorke turns to hit Elias, that's your chance. Hit the **Interact** button as fast as possible to slip free of the bonds. Once free, Logan automatically grabs Rorke's gun.

Escaping is Difficulty-Dependent

The number of presses needed to break free of your bonds is dependent on the game's difficulty. Players on Veteran must hit Interact 40 times; players on Regular only need to hit Interact 25 times.

"Hesh, Now!"

After the Rorke incident, Logan finds himself surrounded by Federation troops. When the shots start raining down on the Feds, wait for the opportunity to grab a P226 pistol on the floor.

When you've grabbed the pistol, open fire on the soldier to your left. Now, help your team kill the remaining troops. Look for the gun closet to arm up. Inside, find a L115 sniper rifle, a Bulldog, and a Remington R5 rifle. Be sure to grab a long-range weapon and complement it with a short-range weapon like the Bulldog. Now that you're armed, it's time to escape.

A OBJECTIVE

ESCAPE

Move to the big doors where Hesh is readied. When Hesh opens the doors, he takes a nearby soldier as a human shield. Stay in cover and fire on the soldiers at the back of the room.

Keegan reunites with the team in the kitchen. Heed his advice, and take cover in the side room with the rest of the Ghosts as the enemies pass. Don't fire on any enemies or you'll be quickly overwhelmed.

"All right, Keegan. Kick It Off."

Move with the team through the casino exit into the mall area. Find cover at the top of the escalators and wait for Keegan to begin firing.

SPECIALIZED TRAINING **THE CAMPAIGN** MP INTRO & BASIC TRAINING SQUADS MP ARMORY PERKS KILLSTREAKS MP MAPS MP GAME MODES SAFEGUARD EXTINCTION CLASSIFIED ACHIEVEMENTS & TROPHIES

81

The Federation wear a new type of black-leather uniform on this level.

Your primary concern here is to eliminate the enemies arriving on the top of the bar to your left, and the club on your right. Use your long-range weapon to pick off the enemies that rappel down. If you take some damage, go prone behind the center divider.

Casino Mall

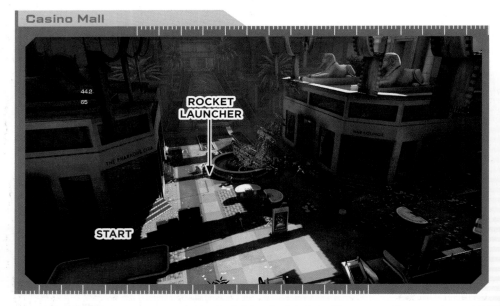

When you've cleared the enemies above, turn your attention to the enemies below. They have now filtered into the club and bar areas. Stay back and exercise some patience, waiting for the enemies to move from cover.

When your team moves, stay behind cover and let them lead the charge to mop up the remaining Federation forces. When the fire dies down, move to the fountain level and use the generous cover there to defend against a second wave of Federation reinforcements.

When you've downed the second wave of enemies, move to the second set of escalators. More Federation defenders are in the casino area below. These defenders are well spread out. Use the upper railing for cover and fire down on the scrambling enemies.

I'm Running Out of Ammo!

The sheer number of enemies may cause you to run out of ammo for your long-range weapon. If you run out, search the corpses near the fountain and in the club and bar for another rifle or more ammo.

Many enemies are in the lower area, along with a couple waves of mini-reinforcements. Continue using cover and pick off the enemies from safety until the casino floor is silent.

JACK-POT

You must destroy 21 slot machines to earn this achievement. The first 20 slot machines are in the lower casino floor. The last five slot machines are harder to find. After going through the gate, the team leads you down a curving escalator. Before going down the escalator, look across the majestic lobby. Notice two Egyptian women on a billboard with a stylistic sun. The last row of slot machines is just to this billboard's left.

ACHIEVEMENT/TROPHY

"We Need to Get Through That Gate."

With the area temporarily safe, proceed down the escalator. Switch to your short-range weapon in case you run into any enemies still hiding behind cover. Keegan opens the door for you. Crouch under it and follow Merrick down the frozen escalators into the hotel area.

"Sin City" Rorke File

When you go through the gate that Keegan pries open, look to your left. The Rorke File is out in the open among some toppled casino props.

"Back It Up! Back Up!"

When Merrick stacks up on the door, you run into a huge team of Federation troops. You definitely don't want to tangle with that many enemies out in the open. Unfortunately, your retreat has been blocked by another platoon.

Sprint after Keegan down the opposite hall. Yet another platoon arrives to corner your squad. Crouch down for some cover, and wait for your team to move through the door on the left. As soon as Merrick is through the door, sprint after him.

Jump out the casino window.

"Take It Slow, We're Going to be Outnumbered."

After your less-than-graceful landing, you're immediately besieged by enemies arriving via helicopter on the outside of the casino. Stay away from the large windows and find cover in the middle of the room you wake up in. Clear out most of the enemies, and then move toward the big doors.

CARRY RILEY TO THE EXTRACTION POINT

Unfortunately, Riley takes a bullet. You must carry him to the extraction zone.

NEVER LEAVE A DOG BEHIND!

While you can move forward without Riley, never leave him too far behind. If you get too far ahead, you fail the mission.

Press and hold the **Interact** button to pick up Riley and move him to the cover of the blown-out police car. Put Riley down and open fire on the helicopter hovering in the courtyard. Shoot at the soldiers in the helicopter until it crashes. If you can find a LSAT LMG from a downed enemy, it makes taking out the choppers much easier.

Carry Riley again and move up the area's left side. Put him down near the Hiero monolith, and open fire on the second helicopter.

When you've destroyed the helicopter, leave Riley and move to the courtyard with the wrecked subway cars and miniature sphinxes. You must clear out this courtyard before moving up with Riley. About a half-dozen enemies are scattered throughout this area. Wait for them to reveal themselves from cover and pick them off.

When the area is quiet, pick up Riley and move to one of the mini sphinxes. More enemies are arriving on the left. Stay in cover and fire on the reinforcements arriving via helicopter. Once you've cleared the area, pick up Riley and move to the next subway car. The subway car and the sphinxes provide plenty of cover against another helicopter full of reinforcements. Continue fighting and progressing from cover to cover until your air support arrives.

"Ghost Six, We Got a Ride Home for You Guys If You Want It."

With your air support inbound, your team advances, clearing out any remaining hidden Federation troops. Grab Riley and sprint down the path through the wrecked automobiles to the level exit.

 SIN CITY

Complete this mission on any difficulty to earn the "Sin City" achievement.

ACHIEVEMENT/TROPHY

SPECIALIZED TRAINING **THE CAMPAIGN** MP INTRO & BASIC TRAINING SQUADS MP ARMORY PERKS KILLSTREAKS MP MAPS MP GAME MODES SAFEGUARD EXTINCTION CLASSIFIED ACHIEVEMENTS & TROPHIES

83

15 ALL OR NOTHING

U.S.S. LIBERATOR, PACIFIC OCEAN | JULY 5, 2028 — 08:16:50

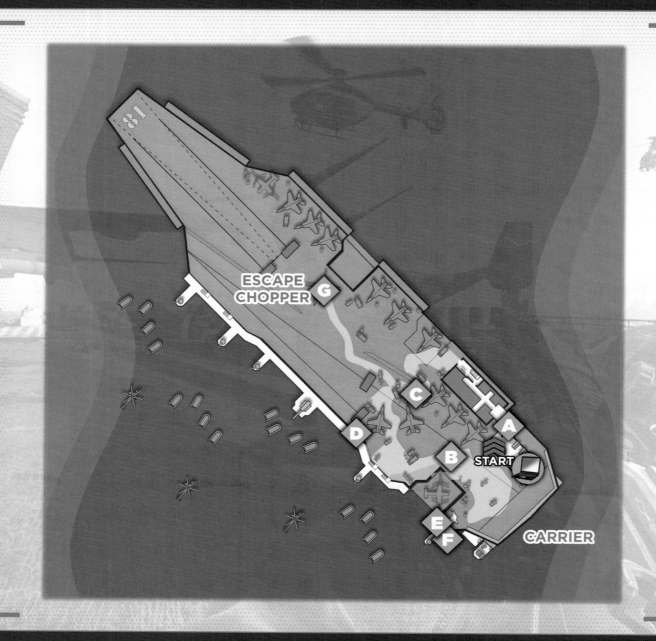

ESCAPE CHOPPER **G**

D

C

A

B START

E

F

CARRIER

OPERATIVE

LOGAN WALKER

SUPPORT

HESH WALKER

MISSION DETAILS

Defend the U.S.S. Liberator during the
assault on the Federation.

OBJECTIVES

- **A** Get to the flight deck.
- **B** Clear the flight deck.
- **C** Regroup with Hesh.
- **D** Defend the carrier.
- **E** Take control of the Sparrow launcher.
- **F** Destroy the Federation gunship.
- **G** Escape the sinking carrier.

LOADOUT

PRIMARY	SECONDARY

MSBS HOLOGRAPHIC	MR-28 ACOG SIGHT

GRENADES & EQUIPMENT

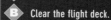

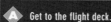

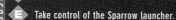
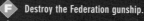

A OBJECTIVE

GET TO THE FLIGHT DECK

"All or Nothing" Rorke File

Before following Hesh to start the mission, search the bunks for the Rorke File. It's on a lower bunk adjacent to Logan's starting point.

You now join the US Invasion fleet as it heads deep into Federation territory to stop the Federation satellites from coming online. March after Hesh and he leads you through the lower carrier area and up to the carrier deck. The battle has already begun.

B OBJECTIVE

CLEAR THE FLIGHT DECK

U.S.S. Liberator

E ENEMY

CART COVER
ENEMY HELICOPTER REINFORCEMENTS
CART COVER

Topside, a strong force of Federation enemies is wreaking havoc on the deck. Move to the golf cart-like vehicle, take cover, and pick off enemies. Eventually, Hesh points out the Ospreys (a special helicopter that can fly like a jet) to your left. You must fight your way to that position. Stay crouched and use the parked fighter jets for cover.

When you make it about halfway to the Osprey, a group of enemy choppers arrives to your left. Fire at the choppers to drop as many enemies as possible before they land. Stay in cover and shoot any remaining reinforcements until Hesh gives the order to move on the Osprey.

C OBJECTIVE

REGROUP WITH HESH

Follow the objective marker to Hesh. When Hesh instructs you, press the **Interact** button to acquire the Osprey MG controls.

SPECIALIZED TRAINING **THE CAMPAIGN** MP INTRO & BASIC TRAINING SQUADS MP ARMORY PERKS KILLSTREAKS MP MAPS MP GAME MODES SAFEGUARD EXTINCTION CLASSIFIED ACHIEVEMENTS & TROPHIES

85

OBJECTIVE

DEFEND THE CARRIER

Shortly after the Osprey takes off, the Federation attacks with a full force of Zodiac tactical rafts on the ship's left side. Follow Hesh to the carrier's side and fire on the raiders below.

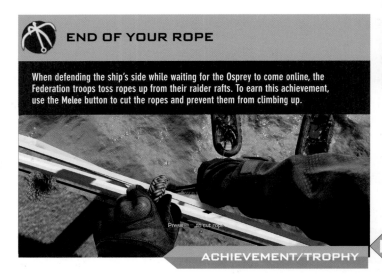

END OF YOUR ROPE

When defending the ship's side while waiting for the Osprey to come online, the Federation troops toss ropes up from their raider rafts. To earn this achievement, use the Melee button to cut the ropes and prevent them from climbing up.

ACHIEVEMENT/TROPHY

It's only necessary to hold off the enemies for about a minute before the Osprey's guns are in position to rain havoc on the invasion force. Press the **Inventory** button to activate the Osprey.

While controlling the Osprey's guns you have two weapons, the minigun and the rocket launcher. Unlike other machine guns used up to this point, this one never overheats. That means you should always hold down the **Aim Down Sight** button to keep the machine gun spun up and raining lead on the Federation. Use the **Fire** button to release rockets at enemies in the Osprey's crosshairs. These rockets are powerful and will down ships that are anywhere near where the rocket hits the water.

After your initial run with the Osprey, control returns to Logan. Don't worry too much about defending the ship from this position. Prioritize finding cover as you wait for the Osprey to ready a second time.

When the Osprey is ready, reactivate. This time you have the option to hit some of the Federation's destroyers. Use the Osprey missiles to demolish the highlighted targets on the side of the ship. Destroy as many targets as possible before control returns to Logan.

E **OBJECTIVE**

TAKE CONTROL OF THE SPARROW LAUNCHER

It's time to really hit back at the Federation. Follow Hesh as incoming mortars begin striking the deck. Slide down the destroyed section and open fire on the two Federation enemies on the right while sliding to the Sparrow deck in slow-motion. Climb to the upper area and hit the **Interact** button to remove the dead navy officer from the Sparrow's control laptop.

OBJECTIVE

DESTROY THE FEDERATION GUNSHIP

The Sparrow rocket launcher has a special lock-on system. Get any enemy in its square crosshairs, and the Sparrow automatically locks on. A wireframe representation of the target appears at the HUD's right. At the bottom of the screen, a radar graphic displays enemies as red dots. Use it to locate and lock on to enemies throughout this sequence. When you've locked on to an enemy, press the **Fire** button to unleash a series of powerful rockets.

The first target is the gigantic gunship floating directly ahead. You can only lock the gunship once. When you have one hit, turn your focus to the helicopters flying behind the gunship.

Now, use your radar to locate incoming Hind attack choppers. Target and down them before they get close enough to open fire on your position.

Between helicopter runs, the gunship returns to attack your position. Whenever it's in range and vulnerable, an onscreen indicator appears. Hit the gunship as quickly as possible, then return to targeting and firing on the Hinds. After three hits with the Sparrow, the gunship crashes.

OBJECTIVE

ESCAPE THE SINKING CARRIER

The Federation threat is online—the US must make its attack or be wiped out. Follow Hesh up the ladder to the carrier deck. Unfortunately, a Rod of God crashes into the carrier causing it to begin sinking. Sprint after Hesh across the deck. Avoid the sliding debris on the right. As long as you stay reasonably close to Hesh, you should have no problems clearing this area and making it to the chopper.

Reach the helicopter, and don't let the blast deter you. Get back up with the **Jump** button and sprint to the side of the chopper.

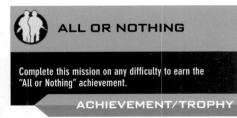

ALL OR NOTHING

Complete this mission on any difficulty to earn the "All or Nothing" achievement.

ACHIEVEMENT/TROPHY

SPECIALIZED TRAINING   **THE CAMPAIGN**   MP INTRO & BASIC TRAINING   SQUADS   MP ARMORY   PERKS   KILLSTREAKS   MP MAPS   MP GAME MODES   SAFEGUARD   EXTINCTION   CLASSIFIED   ACHIEVEMENTS & TROPHIES

87

START

OPERATIVE

BADGER, 2ND TANK BATTALION

MISSION DETAILS

Lead a desperate attack against the Federation's Ground Array.

OBJECTIVES

A Rendezvous with Bravo Company.

B Reach the airstrip.

C Eliminate airstrip defenses.

A OBJECTIVE

RENDEZVOUS WITH BRAVO COMPANY

This mission doesn't start as planned. Your tank takes an early exit from the carrier plane, and you hit the ground at speed. You may have missed your drop zone, but your mission is the same: move up and reinforce Bravo Company.

Use the **Movement** controls to blast forward through the solar farm. Over the next ridge, you encounter your first enemies while controlling the tank. The following explains the special tank controls:

The Fire button releases the tank's main cannon.

The Frag Grenade button fires the tank's machine gun.

The Tactical Grenade button releases a line of smoke.

The Interact button toggles on thermal vision. Thermal makes it easy to see through the smoke and ID your targets (inside or outside of smoke walls).

The Switch Weapon button switches to the Patriot XM11 guided missile. When this special weapon is fired, you can steer it directly into your target.

B OBJECTIVE

REACH THE AIRSTRIP

When you reach the satellite dish farm, enemy tanks are retreating from your advance. Use your tank's cannon to pick them off while continuing to speed through the farm.

KNOW YOUR ENEMY

It can be very difficult to tell the Federation tanks from the army tanks. Before firing, look for your targeting reticule to turn orange. This indicates you are about to fire at an enemy.

On the satellite farm's far side, some Hinds fly in to attack your position. Hit the Hinds with the Patriot XM11 guided missiles.

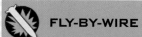

FLY-BY-WIRE

To earn this achievement, hit all three helicopters with the XM11 guided rockets. If you make a mistake, you can always restart the level (since this is so close to the level's start).

ACHIEVEMENT/TROPHY

Reach the opposite side of the satellite farm, drive up the hill, and blast through the concrete barriers to the mountain path on the other side. Continue moving forward to avoid getting hit by the mortars. The airstrip is just through the thin fence ahead.

C OBJECTIVE

ELIMINATE AIRSTRIP DEFENSES

Now that you've made it to the airstrip, you must destroy the four anti-aircraft vehicles hidden among the hangars. Keep moving and use the objective indicators to locate the missile batteries. If one of the rocket soldiers or Hinds manages to get a lock on you, pop a wall of smoke and use your thermal to evade the enemies.

You can charge through this section focusing entirely on offense, popping smoke to avoid missile attacks. Alternatively, you can take a more careful approach, downing the incoming Hinds with your XM11 missiles. Charging is a bit easier, but if you're playing on Veteran, you might want to try taking the more careful approach since your tank cannot take much damage.

When all four anti-air vehicles are in pieces, the first part of this mission is complete. It's time for the Ghosts to move in.

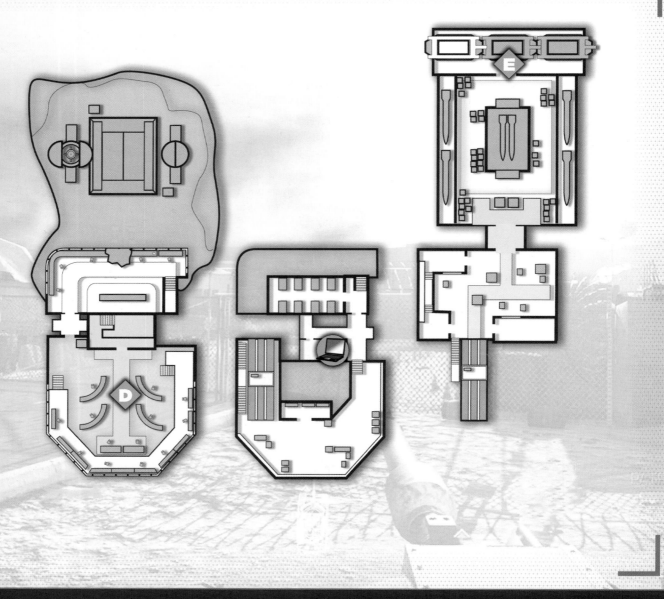

E

D

OPERATIVE

LOGAN WALKER

SUPPORT

HESH WALKER

LOADOUT

PRIMARY	SECONDARY	GRENADES & EQUIPMENT

LSAT LMG	VECTOR CRB HOLOGRAPHIC	FLASHBANG, FRAG GRENADES

OBJECTIVES

SECURE THE CONTROL ROOM AND LAUNCH THE MISSILE

In this next part of the mission, you lead the Ghosts into the Federation base to launch a missile at the station. As Logan, you control a minigun on the side of an attack chopper. Use the minigun to strafe the enemies you can spot on the exterior of the buildings.

When you approach the building with the large glass windows, open fire into the windows and kill as many enemies as possible. You're about to rappel into this room, so it's important that most of them are dead to ensure a safe entry.

Stay on the MG until most of the enemies are clear. Then hit the **Jump** button to breach the air traffic control room. Use the railing for cover and clear out any surviving enemies.

"Time to Improvise, On Your Go."

Follow Hesh through the air traffic control room to the lower double-doors. Press the **Interact** button to start the breach. Hesh throws a fire extinguisher toward the large group of enemies on the other side. Blow the extinguisher to stun the enemies, and then mow them down with your LSAT. In the next room, follow Hesh's orders and **Interact** with the glowing button to launch the missile.

REACH THE TRAIN

Launching the missile starts a nine-minute timer. However, radio chatter indicates that Rorke is nearby. The plan has changed! Follow Hesh to the lower area and start the fight toward Rorke.

"Severed Ties" Rorke File

When descending the stairs to follow Hesh, instead of continuing to the next room with enemies, explore the hallway on your right. Duck into the room on the left. Several computers are inside. The Rorke File is at the back of the room, on the left.

Nine minutes is plenty of time to make it to your goal, so don't feel too rushed in this section. Stick to the basics, as these enemies are very challenging. Stay in cover and fire on enemies when they pop out. The enemies here are very difficult, and they're well-armed. They will kill you quickly if you don't use caution.

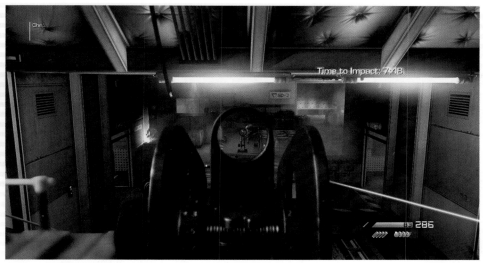

Continue fighting until you make it to the cargo elevator. As the cargo elevator descends, several enemies are working on the missiles in the next room. Use the large crates for cover and open fire on the enemies. Several Federation troops are in the bottom area, and as you advance, some more reinforcements arrive on the overhead walkway.

When you get to the back of the area, the train begins to move. Ignore any remaining enemies and sprint for the train car's side. Use the rails for cover and ride the train out of the area.

SPECIALIZED TRAINING   THE CAMPAIGN   MP INTRO & BASIC TRAINING   SQUADS   MP ARMORY   PERKS   KILLSTREAKS   MP MAPS   MP GAME MODES   SAFEGUARD   EXTINCTION   CLASSIFIED   ACHIEVEMENTS & TROPHIES

91

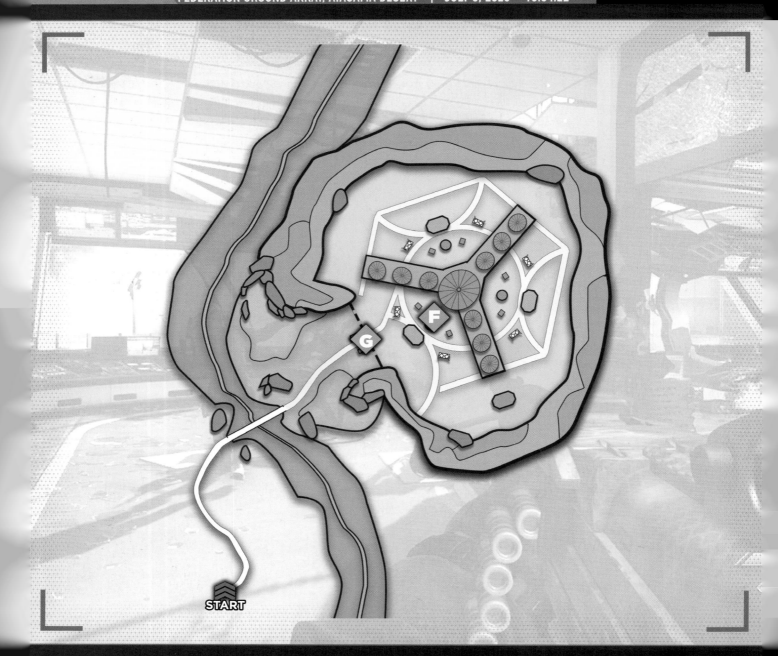

START

G

F

MISSION DETAILS

Lead a desperate attack against the Federation's ground array.

OBJECTIVES

F Destroy the Ground Array Defenses.

G Escape before the missile hits.

OBJECTIVE

DESTROY THE GROUND ARRAY DEFENSES

You are now in control of the Badger One tank. Blast through the enemy barricade and over the bridge. Drive up the steep hill and use the tank's MG to destroy the gun trucks at the top. As your tank crests the hill, your target is visible—a base situated around a gigantic satellite dish.

Within the base, a battery of anti-air defenses is attempting to shoot down the missile the Ghost team launched. You have plenty of time here to take out all the AA turrets. As with the previous tank sequence, you have the option of charging through your targets, or carefully picking off the defenses in all areas before blowing up

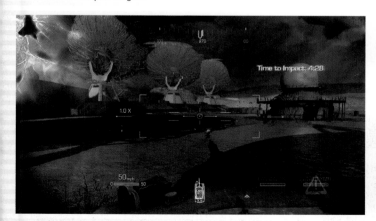

Be warned, as you blow up each turret, your Badger takes a hit from inbound seekers. Each turret battery destroys another part of your tank, making it harder and harder to find your targets.

When you've destroyed all the targets, your tank is disabled.

G OBJECTIVE

ESCAPE BEFORE THE MISSILE HITS

When you've regained consciousness, sprint toward your objective marker to board Badger One. On top of Badger One, you control a grenade launcher. Use the launcher to tear a hole in the Federation's line of defense as your tank attempts to exit the incoming missile's blast radius.

When time slows down, focus your grenades on the hovering Hinds. This will clear the way with only a few seconds remaining on the clock. Mission complete!

SEVERED TIES

Complete this chapter on any difficulty to earn the "Severed Ties" achievement.

ACHIEVEMENT/TROPHY

SPECIALIZED TRAINING   **THE CAMPAIGN**   MP INTRO & BASIC TRAINING   SQUADS   MP ARMORY   PERKS   KILLSTREAKS   MP MAPS   MP GAME MODES   SAFEGUARD   EXTINCTION   CLASSIFIED   ACHIEVEMENTS & TROPHIES

93

17 LOKI

FRIENDLIES
ENEMIES

OPERATIVE

SGT. THOMPSON, ICARUS 1–2

SUPPORT

COLLINS

MISSION DETAILS

Join Icarus Team as they assault the Federation space station and attempt to take control of its orbital weapon.

OBJECTIVES

A Assault the station.

B Locate an entrance to the station.

C Enter the station through the open hatch.

D Locate the control module.

E Breach the control room.

F Activate the Kinetic Rod targeting controller.

G Eliminate the incoming Federation forces.

H Defend the allies.

I Target the train.

LOADOUT

PRIMARY

ARX–160, GRENADE LAUNCHER, ACOG SIGHT

OBJECTIVE

ASSAULT THE STATION

You're now in control of the Icarus team that's assaulting the LOKI space station moments after the previous mission's end. It's been awhile since you've had to fight in zero gravity, so take a moment to re-familiarize yourself with the controls. Press **Tactical Grenade** or **Jump** to move up, and **Frag Grenade** or **Crouch** to move down. You don't have too much time to float around aimlessly, so move to the gold structure and use it for cover. Fire on the enemies floating ahead.

OBJECTIVE

LOCATE AN ENTRANCE TO THE STATION

When you've killed the enemies in the initial area, more arrive from the hatch ahead. Try to kill as many as possible as they exit the hatch. Any survivors make a dash for cover. You don't need to move up, just wait for them to pop out of cover.

OBJECTIVE

ENTER THE STATION THROUGH THE OPEN HATCH

When all of the Federation are dead and floating, you get the order to move on the hatch. Doing so automatically triggers an explosion in the fuel lines. Wait to regain control after the blast.

OBJECTIVE

LOCATE THE CONTROL MODULE

Hang back in the structure as Collins moves up. Pick off the Federation that float into view. When Collins continues to proceed further, follow him.

"Loki" Rorke File

This is another very tricky file to find. It's actually floating in free space after the explosion. Wait for it to float into view near the large orange panel on the left while exiting the pod you landed on after the fuel line blast. Look just to the left of the orange panel. It's exact location changes as it floats away from the base.

Find cover near the large, white, rectangular containers in the next area. The enemies are well hidden throughout this section. Hang back behind cover and wait for the enemies to reveal themselves. You might need to get a better angle, so move from cover to cover if you don't see any enemies in view.

Glinting Suits

Keep an eye out for flares reflecting off space suits. They can give away a well-hidden enemy's position.

SPECIALIZED TRAINING **THE CAMPAIGN** MP INTRO & BASIC TRAINING SQUADS MP ARMORY PERKS KILLSTREAKS MP MAPS MP GAME MODES SAFEGUARD EXTINCTION CLASSIFIED ACHIEVEMENTS & TROPHIES

95

BREACH THE CONTROL ROOM

When your squad has completely cleared the area of Federation, it's time to move into the control room and attempt to activate Loki. Follow Collins to the control room entrance. Press the **Interact** button near the glowing charge indicator to begin the breach. You must target three Federation astronauts during the breach. Kill them all to clear the control room.

ACTIVATE THE KINETIC ROD TARGETING CONTROLLER

Interact with the glowing console near where you entered. Press the **Fire** button to begin the Loki Kinetic Rod volley.

Checkpoint Reached.

You now automatically connect to a targeting drone that gives you eyes on your targets. Pressing **Fire** while in this view allows you to specify where Loki's incoming rods land.

ELIMINATE THE INCOMING FEDERATION FORCES

A huge Federation armored battalion is moving through the satellite field. Open fire on the orange-highlighted targets to absolutely devastate the area.

THEY LOOK LIKE ANTS

To earn this achievement, hit every single orange (enemy) target that's on the ground, and avoid the blue (friendly) targets. The flyby enemies can be very difficult to hit, so don't worry about them. Just focus on wiping out all the ground forces.
In the first volley, be sure to target the group on your bottom-left. It can be tricky to see. If you're admonished in the second volley, it means you hit a friendly or two and need to try again.
This may take a few tries. If you miss any orange targets in the first two volleys, use "Last Checkpoint" to try again. A new checkpoint triggers in the third volley, meaning you only get one shot to get this right and score the achievement.

ACHIEVEMENT/TROPHY

Watch out for the blue-marked train moving slowing through the area from the right. Hesh and Logan are on this train, so don't target it.

OBJECTIVE

DEFEND THE ALLIES

More friendly targets are past the train. Be very careful to avoid hitting the blue-marked targets when firing on the remaining Federation forces.

OBJECTIVE

I

TARGET THE TRAIN

When you've hit the majority of the orange Xs, you get some special orders. The orders may seem strange, but hit the **Fire** button to successfully complete the mission.

LOKI

Complete this chapter on any difficulty to earn the "Loki" achievement.

ACHIEVEMENT/TROPHY

SPECIALIZED TRAINING   THE CAMPAIGN   MP INTRO & BASIC TRAINING   SQUADS   MP ARMORY   PERKS   KILLSTREAKS   MP MAPS   MP GAME MODES   SAFEGUARD   EXTINCTION   CLASSIFIED   ACHIEVEMENTS & TROPHIES

97

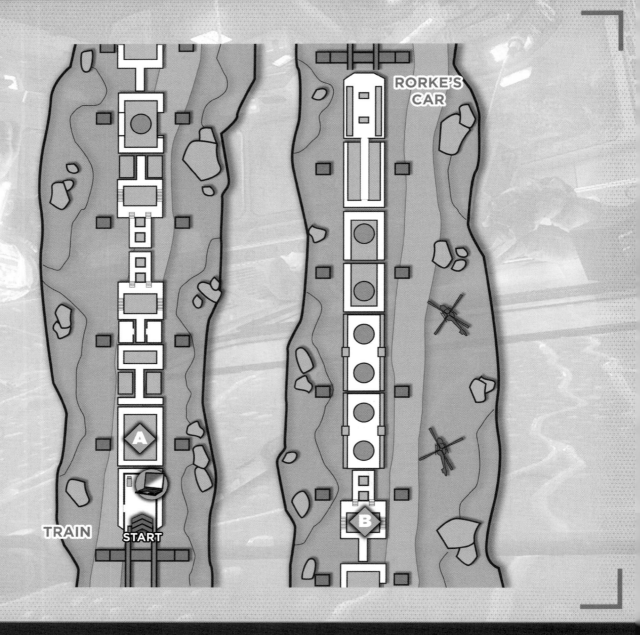

RORKE'S CAR

A

TRAIN

START

B

OBJECTIVES

OPERATIVE

LOGAN WALKER

SUPPORT

HESH WALKER

- ◇ A Find Rorke.
- ◇ B Jump to the rooftops.
- ◇ C Take out enemy helicopters.

MISSION DETAILS

LOADOUT

PRIMARY	SECONDARY	GRENADES & EQUIPMENT

FAD ACOG SIGHT	K7 RED DOT SIGHT	FLASHBANGS, SEMTEX

FIND RORKE

This mission takes place 15 minutes prior to the events in "Loki." Logan and Hesh are on the same train as Rorke. It's time to get revenge for Elias.

"The Ghost Killer" Rorke File

Before following Hesh outside of the first room, find the Rorke File behind the gun truck.

WATCH YOUR STEP

This level takes place on a moving train with lots of gaps. When pushing forward, look toward the ground to make sure you don't accidently step into a hole and fall off!

Follow Hesh outside to the train's side. The train walkway leads forward. When it branches out, find some cover. There's no rush to kill the Federation here. Hang back in cover and pick them off.

When you've killed the troops, move forward up the stairs to the next train car. This leads to another separated train car. Jump over the gap to clear it.

"Take Cover in the Cargo."

When you clear the gap, run behind Hesh on the car's left side. Jump into the cargo container and use it for cover. Ahead, several enemies are using the metal train car pieces for cover. These enemies are vicious, so use extra caution when popping up to pick them off. If you take some hits, go prone to get complete cover and heal. Be careful not to fall out of the cargo crate. There is a Chain SAW hidden in the hangar car.

When Hesh moves up, follow him. Search the bodies for an LSAT LMG; it makes the helicopter sequence later in the mission easier.

SPECIALIZED TRAINING THE CAMPAIGN MP INTRO & BASIC TRAINING SQUADS MP ARMORY PERKS KILLSTREAKS MP MAPS MP GAME MODES SAFEGUARD EXTINCTION CLASSIFIED ACHIEVEMENTS & TROPHIES

99

JUMP TO THE ROOFTOPS

The stairs at the cargo area's back lead to train car rooftop access. Jump to the train car rooftop. Stay in the rooftop's center to avoid getting blown off by incoming blasts.

C **OBJECTIVE**

TAKE OUT ENEMY HELICOPTERS

When the Little Birds arrive, sprint to the left side of the train cars and take cover behind the rail attachment piece. Shoot at the soldiers in the side of the chopper to down the helicopter.

If you grabbed the LMG earlier, taking out the helicopters is not difficult. If you don't have the LMG, stay in cover and try to pick off the soldiers.

When Hesh says all the choppers are down, sprint after him and jump to the next car.

Several more soldiers are defending the next two train cars. Stick to the left and right sides of the train cars and use the railings and rail attachment pieces for cover. It's best not to move to another car until you're sure it's clear. When you've cleared the last car, jump down and join Hesh to breach the door.

This is the hardest breach in the game. Enemies are on the left and right, plus there's a third enemy at the back that fires a rocket at your position.

Kill the enemy before he manages to aim his rocket, or fire at the rocket to blow it up and avoid getting caught in the blast. Regardless, when the rocket explodes, you're sent tumbling into the train's engine room. Now use Rorke's gun to kill the enemies ahead.

🏆 TICKETS PLEASE

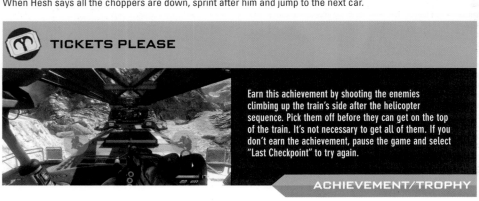

Earn this achievement by shooting the enemies climbing up the train's side after the helicopter sequence. Pick them off before they can get on the top of the train. It's not necessary to get all of them. If you don't earn the achievement, pause the game and select "Last Checkpoint" to try again.

ACHIEVEMENT/TROPHY

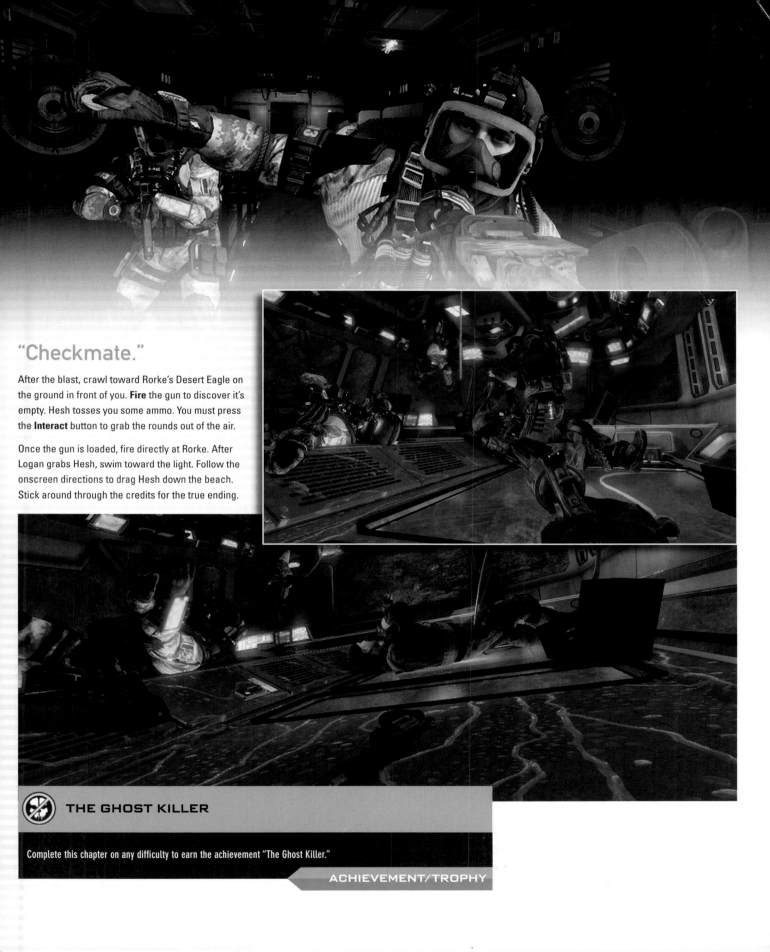

"Checkmate."

After the blast, crawl toward Rorke's Desert Eagle on the ground in front of you. **Fire** the gun to discover it's empty. Hesh tosses you some ammo. You must press the **Interact** button to grab the rounds out of the air.

Once the gun is loaded, fire directly at Rorke. After Logan grabs Hesh, swim toward the light. Follow the onscreen directions to drag Hesh down the beach. Stick around through the credits for the true ending.

THE GHOST KILLER

Complete this chapter on any difficulty to earn the achievement "The Ghost Killer."

ACHIEVEMENT/TROPHY

SPECIALIZED TRAINING   **THE CAMPAIGN**   MP INTRO & BASIC TRAINING   SQUADS   MP ARMORY   PERKS   KILLSTREAKS   MP MAPS   MP GAME MODES   SAFEGUARD   EXTINCTION   CLASSIFIED   ACHIEVEMENTS & TROPHIES

101

MP BASIC TRAINING

This part of the guide was designed and written in consultation with the team at Infinity Ward. We worked closely with the multiplayer designers who created the game you are now playing.

This multiplayer guide arms you with all the information needed to make decisions about character loadouts, maps, game modes, and more.

We have highly detailed statistical breakdowns of every weapon in the game, and detailed information on how perks and killstreaks work for you. Hand-drawn maps give you clean, clear views of the multiplayer battlefields.

Use the information here to improve your game online—and have fun out there!

WEAPON USAGE

Handling your weapon properly in combat is vital to your survival. Here's a breakdown of some of the mechanics, along with advice for how to best use your tools in *Call of Duty: Ghosts*.

AIM DOWN SIGHTS (ADS)

Aiming down the sights is simply the act of bringing your gun's iron sights or scope up to your face so you can aim accurately at a distance. In any mid-range or longer combat, you should always have your sights up when firing, as it is the most accurate method of shooting.

When you ADS, your first shot is always perfectly on target—after that, recoil forces pull your aim off target. Careful trigger control is the way to handle this when firing at distant targets with fully automatic weapons. Short controlled bursts!

Going into ADS slows your movement speed, making you an easier target in CQB, so be careful about staying in ADS longer than necessary. Bring up the sights, take the shot, and move on.

The Quickdraw perk halves the time it takes to bring up your sights.

The Stalker perk lets you move at full speed while ADS.

Different weapons have different ADS times, and Sight attachments can affect these times. See the Armory section for more details.

HIPFIRE

Hipfire is exactly what it sounds like—firing your weapon from the hip, without ADS. This is an inaccurate and wasteful method of firing for anything beyond short-range combat, but certain weapons are designed for effective hipfire in CQB—specifically SMGs, shotguns, and dual-wielded pistols. If you plan to hipfire often with an automatic weapon, take the Scavenger or Fully Loaded perks to help your ammo supply.

The Steady Aim perk reduces hipfire spread.

Jumping, crouching, or going prone all affect your hipfire spread.

Sniper rifles use their hipfire accuracy profile when firing unless you are *fully* ADS *and* stationary.

ACCURACY

Accuracy in combat is affected by weapon type, whether you're firing from the hip or while ADS, and if it's full-auto, semi-auto, or burst fire.

Semi-automatic and burst-fire weapons are naturally more accurate than fully auto ones, simply because their fire rate is automatically slower and more controlled. Fully auto weapons quickly become inaccurate at a distance if you hold down the trigger, so firing in short bursts is crucial for accurate long-range fire.

Sights do not directly impact accuracy in any way, but they can make landing long-range shots much easier, as they bring distant targets into focus for accurate shots.

Your stance in combat matters for accuracy—if crouched or prone, you have more accurate hipfire.

Accuracy is particularly important for all weapons, but it's vital for sniper rifles, which deal killing shots based on *where* you hit the target.

Each time you hit an enemy, the location is checked—headshots deal the most damage with almost all weapons, and sniper rifles can deal lethal shots to the chest or above. The Lynx and the L115 sniper rifle are deadly from the knee up by default, even without Chrome Lined Barrel.

Certain attachments can affect locational damage, specifically the Semi-Automatic and Burst Fire attachments for assault rifles, and the Chrome Lined Barrel for sniper rifles.

For all weapons except sniper rifles, your sights are 100% accurate when you bring them up. Sniper rifles require holding your breath to steady your aim—you can only do this for a few seconds. Taking too long causes you to lose control and your sights sway wildly. So line up your shot as you hold your breath, and quickly shoot—don't hold your breath looking for a target.

SWAY AND FLINCH

Sight sway is a subtle but important part of accurate fire. When you ADS with a weapon, your sights are momentarily perfectly steady and accurate. But after a moment, your sights begin to gently drift—this is sway.

You can reset this sway by dropping ADS and bringing it up again. Be aware of this effect if you are in ADS and watching a long-distance area for an extended period of time—the sway can throw your otherwise normally accurate first shots off.

Flinch is what occurs when you get shot. This does bad things to your accuracy, as your gun's sights kick upwards from the impact.

Sway and Flinch can both be greatly reduced by the Focus perk.

RELOADING

Reloading is a simple and common action on the battlefield, but there are a few quirks you should be aware of.

Weapons in *Call of Duty: Ghosts* reload in three stages: adding ammo, reloaded, and reloaded after an empty magazine.

SPECIALIZED TRAINING   THE CAMPAIGN   **MP INTRO & BASIC TRAINING**   SQUADS   MP ARMORY   PERKS   KILLSTREAKS   MP MAPS   MP GAME MODES   SAFEGUARD   EXTINCTION   CLASSIFIED   ACHIEVEMENTS & TROPHIES

103

Reload Cancelling

The first and fastest part of reloading is when the ammo is added to the gun—this happens *before* the reloading animation is complete. There's usually both a visual and audio cue on each weapon when this happens.

The instant the ammo is considered reloaded, you can sprint or switch weapons and cancel the remaining animation. This is reload cancelling, and for some weapons it can save you a second or more on the reload time. That's long enough to save your life if an enemy comes around the corner!

You can cancel an animation with a single-step sprint or a double-tap weapon switch, and your gun will be up and ready for use immediately.

The Sleight of Hand perk halves reload times. For most weapons, this is so fast that you don't need to bother reload cancelling (but the option to do so still exists).

Reloads

Normal reloading is simply allowing the reload animation to finish completely. There's no penalty for doing this, beyond the time lost from not reload cancelling manually.

To chamber the first round on a new magazine, pull the charging handle on a rifle or rack the slide on a pistol. This extra animation adds even more time to the total reload animation. For some weapons, this can be a considerable amount of extra time.

Regardless of the animation triggered when reloading, it can be reload cancelled.

Note that some weapons don't have an "empty magazine" reload—because they don't have a magazine! This applies to some belt-fed LMGs and shotguns that reload shells manually.

SWITCHING WEAPONS

Switching weapons seems like a simple enough act, but you need to be aware that different weapons have different times for switching *to* them and switching *from* them. These are known as the *raise* and *drop* times, and they are longer and slower for heavier, more unwieldy weapons. LMGs and sniper rifles are very slow to bring to bear or drop, while pistols are lightning fast and most SMGs are quick.

Weapon switch speeds tend to follow a certain baseline speed for their weapon class (pistols and SMGs being faster than LMGs or snipers), but there are variations between weapons within a given class.

See the Armory section for more specifics—the total time it takes to switch from one weapon to another is the combination of one weapon's drop time with the second weapon's raise time. This is important information because being mid-swap when an enemy comes around the corner can get you killed! These times also apply when picking up a weapon off the battlefield, so be careful about scavenging a weapon from a downed enemy if you suspect other foes are nearby.

Quick (and Not So Quick) Switching

The Reflex perk halves weapon switch times. This is particularly important for sniper rifles that *need* to switch to a close-range backup weapon quickly if you're ambushed while using one.

The Overkill perk lets you carry two primary class weapons—keep in mind this means your weapon switch times are likely to be slow, as switching from a marksman rifle to a shotgun is much slower than switching to a pistol.

Pistols are ideal backup weapons because they switch so quickly. Switching to a pistol and firing is typically faster than reloading for any weapon. Learning and mastering this skill can keep you alive.

EXPLOSIVES

Explosives are useful backup weapons. You gain access to them through your Lethal and Tactical equipment slots, from the secondary Launcher weapon category, or the Under-Barrel Grenade Launcher attachment on rifles and LMGs.

Explosives are useful for dealing with entrenched enemies, groups of enemies, and clearing objective areas. Explosives deal a certain minimum amount of damage no matter how far from the detonation's center an enemy is located. If you get a hitmarker with an explosive, you know your targets are weakened.

There are quite a few perks that interact with explosives:

- The Blast Shield and Tac Resist perks protect you from explosives and tactical explosives respectively.
- The Danger Close perk boosts explosive damage output significantly.
- The Extra Tactical and Extra Lethal perks give you an extra Tactical or Lethal grenade respectively.
- The Strong-Arm perk lets you throw grenades farther and safely toss back Frag Grenades or Canister Bombs by resetting their timers.
- The Reflex perk lets you throw grenades and deploy equipment at double speed.

Note that the Scavenger and Fully Loaded perks have *no* effect on explosives. You can't resupply them and you don't start with extras.

MELEE

Your soldier is a trained combat operative skilled in all forms of combat, including up-close-and-personal. You can instantly kill any enemy player by getting close to them and tapping the Melee button—this causes you to enter a special animation with your combat knife, silently dispatching your foe.

There are a few different melee options in *Call of Duty: Ghosts*. The most basic is your backup combat knife; you always have access to this even while your gun is raised.

Be careful about stabbing if you aren't sure of a hit. Performing a missed stab drops your gun, and it takes a second to raise again. This can get you killed in a CQB situation.

Animation Lock

New to *Call of Duty: Ghosts* is the special stabbing animations when you attack someone with your combat knife. These look cool, but be aware that they freeze you in place while performing the animation. If an enemy has a teammate nearby, don't expect to survive the encounter!

Get in the habit of using your knife to dispatch lone enemies; don't use it to attack in a room with more than one foe.

The Tactical Knife attachment for pistols does *not* have this extra animation—it kills in a single quick stab. If you like wielding your knife often, that's the attachment to use!

SPECIALIZED TRAINING   THE CAMPAIGN   **MP INTRO & BASIC TRAINING**   SQUADS   MP ARMORY   PERKS   KILLSTREAKS   MP MAPS   MP GAME MODES   SAFEGUARD   EXTINCTION   CLASSIFIED   ACHIEVEMENTS & TROPHIES

105

The next melee option is the *actual* combat knife weapon. You can only gain access to this weapon by dropping your primary weapon entirely. In exchange, you get a main-hand combat knife. This weapon functions identically to your normal backup knife (though you can also swing it with the Trigger button, not just your Melee button).

The combat knife has two important perks. First, holding it gives you the fastest possible movement speed in the game (105% of baseline movement speed). And second, you can sprint *twice as far* while holding the combat knife.

Combining this with the Agility perk can get you around on the battlefield very fast indeed.

Finally, there is a Tactical Knife attachment for pistols only. This specialty weapon has the same range and stealthy instant kill properties as either of the regular combat knives, with one important difference—there is *no* animation freeze after a stab. You can sprint into a room using a Tactical Knife with Marathon and Dead Silence and quickly stab every foe before they're even aware you're attacking.

COVER

Cover is simple, basic, and *absolutely critical* to your survival. Cover can protect you directly (by stopping bullets from hitting you) or indirectly (by preventing an enemy from spotting you in the first place).

When traveling around the battlefield, always

move with your flank to a wall or other large surface, minimizing your exposure. When moving down a hallway or other enclosed space, always keep the largest line-of-sight-blocking cover in front of you so you can duck behind it if an enemy appears. When reloading, duck behind a wall or crouch behind hard cover.

Enemy Spotted

Because *Call of Duty: Ghosts* has the new automatic enemy sighting system, an enemy *player* may miss you, but their soldier may well spot you and call out your location to the team. The only way to prevent this is to avoid being seen in the first place—good combat policy to begin with.

The Incognito perk prevents automatic voice callouts of your position. It also removes the red nametag over your head, which can help with moving stealthily around the map.

Leaning in Cover

The new leaning system changes the way cover affects firefights—there are *many* new potentially strong defensive positions due to leaning. Every corner, doorway, window, and solid block of cover can potentially be used for leaning. Be aware of how this influences likely hiding spots on offense and defense, and make cover work for you.

Walled Him

Most weapons have some level of penetration; they can fire through thin surfaces. High-powered ammunition can punch through thicker surfaces. If you can get a round through a wall or a piece of cover, you can hit and kill enemies on the other side.

Armor-piercing ammunition dramatically improves your ability to penetrate cover. With a suitable automatic weapon and enough ammunition, you can easily take out targets who think they are safe hiding in a room or leaning out beside a wall.

Experiment with penetration by using an LMG, or an AR with armor-piercing ammo and Scavenger or Fully Loaded. Learning how and where to shoot enemies through walls and where they are likely to hide when ducking behind cover is a useful skill to master.

MOVEMENT

Movement is fundamental to your survival on the *Call of Duty: Ghosts* multiplayer battlefield. Moving from place to place swiftly and safely is crucial in every single multiplayer game mode. Using all the options at your disposal for quick and stealthy movement is critical to flanking and surprising the enemy team. Aiming your weapon is important, but knowing how to *move* is just as (and possibly more) important.

MOVEMENT SPEEDS

Your movement speed is affected by the weapon you're holding. This means that you can change your movement speed by carrying a fast secondary weapon.

Fastest 105%: Combat Knife (and double length Sprint)

Fast 100%: Shotgun, SMG, Pistols

Quick 95%: Kastet

Medium 90%: Assault Rifles, Marksman Rifles, Chain SAW, USR Sniper Rifle

Slow 85%: VKS and L115 Sniper Rifles

Slowest 80%: Other LMGs, Lynx Sniper Rifle, Riot Shield, Panzerfaust, and MAAWS

Be mindful that while switching to your pistol and running around is a good idea with a slow weapon, the delay in bringing your primary weapon up can get you killed if you encounter an enemy mid-sprint. Be sure to switch back to your primary weapon as you get closer to expected enemy contact.

The Agility perk increases your movement speed by 7% at all times.

SPRINTING AND SLIDING

Sprinting lets you move more quickly, at the cost of lowering your weapon and making more noise while running. You can sprint for a short distance before running out of breath, and you recover your "sprint time" gradually while walking.

The Marathon perk grants unlimited sprint time. This is a powerful mobility perk, but be careful about running into enemies headlong.

The Ready Up perk brings your weapon up 40% faster after coming out of a sprint. This is very useful for fast-moving CQB builds.

Combat Slides

Sliding is a new type of movement in *Call of Duty: Ghosts*. Sliding allows you to transition from a sprint into a sliding crouch.

Combat slides are performed by holding the Crouch button while sprinting. Doing so causes you to go into a quick evasive slide—very useful for rounding corners or getting into cover quickly. You can freely turn and aim once a slide has started.

Sliding can protect you from mid-range enemies when moving from cover to cover. It can be used to quickly enter cover, allowing you to crouch and prepare to fire immediately.

While sliding is a useful and versatile method of movement, it does have its limitations. Sliding has limited range, and at the end of a slide you're immobile and either crouched or prone.

> ### Cover Slides
> To get a little extra distance on your slides, slide *toward* cover. There's a very slight increase in the distance when sliding toward cover compared to sliding in the open.

SPECIALIZED TRAINING   THE CAMPAIGN   **MP INTRO & BASIC TRAINING**   SQUADS   MP ARMORY   PERKS   KILLSTREAKS   MP MAPS   MP GAME MODES   SAFEGUARD   EXTINCTION   CLASSIFIED   ACHIEVEMENTS & TROPHIES

107

A slide normally ends in a crouch, so don't slide if you plan to continue moving quickly. If you continue to hold Crouch while sliding, you transition to a prone position at the end of the slide. This is particularly useful for sliding around a corner when expecting a hostile in a specific position, as it can throw off their aim. Consider this an alternative to the jump shot around a corner.

It's possible to perform a slide and immediately transition into a sprint again. But be careful about using this to make yourself a more difficult target—sliding isn't as fast as sprinting, and the shift from a sliding crouch into a sprint may not always be perfectly smooth. This can get you killed if a hostile is tracking your movement.

Spend the first few weeks of play intentionally overusing sliding to learn its quirks. If you really want to get serious about using (and abusing) slides, hop in a private match with a few friends and see exactly how it looks from a shooter's perspective. You can also discover how, where, and when sliding is useful on various maps.

MANTLING, CLIMBING, AND JUMPING

Mantling

Mantling has been in *Call of Duty* for years, but *Ghosts* amps up the mobility and speed of mantling. This time around, you can mantle over low cover and keep your momentum. If you're sprinting at a low wall or ground-floor window, you can mantle the cover and continue sprinting on the other side.

Additionally, you now keep your gun up during this combat mantle maneuver. This allows you to fire from the hip while mantling, potentially gunning down any target in immediate view on the other side of cover. Plus you look pretty awesome while doing it. The combat mantle can be performed while pressing forward or sprinting.

The soft mantle is useful for pulling yourself onto a fence, windowsill, ledge, or otherwise narrow surface. You can pull yourself up and look around without dropping over the edge—this is important if your mantle target is high in the air! Perform a soft mantle by pressing Jump near an obstacle, *without* pushing forward.

Mantling Behavior

You can now mantle onto any narrow surface by pressing Jump while against a ledge, railing, or fence. As long as you don't move forward, you can do this without automatically falling over the other side.

If you're moving or sprinting toward cover and mantle, you automatically continue your movement on the other side.

Climbing

Climbing ladders is as simple as moving to one and pressing forward while looking up to climb (or backwards to climb down). You can press Jump to detach from a ladder quickly. It's also possible to jump *onto* a ladder and begin climbing. Your gun is down and you cannot fire while climbing a ladder.

Jumping

Jumping lets you get around a level more swiftly by clearing small gaps and utilizing objects. You can jump through windows, onto ladders, and mantle onto ledges.

With practice, you can find shortcuts on different maps that let you get around the level and ambush enemies from unexpected directions. Just be careful with your trick jumps—some take a lot of practice and time to pull off, and you're quite exposed while trying to jump around and mantle.

You can perform one full-strength jump at a time. If you attempt to jump again immediately, only a short hop is performed. It takes a few seconds to get the strength to jump at full height again.

Keep in mind that jumping causes your hipfire accuracy to degrade severely, both during the jump and just after. Jumping out a window and opening fire like an action-movie hero sounds like a great idea, until you land hard, damage yourself, slow your movement, and kill your accuracy.

CROUCH AND PRONE

Crouching and prone positions are both very useful and important for concealing yourself from enemies at a distance. By crouching, you can minimize your silhouette at a distance and still peek over low cover or out windows. Going prone restricts your field of view more heavily, but it can also be used to take cover behind even the shortest cover at long range. Movement is slow while crouched and very slowly while prone.

Sprinting automatically cancels crouching or prone positions, allowing you to move quickly after ducking behind cover to reload.

Crouching or going prone improves accuracy, but your mobility is impaired. Don't spend too long immobile and firing or you risk making yourself an easy target for explosives and flanking enemies.

CORNER ASSAULTS

There are several ways to round a corner and attack an enemy you know is waiting for you. You can ADS, sprint, walk, slide, and jump around the corner.

Rounding a corner in ADS is the slowest method, but it also allows you to fire instantly if you spot a target. The Stalker perk lets you ADS and move at full speed. This means you can round corners at full walking speed—very useful for moving quickly and firing accurately.

Sprinting around corners is usually a very bad idea, but you can potentially sprint and utilize a knife stab. Otherwise, it takes a moment to bring up your weapon and fire.

Walking around a corner without ADS is a bad idea, unless you have a good hipfiring weapon. A shotgun, SMG, dual pistols, the Chain SAW LMG, or an AR with Steady Aim are all viable options.

You can also slide around a corner. This looks cool, and it does present a different silhouette to the enemy, potentially causing them to miss. But it only takes a split second for them to adjust. Even worse than that, you're left immobile and crouched at the end of a slide. Not a great position to attack from. That said, you can surprise

people by sliding occasionally; if their aim is off, you may get the killshot before they can compensate.

Finally, you can jump around a corner while firing. This is usually a bad idea for most weapons, but it can score a kill with accurate hipfire weapons. The only real advantage to going around the corner in the air is your head is out of line for usual upper body shots. But your center mass is still likely to take plenty of hits.

Your jump's trajectory can also let you land a bit further out from the corner. Jumping from an elevated position around a corner can get you the drop on an enemy who was aiming at chest height. You end up going over their crosshairs and landing to the left or right of their sights. Corners are always dangerous to round, so experiment with different approaches (and throw grenades ahead of you!).

SPECIALIZED TRAINING   THE CAMPAIGN   **MP INTRO & BASIC TRAINING**   SQUADS   MP ARMORY   PERKS   KILLSTREAKS   MP MAPS   MP GAME MODES   SAFEGUARD   EXTINCTION   CLASSIFIED   ACHIEVEMENTS & TROPHIES

109

LEANING

Leaning is an old *Call of Duty* feature reborn in a new form. In *Call of Duty: Ghosts*, leaning is now automatic and context sensitive—instead of discrete lean buttons, you can now simply approach the edge of *any* wall, go into ADS, and automatically lean around the corner. This is extremely useful and powerful when defending an area, especially if you have the drop on incoming enemies who are unaware of your position.

Because you can hide at the edge of almost any wall, doorway, window, or large chunk of hard cover, you can vary your position from encounter to encounter, limiting your exposure and making yourself a very tricky target to spot.

Be aware that while leaning exposes less of your body than standing in the open, it does have the unfortunate side effect of focusing enemy fire at your head. This can lead to quick deaths against accurate opponents. Also keep in mind that even though your body is shielded behind cover, enemy bullets can certainly penetrate the cover, especially if they are using armor-piercing ammunition.

Tough to Spot

The Incognito perk removes the red name over your head when targeted. This is particularly effective when leaning, as it makes you even more difficult to spot.

Leaning Tips

To initiate a lean, move flush with a solid surface. This is easiest at the edge of squared walls, doorways, or windows, but you can lean around any hard cover as long as there's enough of a "flat surface" to press against.

Keep an eye on your reticule—the left or right hashmark changes into a small arrow pointing to the left or right. This indicates that you can now lean by entering ADS. Once in a lean, you're free to strafe left or right to adjust your position. Use this to expose as little of your upper body as possible while still providing a view of the area you want to cover. If you strafe too far or back away from the wall, the lean automatically cancels.

Leaning is a boon for defensive play. If you're an aggressive player, be aware that enemies can and will be hiding around corners and beside windows and doors. They'll be a bit tougher to spot than if they were simply standing at the edge of their cover.

Advanced Cover Slides

It's possible to slide into cover and immediately begin a lean, although this is difficult to pull off consistently.

First, you must be perfectly lined up with the edge of the cover you're sliding into so that you're in range to lean. Second, you must begin the lean just as your slide is completing.

This is tough to do without practice. But as long as your slide is lined up with good solid cover, you don't risk anything by trying it. Worst case, you end up behind hard cover and can line up the lean a second later.

HUD

The basics of your HUD are very simple and easy to use, but we're going to touch on a few key aspects that are important for combat.

HITMARKERS AND INFO MARKERS

Hitmarkers

Your crosshair conveys a lot of useful information at a glance. When you aren't in ADS, it shows the rough radius of your hipfire spread.

When you score a hit on an enemy, you get a red flare and an audio cue; we call this a *hitmarker*. This is an indication that you scored a hit, and it's useful for confirming long-range shots and detecting enemies.

You can use hitmarkers to locate enemies by shooting them through walls. But more commonly, throwing a Lethal or (especially) Tactical grenade can give you warning of enemy presence.

If you toss a Concussion or 9-Bang into a room and get a hitmarker, a dazed or partially blinded enemy is inside. Same story around objectives, around corners, in sniper perches, or anywhere you suspect an enemy might be lurking.

Info Markers

The other important cues to watch for are the info markers over objectives in objective game mode play and the death icons that indicate fallen teammates.

The objective markers typically convey immediately useful information—if the objective is under assault, which team holds it, and so on. You can use these to instantly identify a position that has an enemy presence and needs backup.

Death icons appear on your HUD whenever a teammate dies. The skull over where they died can give away a nearby enemy if they were killed in close- or medium-range combat. This is less useful if they were sniped from across the map. But in general, if a death marker pops up nearby, stay alert.

The reverse of this is true as well. If you kill an enemy, expect nearby enemies to investigate.

The Takedown perk removes the death marker when you score a kill, which is particularly valuable for stealth and CQB builds. This suppresses the warning and gives you an edge in ambushing more targets.

MAP AND MINIMAP

Your minimap is a simple but vital part of the HUD. In non-hardcore modes (where you have no minimap without SATCOM coverage!), your minimap is a constant source of local information.

Friendly players show up fully with directional indicators so you can see what they are covering. Enemy indicators show up as filled red dots (if they're firing an unsilenced weapon) or empty red dots (if they're being spotted by Eyes On coverage from a single active SATCOM).

Multiple SATCOMs cause a scanner sweep that makes enemies appear periodically (with or without friendly eyes on the target). Be aware that players with the Off the Grid perk are immune to SATCOM coverage.

Various equipment and perks can also give local enemy positions—the Ping perk, the Radar attachment on the Riot Shield, Juggernaut Recon, and the Night Owl.

Enemy positional indicators are also marked with a tiny up or down arrow, indicating whether they're above or below you—important to know on many maps that have complex, multi-level environments.

Your main map (accessible by hitting the Main Menu button) displays the entire level. This map respects SATCOM and other forms of intelligence information, so bringing it up occasionally can be useful to get a full map view of enemy positions and to see your team's location.

SPECIALIZED TRAINING   THE CAMPAIGN   **MP INTRO & BASIC TRAINING**   SQUADS   MP ARMORY   PERKS   KILLSTREAKS   MP MAPS   MP GAME MODES   SAFEGUARD   EXTINCTION   CLASSIFIED   ACHIEVEMENTS & TROPHIES

111

Even without SATCOM coverage, you can often infer the enemy team's location based on objective control and teammate positions. It's likely they're where your team and your objectives are not, though this varies by game mode.

KILLCAM

The killcam might be an obvious game element, but it's a very important one. Veterans can skip this, but for new players—use the killcam.

The killcam tells you who killed you, from where, with what, what loadout they were using, and if any of their teammates are nearby. You can use this information to figure out where players commonly camp out, what sort of loadouts they're using, how they attacked you, and a lot of other information that can help improve your play.

Don't mash past killcams when you're learning the game and the maps. You can learn a lot by paying attention to the killcam.

SOUND

Sound is one of the key pillars of your situational awareness. Hearing enemies move, fire, climb, or even call out enemy positions can give away their location.

Sound is extremely important for catching threats that are nearby but not immediately in view. It's also important to be aware of the noises you are making— something as simple as priming and throwing a grenade can give away your position and get you shot if you're deep in enemy territory.

The Amplify and Dead Silence perks directly impact your ability to hear or be heard by enemy players. Amplify doubles your hearing range; Dead Silence cuts your noise level in half. Moving while crouched or prone is quiet, while sprinting or moving on noisy surfaces is louder. All gunfire makes noise, even a silenced weapon.

HEARING DISTANCES

You can hear other players at around 1000 units away. Awareness roughly doubles this range; Dead Silence halves it.

The actual distance is going to vary depending on the quality of your sound system, the amount of nearby ambient noise, and the type of in-game activity taking place.

EQUIPMENT AND KILLSTREAKS

We touched on explosives briefly earlier in this chapter, but the other forms of Lethal, Tactical, and Killstreak equipment are also important parts of your arsenal.

The Trophy System, Motion Sensor, SATCOM, I.M.S., Sentry Gun, Weapon Crate, and Ballistic Vests can all be placed on the ground.

You can pick up a Trophy System or Motion Sensor, as well as undetonated C4 or IEDs. You can also move the IMS and Sentry Gun around once they're placed.

Try to choose your placement locations carefully, and avoid setting up equipment while exposed to enemy view—it's a great way to get killed and end your streak. This is particularly important in the case of the Sentry Gun, which may be part of a run to a 9 or higher Assault killstreak.

The Sitrep perk allows players to see all equipment at a distance and through walls. Players with the Armor-Piercing attachment can deal increased damage to any equipment.

GAME MECHANICS

Most of the number crunching that goes on behind the scenes isn't important for moment-to-moment gameplay, but there are a few topics worth knowing more about.

DAMAGE

Players in *Call of Duty: Ghosts* have 100 health as a baseline. Ballistic Vests can add 150 armor to this value, and the ICU perk causes you to regenerate health
more quickly.

Most weapons deal in the neighborhood of 35 damage per bullet, but this value varies heavily from gun to gun. Also, with few exceptions, most weapons deal less damage the farther away from your target. This is known as *damage falloff*. As a result of this, the number of shots it takes to down a target can rise from 3 to 4 to 5, or even more, depending on the specific weapon.

Most weapons fall from their maximum damage to some minimum value. Once that minimum is reached, they cannot lose any more damage at a distance, regardless of how far away the target. See the Armory section for details on the damage profiles for every weapon in the game.

Most explosives deal a high (and lethal) amount of damage at the center of their blast, and decrease to a certain minimum damage at the blast's outer edge. This means that even a grazing hit can leave a player near death from an explosion.

Shotguns and sniper rifles both bear special mention. Shotguns have a maximum effective range, beyond which their shots do *no* damage. Don't use a shotgun for ranged combat. Even your backup pistol is a better option! Sniper Rifles on the other hand, do not lose damage at a distance at all. Instead, they deal a very high, static amount of damage, and rely on damage multipliers to ensure a lethal one-shot kill if you're accurate with your shot.

Most weapons (except shotguns) deal increased damage with headshots. This is usually enough damage to drop the number of needed shots to kill by one. Sniper rifles have damage multipliers from the lower torso up to the head. A sniper rifle with the Chrome Lined Barrel attachment can even kill with shots to the upper legs or arms. A few weapons or attachments can modify damage multipliers. See the Armory for more details.

MODIFYING WEAPON RANGE

Several attachments bear special mention when it comes to dealing damage with any gun.

The Silencer *reduces* effective damage range by causing a 20% increase in damage falloff. This means you hit your *minimum* damage range more quickly, requiring more shots to kill at a distance. The Muzzle Brake does the exact opposite—it *increases* effective range by 20%.

Both attachments can be very valuable and useful for different reasons. Some weapons have damage profiles that are especially well suited to one attachment or the other. Certain weapons have such excellent damage profiles that a Silencer barely has an impact on their performance. Others benefit significantly from a Muzzle Brake to extend their low shots-to-kill range.

In addition to the Silencer and Muzzle Brake, the Semi-Auto, Burst Fire, and Full Auto attachments for assault rifles have a dramatic impact on the damage profiles— enough to essentially change them into different types of guns entirely.

Slug Rounds for shotguns are another important tweak. They change not only the range profile of the shotguns, but also the way that they deal damage. This changes them from buckshot-firing, hipfire specialists to single-shot, short-range surgical weapons.

SPECIALIZED TRAINING   THE CAMPAIGN   **MP INTRO & BASIC TRAINING**   SQUADS   MP ARMORY   PERKS   KILLSTREAKS   MP MAPS   MP GAME MODES   SAFEGUARD   EXTINCTION   CLASSIFIED   ACHIEVEMENTS & TROPHIES

113

PENETRATION

Penetration is an important part of combat in *Call of Duty: Ghosts*. Almost any weapon can penetrate thin surfaces, and more powerful weapons can punch through thick surfaces.

The thickness of the cover (or wall) fired through and the shot's angle affect the damage of the round that comes out the other side. Ideally, you want to shoot a thin surface dead on at a clean 90-degree angle. The sharper the angle and the thicker the surface, the less damage done.

Shooting enemies through walls and cover tends to be an ammo intensive endeavor, so bring Extended Mags, Fully Loaded, or Scavenger if you intend to take advantage of penetration in combat. The Armor-Piercing attachment triples penetration values, increasing the punch from bullets that do penetrate and hit a player through cover.

Penetration Values

Low: Pistols, all other SMGs, Shotguns

Medium: ARs, Shotguns with Slug attachment, Vector SMG

High: Sniper Rifles, Marksman Rifles, LMGs

TARGETING ASSISTANCE

Call of Duty: Ghosts uses a sophisticated system for targeting and tracking enemies—different weapons and different scopes influence how easily you can get your crosshairs on a target. While this largely happens behind the scenes, there are two areas where you can impact it, and that comes from the weapon you have in hand.

Long-range weapons have longer aim assist ranges, and they have longer spotting distances for sighting enemy names while ADS.

Unsurprisingly, a pistol isn't as good as a marksman rifle or sniper rifle for picking off long-range targets, and not just because of the damage that it does at a great distance. The Tracker and Thermal sights increase aim assist distance for any weapon using them, though the Tracker sight lacks the long-range zoom capability of the Thermal sight. Remember that Incognito enemies don't have red names visible. If you're using a long-range weapon and can't spot a hostile's nametag, that's likely the reason.

WHAT'S NEW

There are many changes, large and small, in the *Call of Duty: Ghosts* multiplayer experience. The following includes the changes that most directly impact your moment-to-moment gameplay.

There have also been a lot of additions and changes to "meta" aspects of the multiplayer gameplay—expanded support for clan play, automatic clan wars, a unified account system (accessible in-game, or from your PC or smartphone), new customization for your squad member models, and tweaks that enhance everything surrounding the core multiplayer game.

MOVEMENT

Mantling has been revamped, sliding has been added, and leaning has new easy-to-use context sensitive controls. Experiment with all three—they greatly smooth out battlefield travel and add new tactical options for engaging in combat.

PERK SYSTEM

The perk system in *Call of Duty: Ghosts* has been revamped, giving you total control over your perk loadout.

You are given 8 perk points that can be spent on any perks of your choice. Perks now cost from 1 to 5 points to equip, and you can equip any mix of perks up to your perk point limit.

Acquire additional perk points (up to 12 maximum) by giving up your primary or secondary weapon, and your Lethal or Tactical equipment. This allows you to pick and choose the precise makeup of your perk loadout, and lets you swap your main gear in exchange for more or less perks as you see fit.

Under-Barrel Attachments

The Grenade Launcher and Under-Barrel Shotgun attachments both take up your Lethal equipment slot. This also means they consume that perk point, so keep this in mind if you choose to use either item.

Specialist

The Specialist Killstreak has changed a bit from *Modern Warfare 3*. Instead of granting all perks, you are now allowed to choose an additional 8 points worth of perks to unlock as your Specialist Bonus.

FIELD ORDERS

Field Orders are a new dynamic item that appears on the battlefield as a small blue briefcase when the first player in a match is killed. Whoever picks up the Field Orders is given a simple mission to accomplish, such as killing three players, earning a melee kill, etc. Completing this mission awards you with an Assault Care Package.

If a player carrying the Field Orders dies before they complete their objective, the Field Orders are dropped on the battlefield again for another player to pick up.

There is always one set of Field Orders making its way around the battle between both teams as the match progresses. Note that this is now the only way to earn a regular Assault Care Package; it's no longer a killstreak!

When you earn a Field Order mission, you won't be given an impossible mission (no explosive kill challenge with no explosives equipped; no secondary weapon challenge without a secondary weapon).

If you are (or become) a Juggernaut, you gain access to a special set of Juggernaut-only missions.

FIELD ORDERS

TYPE	MISSION
Prone	Earn 1 kill while prone
Jumping	Earn 1 kill while jumping
Found	Earn 2 kills with a weapon you picked up
Kills	Earn 3 non-killstreak kills
Crouch	Earn 2 kills while crouched
Melee	Earn 1 kill with melee
Explosive	Earn 1 kill with a non-killstreak explosive
Behind	Earn 1 kill from behind
Headshot	Earn 1 kill with a headshot
Humiliation	Humiliate your opponent after killing them
Secondary Weapon	Earn 1 kill with your secondary weapon

JUGGERNAUT-ONLY FIELD ORDERS

TYPE	MISSION
Maniac Knife	Earn 6 kills with melee only
Maniac Throwing Knife	Earn 4 kills with throwing knives only
Maniac Back Kills	Earn 3 kills from behind, throwing knives or melee
Assault Juggernaut	Earn 7 kills, any method
Recon Shield Kills	Earn 3 kills with Riot Shield
Recon Pistol Kills	Earn 4 kills with the .44 Magnum

Dynamic Map Orders

Field Orders are used to trigger special events on several maps. If you get lucky when calling in the Care Package drop, you may acquire the special map-specific reward—this essentially functions as a specialized killstreak. Activate it to fire the map event.

WHITEOUT: Trigger a satellite crash, granting your team permanent Level 1 SATCOM coverage for the rest of the match.

SIEGE: Call down a missile strike.

WARHAWK: Call in a field artillery barrage. Watch your head if you called it in!

SOVEREIGN: Sabotage the tank assembly line; release clouds of gas.

STRIKEZONE: Trigger a KEM strike, devastating the entire map and killing the entire enemy team.

When a special map-specific reward appears, it shows up as a Care Package with a Grim Reaper icon instead of a normal killstreak icon. Don't let it fall into enemy hands!

DYNAMIC MAP EVENTS

Maps in *Call of Duty: Ghosts* now have dynamic elements. These range from very simple changes (doors that can be opened or closed, walls that can be blown out) to massive changes (the entire map getting bombed and shattered).

Typically, the more devastating level-wide effects are restricted to the Field Order packages, but some large-scale effects are automatic. On

Tremor, for example, the level experiences periodic earthquake aftershocks that affect everyone on the map equally.

SPECIALIZED TRAINING   THE CAMPAIGN   **MP INTRO & BASIC TRAINING**   SQUADS   MP ARMORY   PERKS   KILLSTREAKS   MP MAPS   MP GAME MODES   SAFEGUARD   EXTINCTION   CLASSIFIED   ACHIEVEMENTS & TROPHIES

115

SQUADS

Call of Duty: Ghosts introduces a new way to play the multiplayer game: Squads. With Squads, you can set up a team of six customized Squad members , five of which will will fight by your side in online multiplayer matches.

You can challenge your friends' teams one-on-one, even when they are offline.

The really great feature of Squads is that you can earn multiplayer XP and Squad points by playing against bots. The full *Call of Duty* online multiplayer experience isn't for everyone, and Squads offers up a great alternative.

LOCAL VS. ONLINE SQUADS

Local Squads are different than your online Squads. Online Squads require that you earn Squad points to unlock additional Squad members to customize.
These Squad points are the same ones you earn playing online in the regular multiplayer game. Additionally, you need to earn more Squad points to unlock killstreaks, weapons, and perks.

If you play a local game, you can fully customize your loadout, and everything is available to you. This is beneficial if you want try out certain weapons or abilities but haven't reached a high enough level in multiplayer to earn them.

In local mode, there are only two game types available: Safeguard and Wargame. Wargame allows you to set up an offline game of your choice. Your custom Squad is not utilized, but you can customize your personal loadout.

In online Squads play, you can play four game types: Squad Assault, Squad vs. Squad, Safeguard, and Wargame.

Playing the following online Squads mode earns you Squad points that carry over into multiplayer.

SQUAD ASSAULT

With Squad Assault, you can challenge your friends even if they aren't currently online. When you battle, the team your friends have set up becomes your opponents in a multiplayer game of your choice. All multiplayer maps and game modes are available.

When you first log on to play *Call of Duty: Ghosts* multiplayer, the game automatically sets up your team with default settings. If one of your friends attacks your Squad, they will encounter the Squad you have set up.

If you don't have any friends you want to challenge, you can search online, and the game will automatically find someone for you to play against. If your Squad defeats another team while you are offline, you will be notified when you return (and may get some nice XP bonuses).

SQUAD VS SQUAD

In Squad vs. Squad, you can challenge someone online to a versus match where you both lead your Squad of bots. The standard multiplayer Wargame game types are available. The game type and map are randomly determined once you find an opponent.

WARGAME

Wargame is a bots versus game where you can invite friends to fight alongside you. Bring a party of friends into the Wargame lobby, or invite them from the lobby to battle together.

If you don't have enough friends to fill up your team, the game automatically assigns bots to fight on your team to even it out.

CUSTOMIZING YOUR SQUAD

When you are online, you can enter the Squad Customization screen at any time by selecting the "Create a Soldier" option. You start with one soldier in your Squad, but as you play and unlock more Squad points, you can unlock up to 10 Squad slots.

Until you unlock the Squad slots, those Squad members are automatically added (uncustomized) to your Squad when you start a Squad Assault or Squad vs. Squad game type.

On the Select Squad Member screen, you can select Squad Order, which determines which members of your Squad are active. You can even do this before you have unlocked the slot. The squad member you have selected will show up as a gold icon, while the other active members will display a silver icon. When you change the active member you are playing, it will not move the gold icon player to the top.

Once a slot is unlocked, you can change the Squad member's name and edit their appearance, gender, and outfit.

SQUAD BASE AND GAME TYPE

Your Squad base and game type can be set to any of the available options, which include all the maps in the standard rotation and all the standard multiplayer game types (including the new ones, like Blitz).

When any online opponent attacks your Squad, the battle occurs on the map and game type of your choosing.

SPECIALIZED TRAINING   THE CAMPAIGN   MP INTRO & BASIC TRAINING   **SQUADS**   MP ARMORY   PERKS   KILLSTREAKS   MP MAPS   MP GAME MODES   SAFEGUARD   EXTINCTION   CLASSIFIED   ACHIEVEMENTS & TROPHIES

117

MP ARMORY

This chapter has been prepared to guide you through all of the options available to you in the Squad customization system. Brush up on your multiplayer basics, and dig into details on every weapon, perk, killstreak, and piece of equipment in the game. The Squad customization system in *Call of Duty: Ghosts* allows you to maintain a roster of highly trained, individually equipped special forces.

However you choose to develop your Squad, this chapter has the information you need to make informed decisions about how to use every piece of gear in the game.

Each member of your team can be leveled, equipped, and customized individually. You can choose to focus on a single Squad soldier and maximize their loadout options, or spread your attention over multiple Squad members. Browse the weapons, attachments, and equipment to get an idea of the options available for arming your Squad. Refer to the Perks and Killstreaks sections for customizing their capabilities and support options.

USING THE ARMORY

This guide includes some of the most comprehensive statistical and informational breakdowns of the weapons in a *Call of Duty* title ever. To guide you through how this information is presented and what it means, read on.

Use the statistics presented here to guide and aid in your choice of weapon, but don't be a slave to the numbers. The most important factor in choosing a weapon is what feels best to you.

Rate of fire, recoil pattern, damage range, handling characteristics, iron sights, available attachments, all of these things and more influence the way a gun feels, and that's ignoring pure personal preference if you love the way a certain gun looks or sounds.

If you narrow down your favored weapons to a few specific guns within one category, use these stats to inform you about choosing between them. Experiment, explore, and enjoy!

RECOIL PLOTS

These scatter plots are simulations of thousands of shots fired with a given weapon in 10-shot spreads.

The plots are shown in two colors: the inner color shows an approximation of the first three shots fired, while the outer color shows the next seven shots.

For burst-fire weapons, they simulate multiple bursts fired in quick succession. Semi-auto weapons are fired at their (theoretical) maximum rate of fire.

Use these recoil plots to give you an idea of how a weapon kicks when it is fired on fully automatic, or if you hammer the trigger on a semi-automatic or burst-fire weapon.

You can also use the plots to compare the performance of one weapon with a recoil-modifying attachment to another weapon in the same class without the mod. This is a useful way of evaluating the recoil patterns of any two weapons, no matter which set of attachments you choose to use.

The way that a weapon recoils can have a dramatic effect on its performance, and it can also affect which types of weapons you prefer. Two weapons that are otherwise very similar may have a clear favorite for you personally simply because you prefer one type of recoil pattern over another.

In general, weapons that kick in a single direction are easier to predict than weapons that bounce around the center of the plot. If a weapon kicks straight up, you can pull down, and if it kicks up and left or right, you can pull down and right or left.

However, a weapon that kicks consistently left and right or up and down is more difficult to predict.

The magnitude of the recoil is also an issue, as some weapons simply have very low recoil overall. This makes them very accurate at a distance, regardless of the pattern of the recoil.

The Grip attachment reduces recoil slightly on any weapon it is attached to. Note it does nothing to change the pattern of the recoil, simply the intensity.

The Rapid Fire attachment increases recoil in two ways: first by simply increasing rate of fire, and second by slightly penalizing kick on top of that. The two effects combined mean that firing a Rapid Fire submachine gun (SMG) or light machine gun (LMG) becomes very unstable very quickly.

GUN KICK

A few weapons have special handling characteristics that affect the *visible* recoil of the weapon (that is, the gun actually jerking around in your hands as you fire).

This can be higher or lower than the normal kick the gun experiences past the first few shots fired.

The result of this is that weapons with *reduced* kick feel a bit more stable simply because the gun doesn't jump around in your hands as much on the first few shots.

Similarly, the guns with increased kick may feel more unstable than they really are (in terms of accurate shots downrange) and can fool you into overcompensating for the perceived recoil.

It's important to understand that these effects are minor, and they're mostly just part of the flavor of a given weapon. Some will feel a little more or less stable on the first few shots.

In terms of actual accuracy, though, pay attention to the recoil plots. They give you a good overall picture of how the weapon is really performing at a distance, however it feels in your hands.

Assault Rifles (ARs), slight reduction: ARX-160, FAD

ARs, very slight reduction: Honey Badger, Remington R5, SC-2010

ARs, very slight increase: AK-12

SMGs, slight reduction: CBJ-MS

LMGs, slight increase: Ameli

LMGs, slight reduction: Chain SAW, LSAT

SPECIALIZED TRAINING   THE CAMPAIGN   MP INTRO & BASIC TRAINING   SQUADS   **MP ARMORY**   PERKS   KILLSTREAKS   MP MAPS   MP GAME MODES   SAFEGUARD   EXTINCTION   CLASSIFIED   ACHIEVEMENTS & TROPHIES

119

WEAPON DAMAGE RANGE

Each weapon category has a chart (or series of charts) that shows you the shots to kill at a given distance.

Most weapons can kill in three to four shots within their optimal ranges, but some can kill in one or two. Short-range weapons used on distant targets can take five, six, or even more shots to down a target.

For all weapons except shotguns, once a gun reaches its minimum damage, it keeps that low damage no matter how far out you hit a target. If a weapon takes six shots at long range, it takes six shots even if an enemy is on the other side of a map.

For shotguns specifically, once they hit their maximum distance, they deal no damage past that point. You can't use a shotgun for long-range combat at all!

In the case of shotguns, these figures reflect pellets to kill, not shots. Each shotgun fires eight pellets at a time (the under-barrel shotgun fires six pellets). Pellets lose damage over distance. Up close, you may only need to hit with a few pellets, but at longer ranges, you may need to hit with most or even all of the pellets to get a kill.

The Tac 12 shotgun can potentially be a one-shot kill out to its maximum damage range, but your chances of consistent one-shot kills are much greater at close range for all shotguns.

The ranges on these charts, like all of the ranges presented elsewhere in the multiplayer sections, are all usable with the maps in this guide. You can eyeball the distance between any two points on any map and get a good feel for how many shots you need with any given weapon.

Silencers, the Muzzle Brake, and the Select Fire attachments can all impact weapon range performance.

Important!

These damage ranges assume an upper torso hit. For most weapons, this makes no difference to their performance regardless of where you hit an enemy, and it's a safe gauge of a weapon's performance at range.

If you score headshots, you're going to do better than the expected shots to kill on these charts (typically one shot less for most weapons). However, the Burst Fire and Select Fire attachments for assault rifles and designated marksman rifles (DMRs) bear special mention because they also affect the damage multiplier behavior of those weapons.

With the Select Fire attachment equipped, the weapons gain neck, upper, and lower torso multipliers, but if you're hitting arms or legs at a distance, you aren't going to be killing as quickly. Keep that quirk in mind before you wonder how an enemy got away when you were sure you hit him enough to down him.

DAMAGE NOTES

For most types of weapons, the damage charts simply display the number of shots to kill at any given range. Check the gun, look at the attachment in use, check the range, and you have your number of shots to kill.

For shotguns, the stats reflect the number of pellets needed to kill at a given distance. You won't always land those pellets, but if you do, that's the minimum number it takes to score a kill. Naturally, at shorter distances, you will see much more consistent one-shot kills.

The regular shotguns fire eight pellets each, whereas the under-barrel shotgun fires six pellets. For all but the Tac 12, their per pellet damage can fall to a point where it takes *more* than eight or six pellets to kill—that is, more than a single shot even if every pellet hit. These ranges are designated on the charts by an 8+ and a 6+ marking on the range bar. Shotguns do not get headshot damage multipliers.

For three of the four sniper rifles, they deal a fixed amount of damage at any distance—just barely less than that needed to kill an enemy.

Sniper rifles have more areas on the body where they get a damage multiplier beyond just the head like most weapons. For the VKS and USR, a body shot or headshot is a kill. For the L115 and Lynx, an upper leg shot, body shot, or headshot is a kill.

The VKS does have damage falloff, so past a certain point, you need to hit the head for a one-shot kill (in exchange, it has an integrated silencer).

Assault rifles and marksman rifles with a Select Fire attachment also have different damage profiles overall (enough so that the multiple charts and recoil plots here display the differences between full auto, semi auto, and burst).

RATE OF FIRE

A simple chart displays the rate of fire for each gun in a given class. Rate of fire can be increased with the Rapid Fire attachment, but this is only available to SMGs and LMGs.

The various Select Fire attachments for ARs also affect the rate of fire of the different ARs and MRs. Semi-Automatic lowers the maximum rate of fire (assuming you can pull the trigger that quickly), while Burst Fire raises the rate of fire within the burst. There is still an inherent delay between bursts!

As a general rule of thumb, high rate of fire weapons are more lethal in close-quarters battle (CQB), and less accurate at a distance. A high rate of fire also means that you see the more extreme patterns in the recoil plots quickly if you aren't careful with trigger control.

RELOADS

Reload times are handled in three stages: the time it takes for the ammo to be loaded, the time for the reloading animation to finish normally, and the time for a reload from an empty magazine to finish. These three stages are marked on the chart as Add Time, Reload Time, and Empty Time.

Shotguns and the P226, .44 Magnum, and PDW pistols do not have an empty time. For the two pump-action shotguns (the Tac 12 and FP6), the reload times shown are per shell.

At any time after the "ammo added" portion of a reload, you can cancel the remaining animation time by either sprinting or switching weapons (switching to and from another weapon by double-tapping the Switch button counts).

The On the Go perk lets you reload while sprinting, at the cost of being unable to reload-cancel with a sprint (you can still switch weapons to cancel the animation). The Sleight of Hand perk halves reload times across the board.

AMMO LOAD

This is a simple breakdown of the magazine sizes, starting ammo, and maximum ammo counts for the weapons.

Extended Mags gives you a 50% boost to magazine size, the Fully Loaded perk starts you with maximum ammo, and the Scavenger perk and Weapon Crate Support streak let you refill ammo on the battlefield.

WEAPON DATA

This is a small collection of extra useful information about each weapon: how long it takes to switch to or from a given weapon, base aim down sights (ADS) times, base penetration strength, and damage multipliers for headshots (or other body parts, for some weapons).

Drop time is the time it takes to put a weapon away. Raise time is the time it takes to equip that weapon. Pistols tend to have very fast drop and raise times, while LMGs or snipers are usually quite slow. The Reflex perk cuts these swap times in half.

WEAPON SIGHTS

The weapon sights are simply a collection of images to give you a quick look at the iron sights or integrated scopes for various weapons.

You definitely need to spend time with the weapons in-game to decide which sights you do or do not like; sights are a very personal part of weapon customization.

Following is a short gallery of various special optics.

Red Dot Sight  Holographic Sight  Thermal Hybrid Sight Scope  Thermal Hybrid Sight Irons

Thermal Sniper Scope  ACOG  Tracker Sight Scope  Tracker Sight Irons

VMR Sight Scope  VMR Sight Reflex

PRIMARY WEAPONS

ASSAULT RIFLES (AR)

PROS	
Flexible, all-around weapon	
Wide range of attachments	
Solid handling characteristics	
CONS	
Less effective than specialized short- or long-range weapons in their preferred engagement ranges	

COMBAT ROLE	All-purpose workhorse
PREFERRED RANGE	Close medium to medium long

Reliable, All-Around Weapons

Assault rifles are powerful, versatile weapons. When you need a reliable weapon for any mode or map, you can always count on an assault rifle. They are at their best at medium range, but with customization and trigger control, you can effectively use them at close-medium to medium-long range.

Assault rifles have a wide range of attachments that you can use to tune their capabilities, from shorter range, high rate of fire models that come close to an SMG, to burst or semi-automatic fire options with magnifying scopes that come closer to a marksman-class rifle.

You can also equip under-barrel mods to give you an edge in CQB with a shotgun, or use a grenade launcher to clear enemies around an objective target.

Assault rifles can work well in almost any situation; while they may fall in combat with very close- or very long-range specialists, at almost any other range band, they are a strong and viable option.

When using fully automatic ARs at long range, be sure to use short, controlled bursts. While the lower fire rate ARs can maintain their accuracy longer when the trigger is held down, you are always going to have better accuracy when you carefully fire in short bursts, emulating a burst-fire rifle.

An assault rifle with a simple Red Dot sight is a great place to start if you can't settle on a weapon to dig into multiplayer with.

MSBS Select Fire

The MSBS is already a three-round burst weapon by default, but it can choose to take a fully automatic Select Fire option. This converts the MSBS from a precision mid-long range AR to a high fire rate, fully automatic rifle. Give it a try!

The MSBS also has the semi-auto option available.

Select Fire

There are seven fully automatic rifles, and one three-round burst rifle (the MSBS).

Assault rifles can be customized with two different Select Fire attachments: one for burst fire, the other for semi-automatic fire.

Taking these attachments shifts an assault rifle from a medium range all-purpose automatic weapon to a mid-long range marksman-style weapon.

These attachments completely change the damage profile for the weapon, giving them additional torso damage multipliers and increasing their effective kill shot ranges *if* you are accurate. This means that if you score on-target chest hits, you can get reliable kills in just a few shots at long ranges, but inaccurate fire is punished.

While this makes them similar to marksman-class rifles, there are a few key differences. First and most obviously, you're giving up an attachment slot for this change in performance.

Next, the damage profiles aren't exactly the same as those in the marksman class, which generally hit harder and at longer ranges without the demand for center-mass hits.

And finally, assault rifles do not have the integrated scopes fitted on marksman rifles, meaning you have to spend another attachment for a precision optic. On top of that, marksman rifle scopes have inherent recoil reduction, making them naturally accurate weapons at long range.

If there is a certain weapon that has a recoil pattern you find very comfortable or you simply want to use your favored AR at a different range on larger maps, give the Select Fire attachments a try. You may find you like the way they handle.

AR TRAITS

The Honey Badger AR features an integrated silencer and has the best overall range profile with its integrated silencer compared to other ARs with a silencer attached.

The MSBS is a three-round burst rifle by default and can be fitted with a fully automatic or semi-automatic Select Fire attachment. The MSBS does not have center-mass multipliers like the other ARs with a Burst Fire attachment; it always deals full damage when hitting a target in any location.

The ARX-160 has reduced hipfire spread, placing it roughly halfway between SMG- and AR-class weapons.

The AK-12 and Remington R5 have slightly lower multipliers when equipped with Burst Fire or Semi-Auto, but they deal higher base damage than other rifles, making the overall impact similar to the other ARs.

Assault Rifle Recoil Plots

AR-12 | AK-12 (Grip) | AK-12 (Semi-Auto) | AK-12 (Semi-Auto, Grip) | AK-12 (Burst Fire) | AK-12 (Burst Fire, Grip)

ARX-160 | ARX-160 (Grip) | ARX-160 (Semi-Auto) | ARX-160 (Semi-Auto, Grip) | ARX-160 (Burst Fire) | ARX-160 (Burst Fire, Grip)

FAD | FAD (Grip) | FAD (Semi-Auto) | FAD (Semi-Auto, Grip) | FAD (Burst Fire) | FAD (Burst Fire, Grip)

Honey Badger | Honey Badger (Grip) | Honey Badger (Semi-Auto) | Honey Badger (Semi-Auto, Grip) | Honey Badger (Burst Fire) | Honey Badger (Burst Fire, Grip)

MSBS | MSBS (Grip) | MSBS (Semi-Auto) | MSBS (Semi-Auto, Grip) | MSBS (Full Auto) | MSBS (Full Auto, Grip)

Remington R5 | Remington R5 (Grip) | Remington R5 (Semi-Auto) | Remington R5 (Semi-Auto, Grip) | Remington R5 (Burst Fire) | Remington R5 (Burst Fire, Grip)

SA-805 | SA-805 (Grip) | SA-805 (Semi-Auto) | SA-805 (Semi-Auto, Grip) | SA-805 (Burst Fire) | SC2010 (Burst Fire, Grip)

SC-2010 | SC-2010 (Grip) | SC-2010 (Semi-Auto) | SC2010 (Semi-Auto, Grip) | SC-2010 (Burst Fire) | SC2010 (Burst Fire, Grip)

SPECIALIZED TRAINING   THE CAMPAIGN   MP INTRO & BASIC TRAINING   SQUADS   MP ARMORY   PERKS   KILLSTREAKS   MP MAPS   MP GAME MODES   SAFEGUARD   EXTINCTION   CLASSIFIED   ACHIEVEMENTS & TROPHIES

123

Assault Rifle Damage: Shots to Kill Over Distance

This chart illustrates the number of on-target shots needed to kill a target from a given distance.

ASSAULT RIFLES, STANDARD FIRE

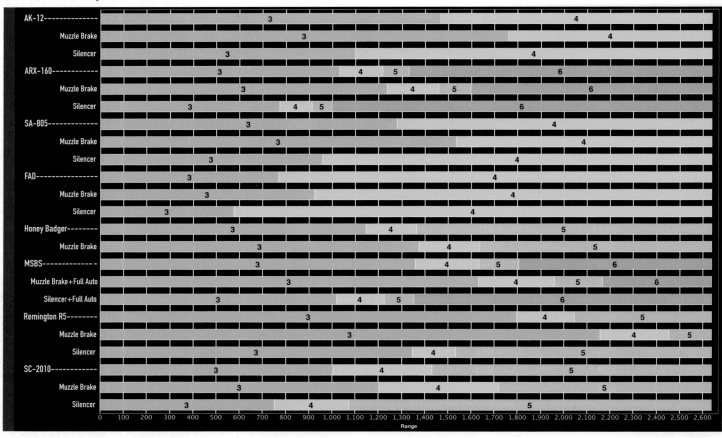

ASSAULT RIFLES, SEMI-AUTO FIRE

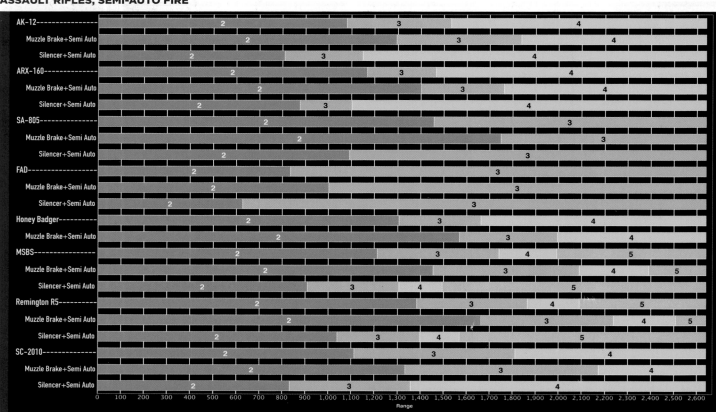

ASSAULT RIFLES, BURST FIRE

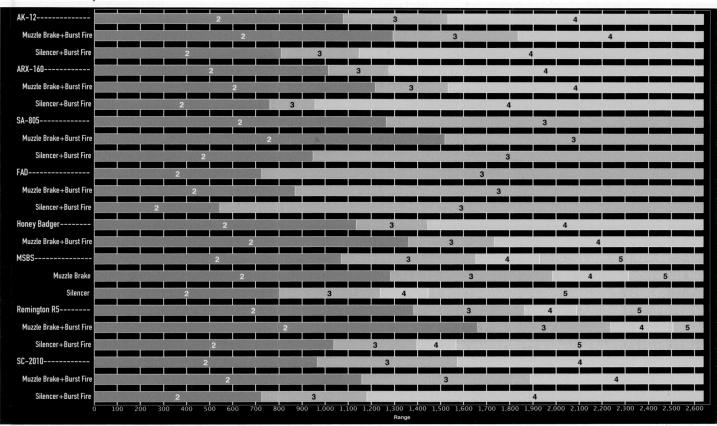

Assault Rifle Rate of Fire: Rounds Per Minute

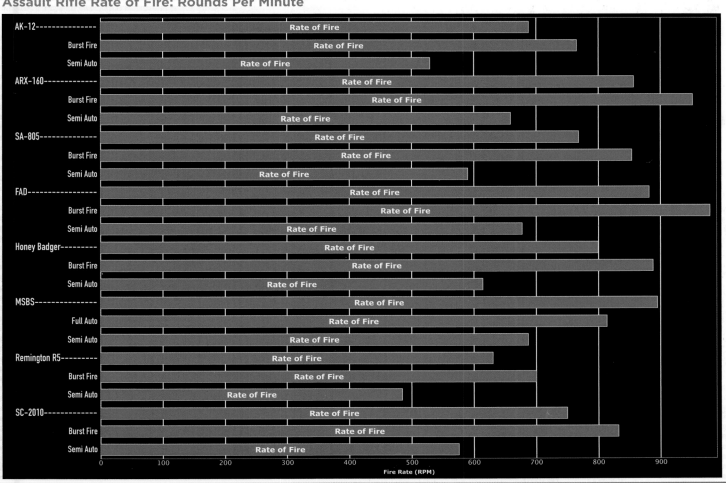

SPECIALIZED TRAINING · THE CAMPAIGN · MP INTRO & BASIC TRAINING · SQUADS · **MP ARMORY** · PERKS · KILLSTREAKS · MP MAPS · MP GAME MODES · SAFEGUARD · EXTINCTION · CLASSIFIED · ACHIEVEMENTS & TROPHIES

125

Assault Rifle Reload: Time in Seconds

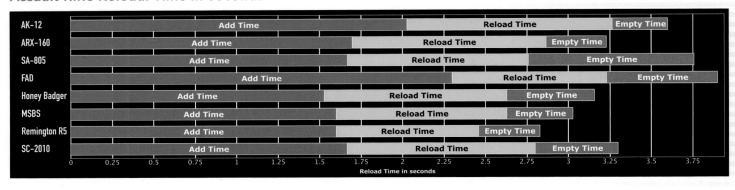

Assault Rifle Ammo Capacity

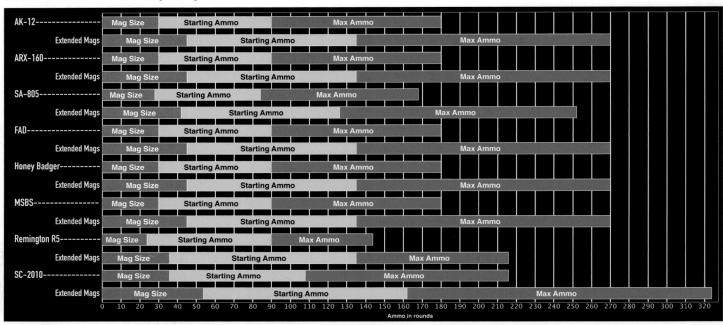

Assault Rifle Attachments

Weapon Name	Extended Mags	Armor-Piercing	Semi-Auto	Burst Fire	Foregrip	Shotgun	Grenade Launcher	Red Dot Sight	ACOG Scope	Holographic Sight	VMR Sight	Thermal Hybrid Scope	Tracker Sight	Flash Suppressor	Silencer	Muzzle Brake
AK-12	✔	✔	✔	✔	✔	✔	✔	✔	✔	✔	✔	✔	✔	✔	✔	✔
ARX-160	✔	✔	✔	✔	✔	✔	✔	✔	✔	✔	✔	✔	✔	✔	✔	✔
SA-805	✔	✔	✔	✔	✔	✔	✔	✔	✔	✔	✔	✔	✔	✔	✔	✔
FAD	✔	✔	✔	✔	✔	✔	✔	✔	✔	✔	✔	✔	✔	✔	✔	✔
Honey Badger	✔	✔	✔	✔	✔	✔	✔	✔	✔	✔	✔	✔	✔			
MSBS	✔	✔	✔	Auto Fire	✔	✔	✔	✔	✔	✔	✔	✔	✔	✔	✔	✔
Remington R5	✔	✔	✔	✔	✔	✔	✔	✔	✔	✔	✔	✔	✔	✔	✔	✔
SC-2010	✔	✔	✔	✔	✔	✔	✔	✔	✔	✔	✔	✔	✔	✔	✔	✔

Assault Rifle Weapon Data

AR	ADS TIME	DROP TIME	RAISE TIME	HEAD	BURST FIRE/ SEMI-AUTO: NECK	BURST FIRE/ SEMI-AUTO: UPPER TORSO	BURST FIRE/ SEMI-AUTO: LOWER TORSO	PENETRATION
AK-12	0.3	0.6	1	1.4	1.4	1.1	1.1	Average
ARX-160	0.3	0.6	1.333	1.5	1.5	1.5	1.5	Average
SA-805	0.3	0.7	1.16	1.5	1.5	1.5	1.5	Average
FAD	0.3	0.7	1.03	1.4	1.5	1.5	1.5	Average
Honey Badger	0.3	0.45	0.9	1.4	1.5	1.5	1.5	Average
MSBS	0.3	0.66	1.23	1.4	1.5	1.5	1.5	Average
Remington R5	0.3	0.7	0.766	1.4	1.4	1.1	1.1	Average
SC-2010	0.3	0.5	1	1.5	1.5	1.5	1.5	Average

SUBMACHINE GUNS (SMG)

PROS
Accurate hipfire
Good mobility and handling characteristics
High rate of fire

CONS
Poor damage at a distance
High ammo consumption

COMBAT ROLE	CQB and high-mobility combat
PREFERRED RANGE	Close to close-medium

CQB Specialists

Submachine guns are specialist CQB weapons, built for speed and close-range engagements. They have excellent mobility and handling characteristics, high rates of fire, and good hipfire accuracy.

SMGs are best used on highly mobile and/or stealthy builds so they can get to a target area quickly to engage and disrupt enemy forces. Stealth allows them to operate in close proximity to the enemy team while picking off isolated targets and then changing positions to lure in more prey, while speed lets them get into CQB where they belong.

SMGs are generally poor at medium range or longer, though a few of the SMGs are somewhat more suited to slightly longer range ADS fire than the others. They don't compare well to long-range weapons, but they can get the job done.

Along with LMGs, SMGs are the only other weapon class to have access to the Rapid Fire attachment. This attachment pushes their already high rates of fire up into truly lethal territory (at the cost of increased recoil and ammo consumption).

SMG TRAITS

The CBJ-MS has built-in armor-piercing rounds. This makes it an excellent weapon for firing through thin walls during indoor engagements, and it also works in a pinch for taking out enemy battlefield equipment.

The K7 has an integrated silencer and the best overall range profile compared to other SMGs with a silencer attached.

The Vector and MTAR-X have notably better long-range performance than the other SMGs.

The Vector has better penetration than the other SMGs, on par with ARs.

Submachine Gun Recoil Plots

Bizon

Bizon (Grip)

Bizon (Rapid Fire)

Bizon (Rapid Fire, Grip)

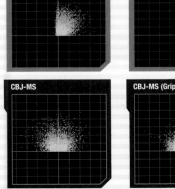
CBJ-MS

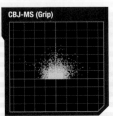
CBJ-MS (Grip)

CBJ-MS (Rapid Fire)

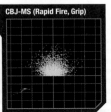
CBJ-MS (Rapid Fire, Grip)

SPECIALIZED TRAINING   THE CAMPAIGN   MP INTRO & BASIC TRAINING   SQUADS   **MP ARMORY**   PERKS   KILLSTREAKS   MP MAPS   MP GAME MODES   SAFEGUARD   EXTINCTION   CLASSIFIED   ACHIEVEMENTS & TROPHIES

127

Submachine Gun Recoil Plots — continued

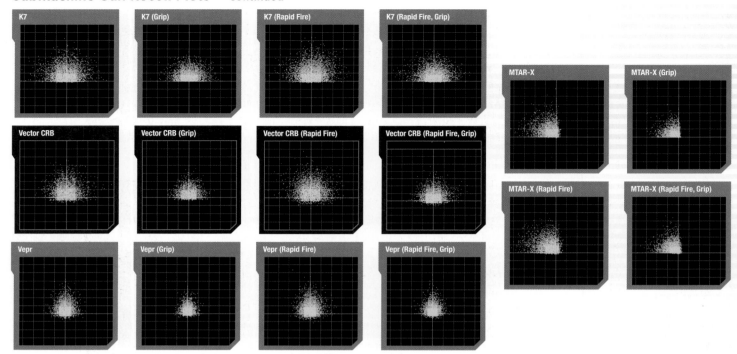

Submachine Gun Damage: Shots to Kill Over Distance

This chart illustrates the number of on-target shots needed to kill a target from a given distance.

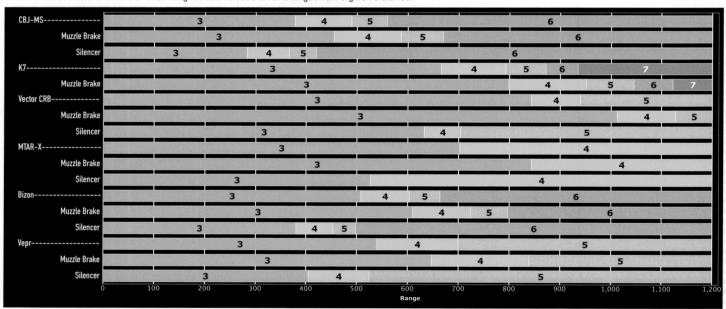

Submachine Gun Rate of Fire: Rounds Per Minute

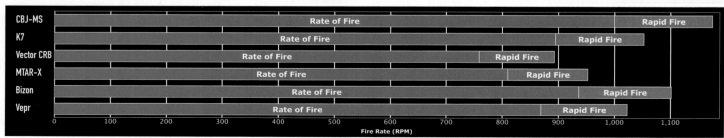

Submachine Gun Reload: Time in Seconds

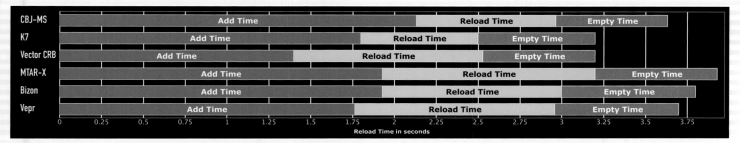

Submachine Gun Ammo Capacity

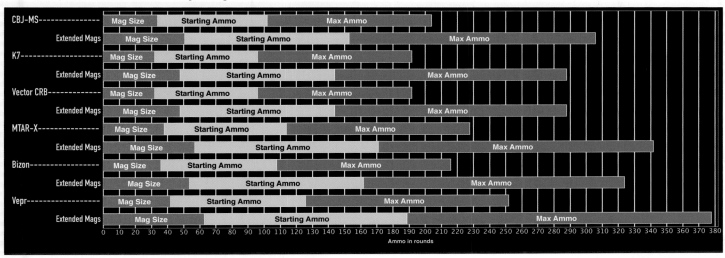

Submachine Gun Weapon Data

SMG	ADS TIME	DROP TIME	RAISE TIME	HEAD	PENETRATION
CBJ-MS	0.2	0.466	1	1.5	Low
K7	0.2	0.5	0.9	1.5	Low
Vector CRB	0.2	0.5	1.06	1.5	Medium
MTAR-X	0.2	0.8	1.93	1.5	Low
Bizon	0.2	0.7	1.36	1.5	Low
Vepr	0.25	0.5	1.066	1.5	Low

SUBMACHINE GUN ATTACHMENTS

Weapon Name	Extended Mags	Armor-Piercing	Rapid Fire	Foregrip	Red Dot Sight	ACOG Scope	Holographic Sight	VMR Sight	Thermal Hybrid Scope	Tracker Sight	Flash Suppressor	Silencer	Muzzle Brake
CBJ-MS	✔		✔	✔	✔	✔	✔	✔	✔	✔	✔	✔	✔
K7	✔	✔	✔	✔	✔	✔	✔	✔	✔		✔		
Vector CRB	✔	✔	✔	✔	✔	✔	✔	✔	✔	✔	✔	✔	✔
MTAR-X	✔	✔	✔	✔	✔	✔	✔	✔	✔	✔	✔	✔	✔
Bizon	✔	✔	✔	✔	✔	✔	✔	✔	✔	✔	✔	✔	✔
Vepr	✔	✔	✔	✔	✔	✔	✔	✔	✔	✔	✔	✔	✔

LIGHT MACHINE GUNS (LMG)

PROS	
High damage at range	
Deep magazines	
Good penetration	
CONS	
Poor mobility and handling characteristics	
Long reload times	

COMBAT ROLE	Defensive suppression
PREFERRED RANGE	Medium to long

Suppression Specialists

Light machine guns are powerful mid- to long-range weapons with massive ammo capacity, great penetration, and high damage even at long range.

The tradeoff: LMGs have very poor handling characteristics, with bad hipfire spreads, movement speeds, slow switch and ADS times, and glacially slow reload times. They're also quite loud and noticeable when you're firing them fully auto!

Because of these traits, LMGs are the wrong choice for mobile "run and gun" combat, or even AR-style generalist mid-range battling. What they do excel at is locking down an area cold.

If you can get into position with a good line of sight and already be in ADS when an enemy (or two enemies, or three, or four, or…) comes around a corner, you can easily mow them all down without breaking a sweat or thinking about a reload.

Ducking around a corner or behind cover to wait for the person firing on you to reload works fine against most other weapons, but it's a terrible idea against an LMG. Not only does the LMG rarely need to reload in a single engagement, but they can also drill you through the wall you're hiding behind!

When using an LMG, watch for players to temporarily take cover from your barrage of fire. Stop your shots, wait, and then cut them down the instant they poke out again. If you know the map well and know where they're likely hiding, simply keep firing on their cover and take them out through the wall.

LMGs have comparable rates of fire to the ARs, but they have access to the Rapid Fire attachment, which ARs do not. This pushes up their lethality considerably (at the cost of increased recoil).

If you expect to be engaging targets at shorter ranges, Rapid Fire works well, but if you intend to keep your distance and pick off enemies at long range, skip it. The increased recoil tends to nullify any time to kill benefits Rapid Fire grants.

LMG TRAITS

The Ameli is the only two-shot kill fully automatic weapon in the game. While it has the lowest rate of fire of the LMGs, it can still kill extremely quickly, especially with Rapid Fire.

The M27 never suffers damage drop-off, as it kills in three shots at any distance.

The Chain SAW is a completely unique weapon: it has no proper ADS and better base hipfire accuracy. Still, "ADSing" only gives a very slight reduction in hipfire spread, while slowing your movement speed. The Chain SAW is essentially a lighter version of the Assault Juggernaut's minigun!

The Chain SAW has better base movement speed than the other LMGs, equivalent to AR speed. The Chain SAW's unusual lack of ADS and increased movement speed make it a better patrolling LMG for mobile mid-range combat than the other LMGs.

Light Machine Gun Recoil Plots

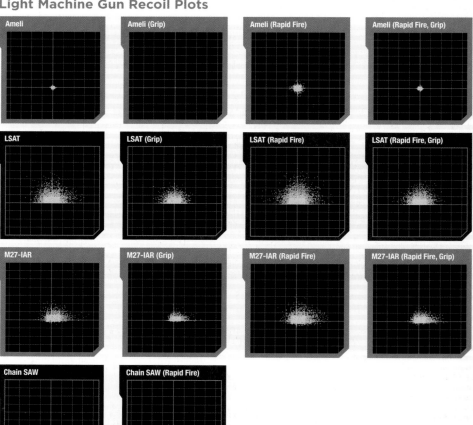

Light Machine Gun Damage: Shots to Kill Over Distance

This chart illustrates the number of on-target shots needed to kill a target from a given distance.

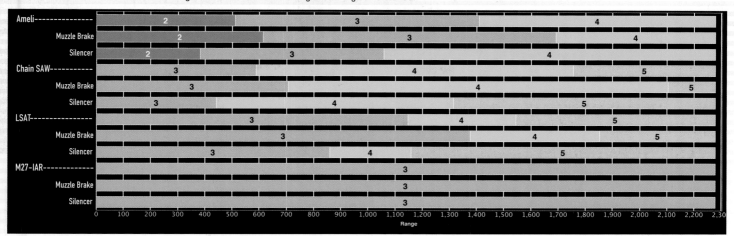

Light Machine Gun Rate of Fire: Rounds Per Minute

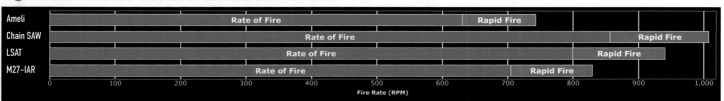

Light Machine Gun Reload: Time in Seconds

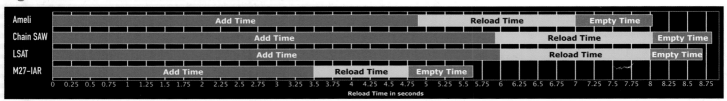

Light Machine Gun Ammo Capacity

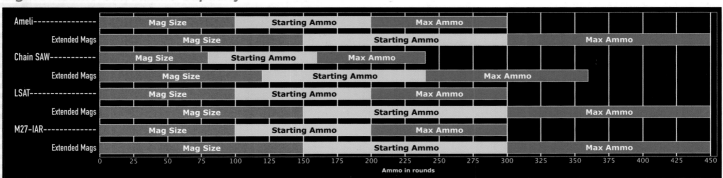

Light Machine Gun Weapon Data

LMG	ADS TIME	DROP TIME	RAISE TIME	HEAD	PENETRATION
Ameli	0.35	1	1.9	1.4	High
Chain SAW	0.35	0.9	1.7	1.4	High
LSAT	0.35	0.633	1.7	1.56	High
M27-IAR	0.35	0.933	1.433	1.4	High

SPECIALIZED TRAINING THE CAMPAIGN MP INTRO & BASIC TRAINING SQUADS MP ARMORY PERKS KILLSTREAKS MP MAPS MP GAME MODES SAFEGUARD EXTINCTION CLASSIFIED ACHIEVEMENTS & TROPHIES

131

LIGHT MACHINE GUN ATTACHMENTS

Weapon Name	Extended Mags	Armor-Piercing	Rapid Fire	Flash Suppressor	Silencer	Muzzle Brake	Red Dot Sight	ACOG Scope	Holographic Sight	VMR Sight	Thermal Hybrid Scope	Tracker Sight	Foregrip	Shotgun	Grenade Launcher
Ameli	✔	✔	✔	✔	✔	✔	✔	✔	✔	✔	✔	✔	✔	✔	✔
M27-IAR	✔	✔	✔	✔	✔	✔	✔	✔	✔	✔	✔	✔	✔	✔	✔
LSAT	✔	✔	✔	✔	✔	✔	✔	✔	✔	✔	✔	✔	✔	✔	✔
Chain SAW	✔	✔	✔		✔	✔									✔

MARKSMAN RIFLES

PROS
Integral high-magnification scopes	
High accuracy	
High damage at range	

CONS
Semi-auto or burst fire modes only	
Poor in CQB situations	
Require an attachment to remove integral long range scope	

COMBAT ROLE	Mobile long-range combat
PREFERRED RANGE	Medium to long

Precision Rifles

MRs bridge the gap between assault and sniper rifles. If you have a fast trigger finger, these highly accurate weapons can down targets extremely quickly, while retaining an AR weapon's mobility.

All marksman rifles feature a recoil-suppressing, high-zoom, integrated scope. They're semi-automatic and deliver very high damage at range.

With its integrated scope, an MR is ideal for long-range combat. If you swap in a Red Dot or Holographic sight, it's suited to mid-range fights. ACOGs split the difference; they're still good for longer-range engagements, but less awkward at short range than their full scopes.

The Thermal Hybrid and Tracker sights provide two specialized options: the Thermal for long range, the Tracker for close-medium range.

All marksman rifles can be equipped with the Burst Fire attachment, giving a three-round option for potential one-shot kills. Be aware that the burst fire's kick is typically greater than firing rapidly and carefully in semi-auto mode. Burst fire can increase instant lethality at shorter ranges, provided you land all shots.

MRs are generally poor in CQB or when hipfired. Though they're slightly better with Burst Fire equipped, carrying a favorite backup pistol is wise. Marksman rifles share mobility and handling characteristics with assault rifles, so they're good for fighting on the move while retaining significant punch at a distance.

MARKSMAN RIFLE TRAITS

All MRs have reduced recoil when using their integrated scopes. For true long-range combat, leave their default scopes attached.

The MR-28 has a built-in grip and the lowest recoil in its class. The SVU is a two-shot kill at any range. All MRs can be equipped with the Burst Fire Select Fire option.

Marksman rifles can take Iron Sights as an attachment. Both the Thermal Hybrid and Tracker sights provide an iron sight that can be toggled on or off.

Marksman Rifle Rate of Fire: Rounds Per Minute

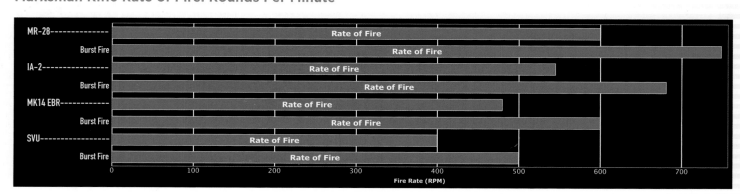

MR-28	Rate of Fire	~600
	Burst Fire	Rate of Fire	~740
IA-2	Rate of Fire	~540
	Burst Fire	Rate of Fire	~680
MK14 EBR	Rate of Fire	~480
	Burst Fire	Rate of Fire	~500
SVU	Rate of Fire	~400
	Burst Fire	Rate of Fire	~450

Fire Rate (RPM)

Marksman Rifle Damage: Shots to Kill Over Distance

This chart illustrates the number of on-target shots needed to kill a target from a given distance.

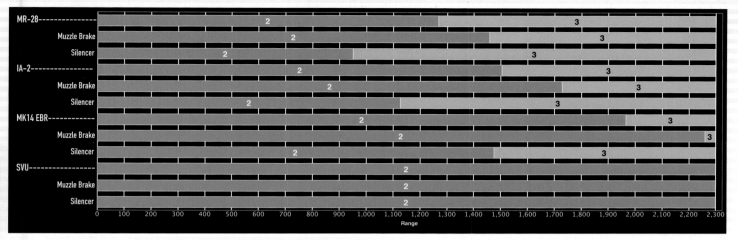

Marksman Rifle Ammo Capacity

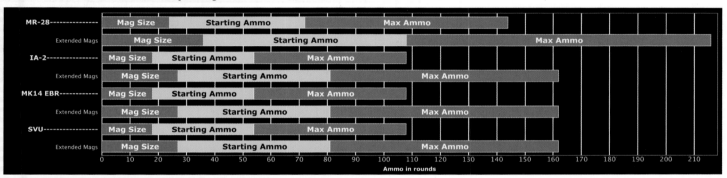

Marksman Rifle Recoil Plots

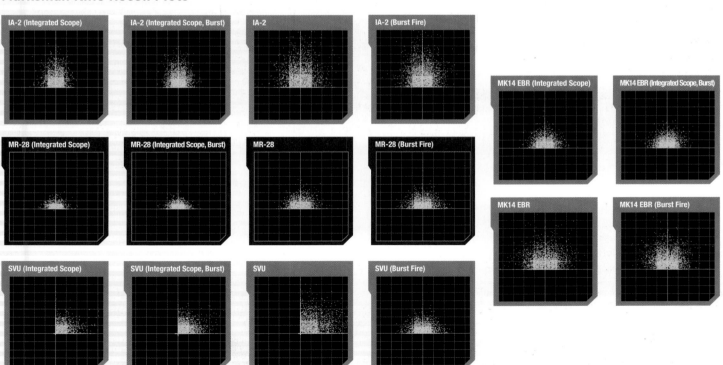

SPECIALIZED TRAINING   THE CAMPAIGN   MP INTRO & BASIC TRAINING   SQUADS   **MP ARMORY**   PERKS   KILLSTREAKS   MP MAPS   MP GAME MODES   SAFEGUARD   EXTINCTION   CLASSIFIED   ACHIEVEMENTS & TROPHIES

133

Marksman Rifle Reload: Time in Seconds

MR-28	Add Time	Reload Time	Empty Time	
IA-2	Add Time	Reload Time	Empty Time	
MK14 EBR	Add Time	Reload Time	Empty Time	
SVU	Add Time	Reload Time	Empty Time	

0   0.25   0.5   0.75   1   1.25   1.5   1.75   2   2.25   2.5   2.75   3   3.25   3.5   3.75   4

Reload Time in seconds

Marksman Rifle Weapon Data

MR	ADS TIME	DROP TIME	RAISE TIME	HEAD	NECK	PENETRATION
MR-28	0.3	0.767	1	1.56	1.56	High
IA-2	0.3	0.93	1.73	1.56	1.56	High
MK-14 EBR	0.3	0.633	1.133	1.56	1	High
SVU	0.3	1.26	0.83	1.56	1.56	High

Marksman Rifle Attachments

Weapon Name	Extended Mags	Armor-Piercing	Burst Fire	Flash Suppressor	Silencer	Muzzle Brake	Iron Sight	Red Dot Sight	ACOG Scope	Holographic Sight	Thermal Hybrid Scope	Tracker Sight
MR-28	✔	✔	✔	✔	✔	✔	✔	✔	✔	✔	✔	✔
IA-2	✔	✔	✔	✔	✔	✔	✔	✔	✔	✔	✔	✔
MK14 EBR	✔	✔	✔	✔	✔	✔	✔	✔	✔	✔	✔	✔
SVU	✔	✔	✔	✔	✔	✔	✔	✔	✔	✔	✔	

SNIPER RIFLES

PROS	
One-shot kills	
High-magnification scopes	
CONS	
Poor in CQB	
Poor handling characteristics	

COMBAT ROLE	Long-range suppression
PREFERRED RANGE	Long range

Long-Range Superiority

Sniper rifles are long-range, precision weapons with powerful scopes and the ability to kill in a single shot at any range. Unlike other weapons, most sniper rifles do not have damage falloff at distance. Instead, they deal fixed damage with multipliers for different parts of the body. Generally, all SRs kill with a torso or headshot, though the specific multipliers vary for each model.

Sniper rifles are very poor at close range, with huge hipfire spread, low fire rate, slow movement speed, and worse handling than CQB specialists. You can get lucky with a hipfire shot, but don't rely on it.

With the Quickdraw perk, it's possible to get by at medium range if you're fast and accurate. However, this depends heavily on both your personal skill and the speed of your connection. Bring a favorite pistol and possibly the Reflex perk when you use a sniper—you want a reliable backup if you get jumped in CQB.

Important! Sniper Rifle Accuracy

A sniper scope's gentle sway can throw off your aim slightly. To steady it, hold your breath by holding the Melee button while you ADS. You can hold your breath for only a short time before the scope sways wildly until you recover.

To take accurate shots, stand stationary, hold your breath, and fire once you're fully stable. Doing so guarantees accurate shots at any distance. If you fire a sniper rifle before you are fully ADS in the scope *or* you move while firing, the shot uses your hipfire accuracy profile—which is very, very bad!

The fastest accurate shots involve using the Quickdraw perk, stopping your movement entirely for a split second, sighting while holding your breath, and firing once stabilized. It's easier to use SRs at their native long distance, where you can rest stationary, scan for targets, and then briefly hold your breath and fire from a crouching or prone position.

Chrome Lined Barrel

Unique to the sniper rifles, this attachment expands the damage multipliers to include upper arms and upper legs for any sniper rifle, at the cost of massively increased recoil and slightly worse sway while ADS. Given that you want to be killing in a single shot to begin with, the downside isn't as significant as the benefit here. For most loadouts, especially those where you intend to stay at a great distance, the Chrome Lined Barrel is an excellent attachment.

The L115 and Lynx already kill with upper leg shots, and the VKS cannot take the Chrome Lined Barrel (it has an integrated silencer). That being the case, only the USR gains two new kill shot zones with the Chrome Lined Barrel. The L115 and Lynx only gain upper arm multipliers, but this is still an increase in overall consistency at a distance.

Choosing between a silencer and the Chrome Lined Barrel is a difficult decision—experiment with both and see which you prefer.

If you prefer to fight at a distance, the Chrome Lined Barrel can increase the consistency of your long-range kill shots slightly, while the silencer can be used to keep you concealed if you expect to be firing within minimap range of hostile targets.

Sniper Rifle Recoil Plots

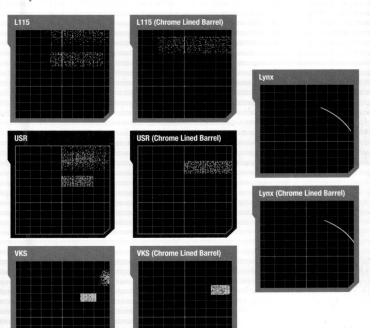

SNIPER RIFLE TRAITS

The USR and L115 have built-in recoil compensators. These special integrated attachments adjust for your shots automatically as you score kills. The display above the scope updates each time you get a kill without dying.

Each kill with the USR or L115 grants you a 3% kick reduction, up to a maximum of 12%. Dying resets the compensation. The USR has good movement speed for a sniper rifle, equivalent to ARs. The Lynx has slow movement speed, equivalent to the LMGs.

The VKS and L115 have an average movement speed between that of the USR and the Lynx. The VKS has an integrated silencer, and it is the only sniper rifle with damage falloff—it drops to a two-shot kill past a certain range, or a one-shot kill to the head.

The Lynx and the VKS have slightly slower ADS times (0.45) compared to the L115 and USR (0.40). You can improve the semi-auto sniper ADS times to 0.40 by attaching an ACOG or Thermal scope, at the cost of losing their integrated precision scopes.

Sniper Rifle Damage: Shots to Kill Over Distance

This chart illustrates the number of on-target shots needed to kill a target from a given distance.

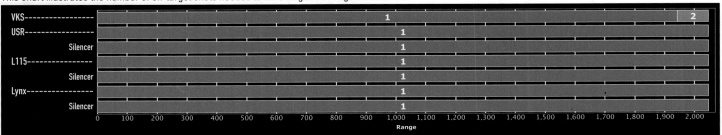

Sniper Rifle Rate of Fire: Rounds Per Minute

SPECIALIZED TRAINING   THE CAMPAIGN   MP INTRO & BASIC TRAINING   SQUADS   **MP ARMORY**   PERKS   KILLSTREAKS   MP MAPS   MP GAME MODES   SAFEGUARD   EXTINCTION   CLASSIFIED   ACHIEVEMENTS & TROPHIES

135

Sniper Rifle Reload: Time in Seconds

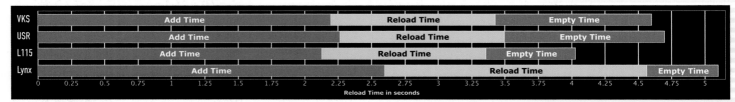

Sniper Rifle Ammo Capacity

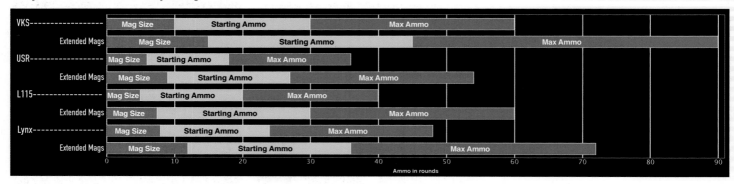

Sniper Rifle Weapon Data

SNIPER	ADS TIME	DROP TIME	RAISE TIME	HEAD	NECK	UPPER TORSO	LOWER TORSO	UPPER LEGS	PENETRATION
VKS	0.45	0.9	1.46	1.5	1.1	1.1	1.1	1	High
USR	0.4	1	1.36	1.5	1.1	1.1	1.1	1	High
L115	0.4	0.8	1.3	1.5	1.1	1.1	1.1	1.1	High
Lynx	0.45	1	1.567	1.5	1.1	1.1	1.1	1.1	High

Sniper Rifle Attachments

SNIPER RIFLE ATTACHMENTS							
Weapon Name	Extended Mags	Armor-Piercing	ACOG Scope	Thermal Scope	Variable Zoom Lens	Silencer	Chrome Lined Barrel
VKS	✔	✔	✔	✔	✔		
USR	✔	✔	✔	✔	✔	✔	✔
L115	✔	✔	✔	✔	✔	✔	✔
Lynx	✔	✔	✔	✔	✔	✔	✔

SHOTGUNS

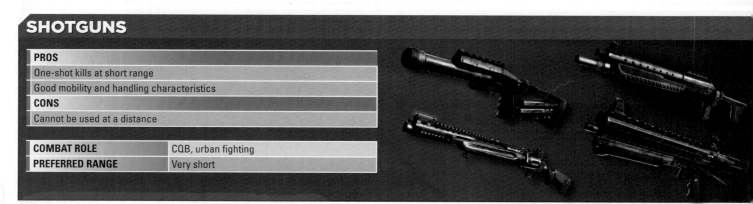

PROS	
One-shot kills at short range	
Good mobility and handling characteristics	
CONS	
Cannot be used at a distance	

COMBAT ROLE	CQB, urban fighting
PREFERRED RANGE	Very short

Short-Range Monsters

All brute force and no finesse, shotguns exist to kick in the door and clear the room with speed and finality. Shotguns are literally useless beyond short range, as their shots cannot inflict damage past a certain range. Unlike SMGs, they must get into CQB to do their work. However, with that weakness in mind, shotguns are also the only weapon class that can get reliable one-shot kills at close range. Unlike sniper rifles, you don't even need to be pinpoint accurate to do so—get your crosshair near your target, and pull the trigger.

Shotguns are also lethal when hipfired, even more so than SMGs. With the Steady Aim perk, you can essentially ignore ADSing entirely, moving and firing at full speed at all times.

Pump-action shotguns have better range profiles (for a shotgun at least), but the tradeoff is a lower rate of fire compared to the semi-automatics. The semi-automatics are better suited for room clearing against multiple targets, but they often require two shots to get the job done, whereas an accurate pump shot is almost always fatal at close range. A stealthy or speedy build is paramount with shotgun usage. Map knowledge will tell you where you can stay out of sight and flank enemy positions without being engaged at a distance.

Shotguns have excellent handling, equivalent movement speed to SMGs, and good hipfire spreads. Because shotguns are so tightly restricted to CQB, picking up a long-range weapon on the field is smart. Without the Reflex perk, switch between your shotgun and your long-range weapon early because of slow primary weapon switch speeds.

SHOTGUN TRAITS

The Tac 12 and FP6 are pump action; the MTS-255 and Bulldog are semi-automatic.

The pump-action shotguns reload one shell at a time, while the semi-automatics have full chamber reloads. Note that the reload times on the chart for the Tac 12 and FP6 are per shell.

The under-barrel shotgun fires six pellets instead of eight like the primary shotguns.

Shotguns can be equipped with slug rounds, giving them a single high-damage bullet capable of killing in one shot. However, in exchange, they demand highly accurate ADS fire to land a kill shot.

Shotgun Tweaks

Shotguns have been tuned in *Call of Duty: Ghosts* to have more consistent spread patterns. They still have random pellet spreads, and at the edges of their damage ranges, you can expect to use more than one shot to kill. However, if you are cleanly on target at short distances, you should find that you get more consistent kills and less frustrating hitmarkers.

Shotgun Recoil Plots

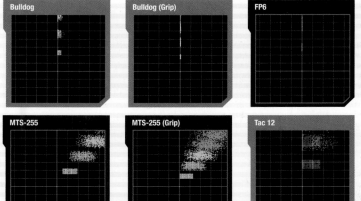
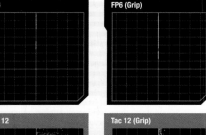
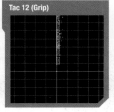

Bulldog | Bulldog (Grip) | FP6 | FP6 (Grip)

MTS-255 | MTS-255 (Grip) | Tac 12 | Tac 12 (Grip) | UB Shotgun

Shotgun Damage: Pellets to Kill over Distance

This chart illustrates the number of on-target pellets needed to kill a target from a given distance. This is distinct from other weapons, which list the number of shots needed to kill. Shotguns can and do frequently kill in one shot. For ranges that indicate 8+ or 6+, you need more than the maximum number of pellets you can fire in a single shot. This means that you need at least two shots to kill at that distance and possibly more, depending on how many pellets actually hit their mark.

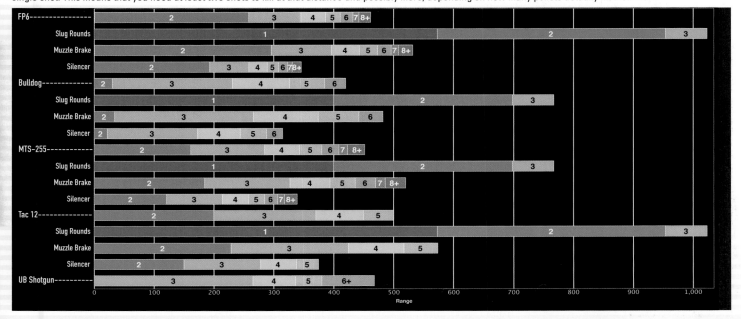

SPECIALIZED TRAINING   THE CAMPAIGN   MP INTRO & BASIC TRAINING   SQUADS   **MP ARMORY**   PERKS   KILLSTREAKS   MP MAPS   MP GAME MODES   SAFEGUARD   EXTINCTION   CLASSIFIED   ACHIEVEMENTS & TROPHIES

137

Shotgun Rate of Fire: Rounds per Minute

Shotgun Reload: Time in Seconds

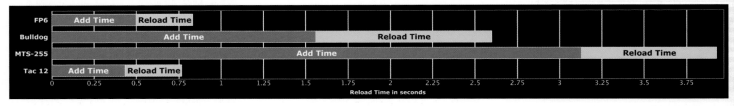

Shotgun Ammo Capacity

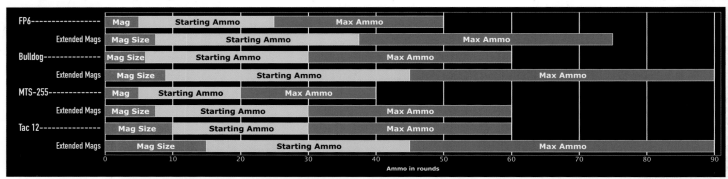

Shotgun Weapon Data

SHOTGUN	ADS TIME	DROP TIME	RAISE TIME	HEAD	PENETRATION
FP6	0.2	0.83	1	1	Low
Bulldog	0.2	0.75	1	1	Low
MTS-255	0.2	1	1.1	1	Low
Tac 12	0.2	0.75	1	1	Low

Shotgun Attachments

SHOTGUN ATTACHMENTS							
Weapon Name	Foregrip	Silencer	Muzzle Brake	Red Dot Sight	Holographic Sight	Slug Rounds	Extended Mags
FPG	✔	✔	✔	✔	✔	✔	
Bulldog	✔	✔	✔	✔	✔	✔	✔
MTS-255	✔	✔	✔	✔	✔	✔	
Tac 12	✔	✔	✔	✔	✔	✔	✔

Front Line Defense

The Riot Shield is a bulletproof shield that can be used to protect you and your teammates from enemy fire. Note that it can only shield you from the front, and while moving, your feet are exposed unless you crouch.

The Riot Shield is extremely useful in some objective modes, but considerably less so in deathmatch modes focused on kill scores. Don't expect to rack up a great k/d in a round, but you can seriously help your team with proper Riot Shield usage.

If you take a pistol secondary (especially with the Reflex perk), you can easily kill opponents armed with automatic weapons when they open fire, then stop and back off or reload. Wait for the hail of bullets to end and watch for the reload, then switch and pick them off.

At very close range, you can still turn and block incoming fire, but because of the realities of internet latency, expect enemies to be able to sneak around your flank and either shoot you or knife you.

The Riot Shield works best at medium distances where you can crouch and face your target squarely; it is extremely difficult to kill a Riot Shield user under these circumstances.

Riot Shield Attachments

| Scrambler | Titanium Frame | Radar |

Pair the Riot Shield with extra Tactical and Smoke grenades or the Trophy System, and you can capture and hold objectives all on your own. With team backup, you can lead the charge into a defended area and break their defenses.

In CQB, you can melee an enemy twice to kill them, but at these ranges, don't be surprised if you get stabbed or shot in retaliation! Still, there's nothing quite as humiliating as a good Riot Shield bash kill.

The Riot Shield works very well when your teammates guard your back while you take point. When adversaries spot you and open fire on your impregnable front, this gives away their location and lets your teammates pick them off with ease.

The Riot Shield is a great tool for a teamwork-oriented player. It's not the right choice if you want to be running and gunning or sniping at long ranges!

Rear Guard

When you switch to a secondary weapon, the Riot Shield goes on your back, and it can block some shots (or even explosions, if you happen to be prone and something goes off above you). However, don't rely on this to save your life.

It's a nice perk if it sponges a bullet or two, but don't expect immunity to gunfire from the rear!

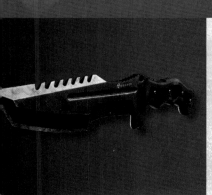

Blade Running

The combat knife can only be "chosen" by removing your primary weapon entirely.

The combat knife is simply a main hand knife that functions almost identically to your normal knife stab, except that you can press your Trigger button to stab in addition to your dedicated Melee button.

While in theory being stripped of your primary weapon is only useful for the perk point it provides, there is one somewhat hidden bonus to the combat knife: while using it, you can sprint double your normal running distance!

This isn't quite a free Marathon perk, but it comes close in a lot of situations (particularly those involving chasing down an enemy from behind while you have Dead Silence).

SPECIALIZED TRAINING   THE CAMPAIGN   MP INTRO & BASIC TRAINING   SQUADS   MP ARMORY   PERKS   KILLSTREAKS   MP MAPS   MP GAME MODES   SAFEGUARD   EXTINCTION   CLASSIFIED   ACHIEVEMENTS & TROPHIES

139

SECONDARY WEAPONS

HANDGUNS

PROS	
High damage at short range	
Excellent handling and mobility	
CONS	
Low damage at range	

COMBAT ROLE	Secondary backup weapon
PREFERRED RANGE	Short

Reliable Backup

Pistols are very effective secondary weapons with two-shot kill capability at close range for certain types in the class and extremely fast switch speeds.

Pistols have fairly low ammo capacities, and they aren't impressive at long range. However, when used properly, they are very good at supporting your primary weapon.

While you can choose to give up your pistol for a perk point, doing so is a real sacrifice, not a free point gain. It's usually not a good idea at all for sniper rifles or marksman rifles, which need an effective close-range backup weapon.

The Akimbo attachment allows you to dual-wield pistols, trading off any ADS accuracy for the ability to unload a lethal hail of bullets at close range. This is taxing on your ammo supply, but it can increase your close-range power.

Quick Swap and Fire

Learning to switch to your pistol and finish off a damaged enemy is an important skill to master to improve your game. This is particularly important for assault rifles and SMGs, which often get into short-range engagements with multiple enemies.

Rather than reloading when you run dry after your first or second enemy, quickly switch to your pistol and open fire.

Done well, you can all but guarantee a kill against an opponent who has already taken a hit or two, or if you get the drop on an enemy teammate when they come around the corner to investigate the gunfire. With most pistols, two quick shots center mass is enough to put them down.

PISTOL TRAITS

The Magnum can score one-shot kills at close range if you hit the target in the upper torso or head. The PDW is a machine pistol, firing three-round bursts. It has intense vertical recoil and needs all three shots to kill even at short range. Be sure to compensate for the kick to score single trigger pull kills.

The P226 has the best two-shot kill range of the semi-automatic pistols, the MP-443 has the worst, and the M9A1 lies in the middle. All three have distinct handling characteristics and damage profiles past short range. Experiment with each to find your preferred sidearm.

Pistol Recoil Plots

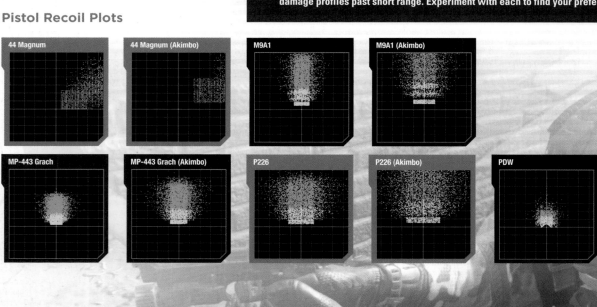

44 Magnum | 44 Magnum (Akimbo) | M9A1 | M9A1 (Akimbo)

MP-443 Grach | MP-443 Grach (Akimbo) | P226 | P226 (Akimbo) | PDW

Pistol Damage: Shots to Kill Over Distance

This chart illustrates the number of on-target shots needed to kill a target from a given distance.

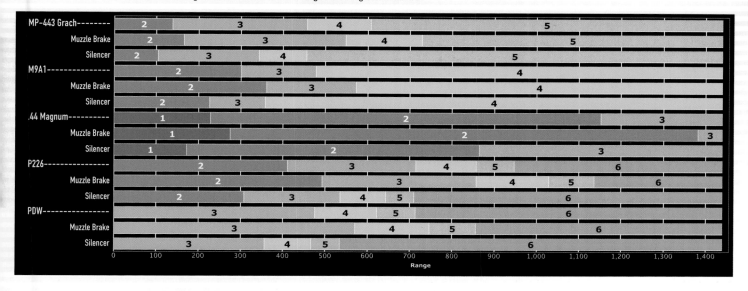

Pistol Rate of Fire: Rounds Per Minute

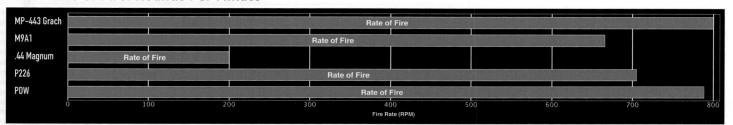

Pistol Reload: Time in Seconds

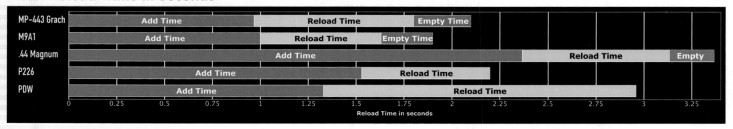

Pistol Ammo Capacity

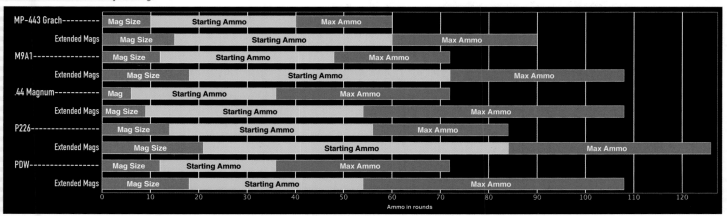

SPECIALIZED TRAINING   THE CAMPAIGN   MP INTRO & BASIC TRAINING   SQUADS   MP ARMORY   PERKS   KILLSTREAKS   MP MAPS   MP GAME MODES   SAFEGUARD   EXTINCTION   CLASSIFIED   ACHIEVEMENTS & TROPHIES

141

Pistol Weapon Data

PISTOL	ADS TIME	DROP TIME	RAISE TIME	HEAD	NECK	UPPER TORSO	PENETRATION
MP-443 Grach	0.2	0.433	0.567	1.4	1	1	Low
M9A1	0.2	0.433	0.7	1.4	1	1	Low
.44 Magnum	0.3	0.2	0.5	1.6	1.6	1.4	Low
P226	0.2	0.533	0.566	1.4	1	1	Low
PDW	0.2	0.4	0.56	1.5	1	1	Low

Pistol Attachments

Weapon Name	Flash Suppressor	Silencer	Muzzle Brake	Extended Mags	Armor-Piercing	Tactical Knife	Akimbo	Red Dot Sight	ACOG Scope	Holographic Sight
MP-443 Grach	✔	✔	✔	✔	✔	✔	✔			
M9A1	✔	✔	✔	✔	✔	✔	✔			
.44 Magnum	✔	✔	✔		✔	✔	✔		✔	
P226	✔	✔	✔	✔	✔	✔	✔			
PDW	✔	✔	✔	✔	✔	✔		✔	✔	✔

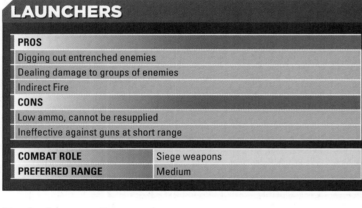

LAUNCHERS

PROS	
Digging out entrenched enemies	
Dealing damage to groups of enemies	
Indirect Fire	
CONS	
Low ammo, cannot be resupplied	
Ineffective against guns at short range	
COMBAT ROLE	Siege weapons
PREFERRED RANGE	Medium

Explosives on Demand

MK32: Lethal to 56, Hitmarker to 180   Kastet: Lethal to 35, Hitmarker to 300   Panzerfaust: Lethal to 104, Hitmarker to 256

Launchers are specialist explosive weapons useful for clearing out enclosed spaces of multiple enemies, bombarding objective locations, or clearing out enemies who are out of reach of a gun.

Launchers have sharply limited ammunition and cannot be resupplied, so be aware that you are giving up the utility of your pistol if you take one.

You need to be getting a few kills with them every time to justify taking one. Ideally, these need to be critical kills removing enemies from objectives or taking out adversaries entrenched in defensive terrain.

All launchers benefit from the Danger Close perk, greatly increasing their lethality and nullifying enemy Blast Shield users.

Of the three launchers, the MK32 has the lowest radius, but it fires two explosives at once. The Kastet shares its attributes with the under-barrel grenade launcher: large radius, low lethality. Finally, the Panzerfaust has the best lethal range but is the most unwieldy of the three launchers.

Each of the launchers is unique and serves a different role on the battlefield.

The MK32 fires two mini-Semtex grenades in quick succession. Be aware that the second shot has extreme vertical kick, so you must aim down quickly to compensate if you want both explosives in the same area. Unlike the other launchers, the MK32 gets three shots total (six mini-Semtex altogether).

This gives the MK32 double the boom with each shot, making it a particularly nice weapon for clearing out a room. Be aware that the delay before the Semtex detonates makes this a poor choice for direct engagement of foes aware of your position. It's better to use this launcher for assaulting an objective area or known enemy position when they are unaware of your presence.

The Kastet is a standard grenade launcher, largely identical to the under-barrel grenade launchers for ARs and LMGs.

The Kastet is a much better launcher for directly engaging targets than the MK32, and with practice, you can lob grenades with great accuracy across the battlefield and even into windows or up onto raised ledges.

Be aware that the Kastet has a minimum arming distance—if you don't give the projectile time to arm, it simply bounces harmlessly. The exception is if you manage to directly impact another target with it, in which case, it kills them instantly.

Finally, the Panzerfaust is a dumb-fire rocket. With two shots and a straight trajectory, the Panzerfaust is generally easier to use than the Kastet (though it lacks the ability for indirect fire over obstacles between you and your target).

The Panzerfaust is a good brute force tool for quickly clearing out enemies around an objective in the open, or blasting the floor just inside a doorway to clear a room. Just be careful not to fire it too close to yourself…

Launcher Weapon Data

LAUNCHER	ADS TIME	DROP TIME	RAISE TIME
MK32	0.3	1	1.33
Panzerfaust	0.5	1.36	1.433
Kastet	0.4	0.6	1.133

ATTACHMENTS

Attachments are modifications for your primary and secondary weapons, as well as the Riot Shield (though not launchers).

Each weapon can have up to two different attachments, and the Extra Attachment perk lets you take a third.

Attachments let you customize a weapon to your personal liking, selecting from a variety of sights, barrels, modifications, and under-barrel attachments.

A carefully customized weapon should suit your personal preferences above all else. There are no right or wrong ways to modify a weapon, only the way that feels best to you.

That being said, this guide provides advice about all of the attachments so you can make an informed decision on how to pair a customized weapon with a specific perk setup to suit different combat roles on the battlefield.

New Attachment Rules

Attachment options for weaponry has been simplified, as all attachments now belong to one of four categories: Sights, Barrel, Under Barrel, and Mod. You can pick a single attachment from any category…simple!

You normally get two attachments of your choice for your primary and secondary weapon, though some perks can affect this (notably Extra Attachment and Overkill).

Integrated Attachments

Some weapons have an integrated attachment that cannot be changed, but this also frees up an attachment slot for other options.

For example, the Honey Badger AR, the K7 SMG, and the VKS Sniper have integrated silencers.

This means you cannot select a different barrel attachment, but you can select any two of sights, under-barrel, or mod attachments and get a weapon with three attachments for "free" without using the Extra Attachment perk. (*With* that perk, you can get a weapon with an attachment from every single category.)

SPECIALIZED TRAINING   THE CAMPAIGN   MP INTRO & BASIC TRAINING   SQUADS   **MP ARMORY**   PERKS   KILLSTREAKS   MP MAPS   MP GAME MODES   SAFEGUARD   EXTINCTION   CLASSIFIED   ACHIEVEMENTS & TROPHIES

143

ALL ATTACHMENTS BY WEAPON

ASSAULT RIFLE ATTACHMENTS

Weapon Name	Extended Mags	Armor Piercing	Semi-Auto	Burst Fire	Foregrip	Shotgun	Grenade Launcher	Red Dot Sight	ACOG Scope	Holographic Sight	VMR Sight	Thermal Hybrid Scope	Tracker Sight	Flash Supressor	Silencer	Muzzle Brake
AK-12	✔	✔	✔	✔	✔	✔	✔	✔	✔	✔	✔	✔	✔	✔	✔	✔
ARX-160	✔	✔	✔	✔	✔	✔	✔	✔	✔	✔	✔	✔	✔	✔	✔	✔
SA-805	✔	✔	✔	✔	✔	✔	✔	✔	✔	✔	✔	✔	✔	✔	✔	✔
FAD	✔	✔	✔	✔	✔	✔	✔	✔	✔	✔	✔	✔	✔	✔	✔	✔
Honey Badger	✔	✔	✔	✔	✔	✔	✔	✔	✔	✔	✔	✔	✔			
MSBS	✔	✔	✔	Auto Fire	✔	✔	✔	✔	✔	✔	✔	✔	✔	✔	✔	✔
Remington R5	✔	✔	✔	✔	✔	✔	✔	✔	✔	✔	✔	✔	✔	✔	✔	✔
SC-2010	✔	✔	✔	✔	✔	✔	✔	✔	✔	✔	✔	✔	✔	✔	✔	✔

SUBMACHINE GUN ATTACHMENTS

Weapon Name	Extended Mags	Armor Piercing	Rapid Fire	Foregrip	Red Dot Sight	ACOG Scope	Holographic Sight	VMR Sight	Thermal Hybrid Scope	Tracker Sight	Flash Supressor	Silencer	Muzzle Brake
CBJ-MS	✔		✔	✔	✔	✔	✔	✔	✔	✔	✔	✔	✔
K7	✔	✔	✔	✔	✔	✔	✔	✔	✔				
Vector CRB	✔	✔	✔	✔	✔	✔	✔	✔	✔	✔	✔	✔	✔
MTAR-X	✔	✔	✔	✔	✔	✔	✔	✔	✔	✔	✔	✔	✔
Bizon	✔	✔	✔	✔	✔	✔	✔	✔	✔	✔	✔	✔	✔
Vepr	✔	✔	✔	✔	✔	✔	✔	✔	✔	✔	✔	✔	✔

LIGHT MACHINE GUN ATTACHMENTS

Weapon Name	Extended Mags	Armor Piercing	Rapid Fire	Flash Supressor	Silencer	Muzzle Brake	Red Dot Sight	ACOG Scope	Holographic Sight	VMR Sight	Thermal Hybrid Scope	Tracker Sight	Foregrip	Shotgun	Grenade Launcher
Ameli	✔	✔	✔	✔	✔	✔	✔	✔	✔	✔	✔	✔	✔	✔	✔
M27-IAR	✔	✔	✔	✔	✔	✔	✔	✔	✔	✔	✔	✔	✔	✔	✔
LSAT	✔	✔	✔	✔	✔	✔	✔	✔	✔	✔	✔	✔	✔	✔	✔
Chain SAW	✔	✔	✔		✔										✔

MARKSMAN RIFLE ATTACHMENTS

Weapon Name	Extended Mags	Armor Piercing	Burst Fire	Flash Supressor	Silencer	Muzzle Brake	Iron Sight	Red Dot Sight	ACOG Scope	Holographic Sight	Thermal Hybrid Scope	Tracker Sight
MR-28	✔	✔	✔	✔	✔	✔	✔	✔	✔	✔	✔	✔
IA-2	✔	✔	✔	✔	✔	✔	✔	✔	✔	✔	✔	✔
MK14 EBR	✔	✔	✔	✔	✔	✔	✔	✔	✔	✔	✔	✔
SVU	✔	✔	✔	✔	✔	✔	✔	✔	✔	✔	✔	

SNIPER RIFLE ATTACHMENTS

Weapon Name	Extended Mags	Armor Piercing	ACOG Scope	Thermal Scope	Variable Zoom Lens	Silencer	Chrome Lined Barrel
VKS	✔	✔	✔	✔	✔		
USR	✔	✔	✔	✔	✔	✔	✔
L115	✔	✔	✔	✔	✔	✔	✔
Lynx	✔	✔	✔	✔	✔	✔	✔

RIOT SHIELD ATTACHMENTS

Weapon Name	Scrambler	Titanium Frame	Radar
Riot Shield	✔	✔	✔

SHOTGUN ATTACHMENTS

Weapon Name	Foregrip	Silencer	Muzzle Brake	Red Dot Sight	Holographic Sight	Slug Rounds	Extended Mags
FP6	✔	✔	✔	✔	✔	✔	
Bulldog	✔	✔	✔	✔	✔		✔
MTS-255	✔	✔	✔	✔	✔	✔	
Tac 12	✔	✔	✔	✔	✔	✔	✔

PISTOL ATTACHMENTS

Weapon Name	Flash Supressor	Silencer	Muzzle Brake	Extended Mags	Armor-Piercing	Tactical Knife	Akimbo	Red Dot Sight	ACOG Scope	Holographic Sight
MP-443 Grach	✔	✔	✔	✔	✔	✔	✔	✔	✔	✔
M9A1	✔	✔	✔	✔	✔	✔	✔	✔	✔	✔
.44 Magnum	✔	✔	✔	✔	✔	✔	✔	✔	✔	✔
P226	✔	✔	✔	✔	✔	✔	✔	✔	✔	✔
PDW	✔	✔	✔	✔	✔	✔	✔	✔	✔	✔

SIGHTS

Sights allow you to customize your weapon with an optical enhancement.

These can grant you zoom capability, sophisticated target imaging, or simply a clear view with a clean reticle on a target.

If you are comfortable using iron sights, you can save an attachment slot by skipping out on a basic sight, but some of the advanced sights have tactical applications on their own merits. There are certain cases where you may want to take one even if you don't mind irons.

Sniper rifles and DMRs both have integrated scopes rather than iron sights.

Sights Details

A quick but important note about sights.

The same sight on two different weapons can have slightly different attributes.

Generally, these are very minor tweaks to accommodate the purpose of the weapon in question. (A good example of this is the ACOG scope: when attached to a pistol, it has less zoom than when it is on any other weapon.)

BASE ADS TIMES

Several scopes modify the ADS time of a weapon; here are the base values for comparison:

Pistols: 0.2	SMGs: 0.2	LMGs: 0.35
Pistols (Magnum): 0.3	SMGs (Vepr): 0.25	Sniper Rifle (USR and L115 bolt-action): 0.4
Shotguns: 0.2	DMRs and ARs: 0.3 (0.38 for DMR integrated scopes)	Sniper Rifle (VKS and Lynx semi-automatic): 0.45

BASE ZOOM FACTOR

Scopes affect the distance you can zoom by essentially narrowing your field of view, pulling distant targets into focus.

Your baseline field of view is 65, meaning that any scope with a lower number is pulling your view in, giving you increased zoom.

Iron sights on different weapons have slightly different zoom factors. Note that pistols and the Tracker Sight don't zoom your view at all; they simply bring up your sights for accurate ADS fire. ARs and DMRs get slightly increased base zoom over other weapons with iron sights.

Pistols: 65	SMGs: 55	LMGs: 55	Sniper Rifles: 15
Shotguns: 55	ARs: 50	DMRs: 22	

Red Dot Sight (RDS)

Zoom Factor: 50   ADS Times: Default, 0.38 for LMGs

▶ BASIC TARGETING OPTIC, SIMPLE AND CLEAN VIEW

The most basic of all sights, the RDS gives a clear targeting reticle, with a minimally obscuring housing.

The Red Dot sight is a great choice if you're new to the game, as it's easily the most comfortable of all the sights in the game to use. On the other hand, the RDS does nothing special in terms of zoom or target acquisition, so as you grow more comfortable and gain experience, you may want to look to other options for your attachment slot.

Holographic Sight (Holo)

Zoom Factor: 45   ADS Times: Default, 0.38 for LMGs

▶ BASIC TARGETING OPTIC WITH A DAMAGE FALL-OFF DISPLAY

The Holographic is an alternative to the Red Dot sight. In exchange for a slightly more obscuring frame, the Holographic sight has a very slightly higher zoom than the RDS, and it has an integrated rangefinder on the scope.

The rangefinder shows you what percentage of damage you are dealing with your weapon. This gives you a quick eyeball check of how many extra shots you may need to take down a target at a distance. (This rangefinder actually works with the charts provided in the weapon section if you feel like fooling around with distances and shots to kill in a private match!)

Because of the slightly enhanced zoom, the Holographic is a good choice over the RDS if you are using a semi-automatic or burst-fire weapon that is stable enough to use accurately at slightly longer ranges than a fully auto weapon.

ACOG Scope

Zoom Factor: 30, 40 on the Magnum pistol   ADS Time: 0.38, 0.25 for Magnum pistol and SMGS, 0.4 for all snipers

▶ BASIC LONG-RANGE OPTIC, MODERATE ZOOM

The Advanced Combat Optical Gunsight is the most basic of the high-magnification optics. It provides a greater zoom factor than the Red Dot sight or Holographic sight, but it works well for mid- to mid-long-range engagements. The ACOG is poorly suited for close-range engagements, and it's not great at close-mid, either, so be mindful of your engagement distances when using an ACOG.

The ACOG pairs well with marksman rifles, but assault rifles customized with a Burst or Semi-Auto mod also work well. Sniper rifles with an ACOG are a different story—you trade off long-range zoom for faster target acquisition at medium distances and retain the high lethality. Just be aware that snipers have a significant amount of sway with an ACOG in comparison to a perfectly steadied normal sniper scope.

VMR Sight

| Zoom Factor: 25 (zoom active), 50 (reflex active) | ADS Times: 0.38 (zoom active), 0.35 (reflex active). 0.25 for both on SMGs. |

▸ VARIABLE MAGNIFICATION REFLEX SIGHT. SWITCH BETWEEN REFLEX AND ZOOM SIGHTS.

The VMR combines the functionality of a Red Dot sight and a ACOG scope into a single hybrid sight. By pressing your Melee button while in ADS, you can switch between the two optics.

With practice, the VMR is a "best of both worlds" option, but be aware that as fast as the switching is, getting into a fight with the wrong scope up can be fatal.

When you are using an RDS/Holo or ACOG, you know exactly from which distances you want to be engaging enemies. Conversely, the VMR demands that you constantly switch scopes to suit the combat environment.

The zoom on the VMR is also slightly more intense than the ACOG, which makes it even less suited for short-range engagements.

Try to plan ahead and switch to the scope you expect to need momentarily just after you down a target, rather than after you raise your gun on a new target.

If you can master the switching, the VMR can be a remarkably useful sight, but it does require some extra effort from the operator to reach peak effectiveness.

Tracker Sight

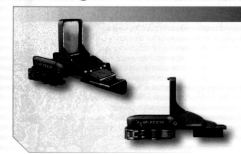

| Zoom Factor: 65 (tracker active), 55 (irons active) | ADS Times: 0.4 (tracker active), 0.38 (irons active). 0.25 for both on SMGs |

▸ ADVANCED TARGETING SIGHT. HIGHLIGHTS ENEMY OUTLINES.

The Tracker sight is a sophisticated targeting optic that outlines hostile players in your line of sight while you are ADS. This can make spotting them in rough cover or obscuring foliage easier, but the Tracker sight also blurs your peripheral vision, dampening your situational awareness.

Incog players are shielded from the highlighting effect of the Tracker sight—you can still see them, but the highlight does not appear. The Tracker sight also has a poor zoom factor, so it is not an ideal weapon for engaging targets at long range, but it is useful at close-medium distances for quickly identifying targets.

The restricted view of your surroundings while you focus on the Tracker sight display makes it risky to hold ADS for extended periods of time. Bring it up occasionally to sweep a likely area for hostile targets, and then move on. You also pay an ADS speed penalty for the aid from this optic, making the Tracker a poor option if engaging in frequent head-to-head quick draw contests is your intent!

The Tracker sight is a hybrid sight that can be disabled, switching to an integrated set of irons. When you don't need the Tracker assistance, or when you want a clear view of your surroundings and a slightly better zoom for longer range targets, flip the Tracker sight off. While the Quickdraw perk is important for all gunfights involving quick ADS combat, it is particularly important with the Tracker sight. The Tracker sight is an optic most useful at close range, and in CQB, fractions of a second count.

With their faster ADS times using this sight, SMGs can get away without it more safely, but be aware that you're still slower than another SMG user or any shotgun user firing from the hip.

Thermal Hybrid Scope

| Zoom Factor: 20 (thermal active), 50 (irons active) | ADS Time: 0.38. 0.25 for SMGs |

▸ ADVANCED OPTIC DETECTS ENEMY HEAT SIGNATURES.
SWITCH BETWEEN THERMAL AND ALTERNATE REFLEX SIGHT.

The Thermal Hybrid gives you a heat-sensing zooming scope that makes target acquisition in poor lighting conditions or through obscuring cover much easier, as it outlines all hostiles in bright white.

Be aware that the Thermal scope has a high zoom factor and fills your view with a color-shifted image of the world, which can dull your situational awareness.

Also watch out for Incog players—they are protected from Thermal highlighting. You can still spot them, but it takes a bit more effort, especially if they are motionless and in cover.

The Thermal is a strong alternative to the VMR, and it can give you an edge in long-range engagements on certain maps. Experiment with it and see if you like the visibility with the Thermal scope. You may find you prefer one or the other depending on the map in question.

SPECIALIZED TRAINING   THE CAMPAIGN   MP INTRO & BASIC TRAINING   SQUADS   **MP ARMORY**   PERKS   KILLSTREAKS   MP MAPS   MP GAME MODES   SAFEGUARD   EXTINCTION   CLASSIFIED   ACHIEVEMENTS & TROPHIES

147

Thermal Sniper Scope

Zoom Factor: 30	ADS Time: 0.4

▶ ELIMINATES MUZZLE FLASH. NO IMPACT ON PERFORMANCE.

Taking this over the other barrel options is a questionable choice, given their performance improvements, but it is worth experimenting with in at least a few games. You may be surprised at how the removal of muzzle flash improves your aim.

Variable Zoom Sniper Scope

Zoom Factor: 65, 30, 15	ADS Time: Default

The Variable Zoom Sniper scope is a flexible upgrade that gives you access to additional lower magnification settings for your sniper scope. Toggle through the three settings by tapping your Melee button while you're zoomed in—you can adjust your field of view to perfectly suit the distance from which you are engaging targets.

The VZS is essentially a straight upgrade in functionality over the regular sniper scope, but you pay for it with the cost of the attachment to modify the default scope.

Iron Sight

Zoom Factor: 50	ADS Time: 0.3

▶ OPTIONAL ATTACHMENT FOR MARKSMAN-CLASS RIFLES, REMOVES INTEGRATED SCOPE.

A special attachment for marksman rifles, Iron Sights allows you to disable the integrated scope and revert to basic iron sights. If you're switching off the integrated scope because you want a less obscuring optic, you may want to consider one of the other sights instead. However, if you simply prefer a clear view of the world while ADS, there's nothing wrong with taking Iron Sights!

Do keep in mind that the integrated scope on marksman rifles provides some additional stability for long-range shots, suppressing recoil slightly, so you are making a long-range accuracy sacrifice by giving it up.

BARREL

Flash Suppressor

▶ ELIMINATES MUZZLE FLASH. NO IMPACT ON PERFORMANCE.

A simple attachment, the Flash Suppressor eliminates muzzle flash entirely. This has no impact on weapon performance, but it can increase your visibility on target for weapons with intense muzzle flash, a high rate of fire, or both.

Taking this over the other barrel options is a questionable choice, given their performance improvements, but it is worth experimenting with in at least a few games. You may be surprised at how the removal of muzzle flash improves your aim.

Accuracy Benefits

Because there are no direct mechanical advantages to the Flash Suppressor, the only way to truly evaluate how well the Flash Suppressor works for you is to test it in-game a lot, and then examine your statistics. If you find that your accuracy is actually higher with it equipped over many shots, you can make a more informed decision between this attachment and the Muzzle Brake. Because accuracy is an entirely personal statistic and the impact of the Flash Suppressor is a subtle one, there is no hard and fast rule for when it is worth taking over other barrel mods. Test it extensively, and decide for yourself!

You can also compare your relative k/d values between the barrel attachments, but be careful with this evaluation. Many other factors play into k/d, from your team to the modes you play, and unless you are very rigorous about testing the difference under controlled circumstances, it's easy to draw incorrect conclusions from the data. Or you can just use it because you like the way it makes your weapon look when you fire it. No judgment.

Silencer

▶ ELIMINATES MINIMAP RED DOT WHEN FIRING, SUPPRESSES GUNFIRE NOISE, REDUCES EFFECTIVE DAMAGE RANGE.

The Silencer is a powerful stealth attachment that eliminates your red dot on the minimap when you fire your weapon. This trait alone makes the Silencer vital for stealth builds and a useful attachment overall, but it also has the effect of reducing your gunfire noise significantly. The tradeoff for these advantages is a loss of effective damage range. You lose about 20% of your effective damage range with a Silencer attached. In general, this tradeoff is worth it for builds focused on stealthy combat, particularly builds that expect to be used in CQB situations where you don't need long range on your weapon.

If you're planning on playing in a more standoff, long-range role, a Silencer is less appealing. The loss of damage at a distance is more of a concern than appearing on the map where most enemies can't reach you easily in the first place!

Silenced Long-Range Death

Sniper rifles do not suffer damage falloff with a Silencer attached, so deciding between the Silencer or the Chrome Lined Barrel attachment is a meaningful choice.

Muzzle Brake

▶ INCREASES EFFECTIVE DAMAGE RANGE.

The Muzzle Brake improves your damage range by 20%, giving any weapon a bit of extra punch at a distance. This is useful on almost any weapon you intend to use at medium range or longer with any regularity. It is even helpful on short-range weapons to keep their highest lethality out to the maximum possible distance.

This is a simple and effective attachment. It should usually be your default barrel attachment unless you need a Silencer or feel that the Flash Suppressor actually improves your personal accuracy to such a significant degree that you can give up the added range safely.

Chrome Lined Barrel

▶ SNIPER RIFLE EXCLUSIVE BARREL ATTACHMENT, IMPROVES KILL SHOT DAMAGE PROFILE AT THE COST OF MASSIVELY INCREASED RECOIL.

The Chrome Lined Barrel attachment improves the damage profile of any sniper rifle, extending the kill shot hit zone out to upper arms and upper legs. This means that a shot almost anywhere near center mass becomes a guaranteed one-shot kill. Given the importance of landing a single-hit kill shot with sniper rifles to begin with, this attachment is useful for improving consistency at long range.

The Chrome Lined Barrel effect is particularly noticeable at very long ranges where even a sniper scope has difficulty picking out your target. At those distances, especially against a moving target, it is easy to score a hit that looked like a kill shot but resulted in a hitmarker instead. This attachment can reduce those occurrences, improving your overall lethality.

The VKS cannot take the Chrome Lined Barrel, as it has an integrated silencer. Note that the L115 and Lynx already kill with shots to the upper leg, so only the USR benefits from the upper leg addition. However, all three gain the upper arm kill shot.

SPECIALIZED TRAINING THE CAMPAIGN MP INTRO & BASIC TRAINING SQUADS **MP ARMORY** PERKS KILLSTREAKS MP MAPS MP GAME MODES SAFEGUARD EXTINCTION CLASSIFIED ACHIEVEMENTS & TROPHIES

149

Grip

▶ REDUCES RECOIL.

The foregrip attachment reduces recoil when you fire your weapon on full auto or rapidly tap the trigger on semi-auto weapons that have high recoil. It can also very slightly improve the shot grouping for burst-fire weapons.

Grip tends to be more useful on weapons with heavy recoil, where even a slight improvement in controllability can increase the number of shots on target at range.

After you have spent some time in multiplayer with all of the weapons and settled down to a handful of favorites, experiment with Grip. While it is almost always effective for any gun you plan to use at medium range or longer, you need to weigh the slightly increased accuracy against the benefits other attachments can provide.

Shotgun

▶ UNDER-BARREL SHOTGUN. FIRES INSTANTLY WITH GRENADE BUTTON.
  REPLACES LETHAL SLOT, CONSUMES A PERK POINT.

A powerful close-range backup tool, the under-barrel shotgun fits your AR or LMG with a shotgun that can be fired with a single tap of your Grenade button. The price you pay for this easy access is the loss of your Lethal equipment slot and its attendant perk point. You cannot equip any Lethal equipment with this attachment. Because of the ready access to this weapon via a single button press, the under-barrel shotgun is considerably more effective than it has been in past *Call of Duty* titles. Rather than switching to your backup pistol in CQB situations, you can simply rely on your always-ready shotgun to deal with ambushes or surprise encounters.

This attachment is especially useful for semi-auto or burst-fire ARs and any LMGs if you aren't running Rapid Fire, but it is helpful on any AR or LMG in general. The under-barrel shotgun is not as powerful as any of the primary shotguns, but it does its work well enough at extreme close range if you are on target with your shots. Aim for one-shot kills but expect two to three shots. Oh, and be careful when using the under-barrel shotgun on a silenced weapon: it can give away your position!

Grenade Launcher

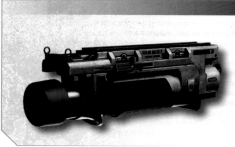

Radius: Lethal to 35, Hitmarker to 300

▶ UNDER-BARREL GRENADE LAUNCHER. FIRES INSTANTLY WITH GRENADE BUTTON.
  REPLACES LETHAL SLOT, CONSUMES A PERK POINT.

Improved in the same manner as the under-barrel shotgun with quick-fire capability, the under-barrel grenade launcher gives you instant access to a ranged explosive weapon. This can be useful for giving some added punch to a build built for sieging defended positions or objectives, but keep in mind that you're giving up your Lethal equipment slot

How you configure an explosives-heavy build comes down to whether you prefer the flexibility of the various Lethal options or the ease of access to another launcher-class explosive weapon on your Grenade button. In general, avoid taking this attachment in isolation.

It tends to be more effective if you commit fully to its use with some combination of Danger Close, Extra Tactical, and a secondary launcher-class weapon. But that being said, if you coordinate with your teammates well, you can almost always ensure easy kills at known enemy positions. Even the slightest graze from the grenade launcher explosion puts opponents into two-shot kill territory for most weapons. You're also completely avoiding the potential deaths that come from having your weapon down when you cook or throw a Lethal grenade.

One other warning: while this launcher has a good radius on the blast, it is only lethal on a near direct hit, and it drops to a lower minimum damage at the edges of its blast than the other explosives. Most other explosives leave their target half-dead with even a grazing strike; this leaves them at close to three-quarters full.

Tactical Knife

▶ OPTIONAL ATTACHMENT FOR PISTOLS. PROVIDES OFFHAND COMBAT KNIFE FOR RAPID LETHAL KNIFE STABS.

The tactical knife is a special pistol only attachment that gives you access to a combat knife held in your off hand while you still retain full use of your pistol. This specialized knife gives you faster knife stabs. Normally, you "stick" in your target for a moment while performing a knife animation kill, but with the tactical knife, kills are a quick instant kill stab.

This is a surprisingly powerful attachment if you are aggressive about using melee in CQB, and it is vital if you're running a dedicated knifing class. However, don't take the tactical knife if you're not planning on using it heavily. Indecision about whether to knife or shoot a target is a great way to get yourself killed. The tactical knife shares the benefits of stealthy kills with the regular knife, being quieter than even a silenced pistol.

Akimbo

▶ DUAL-WIELD PISTOLS. DOUBLE FIREPOWER AT THE COST OF ADS PRECISION AND LEAN.

Akimbo is an attachment that can only be used on some of the pistols, giving you dual-fisted combat action. This completely eliminates your ability to use ADS or lean around corners, so you can't expect to use your pistol for even close-medium combat.

In exchange, however, you gain greatly increased lethality at short range. In CQB encounters, Akimbo pistols stack up favorably against the under-barrel shotgun, and you can often come out on top against almost any primary weapon except a shotgun if the distance is short enough.

You need to be quick on the triggers if you use this attachment, and getting a lot of lead on your target with the twin pistols is important. Accuracy is not a defining trait of dual wielding. It is possible (though very unpredictable) to land a "one-shot kill" when you pull both triggers and the first two bullets hit your target. This can down an enemy in close range as quickly as a shotgun, Magnum, or lucky hipfired sniper. Ammo quickly becomes an issue when using Akimbo pistols due to their inaccuracy and rapid ammo expenditure, so bring Extended Mags, Scavenger, or Fully Loaded if you expect to rely on them often. Get in the habit of pulling out your twin pistols before you move into a CQB situation to have them at the ready.

MOD

Extended Mags

▶ 50% INCREASE IN AVAILABLE AMMO PER MAGAZINE.

A simple and effective attachment, Extended Mags is almost always a good choice on any weapon with a high fire rate, particularly SMGs and some ARs. On slower firing weapons and semi-automatic or burst-fire weapons, it is less critical, though the free extra ammunition can be a boon. For weapons without an actual magazine, Extended Mags still increases your available ammo supply (like LMGs or shotguns).

Full Auto

▶ CONVERTS THE MSBS TO FULLY AUTOMATIC.

A unique mod attachment specific to the MSBS, this converts the only natural burst-fire AR in the game to full auto.

This changes the damage profile of the weapon, as well as its fire rate. But just as with the other Select Fire attachments for the regular ARs, remember that you're paying an attachment slot for this privilege.

SPECIALIZED TRAINING   THE CAMPAIGN   MP INTRO & BASIC TRAINING   SQUADS   **MP ARMORY**   PERKS   KILLSTREAKS   MP MAPS   MP GAME MODES   SAFEGUARD   EXTINCTION   CLASSIFIED   ACHIEVEMENTS & TROPHIES

151

Armor-Piercing

▶ TRIPLES PENETRATION, BYPASSES BALLISTIC VESTS,
DEALS 50% INCREASED DAMAGE TO JUGGERNAUT ARMOR AND KILLSTREAKS.

Armor-piercing ammo significantly increases your baseline penetration, delivering more damage when you shoot through walls. This is especially valuable with deep magazines, as you can afford to burn the extra ammo to score a kill on a target hiding in cover or in a room. LMGs are practically purpose-built for this attachment: it lets them slice through concrete like butter. Their deep magazines and high damage at range make them effective at eliminating enemy equipment or armored killstreaks. If you plan on using armor-piercing ammo extensively, consider taking Fully Loaded or Scavenger to handle the increased ammo expenditure.

Armor-piercing deals 50% more damage against all types of Juggernaut armor, the IMS, Sentry Guns, helicopters of all types, and other hostile killstreaks. Note that armor-piercing ammo has no effect on Guard Dogs or the Support Squadmate. Keep a class with an LMG, the Blind Eye perk, and armor-piercing rounds—an instant remedy for an enemy Battle Hind, Helo Pilot, or Heli Sniper.

Semi-Automatic

▶ SWITCHES AN ASSAULT RIFLE FROM FULLY AUTOMATIC TO SINGLE SHOT.
REDUCES FIRE RATE. ADDS DAMAGE MULTIPLIERS TO TORSO AND NECK HITS.

While equipped with the Semi-Automatic mod, your weapon has a better damage profile at a distance and gains damage multipliers to the torso and neck. This shifts your assault rifle's ideal engagement range out to a greater distance, similar to a marksman rifle. Keep in mind that, compared to a marksman rifle, your AR lacks the integrated zooming scope, and you're paying an attachment for the semi-automatic fire mode. Additionally, you need to land body or headshots to benefit from the increased damage multipliers, so accurate fire is important. Consider pairing this attachment with a zooming scope if you intend to engage at long ranges.

Burst Fire

▶ SWITCHES AN ASSAULT RIFLE FROM FULLY AUTOMATIC TO THREE-ROUND BURSTS.
INCREASES FIRE RATE WITHIN BURST. ADDS DAMAGE MULTIPLIERS TO TORSO AND NECK HITS.

The Burst Fire mod changes your assault rifle from fully automatic to a three-round burst. This raises the fire rate (within the burst, not between trigger pulls) and adds body shot multipliers, similar to the way that the Semi-Automatic mod works.

Burst Fire can potentially kill a target in one "shot," but you have to be precisely on target and land center-mass hits. This is different from the natural burst rifle (the MSBS), which does not require landing perfect hits to deal its full damage.

Like Semi-Automatic, Burst Fire is useful to extend your AR's average range, so experiment with the two on your favorite assault rifles to see which you prefer. Of the two, Burst Fire is more effective at closer range, as it's more likely that you can land all three shots from the burst on target at medium distance than at very long range. Burst Fire is a bit harder to use on targets running perpendicular to your line of sight—they often sprint away from the follow-up shots, and landing clean body shots is tough with their arms in the way.

Titanium Frame

▶ FASTER MELEE ATTACKS WITH RIOT SHIELD.

The Titanium Frame upgrade for the Riot Shield lessens the burden of slinging around the heavy protective chunk of metal, allowing you to perform multiple shield bashes more quickly than normal.

It takes two melee strikes with a Riot Shield to down a target, and even with the titanium frame, you're not going to be performing any amazing multi-kills with a shield equipped (usually). However, this mod does give you the option of having slightly improved lethality at close range without the risk of switching to your pistol.

Rapid Fire

▶ INCREASES RATE OF FIRE AND RECOIL OF SMGS OR LMGS.

Rapid Fire raises your weapon's rate of fire, increasing its lethality significantly at the cost of a very noticeable recoil increase. Only SMGs and LMGs can take this attachment. In SMGs, it boosts short-range power but makes accurate fire at a distance extremely difficult. On LMGs, it can increase the slow-firing models to a moderate fire rate without an uncontrollable recoil penalty. Experiment with all the LMGs to get a feel for how the increased fire rate impacts their handling.

Generally, Rapid Fire is more effective at improving your gun's power at short range, trading off accuracy at a distance. Depending on the weapon, the Grip can reduce the recoil to manageable levels for longer-range fire if you're careful with the trigger.

Because of the increased fire rate, you'll burn a lot more ammunition—less of an issue with LMGs, but still a concern. Fully Loaded or Scavenger are advisable. One other note: Rapid Fire works quite well with the Deadeye perk. Because Deadeye has a percentage chance to raise your damage on every hit, more hits in less time gives you more damage potential.

Slug Rounds

▶ CHANGES SHOTGUN AMMUNITION TO SLUG ROUNDS. INCREASES PENETRATION TO MEDIUM. GRANTS A HEADSHOT MULTIPLIER.

Slug Rounds changes your shotgun's default buckshot into a single slug round. This provides a pinpoint-accurate "sniper" in the form of a shotgun. Note that you do *not* have sniper rifle range, but you can indeed score accurate one-shot kills at short distances.

Pump-action shotguns have slightly better range with slug rounds, while semi-automatics can more easily follow up a missed shot or a second killing shot at greater distance. Using Slug Rounds grants shotguns a headshot damage multiplier of 1.2, which can extend their effective one-shot kill range if you're highly accurate.

Slug rounds demand extreme accuracy, and unlike normal shotgun hipfire, hipfiring a slug round is usually only marginally more effective than hipfiring a sniper rifle. Quickdraw and possibly Stalker are advisable if you're serious about using slugs; you need fast ADS and quick movement to take down targets with slugs. Much like Select Fire for ARs, slug rounds aren't necessarily any better or worse than regular buckshot: they're simply a different way to use the weapon. Experiment and see!

Radar

▶ GRANTS THE RIOT SHIELD A PERSONAL RADAR WHILE IN HAND.

Radar should be your default attachment for the Riot Shield unless you have a strong reason for choosing other options. Radar periodically emits a ping on the minimap, equivalent in size to the Ping perk or Night Owl.

This is extremely useful in conjunction with your teammates. With one or two supporting gunners, you can push into an area with your Riot Shield up, detect nearby enemies, and move in on them with your teammates alerted to their presence. On this attachment's receiving end, be wary if you spot adversaries using a Riot Shield nearby. It's very possible they've alerted their teammates to your position.

Scrambler

▶ ATTACHES A RADAR SCRAMBLER TO THE RIOT SHIELD.

The Scrambler generates a short-range broadcast that scrambles nearby enemy minimaps, completely whiting them out if you get close enough. While this seems helpful, there are two problems: firstly, the range is extremely short; secondly, it alerts enemies to your proximity, instead of the other way around with Radar.

Unless you work with a teammate in a building or other enclosed area to draw enemies inside, stick to the Radar or Titanium Frame. It's possible to stand below or above a camping enemy on a different level and get close enough to shut down their minimap. However, this requires knowledge of an adversary's position and alerts them to your presence.

SPECIALIZED TRAINING   THE CAMPAIGN   MP INTRO & BASIC TRAINING   SQUADS   **MP ARMORY**   PERKS   KILLSTREAKS   MP MAPS   MP GAME MODES   SAFEGUARD   EXTINCTION   CLASSIFIED   ACHIEVEMENTS & TROPHIES

153

EQUIPMENT

Equipment options give you a variety of expendable explosives and tactical tools to aid you on the battlefield. You can expand your equipment options with perks in the Equipment category.

The SitRep perk can spot almost any type of equipment through walls. It can also be useful out in the open, as it highlights even small explosives like the Frag grenade or Semtex.

It is especially helpful on the placed equipment, like the IED, C4, Trophy System, and Motion Sensor. Not only does it warn you of their presence, but it can also give away the enemy who planted the equipment and is still lurking nearby.

All types of explosives in the Lethal and Tactical categories can be used to tag enemies with the Recon perk.

Strong-Arm Cookin'

The Frag grenade and 9-Bang grenades can both be cooked at double speed with the Strong-Arm perk. This is most useful on a build loaded with Equipment perks to emphasize your Lethal and Tactical armaments. Strong-Arm also adds roughly 50% to throwing ranges for all thrown Lethal and Tactical grenades and explosives.

LETHAL

Lethal equipment offers a variety of explosive tools to bombard the enemy or defend an area.

Excepting the throwing knife, all explosives are lethal when detonated in close proximity to an enemy. They inflict serious damage if an adversary is even scratched, typically knocking them down to a two-shot kill at most.

Blast Shield protects against explosives, while Danger Close increases their power and also nullifies the effect of enemy Blast Shields.

The various Equipment perks can improve your ability to take advantage of Lethal gear.

Frag Grenade

Radius: Lethal to 102, Hitmarker to 256	Throwing Distance (approximate): 1200

▶ BASIC COOKABLE GRENADE. FOUR-SECOND FUSE.

The simplest type of grenade is the classic Frag grenade. You can hold and cook this grenade by holding it before throwing for up to four seconds.

Mastering this fuse is vital for using the Frag grenade to its full effectiveness. Not only can enemies simply run away from an uncooked grenade, but they can also throw it back!

While rare, any opponent with the Strong-Arm perk who happens to be near a Frag grenade can also pick it up and throw it back safely regardless of the fuse time remaining. This is usually not something to worry about, but it can happen from time to time.

However, when a Frag grenade throw is cooked and you time it correctly, you can detonate the grenade in midair precisely near your intended target, causing an instantly lethal airburst explosion. This is especially useful for flushing enemies out of windows and enclosed rooms.

Near objectives, it's reasonably effective to briefly cook a Frag grenade and toss it into the objective area. You can score easy kills on heavily contested points and flush out adversaries nearby.

Strong-Arm is helpful with Frags, letting you cook them in half the time. Just be sure to practice with Strong-Arm if you're used to timing your throws at a certain distance without it!

Semtex

Radius: Lethal to 102, Hitmarker to 256	Throwing Distance (approximate): 1200

▶ STICKY EXPLOSIVE, FIXED TWO-SECOND FUSE.

Cousin to the Frag grenade, Semtex is a throwable explosive that sticks to any surface, including enemy players.

It is possible to airburst a Semtex, but as the "fuse" is fixed, doing so is tricky because your detonation range is inflexible.

You can throw Semtex to stick to a wall or ceiling near an opponent, particularly when you are on a lower level relative to your target.

Semtex is quicker than a Frag grenade in the sense that you don't need to cook it. You can always simply throw it and then keep moving, but the cost of that is the loss of a precision detonation.

Get used to the distance at which you can throw and cause Semtex to detonate; landing a Semtex near an enemy just as it is about to explode is quite effective.

Throwing Knife

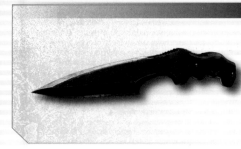

▶ LETHAL THROWING BLADE.

The throwing knife is a specialized piece of Lethal equipment. You can throw it for instant one-hit kills and even bounce it off of surfaces to score kills.

It takes a lot of practice to master the throwing knife, however—this is not the Lethal item to take if you're looking for ease of use!

It is possible to automatically retrieve your knife by simply stepping on top of it after it lands.

IED

| Radius: Lethal to 96, Hitmarker to 256 | Throwing Distance (approximate): 500 |

▶ STICKY PROXIMITY MINE.

The improvised explosive device is a proximity-triggered charge that can be thrown a short distance and sticks to any surface.

This makes the IED ideal for guarding your back, blocking a narrow passageway, or covering an objective. Careful placement can all but guarantee a kill against any enemy who stumbles across your trap.

Stick IEDs in out-of-the-way places—above doorways, on ceilings, on walls around corners, tucked behind cover near objectives, and so on.

It is possible to shoot and destroy an IED or detonate it with another explosion nearby.

C4

| Radius: Lethal to 171, Hitmarker to 256 | Throwing Distance (approximate): 500 |

▶ REMOTE DETONATED HIGH-POWER EXPLOSIVE.

C4 is an alternate remote explosive to the IED, but where that explosive has a proximity fuse, this one is manually detonated. C4 is most useful for covering part of an area you are already watching or an objective.

You need to have eyes on the target area, be watching for an objective HUD element to change colors, or have an announcer voice warning you of an enemy near an objective so that you can detonate it in time.

When you are covering an area defensively, placing a C4 on one path and covering the other with your gun lets you deal with two possible avenues of approach without the risk of being aimed in the wrong direction when an opponent appears. Simply detonate the C4 if they come down the wrong path.

Like an IED, you can stick a C4 to basically any surface (though not other soldiers, nice try), so try to place it out of view whenever possible, as enemy fire or explosions can destroy it.

Remember you can quickly detonate a C4 by double-tapping the Reload button. This also allows you to use the C4 as a sort of short-ranged grenade. If you toss a C4 pack and detonate it quickly enough, you can kill an enemy around a corner or over cover before they can react. This is typically faster than cooking a Frag or throwing a Semtex if you are close enough.

Canister Bomb

| Radius: Lethal to 171, Hitmarker to 256 | Throwing Distance (approximate): 500 |

▶ HIGH-POWERED SHORT-RANGE EXPLOSIVE.

The Canister Bomb is a specialized explosive, considerably more powerful than the Frag grenade and on the level of a C4 blast.

However, you pay for this increased lethality with a much shorter throwing distance and a fixed two-second fuse. This makes the Canister Bomb a specialized tool largely useful for clearing out a packed objective or very small room from short range.

Because you must expose yourself to more risk to get the Canister Bomb on target, it is a riskier piece of Lethal equipment to use than either Frags or Semtex.

Also, note that you can use a C4 pack for essentially the exact same task, as it has the same damage profile and blast radius.

SPECIALIZED TRAINING   THE CAMPAIGN   MP INTRO & BASIC TRAINING   SQUADS   **MP ARMORY**   PERKS   KILLSTREAKS   MP MAPS   MP GAME MODES   SAFEGUARD   EXTINCTION   CLASSIFIED   ACHIEVEMENTS & TROPHIES

155

Tactical equipment gives you support options for disabling your opponents or protecting yourself.

Unlike Lethal equipment, which is largely a class of explosive weaponry, the explosives in the Tactical category tend to be useful for disabling multiple enemies simultaneously so you can then take them out with gunfire.

The Smoke grenade, Trophy System, and Motion Sensor are all very useful in objective gameplay or for guarding your back.

The Tac Resist perk can protect you from the effects of 9-Bangs and Concussions, along with the Thermobaric's armor-stripping effect.

The Reflex perk is particularly useful with Tactical grenades, as it allows you to toss them in half the time. This lets you bring your gun up to take down any nearby disoriented targets from your toss.

9-Bang Grenade

Radius: 800 for blinding, 512 for EMP.	Throwing Distance (approximate): 1200

▶ MULTI-DETONATION FLASHBANG GRENADE WITH INTEGRATED EMP.

The 9-Bang is a specialized form of flash grenade that can explode up to five times with the blinding and disorienting effect of a Flashbang grenade each time. If the 9-Bang is fully cooked before being thrown, it also finishes its detonations with a final EMP blast that can disable enemy equipment and shut down hostile minimap usage for a short time. The 9-Bang takes 2.5 seconds to charge fully, and each .75 second increment adds another flash when you throw the grenade. You must charge it fully to get the EMP effect.

The 9-bang has a 1.5 second fuse, so you can airburst it over a target area. There is an 800-unit radius for the flash effect and a 512-unit radius for the EMP, both of which are large by regular explosive standards. Be sure to land it near an offending Sentry Gun or IMS to ensure the EMP hits.

The EMP lasts for eight seconds if it hits an adversary. However, the flash blind effect varies based on whether or not your opponents were looking directly at the 9-Bang when it detonated, and how far from the center of the blast they were. Looking full on at a 9-Bang when it detonates completely whites out your screen, on top of deafening you. If you are turned away, you are still disoriented slightly, but the blinding effect isn't as bad.

Strong-Arm's fast cooking is especially useful for the 9-Bang, letting you ramp it up to its full effectiveness in half the time. Oh, and be careful, as you can blind yourself!

Concussion Grenade

Radius: 512	Throwing Distance (approximate): 1200

▶ DISABLING STUN GRENADE.

Concussion grenades are stunning grenades that disable enemy movement, rendering them helpless if they are stuck facing the wrong direction when you hit them with the grenade. Concussion grenades are ideal for stopping a fast-moving target, and if you ambush an opponent's position from the flank or rear, odds are they won't be able to turn in time to prevent you from cleaning house.

The Concussion grenade has a 512-unit radius and a six-second maximum duration on the stun effect. How long it lasts exactly depends on the distance from the center of the blast, scaling from the center to the edge.

Like the 9-Bang, don't drop Concussion grenades near you; stunning yourself is embarrassing and usually fatal.

Smoke Grenade

Throwing Distance (approximate): 1200

▶ CREATES AN OBSCURING CLOUD OF IMPENETRABLE SMOKE.

The Smoke grenade is a quick-detonating Tactical grenade that creates a huge cloud of smoke at its detonation point. This cloud is extremely useful for creating instant visual cover in the open or for obscuring an objective area. In a pinch, you can use it on an enemy position, but it is usually better to block their line of sight and move behind the cloud.

If you are pinned down, you can also toss the grenade at your feet (how often is that a good idea?) and create a smokescreen to sneak out from suppressing fire.

It's not a guaranteed method of escape, but it's much better than running in the open! Smoke grenades are easy to underestimate compared to other equipment options, but they are invaluable in objective modes. Using the cover from smoke intelligently (especially in concert with a Riot Shield and defensive perks), you can seize an objective area from under the opposing team's nose. Even if they know you are taking a point, with smoke cover, it is all but impossible to land accurate shots. If there is any decent cover near the objective, you can hide behind it while the smoke makes it impossible for them to discover where you are located.

Trophy System

Defensive Radius: 256 units, longer for Battle Hind rockets (384) or the Trinity Rocket projectiles (1024)

▶ SOPHISTICATED ELECTRONIC ANTI-EXPLOSIVES DEVICE.

The Trophy System is a point defense unit that can intercept and destroy any two incoming projectiles.

This includes all forms of thrown Lethal and Tactical grenades, IMS projectiles, and even the Trinity Rocket missiles!

The Trophy System is particularly useful for securing a contested objective area that is being bombarded with explosives on a regular basis, though whether to take a Trophy System or a Smoke grenade depends on the map and mode in question.

With the Reflex perk, you can set up a Trophy System fast enough to catch an incoming explosive or Trinity Rocket before it hits, which is always a nice party trick.

Motion Sensor

Detection Radius: 100 Units (no higher than 20 units above it)

▶ PROXIMITY-ACTIVATED ENEMY DETECTION DEVICE.

The Motion Sensor is a one-shot proximity mine that trips when an enemy player gets in range and explodes, "painting" them on your HUD with an outline for eight seconds.

The outline is identical to that provided by the Oracle Support streak, and it makes the adversary extremely easy to spot and eliminate once tagged.

However, a good part of the value in the Motion Sensor is simply being able to guard your back—when you hear the Motion Sensor trip, you know someone is coming.

Two points here: first, Incog perk users don't get tagged by the Motion Sensor (but they do still set it off), and second, anyone tripping a Motion Sensor when they enter a building is going to be looking for whoever placed it.

The Motion Sensor prevents you from being completely blindsided, but it isn't a total safeguard against an enemy attack.

Thermobaric Grenade

Radius: 400   Throwing Distance (approximate): 1200

▶ SPECIALIZED ARMOR-STRIPPING GRENADE.

The Thermobaric grenade is the most directly dangerous of the Tactical grenades, dealing 50 damage anywhere in its 400-unit wide blast radius and stripping the armor from anyone hit by the blast.

For five seconds after being tagged by a Thermobaric grenade, any equipment or enemy hit with it suffers 85% increased damage from any explosive.

This means that with the Extra Tactical perk, a second Thermobaric is lethal, and essentially, any primary Lethal explosive is guaranteed to be fatal if it even tags someone hit by a Thermobaric grenade.

Thermobarics are best used as part of a one-two punch on a highly populated area. Throw the Thermobaric, then toss the Lethal immediately after.

The Reflex perk makes this combination especially nasty, as you can get both explosives in the air before your nearby opponents can react to the Thermobaric going off.

Similarly, Thermobarics work extremely well with the fast-firing under-barrel grenade launcher, and quite well with a secondary launcher if it is already in your hands when you toss the Thermobaric grenade.

Thermobaric grenades are also useful for aiding in the takedown of Juggernauts, enemies with Ballistic Vests, or any kind of emplaced equipment or killstreak, though the EMP from the 9-Bang serves as a more direct answer to equipment in general.

SPECIALIZED TRAINING   THE CAMPAIGN   MP INTRO & BASIC TRAINING   SQUADS   **MP ARMORY**   PERKS   KILLSTREAKS   MP MAPS   MP GAME MODES   SAFEGUARD   EXTINCTION   CLASSIFIED   ACHIEVEMENTS & TROPHIES

157

PERKS

Perks let you break the rules of the game, hiding you from SATCOM sweeps, dampening your movement sounds, speeding your weapon handling, and providing many, many other options.

Choose up to eight points' worth of perks from any categories to build your custom loadout.

Disable your primary or secondary weapons and your Lethal or Tactical equipment slots to gain up to four more perk points, one for each slot you disable.

Remember that the under-barrel grenade launcher and shotgun both take the place of your Lethal slot (and consume the "free" perk point from that space).

SPEED >>>>>>>>>>>>>> ENHANCE YOUR MOBILITY.

READY UP
BRINGS UP YOUR WEAPON 40% FASTER AFTER SPRINTING.

1

Ready Up brings your weapon up more quickly after ending a sprint. While this is extremely important for CQB weapons like SMGs and shotguns, it is still useful for assault rifles on mobile builds.

For slower or longer-range weapon setups, Ready Up is less critical, as you typically have time to get set up and aim down your sights (ADS) before you engage your targets. But for in your face, around the corner surprise engagements, Ready Up is a powerful perk for aggressive setups.

SLEIGHT OF HAND
RELOAD YOUR WEAPON TWICE AS QUICKLY.

2

Sleight of Hand is a useful utility perk that gives you much faster reloads.

This is particularly helpful for weapons with a high rate of fire and low ammo capacity, notably SMGs or some ARs without extended magazines.

Sleight of Hand is not a direct combat perk, but it can save your life in CQB engagements by allowing you to down one or two enemies, then reload in time to deal with any nearby adversaries who come to investigate the commotion.

Avoid developing bad reloading habits from using Sleight of Hand often. This can get you in trouble when you aren't using it on other setups, especially with moderate fire-rate ARs or marksman rifles that don't always need an immediate reload after every kill.

Bear in mind that a quick switch to your backup pistol can be just as effective in CQB situations as double speed reloads, but Sleight of Hand can potentially free up your pistol slot for another perk point, and it provides overall benefits for your combat momentum.

AGILITY
MOVE 7% FASTER.

2

Agility is a useful mobility perk that increases your movement speed at all times. This is especially useful for CQB builds where you rely on mobility to stay alive, and it is also useful in game modes that require rapid movement between objectives.

Agility combos particularly well with Stalker, Steady Aim, or Marathon, giving you even faster ADS movement, quicker movement while hip-firing, or the ability to traverse the map very quickly. Agility also pairs best with weapons that are already fast, giving you an even stronger movement edge. Pistols, shotguns, SMGs, or the combat knife complement it well.

While you can use Agility to bump up a slower weapon, this usually isn't worth the perk points, as you're gaining extra mobility on weapons that may not need it quite as much to fight efficiently. Note that Agility does slightly increase your maximum sprint distance when you aren't using Marathon. This is most noticeable on the combat knife, which already has doubled sprint distance, but it is a meaningful bonus on SMG or shotgun builds, or if you move with your pistol out even if you have an AR primary.

MARATHON
UNLIMITED SPRINT.

2

A simple, powerful movement perk, Marathon allows you to sprint indefinitely around the map. This is vital for objective modes that require constant movement and very important on larger maps in general, as it lets you get into key positions more quickly.

A Running Warning

Be very careful using Marathon. Getting into the habit of sprinting everywhere is a great way to get yourself killed. Not only are you defenseless while sprinting, but you also make more noise and easily attract attention while moving in the open.

Get in the habit of stopping your sprints short at corners or when entering a known dangerous lane of fire. Even if you don't slow down to the point of leaning around every new corner, at least check quickly with your gun at the ready!

Marathon is also very useful and important for builds that must get into CQB to be effective (notably shotguns and SMGs).

Slower weapons still benefit from Marathon, as they can use it to get into an effective firing position more quickly. This can be particularly relevant in objective modes that require you to shift positions constantly while lugging around a heavy LMG or sniper.

Marathon's utility also changes significantly based on game mode and map size. On the larger maps in objective modes, Marathon is all but mandatory for any build focused on capturing objectives swiftly. On smaller maps, or when playing on offense is less important to you, Marathon isn't as crucial.

STALKER
FULL-SPEED MOVEMENT WHILE ADS.

3

Stalker is a powerful, game-changing combat perk. It allows you to break the mobility rules of ADS combat—normally, entering ADS slows movement speed considerably, making you an easier target to hit.

With Stalker, however, you can still move at full speed while aiming. This allows you to strafe constantly while ADS, presenting a difficult target for your enemies, especially at longer distances.

In an otherwise evenly matched mid-range encounter, Stalker can give you a powerful evasive edge against an opponent who is ADS without it.

Even in CQB encounters, Stalker lets you move quickly to dodge incoming fire, place cover between you and a target, or back out of an engagement while continuing to put accurate ADS fire on your opponent.

Stalker also allows you the luxury of moving while already ADS around corners and into hotspots on the map, ready to fire at any target that comes into view. You maintain enough movement speed to present a much more difficult target than someone who slowly steps around a corner in ADS without Stalker.

Stalker is most useful on close- to mid-range weapons, from shotguns and SMGs to mid-range ARs. It is less important on longer range setups, though beware of LMG players moving through mid-range combat zones with their guns always up!

SPECIALIZED TRAINING · THE CAMPAIGN · MP INTRO & BASIC TRAINING · SQUADS · MP ARMORY · **PERKS** · KILLSTREAKS · MP MAPS · MP GAME MODES · SAFEGUARD · EXTINCTION · CLASSIFIED · ACHIEVEMENTS & TROPHIES

159

STRONG-ARM
EXTENDS THROWING DISTANCE BY 50%, ALLOWS SAFE RETURN THROWS OF FRAG GRENADES AND CANISTER BOMBS, HALVES GRENADE COOK TIMES.

1

Strong-Arm is a specialty perk for loadouts making heavy use of Lethal and Tactical grenades. It is most useful when paired with equipment perks to expand your explosive arsenal. Strong-Arm allows you to throw grenades across tall buildings and at greater distances than normal. This is particularly useful in objective modes when you know the exact position that you need to target with your grenades.

It does take some practice with Strong-Arm to learn exactly where you can take advantage of the extra throwing distance on each map. If you really want to explore the possibilities, create a private match with a few friends and spend some time lobbing grenades around the map to get a sense for how you need to adjust your aim to hit useful targets.

The second ability of Strong-Arm resets the fuses on Frag grenades or Canister Bombs, allowing you to throw them back safely. This doesn't come up very often, but it is occasionally useful when you are standing near an objective and an errant grenade lands at your feet.

Finally, Strong-Arm decreases the cook time of grenades. This is relevant for Frag grenades and 9-Bang grenades especially, which normally cook slowly and can get you killed if you're "charging" one up and an enemy comes around the corner.

ON THE GO
RELOAD WHILE SPRINTING. DISABLES THE ABILITY TO SPRINT-CANCEL A RELOAD.

1

On the Go is a useful perk for fast-moving mobile classes, as it can provide you with what amounts to a slightly cheaper version of Sleight of Hand on certain builds.

Canceling Your Reload Cancels

Normally, it is possible to cancel a reload animation early to speed up a reload. You can do this by double-tapping weapon swap, or by sprinting. With On the Go equipped, however, you cannot reload cancel by sprinting. If you're newer to the game, this isn't likely to affect you at all, but if you're a veteran who compulsively reload cancels by tapping sprint, keep this in mind!

With On the Go, you can reload your weapon while sprinting, which gives you the ability to down an enemy or two, then take off for another position while reloading your weapon. This speeds your transition from area to area very slightly.

On the Go is also useful for the slug-loading shotguns or belt-fed LMGs, where reload canceling does not apply in the first place.

If you don't mind the lack of reload canceling or you're comfortable switch canceling, you can use On the Go as a cheaper version of Sleight of Hand, enhancing your mobility and aiding your reload speed at the same time.

REFLEX
DOUBLE-SPEED WEAPON SWAP AND EQUIPMENT USAGE.

Reflex is a very useful perk for sniper, marksman, and LMG builds that require quick weapon swapping to a secondary pistol, and it can also be useful on a build utilizing Overkill with a mix of close- and long-range primary weapons.

Reflex also has applications for builds making heavy use of Lethal and Tactical equipment—double speed grenade throws and Trophy System setup are nice bonuses.

You can take Reflex on a build with a short- or long-range weapon with the intent to pick up a matching long- or short-range weapon on the field. This lets you skip out on a secondary weapon for an extra perk point and make good use of scavenged weapons, but it definitely takes some extra work and involves an element of chance.

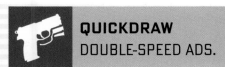

STEADY AIM
REDUCES HIP-FIRE SPREAD BY 35%.

2

Steady Aim is a simple and powerful perk: it reduces hip-fire spread significantly, making SMGs and shotguns especially lethal when fired on the move.

This has a double benefit for those weapons, as it lets you take advantage of their already high movement speeds without needing to pick up the more expensive Stalker and/or Quickdraw perks to make use of accurate fire while moving quickly.

On ARs or LMGs, Steady Aim can tighten the spread about enough to improve them one "class" (from LMG to AR, AR to SMG), but in general, hip-firing with snipers, marksman rifles, and semi-auto or burst fire ARs is a poor choice in close combat.

There is one exception in the LMG class: the Chain SAW is built for mobile combat at medium distances. Using Steady Aim can be helpful for that purpose.

Similarly, the AR class has the ARX-160, which normally has a spread between that of ARs and SMGs. Steady Aim can make it very lethal when hip-fired in CQB.

QUICKDRAW
DOUBLE-SPEED ADS.

3

Quickdraw is a powerful all-purpose gun combat perk. By halving your ADS times, you are always at an advantage whenever you get into an otherwise even firefight with another player and neither of you is already looking down the sights.

Quickdraw gives you the edge in combat with opponents using the same weapon (or an extreme edge against challengers with a slower weapon), but it can also give you the speed advantage even against faster weapons if your target isn't using Quickdraw, too.

Quickdraw is a generally useful perk for any weapon class, but shotguns and SMGs can often get away with using Steady Aim instead to save a perk point. If you're focused on keeping your distance, Quickdraw isn't a critical perk to use for very long-range weapons. Sniper rifles and marksman rifles only receive half the speed benefit from Quickdraw. This is still a potent speed increase, but they are not as fast as other weapons when using Quickdraw.

For mid-range engagements, however, or for mobile builds using ARs or MRs, Quickdraw is a very strong choice.

Quickdraw with Marksman Rifles/Snipers

Quickdraw gives only half its usual speed boost when used with a DMR or Sniper Rifle.

This is still a significant bonus, but keep in mind that you're at a speed disadvantage against someone using a different weapon type with the Quickdraw perk.

SPECIALIZED TRAINING   THE CAMPAIGN   MP INTRO & BASIC TRAINING   SQUADS   MP ARMORY   **PERKS**   KILLSTREAKS   MP MAPS   MP GAME MODES   SAFEGUARD   EXTINCTION   CLASSIFIED   ACHIEVEMENTS & TROPHIES

161

STEALTH >>>>>>>>>>> THE NEXT BEST THING TO INVISIBILITY.

TAKEDOWN
ELIMINATES THE LOCATIONAL SKULL MARKER WHEN DOWNING A HOSTILE PLAYER.

1

Takedown is a subtle but powerful stealth perk, eliminating the "friendly killed here" marker that appears when you down an enemy player.

Experienced players know to watch for these markers and hunt in the immediate vicinity. By denying them this intelligence, you can fight in close proximity to the opposing team without alerting them as easily.

Be aware that this does *not* protect you from an organized enemy team communicating when and where they die to each other, nor does it help with any noise you make, bullet tracers from your weapons, or any other overt warning of your presence.

But with that in mind, Takedown is still a cheap and useful perk that can act as a strong capper for a stealth-focused build.

BLIND EYE
INVISIBILITY TO AIR SUPPORT, THE ORACLE SYSTEM, AND SENTRY GUNS.

2

Blind Eye provides protection against all forms of automated killstreaks, including the IMS, Sentry Gun, Battle Hind, and Vulture. It also provides some limited protection against the Trinity Rocket, Helo Pilot, and Loki by cloaking your signature on an enemy player's HUD.

Blind Eye also protects against the Oracle support streak, but it does *not* protect against radar sweeps of any kind. (See the Off the Grid perk to obtain that protection.)

No Scent Dampening, Sorry

The Guard Dog is not impressed with your usage of Blind Eye; it can and will hunt you down!

Blind Eye is an unusual defensive perk in that its utility is tied strongly to the performance of your team and the loadouts of the enemy team. If the other team isn't even running the streaks that Blind Eye protects against, it won't do you much good. Similarly, if your team is playing well, they aren't likely to earn many dangerous Assault killstreaks to begin with!

Still, it is a good idea to keep a build with Blind Eye around, as it can be extremely useful for destroying enemy Sentry Guns or Battle Hinds. Bring an LMG and armor-piercing rounds to dispatch their streaks with ease. The CBJ-MS SMG also has inherent armor-piercing rounds and can be used for destroying some equipment up close.

DEAD SILENCE
QUIETS YOUR MOVEMENT SOUNDS.

2

Dead Silence is a simple stealth perk—it severely dampens any sounds you make while moving, sprinting, or mantling around the map, halving the distance from which enemies can effectively hear you.

This is useful for CQB builds, particularly those running the tactical knife, shotguns, or SMGs, as it lets you get into range of your prey without alerting them to your presence with an errant footfall on a metal surface.

Keep in mind that while Dead Silence does muffle your movement noises, it does nothing for your weapon. Additionally, nearby enemies can still spot you, of course.

Also, remember that not all players are totally aware of their surroundings based on noises. Dead Silence is best against enemies who are using good audio setups or wearing headphones and are very alert to begin with—and that's not something you can know before going into a match!

Dead Silence pairs quite well with silenced weapons.

INCOG

REMOVES THE RED NAME OVER YOUR HEAD WHEN TARGETED IN ADS. GIVES IMMUNITY TO THERMAL AND TRACKER SCOPES, MOTION SENSORS, AND THE RECON PERK.

Incog is a powerful stealth perk, giving you immunity to most forms of "special" detection while providing a direct combat benefit by removing the red name over your head when an enemy targets you. This last point might seem minor, but in practice, your name tends to give away your position as fast as or faster than your actual body does. Your name often pokes through soft cover, and at longer ranges, an enemy may only see your name if you are well-hidden in shadow or cover.

Incog can cause an enemy to hesitate just long enough when spotting you to give you the drop on them, and this is usually enough time to put a lethal burst of fire in their face. Incog is useful at any distance and on many builds (even those not explicitly running a stealth setup, as it helps with gunfights in general), but it is particularly useful for long-range builds.

When setting up in a building or behind hard cover in deep shadows, you become extremely difficult to spot. As long as you keep your motion to a minimum, it is unlikely that an enemy scanning the battlefield in your direction will spot you before they notice any of your Incog-free teammates running around.

Incog Protection from Voice Location

Incog has one important hidden benefit: it prevents the new location call-out system from calling you as a target! In other words, the soldiers on the battlefield will no longer call your position audibly to their teammates.

Because this system is totally automated, this can cause you to be "spotted" by the game and have a voice warning be thrown, even if the player who "saw" you didn't actually notice you! Incog stops this from happening, preventing enemy soldiers from calling your position.

Incog also protects against detection via the various advanced scopes, including Thermal and Tracker. The scopes can still *see* you, but you aren't highlighted in white or outlined in either scope.

Finally, keep in mind that while Incog prevents you from being *tagged* by the Motion Sensor, it does not prevent the Motion Sensor from actually going off and exploding.

This means that an alert player who is camping near their Motion Sensor will know that it has been triggered. Though you won't be outlined, they will still be on guard. Be careful if you're entering an area with only one likely entry route, as the foe may already be aimed in your direction.

OFF THE GRID

HIDES YOU FROM SATCOM SWEEPS, JUGGERNAUT RECON, RIOT SHIELD RADAR, AND THE PING PERK.

Off the Grid is the cornerstone of any stealth-based build where you plan to fight in close proximity to the enemy team. Paired with a silencer to hide your minimap dot when you fire a weapon, you are invisible to anything but direct visual contact or audio cues (and Incog and Dead Silence can help with those two problems).

Off the Grid is most useful for aggressive builds where you need to get into CQB with the enemy team on a regular basis. Concealing your radar signature is less important if you are planning on playing defense or staying at long range.

The best time to strike when using Off the Grid is when the enemy does have SATCOM coverage. These attackers tend to pay more attention to visible enemy marks on the minimap, giving you an opportunity to blindside them. Be aware that staying near teammates who do *not* have Off the Grid is just as bad as not having it yourself, as an enemy can see them on the minimap, which can give away your location.

Team Invisibility

Off the Grid grows in power as more players run it. An entire team using Off the Grid completely nullifies all SATCOM usage and any other forms of radar detection.

Note that Off the Grid does *not* protect you from the Oracle support streak or from being tagged by a Motion Sensor or the Recon perk.

SPECIALIZED TRAINING   THE CAMPAIGN   MP INTRO & BASIC TRAINING   SQUADS   MP ARMORY   **PERKS**   KILLSTREAKS   MP MAPS   MP GAME MODES   SAFEGUARD   EXTINCTION   CLASSIFIED   ACHIEVEMENTS & TROPHIES

163

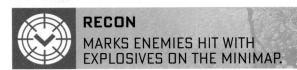

RECON
MARKS ENEMIES HIT WITH EXPLOSIVES ON THE MINIMAP.

1

Recon is a team intelligence perk. While equipped with it, whenever you tag an enemy with any explosive (including all forms of launchers, Lethal and Tactical grenades, and the under-barrel grenade launcher), they are highlighted in the world as though they had been hit with a Motion Sensor or an active Oracle system.

The tag lasts for a second, giving you or nearby teammates enough time to spot and eliminate any reasonably close tagged targets (a cross-map Strong-Arm grenade toss might be a bit out of range for anyone but a sniper).

Recon is most useful when you commit to using it heavily and take the Extra Tactical perk and either the Extra Lethal perk or an under-barrel grenade launcher. For maximum use, add a secondary launcher on top of the above.

Having explosives that can tag enemies can be extremely useful in objective modes when you are attempting to flush out defenders located near an objective.

Recon is less useful if you are running with a regular Lethal and Tactical loadout, and it's not useful at all if you lack explosives!

Recon can be countered by taking the Incog perk, preventing you from being tagged.

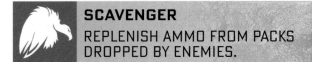

SCAVENGER
REPLENISH AMMO FROM PACKS DROPPED BY ENEMIES.

2

Scavenger allows you to resupply one magazine's worth of ammo from any fallen enemy. Simply step over their body to pick up the pack and reload.

Scavenger is a useful perk for Specialist builds or any playstyle that emphasizes staying alive over taking risks.

When you last a long time, you tend to run low on ammo; Scavenger lets you avoid the risk of picking up a weapon from the battlefield.

While you can maintain a streak with enemy (or friendly) weapons, using a custom weapon that suits you and your build personally is usually a better option. Scavenger lets you keep your fully customized weapon loaded with ammo as long as you stay alive.

Any kill by a teammate or from you generates a pack from an enemy. Just be careful about exposing yourself to pick up a pack out in the open. The whole point to using Scavenger is to stay alive longer and keep topped off, so dying to get a pack is counterproductive in the extreme!

SITREP
HIGHLIGHTS ENEMY EQUIPMENT OF ALL TYPES THROUGH WALLS.

SitRep is a powerful but situational perk that provides visual intelligence on enemy equipment placement. This includes all types of placed Lethal or Tactical equipment, as well as any placed killstreak items like SATCOMs or the IMS.

SitRep lets you spot targets roughly 600 units away, and about 50% farther if you are looking down your sights while ADS. Any enemy equipment is shown as a bright red outline. This means that you can "sweep" a building by going ADS and looking it over; any equipment inside should show up.

SitRep is very helpful not just for locating enemy equipment, but also for locating enemies. Because players tend to camp out near a placed IED or Motion Sensor, SitRep can be helpful to spot them before they are aware of your presence.

SitRep is also helpful for warning teammates of an enemy IMS, as well as for locating and disabling enemy SATCOM emplacements quickly.

Grenade Dodging

SitRep actually highlights all forms of enemy items in the world, not just emplaced equipment.

This means it also highlights thrown grenades—you can actually see the red glow on a grenade through a nearby wall or (more importantly) when it lands near you.

While this won't always save you, the enhanced visibility is often enough to catch your eye and ensure that you dodge in the right direction as quickly as possible.

AMPLIFY
LOUDER ENEMY MOVEMENT.

Amplify is a simple and useful awareness perk that increases the noise made by enemy movement, roughly doubling the distance from which you can hear an enemy.

This increases your ability to hear enemy footsteps, sprinting, and mantling. However, the exact effect depends heavily on the terrain around you and if there is an active firefight occurring nearby.

Amplify is most useful if you have a strong audio setup or a good pair of headphones and you are already attuned to the sounds during a match. The more you practice with it, the more this perk gives you.

Note that if you switch between builds using Amplify and those without, you may find that you have problems identifying enemy positions accurately because you are used to hearing them at a certain range.

Amplify is a very useful situational awareness perk when you are using CQB builds, as it lets you identify new targets to hunt while warning you of incoming threats.

It can also be a valuable perk when defending an area, as it may alert you to an incoming enemy who is otherwise stealthy (Off the Grid, Incog, silenced weapon, etc.).

Dead Silence and Amplify act to cancel each other out, returning sounds to their default range.

WIRETAP
ALLOWS USAGE OF THE ENEMY SATCOM NETWORK.

Wiretap ties your team's SATCOM network into the enemy team's, giving you the benefit of any active SATCOMs the opposition places on the field.

This means that if your team and the enemy team each has a single SATCOM active, you get a regular satellite sweep, while everyone else only has eyes on coverage.

Keep in mind that Wiretap's enhanced SATCOM benefit only applies to you personally, not your entire team.

Consequently, you should make an effort to relay enemy positions as often as possible to your teammates when you are using Wiretap. In an average match, you are typically going to have better SATCOM coverage than your teammates.

Like Off the Grid, Wiretap has an odd quirk in that if the enemy team somehow fails to use any SATCOMs at all, it's essentially a dead perk choice. However, this is an unusual situation, and you can always simply switch to another build without Wiretap if you aren't seeing a lot of enemy SATCOM coverage.

SPECIALIZED TRAINING   THE CAMPAIGN   MP INTRO & BASIC TRAINING   SQUADS   MP ARMORY   **PERKS**   KILLSTREAKS   MP MAPS   MP GAME MODES   SAFEGUARD   EXTINCTION   CLASSIFIED   ACHIEVEMENTS & TROPHIES

165

RESISTANCE

>>>>>>>>>>>>>>> TAKE A PUNCH, STAND BACK UP.

RESILIENCE
ELIMINATES FALLING DAMAGE.

1

Resilience is a cheap perk with a very minor effect: it eliminates falling damage. This is useful on some maps for traversing them more safely, and it can occasionally save your life if you happen to jump (or fall) from a significant height during a combat encounter.

In general, however, you should only take this perk if you have a free point on a build that is focused on battlefield mobility (like using every available speed route during a Blitz game, or running a mobile tactical knife or CQB gun build). Otherwise, the effect is too focused to be useful in all maps and modes.

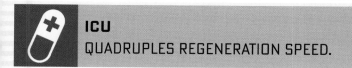

ICU
QUADRUPLES REGENERATION SPEED.

2

ICU greatly increases your ability to recover from combat damage, halving the time it takes to begin regenerating, and doubling the speed of that regeneration.

The total effect means that you should almost always be fully recovered from a firefight before you next encounter an enemy, as long as you have at least a brief span of time to regenerate. ICU is more useful for aggressive builds where you expect to engage in a lot of close- to medium-range firefights, and you are all but guaranteed to come out of a fight having taken some damage.

ICU is an unusual perk in that it is potentially useful on a great many builds, but it is not exceptionally useful in any specific build. As a result, it makes an excellent Specialist reward, but it can be hard to find the perk points to squeeze it into a focused build.

Still, make an effort to experiment with it on your CQB and mid-range builds. You may find that it suits your style of play well if you often emerge from fights damaged and must engage fresh targets soon after.

FOCUS
REDUCES FLINCH WHEN HIT BY ENEMY FIRE, REDUCES WEAPON SWAY.

2

Focus is a powerful general gunfighter perk, both greatly reducing flinch when hit in combat and reducing visible weapon sway, aiding with long-range accuracy.

At mid to long ranges, Focus can mean the difference between winning and losing a firefight, as Focus lets you stay on target even if hit by incoming fire. Furthermore, it ensures that your weapon has less idle sway while you are ADS. Focus is especially useful on builds built to take advantage of sniper rifles, most LMGs, MRs, and ARs with burst fire or semi-auto attachments.

It is also useful on mobile mid-range builds, typically those using Quickdraw and/or Stalker to engage at a medium distance. At short ranges, Focus is less potent. If you're using a truly short-range build like a shotgun or SMG with Steady Aim, there are better perk choices.

TAC RESIST
PROVIDES NEAR TOTAL IMMUNITY TO CONCUSSION AND FLASH GRENADES. NEGATES ALL FORMS OF EMP, RESISTS THERMOBARIC ARMOR STRIPPING.

2

Tac Resist protects you from 9-Bang grenades, Concussion grenades, the Thermobaric armor strip, and any form of EMP effect (including fully charged 9-Bang explosions, the Odin support streak, and the Ground Jammer support streak). Tac Resist is particularly useful for defense when you're guarding an objective area that is likely to be bombarded with explosives.

A quirk that applies to both this perk and Blast Shield is that with the option to completely remove Lethal and Tactical gear from loadouts, you may encounter few (or even zero) enemy Tactical grenades on the battlefield. Keep a build handy with Tac Resist equipped for when you are encountering dedicated Tactical grenade usage, as it does its job very effectively.

BLAST SHIELD
PROVIDES 65% RESISTANCE TO EXPLOSIVES.

2

Blast Shield is a powerful defense against enemy explosives, severely dampening the incoming damage and ensuring survival against all but the most powerful of explosive weapons. It is still possible to be killed by direct sticks or powerful killstreak explosives, but for general protection against nearby grenade detonations, Blast Shield does its job very well.

Blast Shield ensures that you will survive one explosive, no matter what—only one time—so you aren't completely safe in all situations, but the protection is substantial.

> ### Armor Up
> With Blast Shield paired with ICU, you can survive a serious bombardment. If the enemy team is making dedicated use of explosives, especially if they are packing extra grenades and Danger Close, this combo can stop the pain.

SPECIALIZED TRAINING   THE CAMPAIGN   MP INTRO & BASIC TRAINING   SQUADS   MP ARMORY   **PERKS**   KILLSTREAKS   MP MAPS   MP GAME MODES   SAFEGUARD   EXTINCTION   CLASSIFIED   ACHIEVEMENTS & TROPHIES

167

EXTRA TACTICAL
PROVIDES AN ADDITIONAL PIECE OF TACTICAL EQUIPMENT.

1

Extra Tactical does what it says on the box: you get one extra piece of Tactical equipment each time you spawn.

This works on any piece of Tactical gear, and it is particularly useful when paired with Trophy System (to defend an objective against bombardment) or Motion Sensor (to set up a safehouse).

All of the Tactical grenades simply give you an extra usage, providing one extra shot at disabling or crippling your targets, or creating extra cover with smoke.

Extra Tactical fits well on any build set up to support your team, but because it is essentially a one-shot perk, you tend to get more use out of it in modes that have a high body count (or if you naturally tend to play aggressively, with a high risk of frequent deaths).

EXTRA LETHAL
PROVIDES AN ADDITIONAL PIECE OF LETHAL EQUIPMENT.

2

As with Extra Tactical, Extra Lethal gives you more firepower in the Lethal department. You pay extra for the privilege, so be sure to use your explosives wisely—flinging them across the map is a bad idea unless you're tossing them directly at a known occupied objective area.

Extra explosives tend to be most useful in modes that force players to cluster in a small space so you can all but guarantee a kill or at least heavy damage to multiple enemies.

Taking an extra Lethal with the IED also lets you set up nasty defensive traps, while the various offensive options all give you a bit more oomph to clear an objective or severely damage even Blast Shield-equipped targets. As with Extra Tactical, Extra Lethal gives you more usage if you die somewhat frequently, but don't use this as an excuse to play foolishly. Simply remember that a defensive or long-range build may not get as much mileage out of this two-point perk as one that is focused on clearing or taking objectives with it.

FULLY LOADED
PROVIDES A FULL MAGAZINE OR AMMUNITION LOAD FOR ANY EQUIPPED WEAPONS.

2

Fully Loaded is a simple perk: it gives you a full ammunition loadout for your primary and secondary weapons. (Note that it does not affect ammo for launchers or the under-barrel grenade launcher.)

Fully Loaded tends to work out to four extra magazines on most weapons, though this varies slightly depending on the weapon in question (belt-fed LMGs, shotguns, and so on). The overall effect is that you can be a lot more aggressive with your bullets, freely using hip-fire (especially strong with Steady Aim), drilling targets through walls or cover, and burning extra ammunition to ensure kills.

Unlike Scavenger (or the Weapon Crate streak, to a lesser extent), Fully Loaded gives you all of the ammo up front, and you don't have to expose yourself to any risk to get that ammo. The downside is that once you've spent the ammo, your two-point perk is no longer doing any work, so you must be sure to get maximum value out of those extra bullets.

Fully Loaded is most useful with ARs and SMGs that have a high rate of fire, or LMGs with the Rapid Fire attachment. It is effective when used aggressively with armor-piercing ammunition, and it also pairs very well with extended magazines.

It takes practice to learn where enemies tend to hide behind walls on any given map and mode combination, but Fully Loaded gives you the extra ammunition to dig them out, particularly with AP ammo.

EXTRA ATTACHMENT
ALLOWS AN EXTRA ATTACHMENT ON YOUR PRIMARY AND SECONDARY WEAPONS.

Extra Attachment lets you further customize your weapons with a third attachment. You can fill out three of the four possible attachment categories, and if you don't mind skipping a sight, you can make every possible modification to your weapon.

Also note that Extra Attachment has special value for weapons that have an integrated attachment. For example, the Honey Badger AR and K7 SMG have integrated silencers. With Extra Attachment, you can have a silenced weapon with a sight, under-barrel, and mod all at the same time—the ultimate in tricked-out weapons.

Extra Attachment also works with Overkill, allowing you to take two primary class weapons with extra attachments.

The Price of Customization

Extra Attachment lets you trick out your weapons, but be aware this means that you're tied to your weapons tightly with the point investment. Fully Loaded, Scavenger, and the Weapons Crate streak should all be given consideration if you're planning on using it.

Running out of ammo on your primary weapon and then picking up a new one from the battlefield after a few kills is an unimpressive use of three perk points!

Also be aware that taking an ammo perk and Extra Attachment burns up five perk points—be sure that you're getting enough mileage from your custom weapon to justify the cost!

DANGER CLOSE
PROVIDES A 40% INCREASE TO EXPLOSIVE DAMAGE.

Danger Close is an expensive brute force perk that boosts damage from all of your explosives.

Because it is so pricy, using Danger Close encourages you to go all-in on an explosives build, taking Extra Lethal and possibly Extra Tactical and Recon or Strong-Arm, as well. Doing so gives you the armament to bombard an enemy position for frequently lethal damage, and anyone who doesn't end up dead from the barrage gets marked with a tracking outline.

Since taking Danger Close restricts your perk options significantly, it's usually a good idea to have it set aside for a dedicated explosives build that you pull out when an enemy is particularly dug in around an objective.

You can certainly use a Danger Close setup during a normal match, but you lose out on general combat power, stealth, or mobility. This isn't a great tradeoff for a perk that only works while you still have explosives remaining.

Instead, use Danger Close to break an entrenched enemy team, and then swap out of it once your work is done. Danger Close nullifies the Blast Shield perk, returning explosive damage to normal.

Edge Cases 101

Danger Close normally does not affect killstreaks that deal explosive damage in any way.

There is one exception to this rule: if you hit an enemy who has Blast Shield equipped, Danger Close does remove their Blast Shield.

This usually won't have an impact on, say, hitting someone with a Tomahawk or a Loki kinetic strike, but it can come up if you're piloting a Gryphon.

SPECIALIZED TRAINING   THE CAMPAIGN   MP INTRO & BASIC TRAINING   SQUADS   MP ARMORY   **PERKS**   KILLSTREAKS   MP MAPS   MP GAME MODES   SAFEGUARD   EXTINCTION   CLASSIFIED   ACHIEVEMENTS & TROPHIES

169

GAMBLER
GRANTS A RANDOM PERK WHEN YOU SPAWN OR EARN THE PERK VIA SPECIALIST.

1

Gambler gives you a weighted chance at acquiring any other perk besides Overkill when you spawn. What this means is that you are more likely to get a low-cost perk than an expensive perk. Note that Gambler does not respect your current build. That is, if you have no Tactical or Lethal equipment, you can and will acquire Strong-Arm, Recon, Extra Tactical, and so on.

Because Gambler only costs a single point, you can use it as a capper perk if there are no better options. However, Ready Up and Takedown are more applicable to many builds, and even Recon is helpful for your team if you have at least two grenades. That said, if you do want to gamble, you may occasionally luck out with something pricy and appropriate for your build!

HARDLINE
REDUCES KILLSTREAK REQUIREMENTS BY 1. TWO ASSISTS COUNT AS A KILL.

2

Hardline is a unique and useful Elite perk that reduces the kill requirement for killstreaks. Hardline is particularly effective when paired with low requirement Assault streaks, as it allows you to chain together streaks much more easily.

It is less useful for support streaks, where you are essentially guaranteed to secure the streaks once or more every match. It's not amazing on Specialist, either: it cuts the kill requirement by one to reach your Specialist bonus but otherwise does nothing to help you on your way there.

Running a 3/5/7 or a 5/7/9 Assault loadout with Hardline is quite effective, but another option is to run a 3 setup. That is, take a SATCOM, Hardline, and no other streaks. Seem odd? Consider that every uninterrupted double kill you get in a match grants your team a SATCOM. That's a lot of satellite coverage! Running a 3/5 setup is another similar option, giving you the potential to loop SATCOMs with IMS or Guard Dog assistance—not a bad streak combination.

PING
GENERATES A LOCALIZED RADAR PING WHEN YOU KILL AN ENEMY.

2

Ping is a powerful CQB perk that gives you immediate local intelligence on enemy positions after you kill a target.

The sweep from Ping has a 700 radius, like other similar effects (the Riot Shield Radar and Recon Juggernaut), but be aware that it takes two seconds for the sweep to reach the edge of that radius.

This means that you can kill a target, sprint away, and bump into someone nearby who is not yet tagged by the sweep. Get in the habit of getting into cover and reloading while you check the minimap for Ping to complete. Keep in mind that players with Off the Grid won't show up on the Ping sweep, so don't get complacent even if you don't see any targets light up on your minimap.

Ping is very useful for any build that you intend to use in close proximity to the enemy team, as the extra information it provides can save your life and keep a streak going. Ping lets you play offensively or defensively, as well, hunting down extra targets or avoiding them if the situation is unfavorable.

Ping shares some similarities with Amplify in terms of the situational awareness it grants you, but it functions a bit differently. Experiment with both and see which suits you. Note that Ping radar sweeps are personal only and do not show up for teammates. Be sure to warn them if an enemy is nearby!

OVERKILL
ALLOWS A PRIMARY WEAPON TO BE TAKEN IN PLACE OF A SECONDARY.

3

Overkill lets you break the equipment loadout rules—instead of having the option for a primary and a secondary weapon, Overkill grants you the ability to equip two primary weapons. This means you could take a sniper rifle and a shotgun, a marksman rifle and an SMG, or even two LMGs if you're feeling particularly action hero-esque.

Overkill pairs well with a long-range weapon and a short-range weapon, or a Riot Shield and a different primary weapon, along with the Reflex perk to let you switch quickly between your two options.

Extra Attachment and Scavenger or Fully Loaded are also useful options, as the former gives you an even more customized loadout, and the latter two let you use your primary weapons longer on the battlefield.

Overkill is a fairly expensive perk, so if you aren't getting maximum benefit out of your weapon choices by actively switching between them and using them in the proper range bands, you would be better served with a different option.

DEADEYE
GRANTS A CHANCE TO DEAL INCREASED DAMAGE WITH EVERY SHOT.
CHANCE INCREASES BY EARNING KILLS.

5

Deadeye gives you a 10% chance to deal 40% more damage when you hit an enemy. Each time you kill an opponent, this chance increases by 10%, up to a maximum of 50%. This means that after four kills, half of your shots are dealing 40% boosted damage. On average, a single Deadeye hit knocks one shot off the number needed to kill an enemy.

Because the percentage chance of a damage boost is not scaled to fire rate, high fire-rate weapons are naturally more effective with Deadeye. High-fire rate ARs, SMGs, and LMGs with rapid fire are all particularly deadly.

Shotguns are also noticeably nastier with Deadeye because Deadeye has a chance to trigger on each pellet, rather than each shot. A close-range shot is all but guaranteed to make Deadeye fire, frequently making the shot lethal if it was on the edge of fatal damage.

For veteran *Call of Duty* players, you may recognize this damage increase as the same given by the classic Stopping Power perk. Deadeye is a tuned version that gives part of the benefit, but you have to work to earn it!

Because Deadeye is so expensive, you want to be running it with a weapon that can take maximum advantage of it. Also, you may need to give up your Lethal and Tactical slots and possibly even your secondary weapon to squeeze in additional combat perks. Deadeye is effective, but you need to weigh the increased lethality against the challenge of sustaining a long killstreak and the loss of perk points. Deadeye is a very powerful perk to pick up as part of a Specialist bonus.

SPECIALIZED TRAINING   THE CAMPAIGN   MP INTRO & BASIC TRAINING   SQUADS   MP ARMORY   **PERKS**   KILLSTREAKS   MP MAPS   MP GAME MODES   SAFEGUARD   EXTINCTION   CLASSIFIED   ACHIEVEMENTS & TROPHIES

171

PERK BUILDS

Perk builds are listed as eight (or around eight) point setups with an optional bonus addition if you are willing to remove equipment from your build to free up the extra perk points.

These are simple, basic perk setups focused on different aspects of combat rather than purpose-built full classes for specific game modes.

In general, the type of weapon, equipment, and killstreaks that accompany any given perk build should be dictated by the map and game mode you are playing, along with a healthy dose of personal preference.

But in this case, these are simply examples of how to put together perks to support a single focus. With 35 perk choices, it can feel a bit overwhelming putting together builds at first, especially if you are a new player!

The lesson here is straightforward: when you're customizing your classes, always build with some goal in mind. It can be anything from aiding your team in a specific mode to best supporting your favorite weapon setup.

The goal doesn't matter, only that you choose perks that suit your purpose and complement each other well!

ALL-PURPOSE COMBAT

Gain the edge against anyone in direct gun-on-gun combat. Simple, straightforward, and highly effective.

STALKER QUICKDRAW FOCUS

BONUS

SLEIGHT OF HAND OR READY UP AND TAKEDOWN

CQB

Get close, stay close, and use your close-range weaponry to dominate your enemies.

 MARATHON

 AGILITY

 SLEIGHT OF HAND **OR** ON THE GO

 STEADY AIM **OR** QUICKDRAW **OR** STALKER

BONUS

 ICU **OR** AMPLIFY **OR** PING **OR** READY UP

LONG RANGE

Keep your distance, pick off targets at long range, and instantly react with a backup weapon if anyone gets too close.

 INCOG

 FOCUS

 REFLEX

BONUS

 HARDLINE **OR** OFF THE GRID

STEALTH

Stay off the minimap, out of sight, and silent. Eliminate enemies without alerting their teammates.

 INCOG

 OFF THE GRID

DEAD SILENCE

BONUS

TAKEDOWN

KNIFING

Bring a tactical knife with this setup. Sprint around the map at high speed, picking off enemies and vanishing before their teammates can react. Resilience can be useful on some maps!

 MARATHON

 AGILITY

 OFF THE GRID

 DEAD SILENCE

BONUS

 PING **OR** AMPLIFY

EXPLOSIVES

Load up on explosive gear and bombard the enemy team. Clear out objectives, clear out rooms, clear out anyone in your way.

 DANGER CLOSE

 EXTRA LETHAL

 EXTRA TACTICAL **AND** RECON **OR** REFLEX

BONUS

 STRONG-ARM

TEAM SUPPORT

Identify enemy positions, spot enemy equipment, absorb enemy explosives, and claim objectives. Run a low-end Assault streak loop if you go for Hardline.

 SITREP

 WIRETAP

 BLAST SHIELD

BONUS

 TAC RESIST **OR** HARDLINE

SPECIALIZED TRAINING   THE CAMPAIGN   MP INTRO & BASIC TRAINING   SQUADS   MP ARMORY   **PERKS**   KILLSTREAKS   MP MAPS   MP GAME MODES   SAFEGUARD   EXTINCTION   CLASSIFIED   ACHIEVEMENTS & TROPHIES

173

KILLSTREAKS

Call of Duty: Ghosts features three types of killstreak packages: Assault, Support, and Specialist.

Each serves a different role in supporting you and your team on the battlefield. You can equip any one of the killstreak types to your squad members and customize that streak as you see fit. For Assault and Support, you select up to three killstreaks, with no two of the same kill cost. You can select fewer than three if you want to loop lower streaks more quickly.

For Specialist, you choose three perks to earn via kills, and then eight perk points' worth of perks as a "Specialist bonus" if you earn all three initial perks and get two more kills past that point.

ASSAULT

You earn Assault killstreaks by reaching consecutive kill targets without dying. Dying breaks Assault streaks, so these are the hardest type of streaks to earn. In exchange, Assault offers powerful battlefield support and has the most directly lethal killstreaks.

Assault killstreaks can be chained to one another. Kills earned by your streaks while you are alive count toward your next streak.

Running a build with something like 5-7-9 is a traditional Assault technique. For example, you can earn your Guard Dog to aid in acquiring your Trinity Rocket, and then use your Trinity Rocket to propel you to your Battle Hind or Vulture.

Generally speaking, the 3-5 slot items are fairly easy to acquire, 7-9 demand more effort, and anything above 9 requires careful play.

Hardline with 3-5 streaks is especially effective if you like Assault streaks but have a hard time consistently earning higher streaks. Running Hardline and simply SAT COM and IMS or Guard Dog lets you saturate the battlefield with two kill SAT COMs and four kill booby traps or a constant canine companion.

Once you're comfortable with the conservative style of play required to chain Assault streaks, 5-7-9 is a good place to move up to. From there, it's a short jump to 5-7-10 or 5-7-12.

There is no fast and easy way to earn the Loki. You can chain a Trinity Rocket to a Battle Hind or Gryphon, but doing so leaves you with no support for seven kills.

The IMS and the Sentry Gun are slower for earning additional kills than the Guard Dog or especially Trinity Rocket, but they are also very powerful defensive tools that are useful in objective game modes. If you place them well, they can even earn you more kills over time.

Both Juggernauts can be very effective if used with care, a trait you should be mastering if you run Assault regularly. A stick and move Maniac or an Assault Juggernaut used to defend an objective area can be extremely lethal.

SUPPORT

As the name implies, Support streaks are useful for aiding your team.

Unlike Assault streaks, your kill streak for Support does *not* reset when you die. No matter which Support streaks you select, as long as you earn enough kills in a match, you are guaranteed to acquire the streaks.

What this means in practice is that you must decide between looping the low-end (and very useful) Support streaks, or aiming for the higher streaks. You may not be able to earn the higher streaks more than once or twice in a match simply because of kill and/or time limits in any game mode beyond your own personal skill.

Support streaks are also ideal if you're a new player, as they let you play with some fun and useful streaks and don't demand the same perfect play that Assault streaks do.

However, don't infer that you should discard Support streaks once you're good enough to chain Assault streaks. If there's anything more dangerous than a skilled player, it's a skilled player wearing Ballistic Vests with a full ammo load and SAT COM coverage.

Looping SAT COM through Ballistic Vests is a strong baseline setup. This gives your team constant SAT COM coverage, constant ammo supplies, and constant vest upgrades.

You can also simply loop SAT COM (with or without Hardline), though whether this is superior to running Assault SAT COM with Hardline is debatable.

If you're looking to go into the middle tier of streaks, the Night Owl and Ground Jammer are both very useful all-purpose Support streaks.

The MAAWS and Air Superiority are both most useful in specific situations (though you can certainly use the MAAWS as an anti-infantry addition to an explosives build if desired), typically for clearing the skies in the mid to late game.

For the high-end Support streaks, the Oracle and Odin are both exceptional, and they can shift the course of a battle if you and your team use them well.

The Recon Juggernaut is a very powerful streak reward, but its power also partly depends on the strength of your team. A Recon Juggernaut with backup is a serious pain to deal with, but if you're solo and unsupported, you can be flanked and taken out with relative ease.

Finally, the Support Squadmate and Helo Scout are entirely unique rewards. The Support Squadmate gives you an AI combat buddy who faithfully follows you around and attempts to protect you with a Riot Shield. However, he is very vulnerable to enemy fire, so you should weigh the additional momentary distraction against the potential value of the Night Owl or Ground Jammer.

The Helo Scout is something else entirely: it can give you and your team useful recon if you quickly call out enemy positions while in the air, and it can aid your team with sniper support by taking out key enemies on or near objectives.

However, the Helo Scout is very vulnerable to focused enemy fire, so an alert enemy team can cut your streak short. Additionally, your ability to snipe from the chopper largely depends on the map: open maps with little cover make it much easier to pick out targets.

SPECIALIST

Specialist is the personal, lone wolf killstreak package. Rather than rewarding you with aggressive Assault killstreak rewards or team-assisting Support rewards, Specialist gives you and only you more power in the form of extra perks.

You can select any three perks as your first three Specialist rewards. The base perk cost of each perk, plus a few points, sets the kill totals that you need to reach to unlock your first three perks.

Beyond the first three perks, you also get to pick eight perk points worth of bonus perks as your Specialist bonus. Once you have earned the first three perks and two more kills, you unlock your bonus perks.

Specialist can turn a good player into an unstoppable force on the battlefield, but at the same time, it doesn't give you any special resistance from stray bullets. Don't get overconfident.

You must decide if the benefit from Specialist outweighs the power of Assault and Support streaks for you and your team.

A typical Specialist strategy is to start with a general combat supremacy perk setup, pick up key stealth perks as the initial unlocks, and then grab the luxury "power" perks as the final Specialist bonus.

This gives you the advantage in your initial firefights, gradually makes you more difficult to detect, and finally gives you the extra edge you can squeeze out of the final perk points.

Because Scavenger is almost certain to be one of your perk rewards, carefully choosing your weapon is very important. You'll likely use it for a long time if you survive to unlock your bonus regularly.

Shotguns and sniper rifles tend to be too extreme for the all-purpose combat demanded of the Specialist fighter. Consider a silenced submachine gun (SMG) or assault rifle (AR), with the possibility of a marksman rifle on certain maps if it suits your playstyle well. Pairing a silenced weapon with stealth perks keeps you off the map and alive.

One last note about Specialist: you don't need to go for a generalist setup. If you have a very specific sort of defensive or offensive build in mind, you can tailor the perk rewards to fit that particular setup and weapon completely.

Removing an entrenched light machine gun (LMG) gunner guarding an objective can be highly annoying, but an LMG gunner who is also packing Blast Shield, Tac Resist, ICU, and Deadeye on top of his normal perk loadout is an order of magnitude worse.

SPECIALIZED TRAINING   THE CAMPAIGN   MP INTRO & BASIC TRAINING   SQUADS   MP ARMORY   PERKS   **KILLSTREAKS**   MP MAPS   MP GAME MODES   SAFEGUARD   EXTINCTION   CLASSIFIED   ACHIEVEMENTS & TROPHIES

175

Juggernaut Punch

Juggernaut armor in this game functions a bit differently than it has in the past.

Juggernauts do *not* regenerate health and eventually succumb to incoming damage.

Still, all Juggernauts are extremely resilient, only taking a fraction (about 8%) of incoming damage from any bullet attacks.

When you need an answer, use armor-piercing rounds, Thermobaric grenades, or the Panzerfaust as Juggernaut remedies.

KEM Strike

If you earn 25 unassisted kills with your weapon, you can unlock the ability to call in a lethal KEM strike on the map, killing off the entire enemy team.

This is identical to the strike that can be called down on Strikezone, though it does not destroy every other map in the game. It does do a nice job of suppressing the other team, though.

Specialist builds tend to be the most effective if you're seriously pursuing 25 kills—they give you the perk muscle you need to be self-sufficient and have an edge in every combat encounter you get into.

Automated Support

The Vulture, Night Owl, Support Squadmate, Assault Juggernaut from the Loki, Recon Juggernaut from the Odin, and Guard Dog all share a common trait: they are AI-controlled automatic support that follows you around the map.

In general, this is a good thing, but be aware that they do tend to give away your location to alert enemies. This is especially true when you are killed and your killer watches where your AI buddy moves to. In some cases, opponents can track you directly back to your spawn!

This isn't a reason to avoid using them, but be aware that they can give away your position, an important consideration if you are planning on running a stealthy close quarters battle (CQB) build. It's hard to be stealthy with an orbiting death bot and a growling dog nearby!

ASSAULT

SAT COM ❸

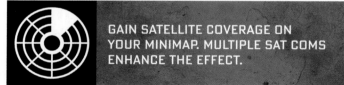

GAIN SATELLITE COVERAGE ON YOUR MINIMAP. MULTIPLE SAT COMS ENHANCE THE EFFECT.

SAT COM lets you place a single satellite communications terminal anywhere on the map. Once placed, the SAT COM links up with any other friendly SAT COM units and provides satellite coverage of hostile enemy targets on your minimap.

There Are Four Levels of SAT COM Coverage

1. Eyes On: Enemy targets are highlighted on your minimap when you or a teammate physically spots them.

2. Scanner Sweep: Periodic sweeps cover the map, revealing enemy positions anywhere on the level.

3. Fast Scan: Same scan as level 2, but the sweep occurs much more quickly.

4. Advanced Satellite Coverage: Provides perfect positional and directional information on all hostile targets.

SAT COMs work best when multiple players on the team are running them (or you have a dedicated SAT COM specialist running Hardline), as the benefits from having two or more SAT COM emplacements are significant.

Note that because SAT COMs are physical terminals that must be placed on the map, the enemy team can find and destroy them. Try to tuck them away in the corners of buildings and behind rough cover; leaving them out in the open or near a high-traffic objective is guaranteed to get them destroyed early.

SAT COMs last for 30 seconds each, and any friendly SAT COM units stack their effects while they are active.

Clearing the Skies

The SAT COM is new to *Call of Duty: Ghosts*, and you need to learn to adapt to it.

Unlike unmanned aerial vehicles (UAVs) in past *Call of Duty* titles, the SAT COM is a ground-based killstreak. As a result, it is considerably harder to spot than a UAV that orbits in the sky on a fixed path.

This means that if you want to completely shut down the enemy satellite communications network, you need to hunt down and destroy enemy SAT COMs.

The SitRep perk is helpful for locating them, Off the Grid lets you avoid their coverage, Wiretap lets you use their SAT COM network, and armor-piercing ammunition lets you destroy SAT COMs more easily (even through walls, and particularly easy to do with SitRep).

IMS ⑤

PLANT A FOUR-SHOT EXPLOSIVE PROXIMITY MINE LAUNCHER.

▌ **Detection Range:** 256 units, 100 units above.

▌ **Blast Range**: Lethal to 178, Hitmarker to 200

The Intelligent Munitions System is a high-tech proximity mine—more specifically, four of them.

When an enemy is detected within a short distance, the IMS targets and launches one of its four explosive payloads at the target.

The IMS is almost always guaranteed to be lethal. The only way to avoid it is via extreme movement speed (say, already sprinting with Agility), or by getting behind hard cover very quickly.

The IMS makes for a perfect objective defense tool. Placed carefully, it can delay an attack, and it is very common to score multiple kills if you place it in a high-traffic pathway.

Avoid placing the IMS in plain view, and instead, tuck it just around a corner that an enemy is likely to pass. By the time they hear the beep from being detected, it's already too late for them to avoid the incoming explosive.

The IMS can be destroyed with regular gunfire or explosives, though it is fairly sturdy—standing out in the open firing at one is a bad idea.

Armor-piercing ammunition can destroy it quickly, a 9-Bang EMP can disable it, SitRep can detect it, and Blind Eye can prevent you from being targeted in the first place. Be careful in the last situation, though: if a

teammate near you doesn't have Blind Eye, the explosion can still kill you!

It is also possible to block IMS explosives with the Riot Shield.

GUARD DOG ⑤

CALL IN A FRIENDLY GUARD DOG TO PROTECT YOU.

Guard Dog brings man's best friend along to protect you. A combat-trained German shepherd, the Guard Dog follows you loyally around the map, attacks any enemies who get too close, and growls to warn you of any nearby threats. He also whines if you tactically defend one spot for too long. You camper.

The Guard Dog lasts until an enemy takes it out, and it faithfully returns to your side even if you are killed and respawn on the other side of the map. It may even pick up a few kills on its way to you!

Of the two five-point Assault streaks, the Guard Dog is the more offensive, but it also serves as mobile protection. It guards your back and ensures that anyone who takes you down instead of your dog is not long for the world (martyr dog!). Indeed, getting into combat with another player who has a Guard Dog at close range is a lose-lose proposition, as you can either shoot at the player and get taken down by the dog, or shoot the dog and get taken down by the player.

Whenever possible, engage the Guard Dog at long range, and when using it yourself, try to move around in hard cover and buildings. Your buddy is especially lethal in enclosed spaces and CQB situations.

SENTRY GUN ⑦

PLACE AN AUTOMATED SENTRY TURRET.

The Sentry Gun is a powerful area denial tool that you can use to lock down an area defensively. This is particularly useful in objective game modes when you know where the enemy is approaching from and what their target is.

The Sentry Gun can quickly take down targets exposed in the open, but it is possible to avoid its fire if there is a lot of hard cover in its line of sight. Try to place the Sentry Gun in an elevated position with a good clear line of sight to the area you are trying to protect. When seeking to avoid or destroy the Sentry Gun, you can disable it with a fully charged 9-Bang EMP blast, shoot it from out of its arc of fire (ideally with armor-piercing ammo), or avoid it entirely by making use of Blind Eye, hard cover, or alternate approach routes.

SPECIALIZED TRAINING   THE CAMPAIGN   MP INTRO & BASIC TRAINING   SQUADS   MP ARMORY   PERKS   **KILLSTREAKS**   MP MAPS   MP GAME MODES   SAFEGUARD   EXTINCTION   CLASSIFIED   ACHIEVEMENTS & TROPHIES

177

The Sentry Gun is only slightly vulnerable to the knife, and it takes three knife hits to down it. This is quick enough if you're unopposed, but it's rather slow if any enemies happen to be nearby and spot you attacking it.

Be careful when placing your Sentry Gun; don't expose yourself to needless risk to get it in place. Also, remember that you can move a Sentry Gun. If the area you place it in becomes irrelevant due to changing battlefield conditions, pick it up and move it to a new position.

A Sentry Gun paired with some defensive Lethal and Tactical equipment (or the IMS, Guard Dog, or Vulture) can also make for a very nasty hidey hole.

Set up shop inside a defensible position with your equipment and streaks protecting you, and pick off enemies while your friends guard your back.

TRINITY ROCKET ⓻

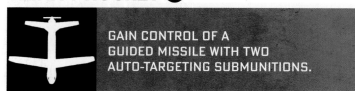

GAIN CONTROL OF A
GUIDED MISSILE WITH TWO
AUTO-TARGETING SUBMUNITIONS.

▌ **Missile Blast Radius:** All three lethal to 200

The Trinity Rocket gives you an aerial view of the battlefield from the mouth of a powerful guided missile. While in the air, you can press the Fire button to launch up to two automated submunitions that home in on a target automatically.

When your two secondary missiles are fired, you can then guide the final main rocket to any target of your choosing, activating the booster rockets to speed up your descent by pressing Fire.

The Trinity Rocket's first two missiles' auto-homing is fast and accurate, but it's not intelligent—if a target seeks cover in a building or under other hard cover, the missile impacts harmlessly on the roof or cover.

The final missile, however, can be guided carefully. This means that you can potentially send it through cracks in a roof, into doorways, or even into some windows.

Landing directly outside of a doorway also often serves to kill anyone inside, as the blast radius can catch them even if you didn't get the missile all the way inside.

With a little luck, you can land triple kills with the Trinity Rocket, and even scoring two is enough to instantly propel you on to a 9 streak. Consequently, the Trinity Rocket is definitely the more useful of the two 7 killstreaks in terms of propelling you toward a higher streak quickly.

The Trinity Rocket is also useful for clearing an area around a crucial objective. If you coordinate an offensive push with your team, you can bomb the area around the target just before they attack, clearing the way for your teammates to secure an area or an objective.

One last note: the final missile of the Trinity rocket inflicts very high damage. You can destroy a Vulture or Gryphon or deal serious damage to a Battle Hind or Helo Pilot, as well as any ground-based equipment.

VULTURE ⓽

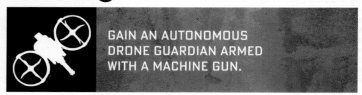

GAIN AN AUTONOMOUS
DRONE GUARDIAN ARMED
WITH A MACHINE GUN.

The Vulture killstreak calls in drone support for you, giving you 60 seconds of robotic escort. The Vulture flies in close proximity to you while active, and it flies to your position on the map should you get killed and respawn elsewhere.

The Vulture automatically targets and attacks enemies within range (about 1200 units), though there is a slight delay before it picks up and begins firing at adversaries.

This makes the Vulture more dangerous when it has a clear line of sight to attackers, but that also typically means you are in a more exposed position.

The Vulture is less effective in cramped quarters or areas with a lot of blocking hard cover, as enemies can duck in and out of view before the Vulture can take them out.

Note that the Vulture can still save your life by detecting an adversary even if it doesn't kill them immediately. Because it turns and highlights nearby foes, it can give you a chance to attack them yourself or retreat to a better position.

The Vulture is fairly vulnerable to small arms fire, particularly with armor-piercing ammunition, though it is dangerous to engage it at close to medium range, where it can retaliate effectively.

Blind Eye serves to protect you from Vulture targeting entirely.

BATTLE HIND 9

CALL IN AN ATTACK HELICOPTER.

The Battle Hind killstreak calls in an attack chopper to strafe the battlefield with cannons, rockets, and bombs for 60 seconds.

This helicopter is noticeably nastier than the Attack Helicopter killstreak from previous *Call of Duty* titles, and the enemy team cannot safely ignore it.

While active, the chopper sweeps the battlefield, seeking targets in the open and gunning them down. It also periodically fires rockets or bombs, often at enemies who think they are safe indoors!

The Battle Hind provides excellent cover for making an offensive push in an objective mode. Otherwise, it simply serves as good support for forcing the enemy team to keep their heads down under hard cover for the duration while it is active.

You can avoid the Battle Hind entirely with the Blind Eye perk (just don't stand near a teammate without it). You can take it down with the MAAWS or Air Superiority Support streaks. Another option is armor-piercing ammo, though only LMGs have enough ammunition to gun down a Battle Hind quickly.

One warning about shooting at the Battle Hind: it generally picks whatever targets it can spot easily in the open, but if you open fire on it, *you* become the priority target!

The Battle Hind is twice as durable as the Gryphon, sharing this durability with the Helo Pilot and Helo Scout.

SPECIALIZED TRAINING   THE CAMPAIGN   MP INTRO & BASIC TRAINING   SQUADS   MP ARMORY   PERKS   **KILLSTREAKS**   MP MAPS   MP GAME MODES   SAFEGUARD   EXTINCTION   CLASSIFIED   ACHIEVEMENTS & TROPHIES

179

GRYPHON

TAKE CONTROL OF A ROCKET ARMED FLYING DRONE.

■ **Blast Radius:** Lethal to 165

The Gryphon is a personally controlled attack drone armed with ground-targeted rockets.

For 60 seconds, you can rain down an infinite supply of rockets onto the battlefield. Control the Gryphon carefully and avoid exposing yourself to needless enemy fire, and you can deal a lot of damage while it is active.

The rockets from the Gryphon kill in a single shot as long as you hit near your target. While targeting with the Gryphon, you get a ground-painted red targeting reticle. Be aware that this also warns your targets that you're looking in their direction, so try to "sweep" the target over their heads and then down onto them to avoid giving any advance warning.

The Gryphon isn't the speediest drone, despite being airborne, so hug building ceilings and use large chunky cover to avoid enemies taking shots at you from a long distance. Because you turn somewhat slowly, getting caught in the open with a long-range gunner firing at you can easily end your run.

While you can fly, you cannot take the Gryphon too high above the battlefield, or you lose radio contact with the Gryphon and end the streak early. You get plenty of warning before this happens, as your screen starts to fuzz when you get too high. On most maps, you're safe to go over any terrain or buildings as long as they're not extremely tall.

Dealing with the Gryphon when you're on the other end of it is best done with an armor-piercing gun (ideally an LMG or an AR with extended mags), though you can take it down with the MAAWS, as well. Curiously, Air Support also targets the Gryphon, but only if it is out in the open.

You can also survive single rocket impacts with the Blast Shield perk, but a second shot is lethal. Otherwise, simply try to avoid it—if you're fast, you can get away from a Gryphon pilot if there is decent cover nearby. The Gryphon is particularly vulnerable when indoors or in other tight spaces, as its lack of maneuverability renders it vulnerable to massed small arms fire. The Gryphon is twice as durable as the Vulture.

MANIAC

GAIN AN ADVANCED SUIT OF MELEE COMBAT ARMOR.

The Maniac Juggernaut lets you call in the airdrop of a care package containing a specialized suit of Juggernaut armor. This armor grants you Juggernaut damage resistance, along with greatly increased movement speed. The catch? Your sole armaments are a combat knife and a throwing knife.

Maniac is built for players who love using the knife. If you're careful while using Maniac, you can go on long sprees with it. Play with a stick and move style (literally…), and don't needlessly expose yourself to enemy fire. You're tough, but you're not invincible.

Unlike other Juggernauts, the Maniac does not automatically appear on the minimap, so you can use your speed and stay stealthy. Move around the outskirts of the map, hide inside buildings, pick off isolated targets, and move on quickly.

Juggernaut Drops

For all types of Juggernaut armor, including Maniac, Assault, and Recon, be careful about using the drop zone marker. You don't want to call in the airdrop of your armor and have it taken by the enemy team! Call for cover, and place the marker in a safe location away from the frontlines. If you're very alert and you hear the enemy team calling in Juggernaut armor, you can often figure out where they are calling it based on the current state of the map. Check the backlines, away from where most of your teammates and the visible enemies are. Get there in time, and you may be able to score a sweet steal.

JUGGERNAUT 11

CALL IN A SUIT OF JUGGERNAUT ARMOR ARMED WITH AN ASSAULT MINIGUN.

Juggernaut calls in an airdrop of a specialized suit of assault armor equipped with a minigun.

The minigun has 250 rounds of ammunition, and even two shots can be lethal. It is a devastating weapon for mowing down enemy infantry.

The Juggernaut is slow and shows up on the enemy minimap, so try to call in the armor near where you need to engage the enemy.

Because of this speed issue, Juggernaut is a poor killstreak in modes that demand mobility, but it is an excellent killstreak for guarding a defensible area. Taking out an entrenched Juggernaut without specialized equipment is somewhere between difficult and suicidal.

Juggernaut is also harder to use on very large maps, so definitely pay attention to the mode and the map before you set this killstreak.

The trick to using Juggernaut well is ignoring the negatives (slow movement, visible on minimap) and forcing the enemy to engage you where your strengths are most evident (high-powered assault cannon, extreme durability).

The Juggernaut comes equipped with a single Canister Bomb—use it to flush out enemies around an objective or to clear a room you want to occupy.

Punching Juggernaut

Use a Panzerfaust to the face as an instant Juggernaut remedy.

HELO PILOT 12

GAIN CONTROL OF AN ATTACK HELICOPTER.

The Helo Pilot killstreak puts you in the pilot's chair of an armed attack helicopter equipped with unlimited high-powered machine gun rounds and two flares to protect from enemy anti-air.

For 60 seconds, you can rain down death on the battlefield. The chopper is quite durable against anything but dedicated anti-air weaponry or an LMG with armor-piercing rounds.

You have full movement control of the chopper, but keep in mind that you must aim the nose down to get a good line of fire on many positions on the map. This means you can't idle in one spot, and you need to make gunning passes that push the nose down as you move forward.

On some maps with larger multi-leveled buildings or elevated areas, you may be able to hover some distance away from them and shoot directly at exposed targets. On denser maps with a lot of cover, though, you often need to reposition the chopper to seek out and pick off targets on the ground.

You have unlimited ammunition for your cannons and they deal slight splash damage, so you don't have to be completely accurate. It's enough to get near your target to take them out.

Use the two flares you have to ward off a MAAWS attack or to save yourself from an Air Superiority attack if you fire the flares in time.

Dealing with an armor-piercing LMG is trickier—you have a short clock to identify where the fire is coming from and take out the gunner before you are shot down.

Typically, you have a short time on the field before any hostiles switch to a build to take you out, so make those seconds count.

If left unchecked, the Helo Pilot can be a devastating killstreak, especially on open maps with little cover. Don't let this happen to your team. If an enemy chopper goes up, switch builds and take it out swiftly, or suffer the consequences.

SPECIALIZED TRAINING   THE CAMPAIGN   MP INTRO & BASIC TRAINING   SQUADS   MP ARMORY   PERKS   **KILLSTREAKS**   MP MAPS   MP GAME MODES   SAFEGUARD   EXTINCTION   CLASSIFIED   ACHIEVEMENTS & TROPHIES

181

TAKE CONTROL OF AN ORBITAL ATTACK SATELLITE.

Large Rod: Lethal to 600

Small Rod: Lethal to 133, Hitmarker to 150

For 60 seconds, you are placed in control of a lethal orbital attack satellite armed with kinetic strikes and the ability to drop an Assault Juggernaut and up to three Assault Care Packages.

The Loki is a powerful, game-changing killstreak. If you can manage to earn the 15 kills required to take control of it, you can lay waste to the enemy team and support your own while doing so.

The Loki's four abilities are Large Kinetic Strike, Small Kinetic Strike, Assault Care Package Drop, and Assault Juggernaut Deployment.

While in control of the Loki, you are given a bird's eye view of the battlefield—a fringe benefit that lets you call out targets for your teammates and get them to flush out the enemy team when they inevitably run for cover.

Drop the care packages quickly. You have a long cooldown before you can drop an additional one, but as long as you get the first one out fairly quickly and then use the next two as soon as they are available, you can always get three Assault Care Packages on the battlefield.

These care packages always contain a random Assault killstreak, the same as the care packages awarded from completing Field Orders.

The Juggernaut deployment lets you drop an autonomous friendly assault Juggernaut on the battlefield, and while in the Loki, you can then order it to move to a specific position on the battlefield. After you exit the Loki, if the Juggernaut is still alive, it moves to escort you on the ground until it is killed.

Finally, and most impressively, the Loki can drop two different types of kinetic bombardment: one larger, one smaller.

The large strike is instantly lethal to enemy players near the impact point, whereas opponents at the outermost edges of the small strike's radius can survive. The large strike is more than double the size of the largest conventional explosives you have access to, while the small strike has a lethal range a little larger than that of a normal grenade.

The large strike reloads every seven seconds, and the small strike has a very fast reload at two seconds. Drop small rods on targets continuously, and drop a large rod whenever you spot a group. Once it is active, the only effective defense against the Loki is to get under hard cover and stay there until the skies are clear again. Unless someone on the other team has earned 25 straight kills against your team…

SUPPORT

Support streaks are used to support and enhance the capabilities of your team.

SAT COM ❹

GAIN SATELLITE COVERAGE ON YOUR MINIMAP. MULTIPLE SAT COMS ENHANCE THE EFFECT.

Identical in effect to the Assault SAT COM, the only difference is the increased killstreak cost. You need an extra kill, but your streak can't be interrupted, so you are guaranteed to get some SAT COMs on the field every match.

AMMO CRATE ❻

DEPLOY A WEAPON LOCKER FOR YOUR TEAM.

The Ammo Crate deploys an ammo resupply box that can refill any primary or secondary gun (not launchers). Additionally, it allows you to pick up a randomized new weapon from the box. You and your team can take up to four new weapons from the crate before it vanishes, or before 90 seconds expire.

Stepping on the crate provides you the equivalent of one Scavenger "pack," usually one magazine. This has a 10-second cooldown, so you can fully load up on ammo, but you'll be out of the match for a short time if you choose to do so. Grabbing one or two magazines at the most and moving out is usually a better use of your time.

Oh, and you have a very small chance of pulling a minigun out of the Ammo Crate…

The Ammo Crate is a generally useful Support streak, and since you often want to be running at least up through Ballistic Vests, there's no reason not to run the Ammo Crate on the way there!

The random weapons you get out of the crate can be just about anything, as it picks a random weapon type and gives it a random set of attachments. This definitely isn't guaranteed to mesh well with your perk setup, but if you need a replacement weapon and don't have time to wait for a full ammo supply, go ahead and grab one.

If your team is particularly coordinated, your team can grab three weapons from a crate and then leave the fourth. This lets you get the maximum ammo resupply time out of every crate because picking up the fourth causes the crate to disappear early.

BALLISTIC VESTS ❽

DEPLOY A PACK OF THREE BALLISTIC VESTS.

Ballistic Vests are a powerful defensive Support streak that gives you and your team the ability to equip up to three Ballistic Vests from one Ballistic Vest "drop." Once placed, you and any players on your team can approach the drop site and pick up a vest. When the last vest is taken (or 90 seconds pass), the vests vanish.

While equipped with a vest, you are bumped up from your baseline 100 health to a total of 250, making you massively more durable in a direct firefight.

Note that Ballistic Vests don't give perfect protection. They don't protect against headshots at all, explosions ignore them, and armor-piercing ammo does what it says, completely ignoring the extra vest armor.

Ballistic Vests also don't help with falling damage, and a knife stab is still instantly fatal. All that said, Ballistic Vests are still very powerful armor, and they can save your life multiple times before wearing off.

A team with one or two players running Ballistic Vests, one or two players running Hardline SAT COMs, and a few Specialists is a very potent combination.

SPECIALIZED TRAINING   THE CAMPAIGN   MP INTRO & BASIC TRAINING   SQUADS   MP ARMORY   PERKS   **KILLSTREAKS**   MP MAPS   MP GAME MODES   SAFEGUARD   EXTINCTION   CLASSIFIED   ACHIEVEMENTS & TROPHIES

183

MAAWS 9

GAIN A TWO-SHOT GUIDED ANTI-AIR LAUNCHER.

The MAAWS is a two-shot guided anti-air launcher that can lock on to any enemy aerial killstreak threats.

Because none of the default launchers is guided, this is your only option for a surefire hit on an enemy Battle Hind, Gryphon, or other nasty offensive killstreak. You can even use it on a Sentry Gun if you want.

Keep in mind that while you can lock on to a Helo Pilot, an alert enemy will use their flares to throw off both of your shots. You may want to save the shots for easier targets.

The MAAWS is laser-guided until it achieves a final lock on an enemy killstreak, but this also means you can use it as a highly accurate anti-infantry launcher if desired!

The MAAWS fires two guided missiles with each shot, which arc out and then converge on their final target. For this reason, give yourself a bit of distance if you're trying to hit an enemy player on the ground.

Also, because each MAAWS shot is two projectiles, MAAWS can disable an enemy Trophy System in a single shot.

NIGHT OWL 10

DEPLOY AN AUTONOMOUS DEFENSIVE SCOUT DRONE.

The Night Owl is a defensive drone that hovers nearby for 60 seconds, providing periodic radar sweeps that extend 700 units every two seconds, and most importantly, destroying all incoming projectiles, just like a Trophy System.

The Night Owl is a very useful defensive Support streak, but its value is also related to how heavily the enemy team is employing Lethal and Tactical grenades. If they are using them heavily, the Night Owl can provide near-immunity while defending an objective area.

The Night Owl radar sweep is also useful for detecting opponents on both offense and defense, though be aware that the Night Owl itself can give away your position occasionally (a hovering drone isn't the stealthiest companion).

The Night Owl can be useful either on defense (to hold down an area), or on offense (to attack a defended position and locate lurking enemies). Be sure to relay enemy positions when you spot them on the minimap so your team gets the full benefit of the Night Owl's intelligence.

SUPPORT SQUADMATE 11

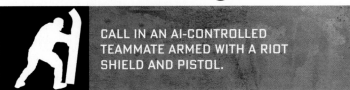

CALL IN AN AI-CONTROLLED TEAMMATE ARMED WITH A RIOT SHIELD AND PISTOL.

Support Squadmate gives you an AI-controlled battle buddy to escort you around the battlefield.

The squadmate tries his best to stay out in front of you and give enemies a ready target to fire at, but keep in mind that he is not especially sturdy. Alert enemies can quickly flank his Riot Shield and gun him down.

The squadmate also occasionally attacks enemies by either bashing close foes or pulling out his sidearm and firing at them. You may even see him pick up an enemy weapon if he lasts long enough!

The squadmate can serve as a more defensive alternative to the Guard Dog when you're running Support streaks, but just be aware of the cost involved in taking the squadmate. It takes a lot of kills to earn a companion who can die fairly easily.

GROUND JAMMER 12

EMPS THE ENEMY TEAM, DISABLING ALL AUTOMATED ENEMY KILLSTREAKS AND EQUIPMENT.

Ground Jammer is a powerful Support streak that shuts down the enemy team's electronic support, disabling their minimaps and destroying all ground equipment and drone support (including the Vulture and Night Owl).

This takes out enemy SAT COMs, the Ammo Crate, Sentry Gun, IEDs, Motion Sensors, C4, and other devices. It does not affect aerial or controlled streaks like the Gryphon or Helo Pilot.

Disabling your opponent's minimaps also gives your team a window while the jammer is active to drive home an offensive push or disrupt an enemy push.

While the Ground Jammer is powerful, it takes a fair number of kills to reach it. You may want to save it rather than firing it off instantly in case the other team calls in any nasty support against your team, or if you're coordinating a team attack.

Oh, and if you get especially lucky, you might just kill the owner of a C4 charge or IED if they happen to be standing near the jammer when you pop it.

AIR SUPERIORITY 12

CALLS IN AN A-10 WARTHOG SWEEP TO ELIMINATE ENEMY AIR SUPPORT.

Air Superiority calls in a friendly CAS sweep that strafes the battlefield twice to eliminate all enemy air support. This takes out Battle Hinds, Gryphons in the open, potentially the Helo Pilot, care package choppers, and the Helo Scout.

Note that an alert Helo Pilot can avoid Air Superiority if they both have flares intact and are very alert.

Given Air Superiority's kill cost and the limited number of targets it works against, this isn't a Support streak you should take regularly, unless you have strong reason to suspect that the enemy team is good enough to call in a lot of air support.

You can accomplish much of the same work with a class using Blind Eye and armor-piercing rounds on an LMG, and the MAAWS also offers a cheaper support option to accomplish a similar goal.

With that said, Air Superiority does do its job well—if the sky is full of enemy support for any reason, it can clear the field nicely.

HELO SCOUT 13

HOP INTO THE SNIPER SEAT IN A HOVERING SUPPORT HELICOPTER.

Helo Scout arms you with a high-powered, low-recoil sniper rifle and puts you in direct control of a hovering helicopter that you can guide around the battlefield airspace to locate and pick off targets below.

The Helo Scout lasts for 45 seconds, and while it is in the air, you can turn the chopper or move it around the map as needed to locate enemy targets.

There are some caveats, though. First off, you are exposed in the gunner seat of the chopper. Alert enemies can and will fire at you directly, and you don't have any special resistance while you are in the chopper.

Additionally, opponents can target and destroy the chopper itself, though it is far sturdier than you, of course.

If you do take light fire, quickly rotate the chopper to break the enemies' line of sight to you, and reposition the chopper to get a different angle of attack.

On top of the ability to simply snipe targets below, the Helo Scout is also a useful reconnaissance tool. While in the air, you can call out targets for your teammates, providing valuable information on enemy positions and movements.

If the enemy calls in a Helo Scout on your team, all you need to do take it down quickly is get your teammates to focus fire on the gunner. A skilled Helo Scout pilot can dodge one or two lazy attempts to take them out, but a whole team gunning for them is all but impossible to avoid.

ORACLE 14

ACTIVATE A SENSOR NETWORK TO DETECT AND OUTLINE THE ENTIRE ENEMY TEAM.

The Oracle network is a very powerful Support streak that periodically pulses a map-wide detection sweep on the enemy team.

Every 10 seconds, the enemy team is highlighted for 1.5 seconds. This outline is visible through walls. This detection works for you and your entire team, so for the 90-second duration of the Oracle, you have fantastic intelligence on enemy positions.

This is a very strong Support streak, and it's definitely one that justifies aiming for a higher kill score. Triggering it even once can tip the balance of a match in your team's favor if it is used well while active.

Because the actual outline duration is very short, you can get maximum use out of the sensor pulse by moving to the edge of a map and facing inward. This gives you the maximum possible chance of spotting enemies, particularly if you aim away from your team's position and toward objectives in hostile territory.

The Oracle can help you (or save you) in CQB situations, as well, but the duration between pings and the short highlight does make it easy to miss enemies who are very near you but on a different elevation, or on your flanks or rear.

JUGGERNAUT RECON 14

CALL DOWN A SUIT OF JUGGERNAUT RECON ARMOR.

This Support streak gives you access to a care package marker that calls in a suit of Juggernaut Recon armor.

This is a defensive and support suit, equipped with a Riot Shield that has the radar attachment, a secondary Magnum, and the Scavenger perk.

You also get one Smoke grenade, which can be useful for forcibly securing a key objective area.

Juggernaut Recon armor is slow-moving, and it does show up on the enemy minimap. However, it has the same damage resistance as the other suits of Juggernaut armor, and with smart use of your Riot Shield, you can be very difficult to kill if you play well.

Be sure to take maximum advantage of your radar-equipped Riot Shield. While it is out, you can advise your teammates of enemy positions near you, and block for them while they take down any hostiles.

If you are alone, you can still use the Riot Shield just as you would normally against a single target, quickly switching to your Magnum to down your opponent when they reload or attempt to disengage.

Juggernaut Recon is particularly useful in objective game modes, as long as you call in the armor drop fairly close to the area you want to reach (remember, you're slow moving!). If you work with your teammates, you can lock down an area very effectively, especially if any of them is running area denial loadouts or killstreaks.

ODIN 16

TAKE CONTROL OF AN ORBITAL SUPPORT SATELLITE.

The Odin is the Loki's support twin. For 60 seconds, you are given control of an orbital support satellite that can mark and EMP hostile targets, drop smoke anywhere on the battlefield, call in a Recon Juggernaut, and deploy up to three Support Care Packages.

While not as overtly destructive as the Loki, the Odin is still a very powerful Support streak, and proper use can turn the match in your team's favor.

The Odin's four abilities are Mark Target, Smoke, Juggernaut, and Airdrop.

While controlling the Odin, just like the Loki, you are given a top-down bird's eye view of the map. This allows you to call enemy positions while you are marking them and smoking areas.

The target mark is a ground-targeted EMP pulse that outlines enemy players in the same manner as a Motion Sensor or Oracle for three seconds, and EMPs their minimap for 10 seconds. The mark has a quick four-second refresh, so you can either keep one player continuously marked, or chain EMPs on a few to disrupt their minimaps if they are near each other.

Marking targets should be your default usage for the Odin. Sweep around the map, call out enemy positions, and mark as many as possible to give your team a serious combat edge. In addition, you can call down a smoke drop that impacts just like a Smoke grenade and has a quick seven-second refresh. This is very useful for creating cover over objectives, or in open areas that your team needs to cross.

Be careful about smoking enemy positions, as this can make it just as hard for your teammates to shoot them as it does for the opponents to see out. Careful use of smoke can give your team a mobility edge by creating areas of safe visual cover, which aids in securing objectives.

The Juggernaut drop allows you to call in an AI-controlled Juggernaut Recon buddy. Once placed, you can order him around the map as long as you are in the Odin.

Unlike the Loki's Assault Juggernaut, try to keep the Recon Jug back in safe territory. If he's still alive when you come out of the Odin, he'll link up with you on the ground, and having a Recon Juggernaut following you is useful.

Plus, the Recon Juggernaut is considerably less dangerous on his own against the enemy team, so it's best to save him as a distraction.

Finally, you can call in up to three Support Care Packages. Be sure to drop these in friendly territory. Each crate contains a random Support streak, all of which can give your team an edge.

Because Odin is much easier to acquire than the Loki, you can expect to see it more frequently in matches, both on your team and the enemy's team. There isn't anything you can do to disrupt an enemy Odin (short of a KEM strike), but try to get maximum benefit out of every friendly one. A skilled Odin controller can give his or her team a very strong informational edge, on top of the other support benefits.

The Odin, the Oracle, and Ground Jammer are some of the stronger arguments for running high Support streaks rather than simply looping low-cost ones. These have enough of a battlefield impact to be worth the extra time it takes to acquire them.

SPECIALIST

Specialist is a unique type of killstreak that rewards you with perks instead of attack helicopters or support satellites.

Specialist lets you choose a set of three perks to unlock with kills. Once all three are unlocked and you earn two more kills, you unlock a Specialist bonus, instantly granting you access to an additional eight points' worth of perks.

PERK UNLOCKS	KILL REQUIREMENT
First Perk	Perk cost in kills +1
Second Perk	Perk cost + 2 + base cost of first perk
Third Perk	Perk cost + 3 + base cost of first and second perks.
Specialist Bonus	Third perk total +2 more kills

The kill cost of the first three perks increases based on the point cost of the chosen perks.

That is, if you choose Incog, ICU, and Focus as your three initial perks, you would acquire them at 4, 7, and 10 kills, with your Specialist bonus unlocking at 12 kills.

By choosing all cheap, one-point perks, you can unlock your Specialist bonus as quickly as possible, but you must weigh the greater ease of earning your bonus against the reduced power of the perks you are acquiring as base kill bonuses.

Specialist is a very selfish sort of killstreak selection. It is focused entirely on improving your performance, and your team does not benefit from its usage in the same way that Assault or Support streaks aid your team.

The upshot here is that if you are a skilled player, comfortable with chaining solid streaks regularly, you can unlock your additional perks very frequently, and a fully loaded Specialist build on top of a strong starting perk setup makes you very dangerous on the battlefield.

It is possible to unlock nearly all of the combat superiority of stealth perks by making use of Specialist, or by adding powerful but normally excessively expensive perks like Deadeye as a "capper" perk to your build.

Always remember that as strong as Specialist is, you're still vulnerable to just a few bullets or an errant explosion or killstreak. Consistently nailing your streaks is important for Specialist to stack up against builds using Assault or Support.

Back Me Up

If you can get a teammate to run Ballistic Vests, this greatly aids your ability to survive and unlock your Specialist bonus every round.

Hardline does affect Specialist unlocks, though the overall impact is fairly minor.

One last note: if you are actually planning on going after the 25 kill reward, a carefully selected Specialist loadout is the way to do it.

SPECIALIZED TRAINING   THE CAMPAIGN   MP INTRO & BASIC TRAINING   SQUADS   MP ARMORY   PERKS   KILLSTREAKS   MP MAPS   MP GAME MODES   SAFEGUARD   EXTINCTION   CLASSIFIED   ACHIEVEMENTS & TROPHIES

187

MULTIPLAYER MAPS

Welcome to our tactical maps chapter. These highly detailed renderings of the levels have been drawn by hand, using the in-game architecture and textures as the basis to give you a clear and clean view of every map in the game

MAP TYPES

We have created four different special map types to give you a different perspective on each of the levels in multiplayer:

1. CLEAN MAP

In previous *Call of Duty* guides, the large number of callout markers and icons that we placed onto the maps often obscured important architecture or terrain. In this guide, the first view of each map is free of these markers. Our intent is provide a clear view of the entire level, without anything placed on top that might otherwise block the map's features. We've enlarged these views as much as the page dimensions will allow.

Also, note that the background of each clean map divides the level into four numbered sectors. These sector numbers can serve as convenient shorthand when discussing regions or quadrants with your teammates.

2. RANGEFINDER MAP

The second map view is a simple gridded map. This map has no other markings on it, but is gridded in 500-unit increments for distance/range.

You can use these range markings with *any* range unit references anywhere in the multiplayer portion of this guide. All of the weapon ranges, explosion ranges, throwing and hearing distances, running distances—all of these measurements correspond to these map grids.

Use these maps to help you decide ideal loadouts and weapons to take into each map and mode.

Along the bottom of each gridded map, you'll see colored bars marked with weapon class abbreviations. These bars serve as a quick-reference tool to judge the *average* effective range for each of the following weapon classes:

| **SG** = Shotgun | **AR** = Assault Rifle | **MARK** = Marksman Rifle |
| **SMG** = Submachine Gun | **LMG** = Light Machinegun | |

These quick "cheat" scales give you average ranges for the weapon classes, but be sure to check the armory for exact numbers on a given weapon.

Sniper Rifles do not need a scale. Excepting the VKS, they all deal full damage at *any* range. Even the VKS's range is longer than other weapons and can still kill in one headshot at ultra-long distances.

Pistols have very similar optimal ranges to Shotguns.

With knowledge of how the weapons perform on every level at any given distance, you can make informed decisions about how to kit-out your squad for combat in CQB, medium-, or long-range combat.

3. OBJECTIVE MAP

The third map is marked with the locations of MP game mode objectives. This has all of the objective locations for all of the various objective-based game modes: Domination points, Grind targets, Blitz points, Search & Destroy and Search & Rescue bomb locations, and so on.

Use this map to identify routes through the levels, key hotspot areas where conflict is likely to erupt, and alternate flanking paths that are not near an objective.

4. TACTICAL MAP

Finally, the last map view is marked with two types of callouts to draw your attention to key features of each level.

The first type is an overwatch indicator, indicated by the letter "O" inside a blue circle. These mark places on the map where you have good, clear line of sight and preferably some hard cover to hide behind. These markers include an arrow pointing in the direction of the line of sight.

The second callout marker is a jump point, represented by the letter "J" inside a red circle. These mark areas where you can climb, jump, or mantle up from one place to another.

Naturally, there are *many* other areas on every level where you can set up in overwatch positions, and tons of other places where you can trick-jump and climb from one spot to another—the map markers in this guide are simply meant to give you a head start on learning the maps.

RANGES

Following is a collection of useful distances that you can use with the Rangefinder maps in this guide. Keep in mind that, while distances for weapons are quite exact, ranges for sprinting, hearing, and throwing can be a little fuzzier depending on terrain, ambient noise, throwing arc, and so on.

Sprint Distance

BASE SPRINT	1100 Units

MOVEMENT SPEED	WEAPONS
105%	Combat Knife (also doubles sprint distance)
100%	Pistols, Shotguns, SMGs
95%	Kastet
90%	Assault Rifles, Marksman Rifles, Chain SAW LMG, USR Sniper Rifle, MK32
85%	VKS and L115 Sniper Rifles
80%	Other LMGs, Lynx Sniper Rifle, Riot Shield, Panzerfaust, MAAWS

Hearing Ranges

HEARING RANGE	DISTANCE
Base	1000 Units
With Amplify	2000 Units
Against Dead Silence	500 Units

Throwing Distances

THROWN ITEM	RANGE	STRONG-ARM
C4, IED, Canister Bomb	500 Units	750 Units
Grenade, Semtex, Smoke, 9-Bang, Concussion	1200 Units	1800 Units

Explosion Ranges

The Claymore (only appearing in Infected) shares the same damage profile with C4, but it only fires in a 60-degree arc from the front of the Claymore; it's not omnidirectional.

Lethal Explosives

EXPLOSIVE	RADIUS	LETHAL TO
C4	256 Units	171 Units
Canister Bomb	256 Units	171 Units
Frag	256 Units	102 Units
Semtex	256 Units	102 Units
IED	256 Units	96 Units

Tactical Explosives

Thermobaric grenades deal 50 damage anywhere inside their radius.

EXPLOSIVE	RADIUS
9-Bang	800 Units
Concussion	512 Units
Thermobaric	400 Units

CHASM

A complex, multi-layered map set in a ruined, bombed-out cityscape. Chasm has a great many broken lines of sight and changes in elevation, as well as twisting routes in and through the wreckage.

Chasm is a large and intricate map. It can take a few games to get your bearings, but there are essentially several large 'chunks' of terrain to fight over: the center, an underground railway area, and two different elevated areas in the wreckage of nearby office buildings.

Chasm can be a comfortable map for anything from close-range engagements to long-range firefights, depending on the mode you're playing and how carefully you choose your battles. Use the alternate routes through the map if you find your progress blocked on one side by heavy enemy resistance.

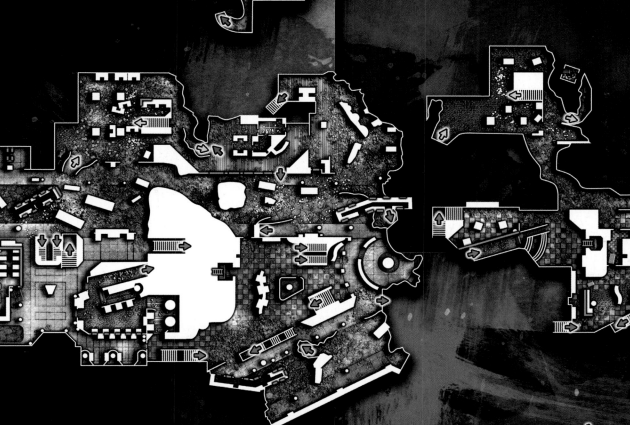

[[sector.3.◇.4.sector]]

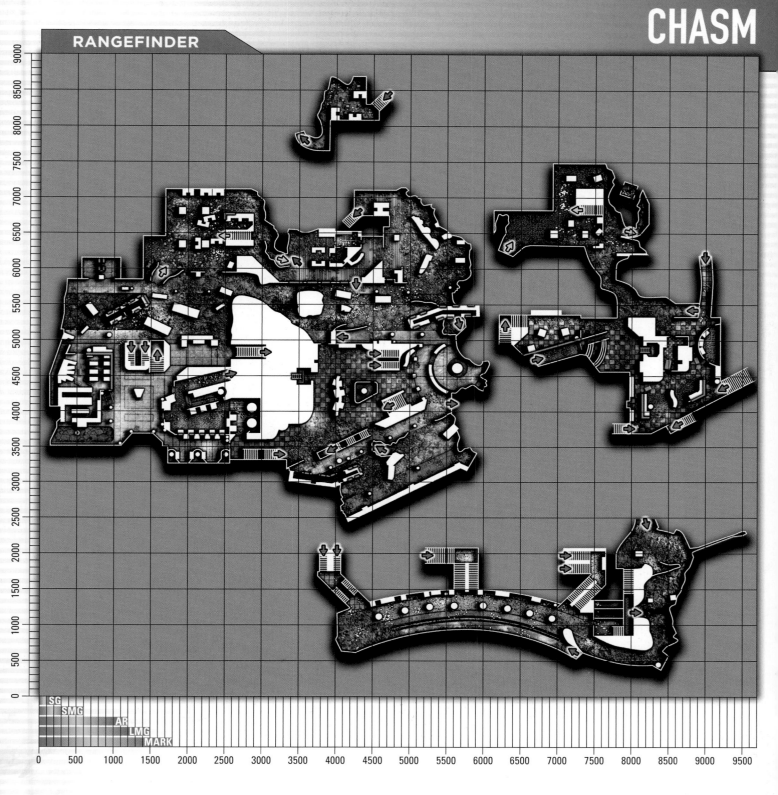

The colored bars marked with weapon class abbreviations serve as a quick-reference tool to judge the *average* effective range for each of the following weapon classes:

SG = Shotgun   **AR** = Assault Rifle   **MARK** = Marksman Rifle

SMG = Submachine Gun   **LMG** = Light Machinegun

SPECIALIZED TRAINING   THE CAMPAIGN   MP INTRO & BASIC TRAINING   SQUADS   MP ARMORY   PERKS   KILLSTREAKS   **MP MAPS**   MP GAME MODES   SAFEGUARD   EXTINCTION   CLASSIFIED   ACHIEVEMENTS & TROPHIES

193

CHASM

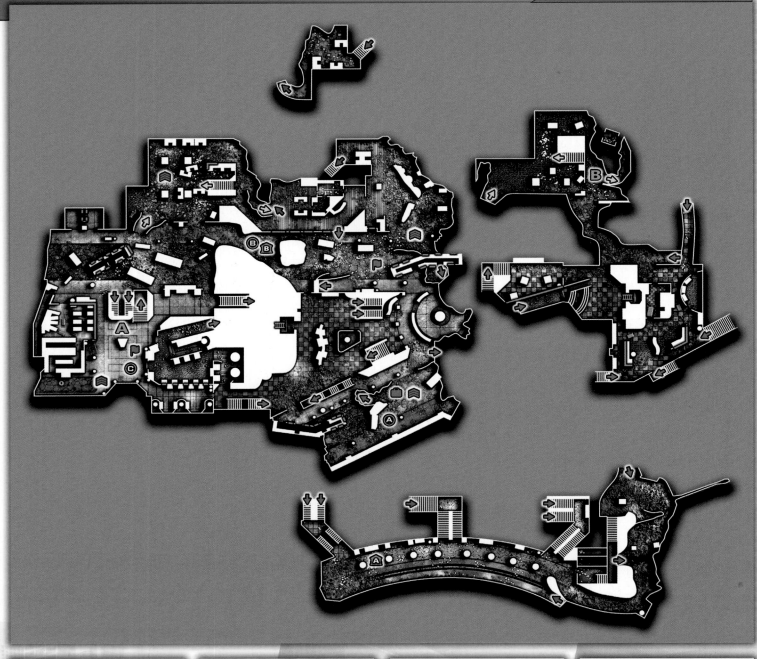

⬜	**DYNAMIC ELEMENT**	🔽🔽	**SPAWN POINT**	⬭	**WINDOW**	💼	**BOMB**
⬜	**OVER/UNDERPASS**	⚑⚑	**BLITZ GOAL**	🪜	**LADDER**	⬆⬆ ⬆⬆	**CONNECT TO SAME-COLORED ARROWS ON MULTI-LEVEL AREAS**
Ⓐ	**CAPTURE POINT**	🅰	**PLANT SITE**	🅰	**BANK**		

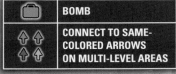

TACTICAL

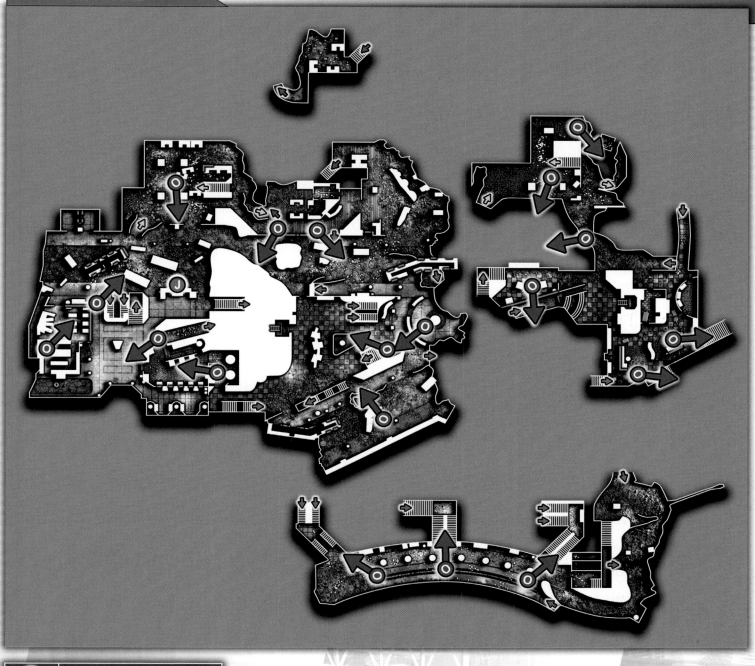

	JUMP SPOT
	OVERWATCH VANTAGE POINT
	CONNECT TO SAME-COLORED ARROWS ON MULTI-LEVEL AREAS

Roof Level

KP Karpark Parking

SPECIALIZED TRAINING   THE CAMPAIGN   MP INTRO & BASIC TRAINING   SQUADS   MP ARMORY   PERKS   KILLSTREAKS   **MP MAPS**   MP GAME MODES   SAFEGUARD   EXTINCTION   CLASSIFIED   ACHIEVEMENTS & TROPHIES

195

FLOODED

This level features a flooded mall and parking garage. A ruined city street with flood waters still raging divides the center of the map.

There are several engagement areas on Flooded: in the offices and shops on two different levels, and on two floors of the parking garage.

Be very careful traversing the center of the level. The footing is unstable and you are exposed to fire from all areas of the map.

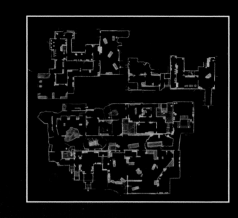

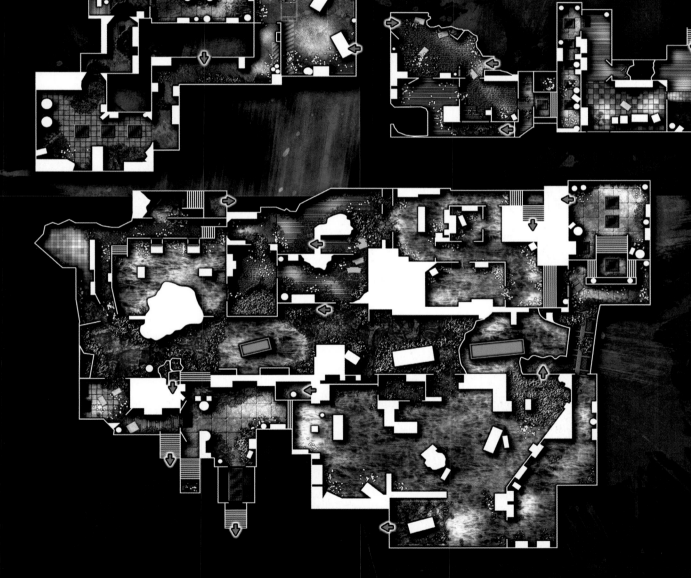

[sector.3.◇.4.sector]

SG												
	SMG											
		AR										
		LMG										
		MARK										

The colored bars marked with weapon class abbreviations serve as a quick-reference tool to judge the *average* effective range for each of the following weapon classes:

SG = Shotgun   **AR** = Assault Rifle   **MARK** = Marksman Rifle

SMG = Submachine Gun   **LMG** = Light Machinegun

SPECIALIZED TRAINING   THE CAMPAIGN   MP INTRO & BASIC TRAINING   SQUADS   MP ARMORY   PERKS   KILLSTREAKS   **MP MAPS**   MP GAME MODES   SAFEGUARD   EXTINCTION   CLASSIFIED   ACHIEVEMENTS & TROPHIES

199

FLOODED

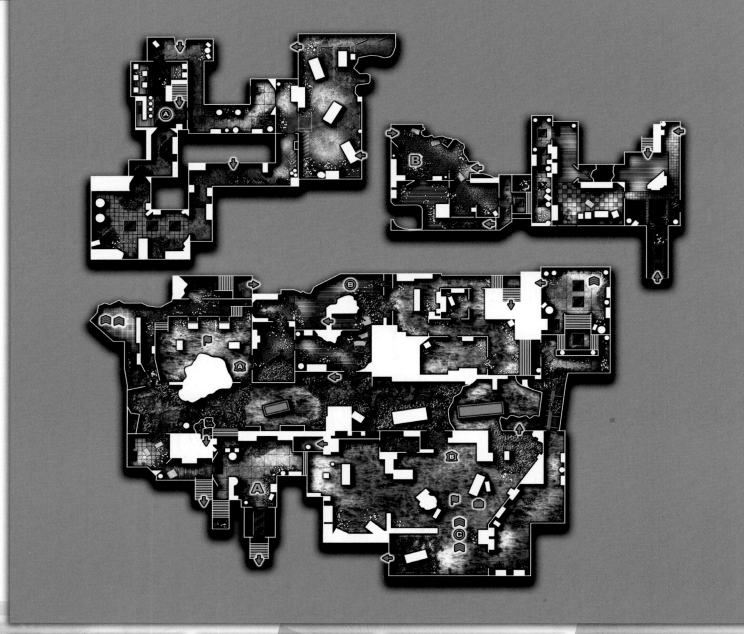

	DYNAMIC ELEMENT			SPAWN POINT			WINDOW			BOMB
	OVER/UNDERPASS			BLITZ GOAL			LADDER			CONNECT TO SAME-COLORED ARROWS ON MULTI-LEVEL AREAS
	CAPTURE POINT			PLANT SITE			BANK			

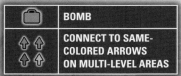

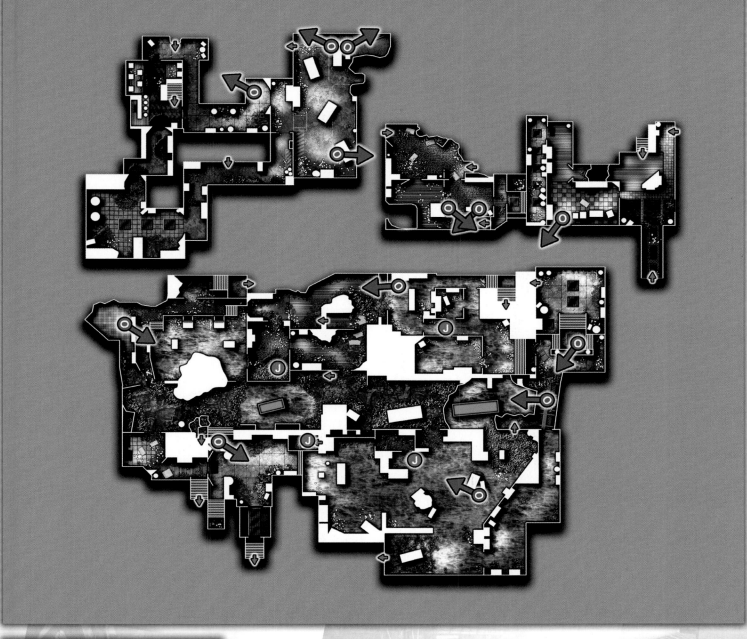

Ⓙ	**JUMP SPOT**
⊙→	**OVERWATCH VANTAGE POINT**
⬆⬆ ⬆⬆	**CONNECT TO SAME-COLORED ARROWS ON MULTI-LEVEL AREAS**

SPECIALIZED TRAINING   THE CAMPAIGN   MP INTRO & BASIC TRAINING   SQUADS   MP ARMORY   PERKS   KILLSTREAKS   **MP MAPS**   MP GAME MODES   SAFEGUARD   EXTINCTION   CLASSIFIED   ACHIEVEMENTS & TROPHIES

201

FREIGHT

Freight is an abandoned snowy rail yard. This is a long, stretched-out map with lots of interior warehouse fighting and a sharp divide down the middle where the tracks cross the map.

Many of the warehouses have multiple floors, so expect enemies above you if you're out in the open. Sweeping and controlling the warehouses is important for maintaining line of sight on the center of the map.

CQB builds can engage effectively at short range and exploit the various doors that can be opened and closed. They can give you early warning to someone trying to sneak into your personal space.

[sector.3.◇.4.sector]

203

5500
5000
4500
4000
3500
3000
2500
2000
1500
1000
500
0

SG
SMG
AR
LMG
MARK

0   500   1000   1500   2000   2500   3000   3500   4000   4500   5000   5500   6000

The colored bars marked with weapon class abbreviations serve as a quick-reference tool to judge the *average* effective range for each of the following weapon classes:

SG = Shotgun **AR** = Assault Rifle **MARK** = Marksman Rifle

SMG = Submachine Gun **LMG** = Light Machinegun

SPECIALIZED TRAINING   THE CAMPAIGN   MP INTRO & BASIC TRAINING   SQUADS   MP ARMORY   PERKS   KILLSTREAKS   **MP MAPS**   MP GAME MODES   SAFEGUARD   EXTINCTION   CLASSIFIED   ACHIEVEMENTS & TROPHIES

205

FREIGHT

	DYNAMIC ELEMENT			SPAWN POINT			WINDOW			BOMB
	OVER/UNDERPASS			BLITZ GOAL			LADDER			CONNECT TO SAME-COLORED ARROWS ON MULTI-LEVEL AREAS
Ⓐ	CAPTURE POINT		Ⓐ	PLANT SITE		Ⓐ	BANK			

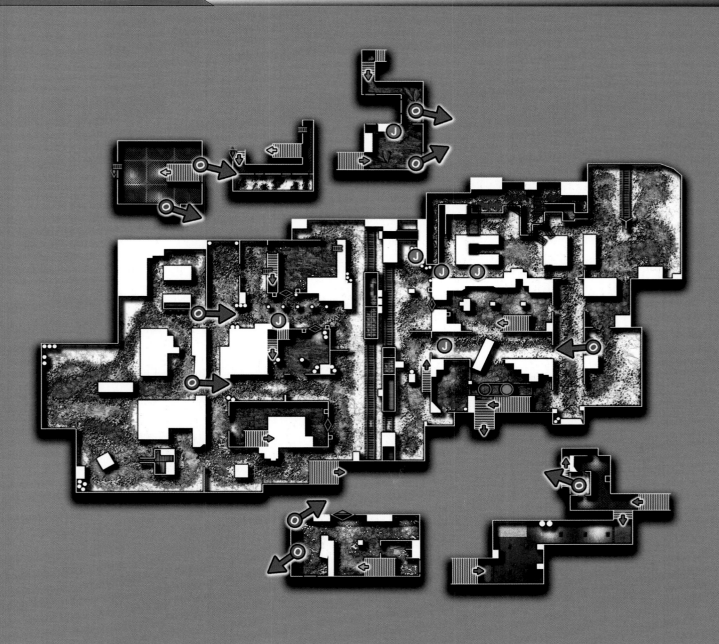

J	JUMP SPOT
O→	OVERWATCH VANTAGE POINT
⇧⇧ ⇧⇧	CONNECT TO SAME-COLORED ARROWS ON MULTI-LEVEL AREAS

SPECIALIZED TRAINING   THE CAMPAIGN   MP INTRO & BASIC TRAINING   SQUADS   MP ARMORY   PERKS   KILLSTREAKS   **MP MAPS**   MP GAME MODES   SAFEGUARD   EXTINCTION   CLASSIFIED   ACHIEVEMENTS & TROPHIES

207

OCTANE

A dusty, abandoned town, Octane is a mix of urban combat in the buildings around the edge of the map, and open firefights in the center street and back alleys.

You can play a distance game by sticking to the buildings' second floors and picking off enemies at range, but watch your back; there's more than one way to cross the street with minimum exposure.

Mobile builds can get around this level quickly, as it is not extremely large. Fast-moving CQB builds can do some work in the building interiors.

Stay away from the center street. A "free" Support Care Package is hidden in the middle of the map. One can reach it via breaching charge or blowing open the doors on the container mid-map. But the area is exposed to fire from all parts of the level. Go for it at your own risk, and avoid the middle unless you have a pressing reason to be there.

In addition to the care package container, it's possible to knock down the gas station by blowing the pumps below it. Several of the rooftop walls can be breached, creating new lines of sight from the southwestern building's second floor.

4500
4000
3500
3000
2500
2000
1500
1000
500
0

SG
SMG
AR
LMG
MARK

0   500   1000   1500   2000   2500   3000   3500   4000   4500   5000

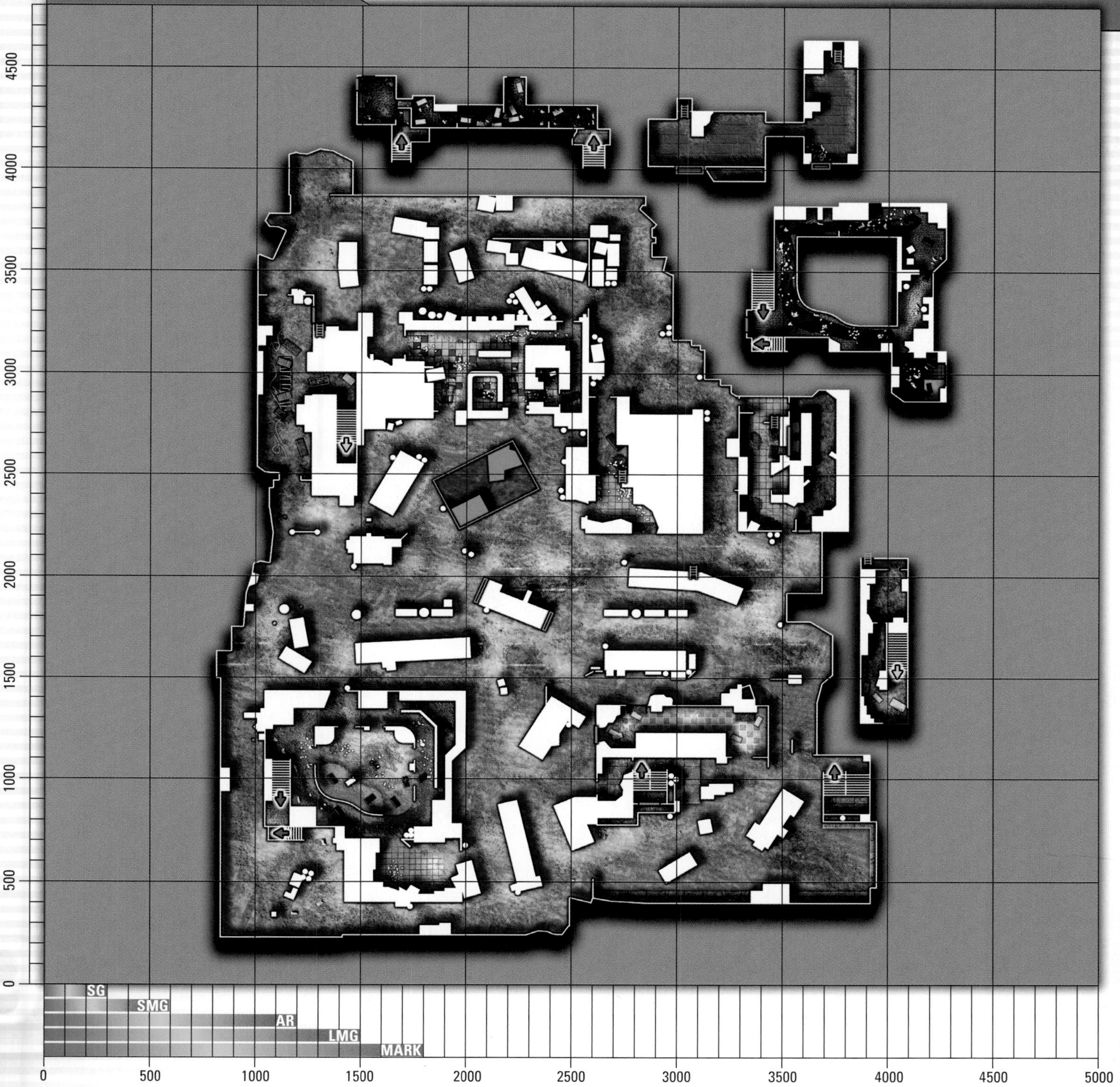

The colored bars marked with weapon class abbreviations serve as a quick-reference tool to judge the *average* effective range for each of the following weapon classes:

SG = Shotgun

SMG = Submachine Gun

AR = Assault Rifle

LMG = Light Machinegun

MARK = Marksman Rifle

SPECIALIZED TRAINING   THE CAMPAIGN   MP INTRO & BASIC TRAINING   SQUADS   MP ARMORY   PERKS   KILLSTREAKS   **MP MAPS**   MP GAME MODES   SAFEGUARD   EXTINCTION   CLASSIFIED   ACHIEVEMENTS & TROPHIES

211

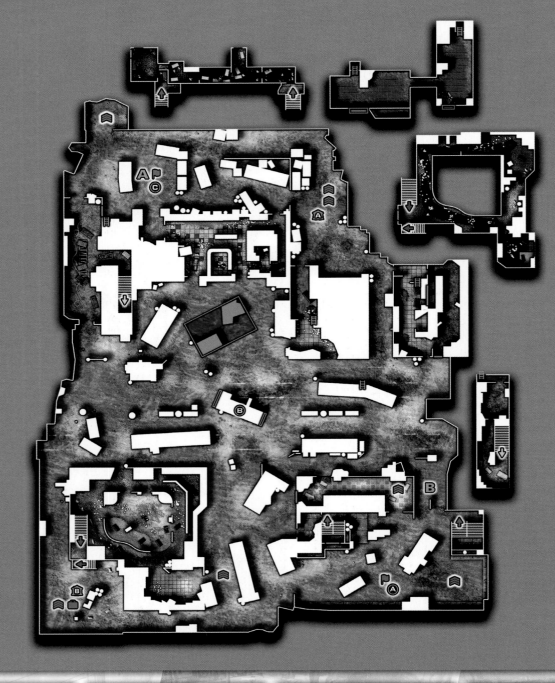

	DYNAMIC ELEMENT		SPAWN POINT		WINDOW		BOMB
	OVER/UNDERPASS		BLITZ GOAL		LADDER		CONNECT TO SAME-COLORED ARROWS
Ⓐ	CAPTURE POINT	Ⓐ	PLANT SITE	Ⓐ	BANK		ON MULTI-LEVEL AREAS

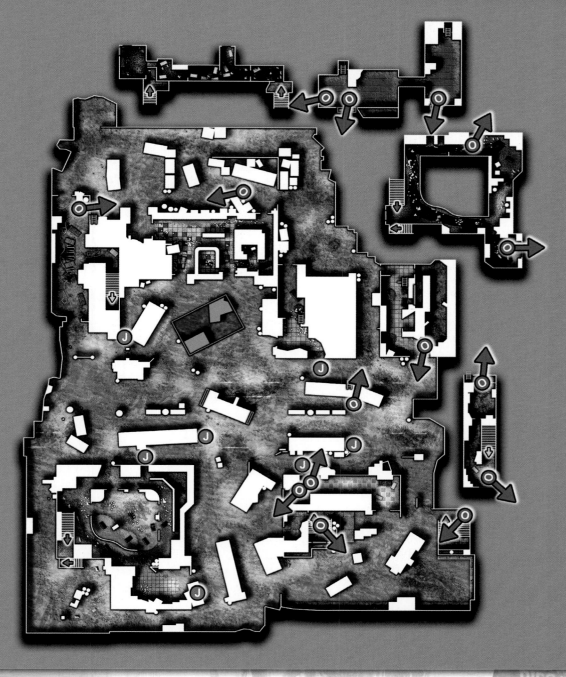

(J)	**JUMP SPOT**
(⊙→)	**OVERWATCH VANTAGE POINT**
⇧ ⇧ ⇧ ⇧	**CONNECT TO SAME-COLORED ARROWS ON MULTI-LEVEL AREAS**

SPECIALIZED TRAINING   THE CAMPAIGN   MP INTRO & BASIC TRAINING   SQUADS   MP ARMORY   PERKS   KILLSTREAKS   **MP MAPS**   MP GAME MODES   SAFEGUARD   EXTINCTION   CLASSIFIED   ACHIEVEMENTS & TROPHIES

213

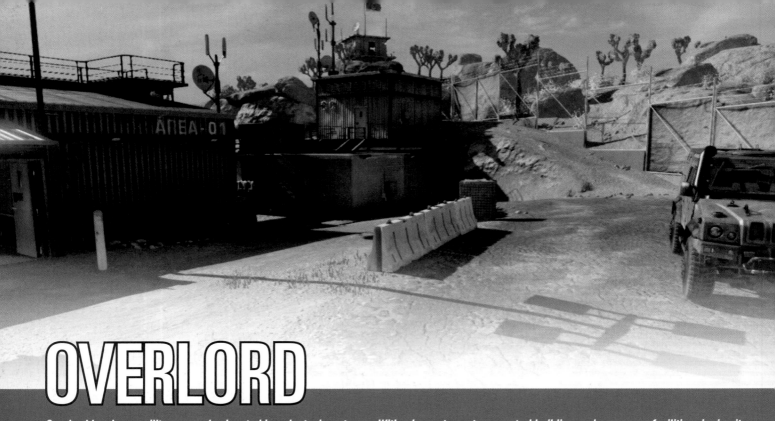

OVERLORD

Overlord is a large military complex located in a dusty desert area. With a large, two-story, central building and numerous facilities ringing it around the map's edges, this is a sizable map with mixed engagement areas.

Given the size of the level, long-range builds work well here, but it is possible to cross the level with minimal exposure if you're careful.

The central building is very dangerous. There are multiple entrances to the first and second floor, and the shutter doors can be opened and closed to block access and warn of enemies using them.

Objective fights over the central building are especially vicious. Bring a good CQB build or stay out of it as much as possible.

You can stalk the map's outer ring, using it either for traversal or simply to hunt down and pick off enemies who are focused on the conflict in the middle. Between the different dusty pathways and the various accessible building rooftops, there's a lot of variance in elevation. Keep an eye open for snipers and long-range shooters up high.

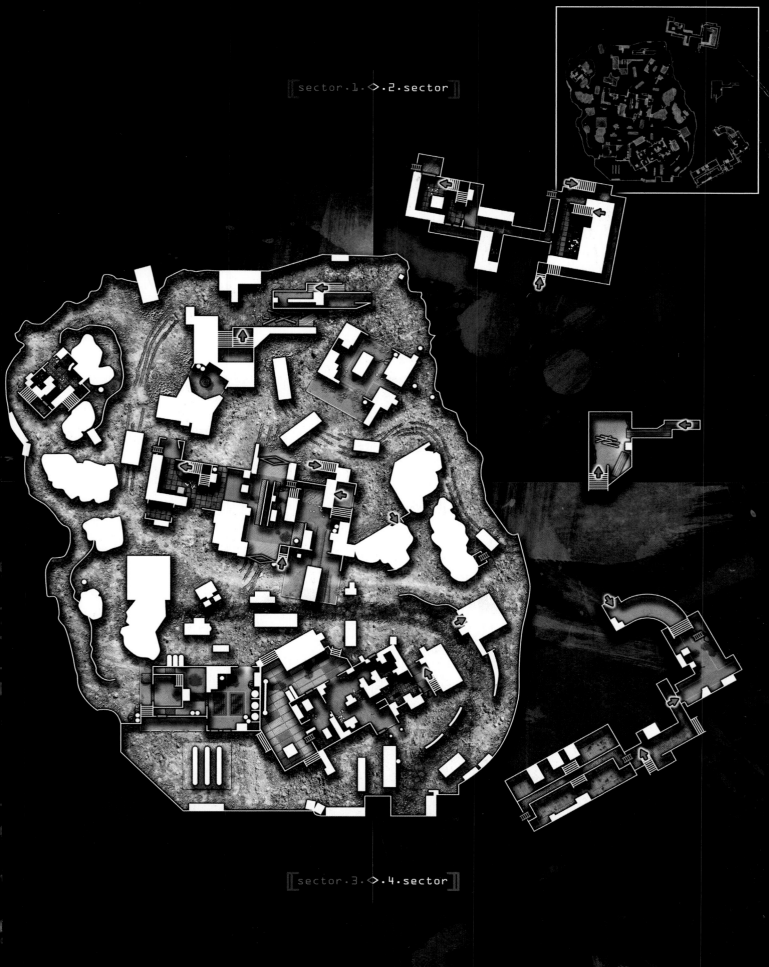

RANGEFINDER

The colored bars marked with weapon class abbreviations serve as a quick-reference tool to judge the *average* effective range for each of the following weapon classes:

SG = Shotgun   **AR** = Assault Rifle   **MARK** = Marksman Rifle

SMG = Submachine Gun   **LMG** = Light Machinegun

SPECIALIZED TRAINING   THE CAMPAIGN   MP INTRO & BASIC TRAINING   SQUADS   MP ARMORY   PERKS   KILLSTREAKS   MP MAPS   MP GAME MODES   SAFEGUARD   EXTINCTION   CLASSIFIED   ACHIEVEMENTS & TROPHIES

217

	DYNAMIC ELEMENT		SPAWN POINT		WINDOW		BOMB
	OVER/UNDERPASS		BLITZ GOAL		LADDER		CONNECT TO SAME-COLORED ARROWS ON MULTI-LEVEL AREAS
Ⓐ	CAPTURE POINT	Ⓐ	PLANT SITE	Ⓐ	BANK		

OVERLORD

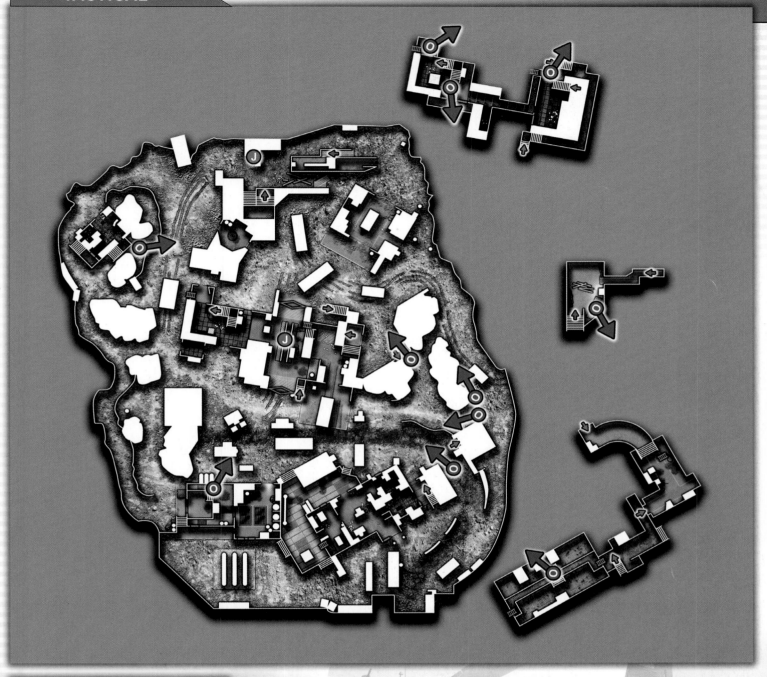

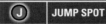	**JUMP SPOT**
	**OVERWATCH VANTAGE POINT**
	CONNECT TO SAME-COLORED ARROWS ON MULTI-LEVEL AREAS

SPECIALIZED TRAINING   THE CAMPAIGN   MP INTRO & BASIC TRAINING   SQUADS   MP ARMORY   PERKS   KILLSTREAKS   **MP MAPS**   MP GAME MODES   SAFEGUARD   EXTINCTION   CLASSIFIED   ACHIEVEMENTS & TROPHIES

219

PRISON BREAK

Prison Break is a small map set in a forested area with a little creek running through the middle. One of the trees by the creek can be shot down, providing a makeshift ramp from the lower part of the map up to the raised hilltop center.

The central hilltop is the focus of a lot of conflict. Other than a bit of foliage and some elevation differences, there's very little cover up there. Be ready for an open firefight at a moment's notice.

Several pathways lead around the map's outer edge, but they lack significant cover, so be careful when moving from one major position to another here.

The small logging camp and the prison entrance area both have a few small buildings and some readily available cover. Use these when you can, and watch out for corner campers when you're passing through.

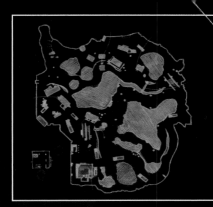

The colored bars marked with weapon class abbreviations serve as a quick-reference tool to judge the *average* effective range for each of the following weapon classes:

SG = Shotgun

SMG = Submachine Gun

AR = Assault Rifle

LMG = Light Machinegun

MARK = Marksman Rifle

SPECIALIZED TRAINING   THE CAMPAIGN   MP INTRO & BASIC TRAINING   SQUADS   MP ARMORY   PERKS   KILLSTREAKS   **MP MAPS**   MP GAME MODES   SAFEGUARD   EXTINCTION   CLASSIFIED   ACHIEVEMENTS & TROPHIES

223

	DYNAMIC ELEMENT			SPAWN POINT			WINDOW			BOMB
	OVER/UNDERPASS			BLITZ GOAL			LADDER			CONNECT TO SAME-COLORED ARROWS ON MULTI-LEVEL AREAS
	CAPTURE POINT			PLANT SITE			BANK			

PRISON BREAK

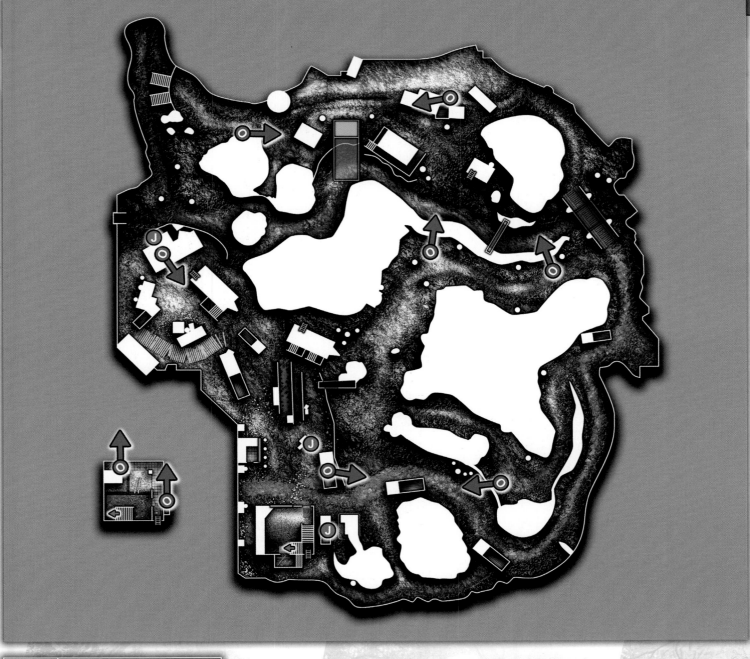

J	JUMP SPOT
⊙→	OVERWATCH VANTAGE POINT
⇧⇧ ⇧⇧	CONNECT TO SAME-COLORED ARROWS ON MULTI-LEVEL AREAS

SPECIALIZED TRAINING   THE CAMPAIGN   MP INTRO & BASIC TRAINING   SQUADS   MP ARMORY   PERKS   KILLSTREAKS   **MP MAPS**   MP GAME MODES   SAFEGUARD   EXTINCTION   CLASSIFIED   ACHIEVEMENTS & TROPHIES

225

SIEGE

An abandoned and overgrown seaside oil complex, Siege is a very large and sprawling map.

Buildings are all around the edges of the level, most with multiple floors. Almost all have numerous entrances in and out of their different levels.

Expect people in any of the buildings on the enemy's side of the map, and don't assume you're in the clear even with two or more active SATCOMs. Off the Grid enemies are a real threat here.

It's possible to engage in long-range combat, but the buildings break up line of sight significantly, so this isn't entirely a sniper's paradise. One can make almost any type of weapon or setup work well here, as long as you stick to weaponry appropriate to the range of engagements you pursue.

Stealth and awareness setups both work well here, either for sneaking up on players hidden in the buildings, or for locating them and rooting them out. You can also get mileage out of advanced scopes, like the Tracker or Thermal, for picking targets out of the busy cover. Stay alert; it's very easy to get flanked if you get immersed in spotting enemies at a distance.

A Field Orders reward can yield a missile strike being called in on the map, instantly killing anyone near its impact!

RANGEFINDER

The colored bars marked with weapon class abbreviations serve as a quick-reference tool to judge the *average* effective range for each of the following weapon classes:

SG = Shotgun   **AR** = Assault Rifle   **MARK** = Marksman Rifle

SMG = Submachine Gun   **LMG** = Light Machinegun

SPECIALIZED TRAINING   THE CAMPAIGN   MP INTRO & BASIC TRAINING   SQUADS   MP ARMORY   PERKS   KILLSTREAKS   **MP MAPS**   MP GAME MODES   SAFEGUARD   EXTINCTION   CLASSIFIED   ACHIEVEMENTS & TROPHIES

229

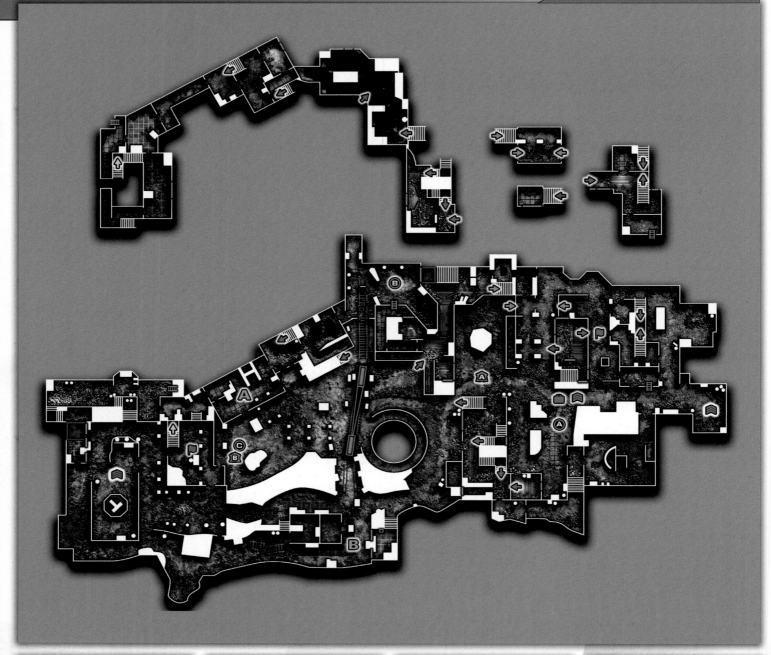

▢	**DYNAMIC ELEMENT**	
▢	**OVER/UNDERPASS**	
Ⓐ	**CAPTURE POINT**	

⛛⛛	**SPAWN POINT**
⚑⚑	**BLITZ GOAL**
Ⓐ	**PLANT SITE**

▭	**WINDOW**
▤	**LADDER**
Ⓐ	**BANK**

💼	**BOMB**
⇧⇧ ⇧⇧	**CONNECT TO SAME-COLORED ARROWS ON MULTI-LEVEL AREAS**

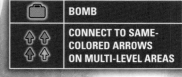

SIEGE

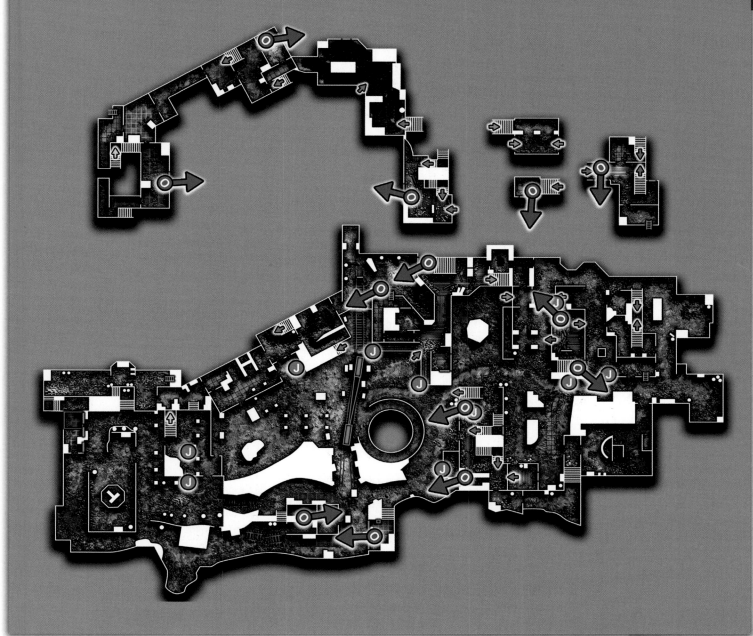

J	**JUMP SPOT**
o→	**OVERWATCH VANTAGE POINT**
⇧⇧ ⇧⇧	**CONNECT TO SAME-COLORED ARROWS ON MULTI-LEVEL AREAS**

SPECIALIZED TRAINING   THE CAMPAIGN   MP INTRO & BASIC TRAINING   SQUADS   MP ARMORY   PERKS   KILLSTREAKS   **MP MAPS**   MP GAME MODES   SAFEGUARD   EXTINCTION   CLASSIFIED   ACHIEVEMENTS & TROPHIES

231

SOVEREIGN

A large, high-tech tank assembly complex, Sovereign is a long and wide factory battleground. The tank assembly line that runs straight through the middle of the map breaks up three levels of conflict.

There are lots of long, straight lines of sight on this map. Be ready for mid-range engagements. Or, if you're using a close-range weapon, be very careful in your movements across the factory floor.

You can use the upper level to get an edge on anyone down on the factory floor. The lower level allows one to traverse from one end of the factory to the other, but be wary of bumping into shotgun or SMG runners down there!

A Field Orders reward triggers demolition charges all along the tank assembly line, killing anyone within and flooding the lower levels with fire suppressant gas.

[sector.1.◇.2.sector]

[sector.3.◇.4.sector]

233

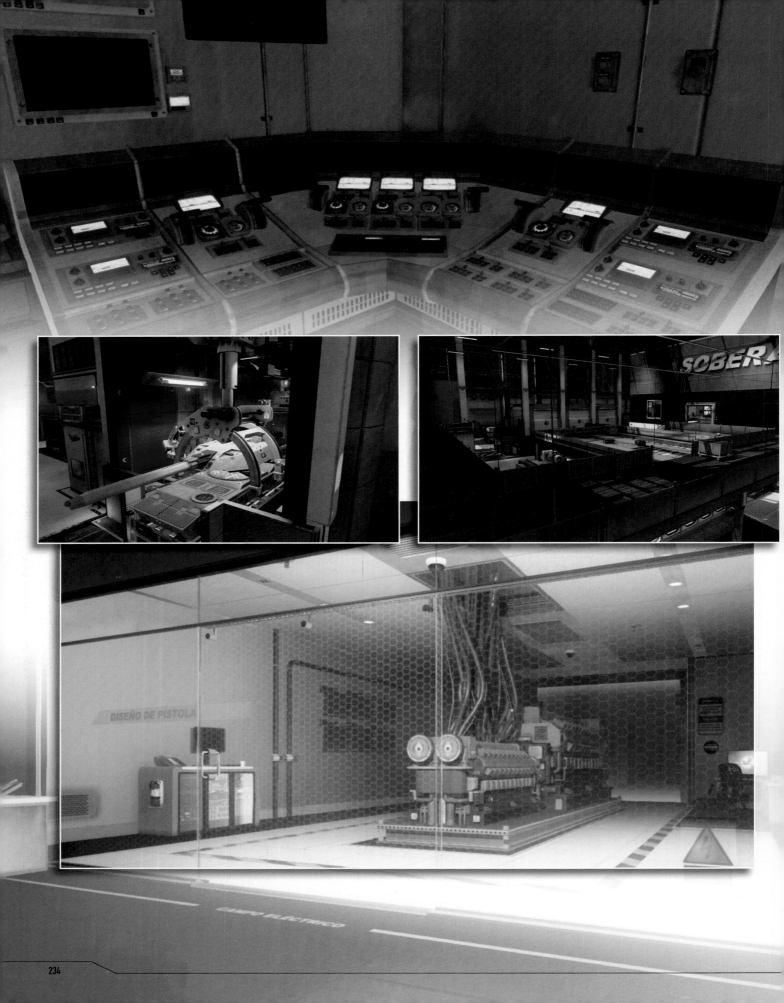

RANGEFINDER

The colored bars marked with weapon class abbreviations serve as a quick-reference tool to judge the *average* effective range for each of the following weapon classes:

SG = Shotgun   **AR** = Assault Rifle   **MARK** = Marksman Rifle

SMG = Submachine Gun   **LMG** = Light Machinegun

SPECIALIZED TRAINING   THE CAMPAIGN   MP INTRO & BASIC TRAINING   SQUADS   MP ARMORY   PERKS   KILLSTREAKS   **MP MAPS**   MP GAME MODES   SAFEGUARD   EXTINCTION   CLASSIFIED   ACHIEVEMENTS & TROPHIES

235

SOVEREIGN

DYNAMIC ELEMENT	**SPAWN POINT**	**WINDOW**	**BOMB**
OVER/UNDERPASS	**BLITZ GOAL**	**LADDER**	**CONNECT TO SAME-COLORED ARROWS ON MULTI-LEVEL AREAS**
CAPTURE POINT	**PLANT SITE**	**BANK**	

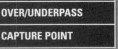

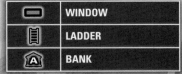
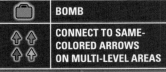

SOVEREIGN

 **J**	JUMP SPOT
○→	OVERWATCH VANTAGE POINT
⇧ ⇧ **⇧ ⇧**	CONNECT TO SAME-COLORED ARROWS ON MULTI-LEVEL AREAS

SPECIALIZED TRAINING   THE CAMPAIGN   MP INTRO & BASIC TRAINING   SQUADS   MP ARMORY   PERKS   KILLSTREAKS   **MP MAPS**   MP GAME MODES   SAFEGUARD   EXTINCTION   CLASSIFIED   ACHIEVEMENTS & TROPHIES

237

STONEHAVEN

Stonehaven features a massive, open field near the ruins of a castle and a small village, as well as one extremely large, crashed satellite at the field's edge.

Stonehaven looks like it is completely open and appears to be a total sniper's paradise, but this isn't entirely true. The terrain is extremely uneven, and there is a surprising number of ways to move across the field without being taken down from long range.

That said, you can expect enemies to use long-range weaponry here, so be careful about the routes you choose. Going around the edges is possible, of course, but several of the map's outer regions actually have cleaner line of sight than some places near the castle ruins and the map's center.

STONEHAVEN

The colored bars marked with weapon class abbreviations serve as a quick-reference tool to judge the *average* effective range for each of the following weapon classes:

SG = Shotgun   **AR** = Assault Rifle   **MARK** = Marksman Rifle

SMG = Submachine Gun   **LMG** = Light Machinegun

SPECIALIZED TRAINING   THE CAMPAIGN   MP INTRO & BASIC TRAINING   SQUADS   MP ARMORY   PERKS   KILLSTREAKS   **MP MAPS**   MP GAME MODES   SAFEGUARD   EXTINCTION   CLASSIFIED   ACHIEVEMENTS & TROPHIES

241

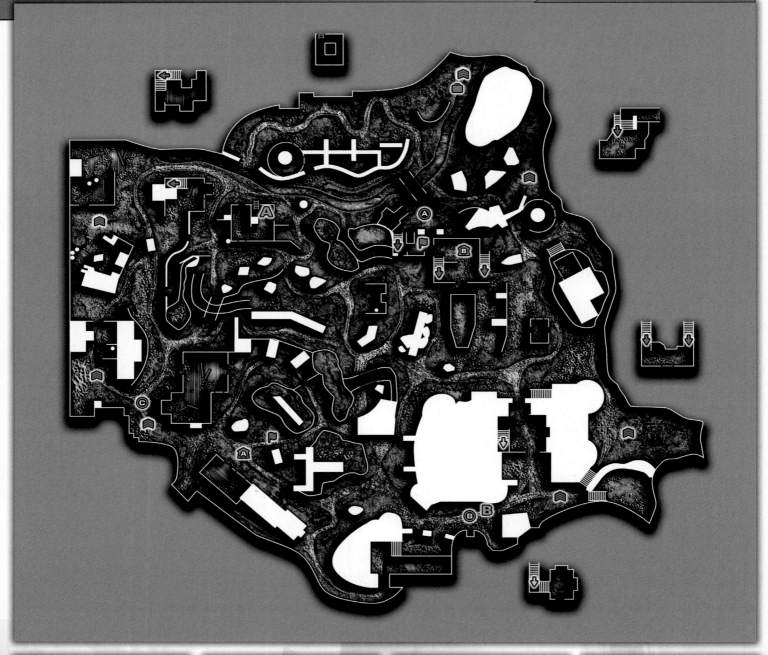

⬚	**DYNAMIC ELEMENT**		⪢⪢	**SPAWN POINT**		▭	**WINDOW**	
⬚	**OVER/UNDERPASS**		⚑⚑	**BLITZ GOAL**		⚏	**LADDER**	
Ⓐ	**CAPTURE POINT**		A	**PLANT SITE**		Ⓐ	**BANK**	

🛄	**BOMB**
⬆⬆ ⬆⬆	**CONNECT TO SAME-COLORED ARROWS ON MULTI-LEVEL AREAS**

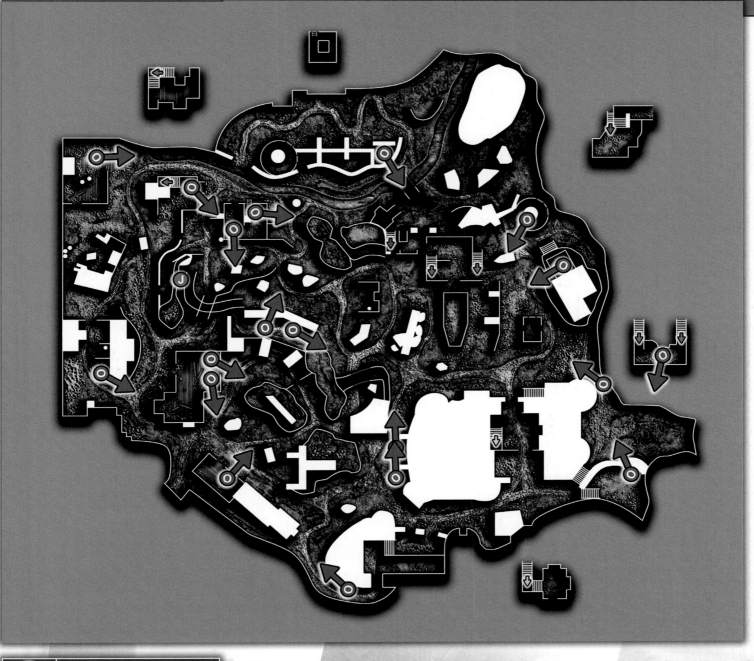

(J)	JUMP SPOT
(o→)	OVERWATCH VANTAGE POINT
⇧ ⇧ ⇧ ⇧	CONNECT TO SAME-COLORED ARROWS ON MULTI-LEVEL AREAS

SPECIALIZED TRAINING   THE CAMPAIGN   MP INTRO & BASIC TRAINING   SQUADS   MP ARMORY   PERKS   KILLSTREAKS   MP MAPS   MP GAME MODES   SAFEGUARD   EXTINCTION   CLASSIFIED   ACHIEVEMENTS & TROPHIES

243

STORMFRONT

Stormfront is a large, urban map set in and around a retail complex, an old library, and the wide street that cuts through the center.

This map is large enough to support multiple areas of simultaneous conflict in deathmatch modes. Meanwhile, objective modes tend to focus combat in specific places around the map.

In either case, be careful about crossing the street—it's exposed to long-range fire from many different directions.

Despite the interior spaces, a lot of combat on Stormfront occurs at medium range or even farther. So, either bring a solid ranged weapon, or be careful about where you engage and how you cross the street.

And yes, the titular storm front does in fact strike the map. Rain eventually starts to fall, obscuring vision slightly, and lightning strikes hammer the battlefield.

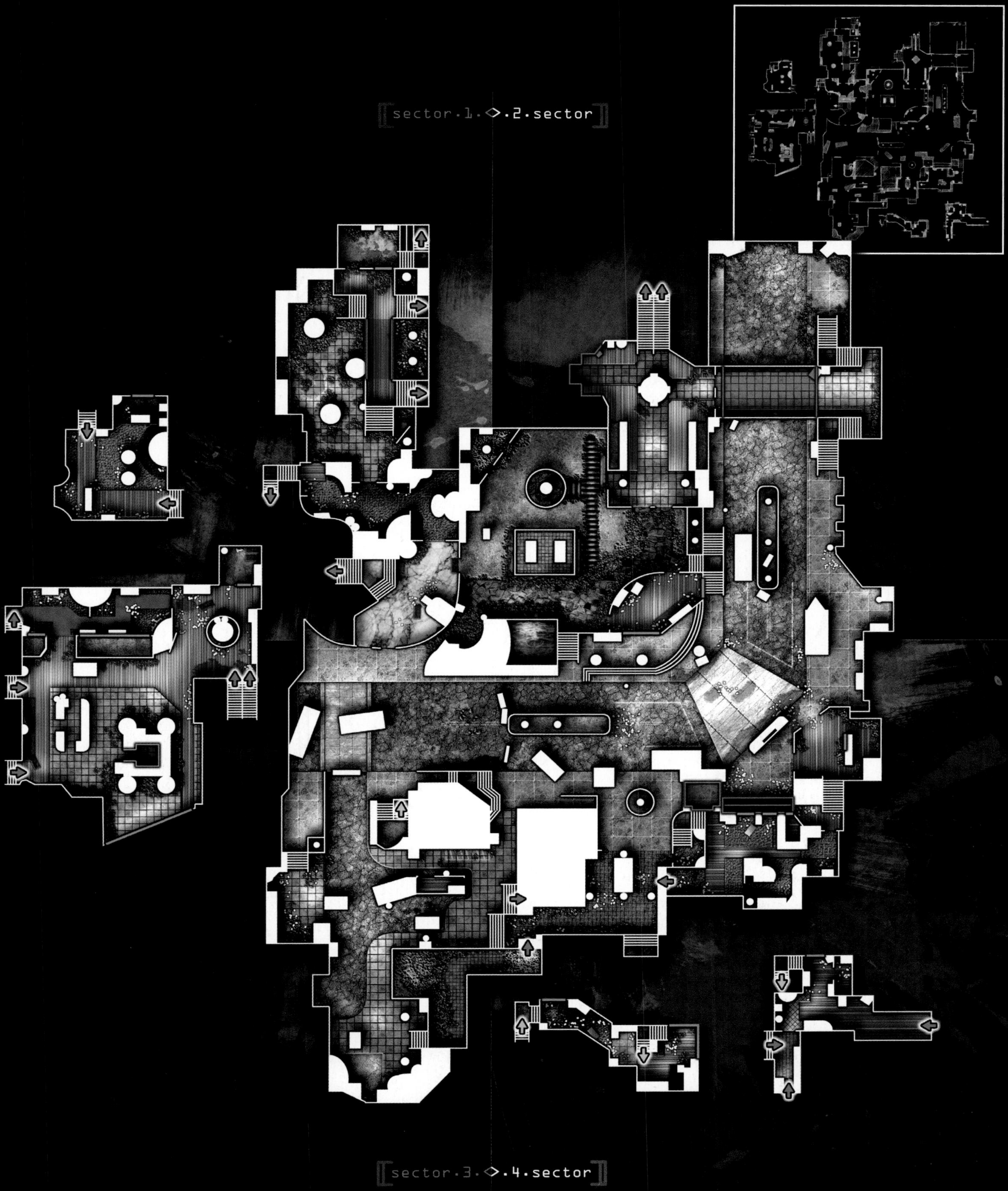
sector.1.<>.2.sector
sector.3.<>.4.sector

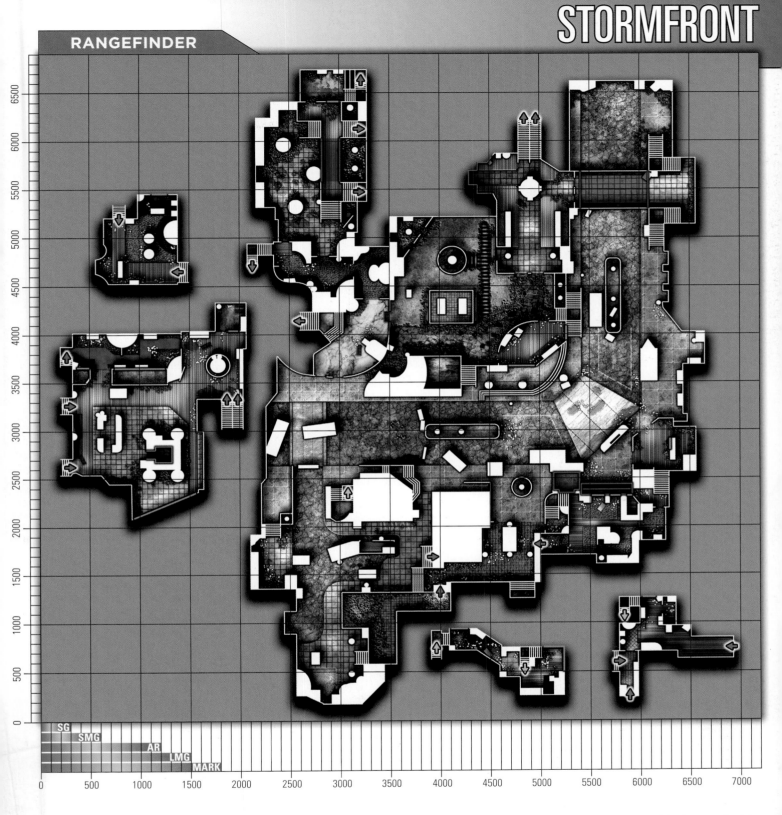

SG
SMG
AR
LMG
MARK

0   500   1000   1500   2000   2500   3000   3500   4000   4500   5000   5500   6000   6500   7000

The colored bars marked with weapon class abbreviations serve as a quick-reference tool to judge the *average* effective range for each of the following weapon classes:

SG = Shotgun   **AR** = Assault Rifle   **MARK** = Marksman Rifle

SMG = Submachine Gun   **LMG** = Light Machinegun

SPECIALIZED TRAINING   THE CAMPAIGN   MP INTRO & BASIC TRAINING   SQUADS   MP ARMORY   PERKS   KILLSTREAKS   **MP MAPS**   MP GAME MODES   SAFEGUARD   EXTINCTION   CLASSIFIED   ACHIEVEMENTS & TROPHIES

247

STORMFRONT

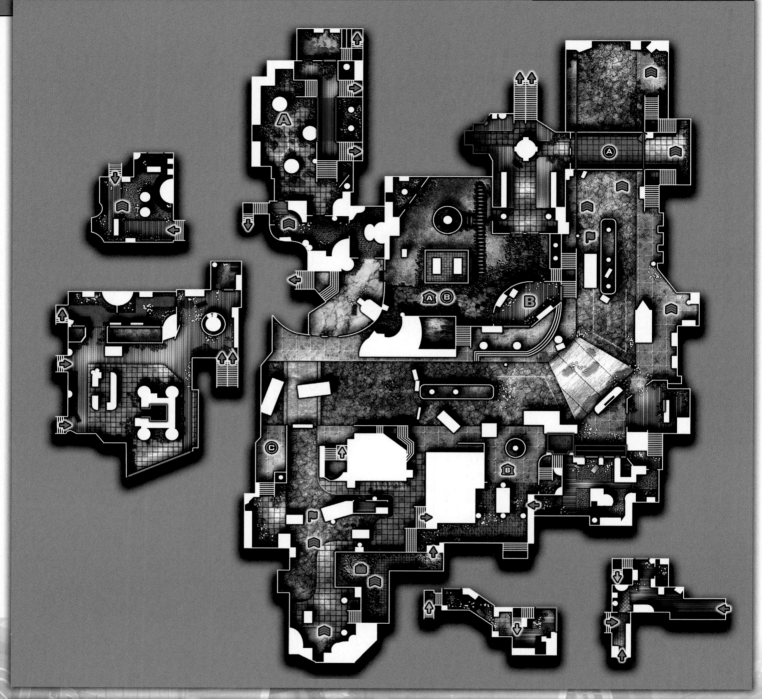

☐ DYNAMIC ELEMENT	SPAWN POINT	▭ WINDOW	🧳 BOMB
☐ OVER/UNDERPASS	BLITZ GOAL	🗄 LADDER	⬆⬆ ⬆⬆ CONNECT TO SAME-COLORED ARROWS ON MULTI-LEVEL AREAS
Ⓐ CAPTURE POINT	Ⓐ PLANT SITE	Ⓐ BANK	

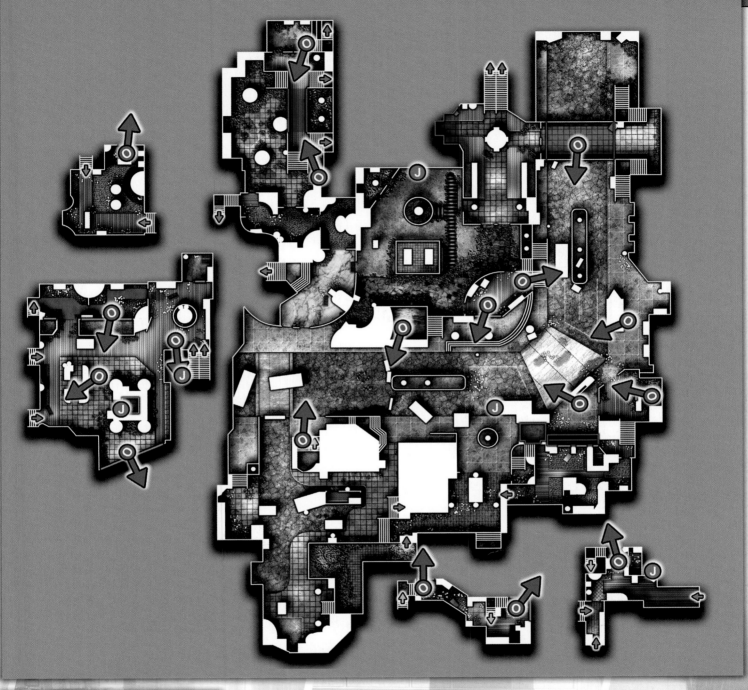

J — JUMP SPOT

O→ — OVERWATCH VANTAGE POINT

⇧⇧ ⇧⇧ — CONNECT TO SAME-COLORED ARROWS ON MULTI-LEVEL AREAS

SPECIALIZED TRAINING   THE CAMPAIGN   MP INTRO & BASIC TRAINING   SQUADS   MP ARMORY   PERKS   KILLSTREAKS   **MP MAPS**   MP GAME MODES   SAFEGUARD   EXTINCTION   CLASSIFIED   ACHIEVEMENTS & TROPHIES

249

STRIKEZONE

Strikezone takes place on the outskirts of a baseball stadium, at the shops and right outside the stands. Alongside Prison Break, it's one of the smallest maps.

Despite its size, Strikezone has considerably more cover and more alternate routes than Prison Break. Mobile and CQB builds fare well here. It's possible to fight at medium range, but don't expect to get much more than that without really solid teammates covering your back.

Expect a lot of close-quarters encounters in the shops' hallways around the map. The open areas outside provide just about the greatest distance can hope to get on this level.

BOOM

Strikezone is aptly named for more than one reason.

Pick up the special Field Orders care package for this level and you can call in a KEM strike, leveling the entire map and killing the enemy team.

This transforms the level, ruining all of it, cutting off some paths, and changing the overall look and feel.

We have two maps prepared for this level, so you can see the before and after.

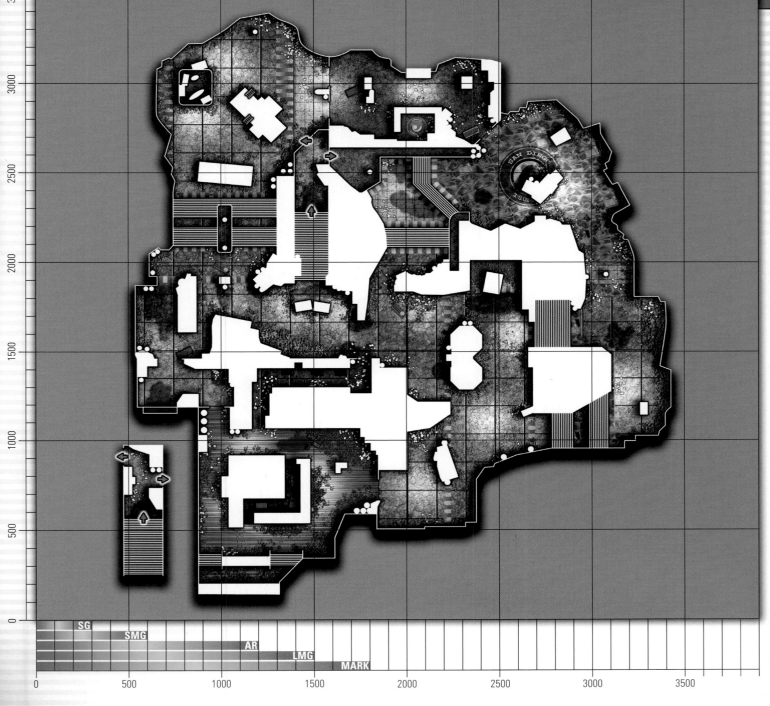

The colored bars marked with weapon class abbreviations serve as a quick-reference tool to judge the *average* effective range for each of the following weapon classes:

SG = Shotgun   **AR** = Assault Rifle   **MARK** = Marksman Rifle

SMG = Submachine Gun   **LMG** = Light Machinegun

SPECIALIZED TRAINING THE CAMPAIGN MP INTRO & BASIC TRAINING SQUADS MP ARMORY PERKS KILLSTREAKS **MP MAPS** MP GAME MODES SAFEGUARD EXTINCTION CLASSIFIED ACHIEVEMENTS & TROPHIES

253

STRIKEZONE: PRE

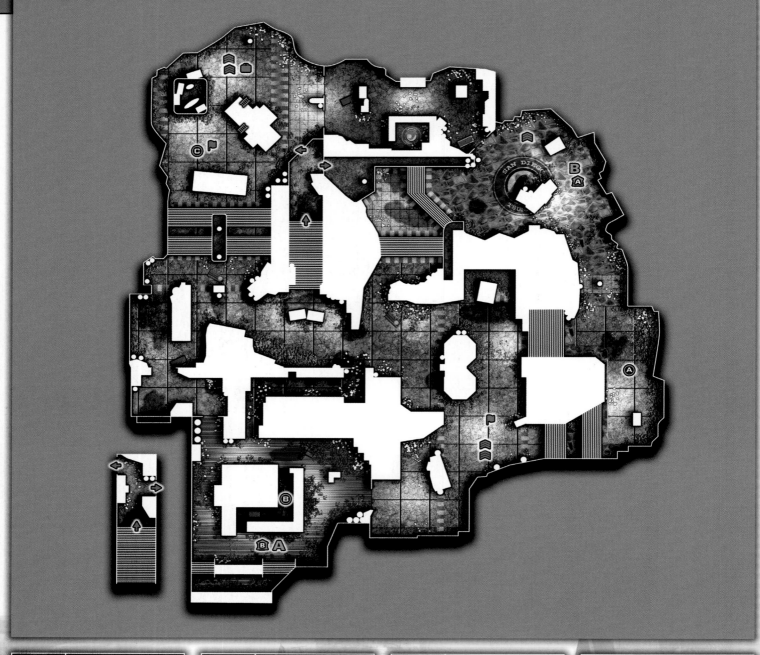

■	**DYNAMIC ELEMENT**	⋙⋙	**SPAWN POINT**	▭	**WINDOW**	📋	**BOMB**
▢	**OVER/UNDERPASS**	⚑⚑	**BLITZ GOAL**	🗏	**LADDER**	⬆⬆	**CONNECT TO SAME-COLORED ARROWS ON MULTI-LEVEL AREAS**
Ⓐ	**CAPTURE POINT**	🅰	**PLANT SITE**	Ⓐ	**BANK**	⬆⬆	

PREMIUM DARK BEER

STRIKEZONE: PRE

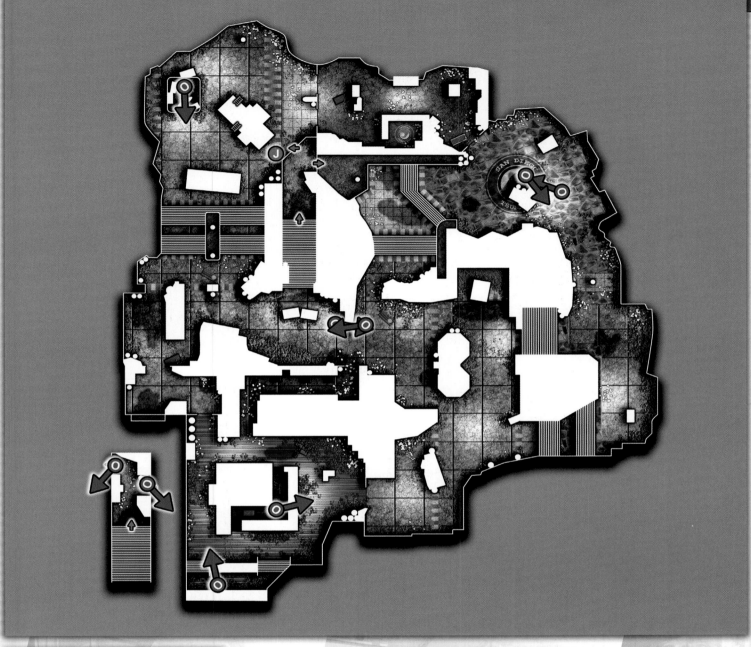

J	JUMP SPOT
⊙→	OVERWATCH VANTAGE POINT
⇧⇧ ⇧⇧	CONNECT TO SAME-COLORED ARROWS ON MULTI-LEVEL AREAS

SPECIALIZED TRAINING   THE CAMPAIGN   MP INTRO & BASIC TRAINING   SQUADS   MP ARMORY   PERKS   KILLSTREAKS   **MP MAPS**   MP GAME MODES   SAFEGUARD   EXTINCTION   CLASSIFIED   ACHIEVEMENTS & TROPHIES

255

3500
3000
2500
2000
1500
1000
500
0

SG
SMG
AR
LMG
MARK

0   500   1000   1500   2000   2500   3000   3500

The colored bars marked with weapon class abbreviations serve as a quick-reference tool to judge the *average* effective range for each of the following weapon classes:

SG = Shotgun   **AR** = Assault Rifle   **MARK** = Marksman Rifle

SMG = Submachine Gun   **LMG** = Light Machinegun

SPECIALIZED TRAINING   THE CAMPAIGN   MP INTRO & BASIC TRAINING   SQUADS   MP ARMORY   PERKS   KILLSTREAKS   **MP MAPS**   MP GAME MODES   SAFEGUARD   EXTINCTION   CLASSIFIED   ACHIEVEMENTS & TROPHIES

257

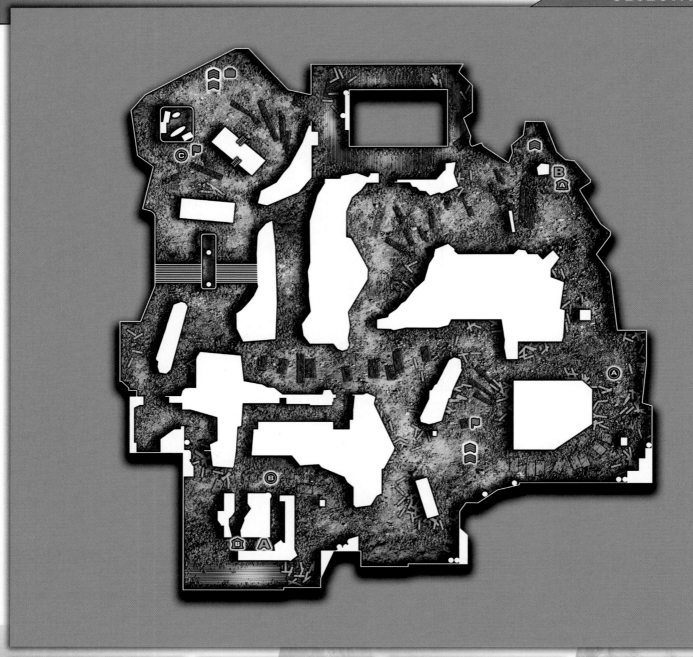

	DYNAMIC ELEMENT		SPAWN POINT		WINDOW		BOMB
	OVER/UNDERPASS		BLITZ GOAL		LADDER		CONNECT TO SAME-COLORED ARROWS ON MULTI-LEVEL AREAS
	CAPTURE POINT		PLANT SITE		BANK		

STRIKEZONE: POST

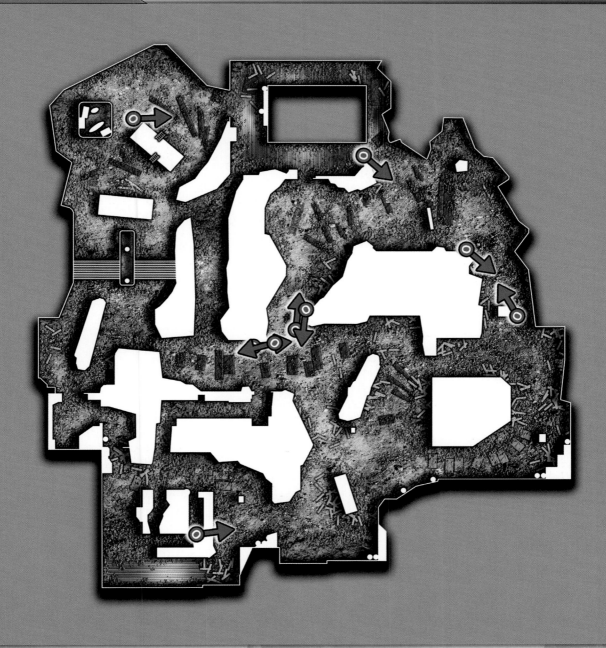

(J)	JUMP SPOT
○→	OVERWATCH VANTAGE POINT
⇧ ⇧ / ⇧ ⇧	CONNECT TO SAME-COLORED ARROWS ON MULTI-LEVEL AREAS

SPECIALIZED TRAINING   THE CAMPAIGN   MP INTRO & BASIC TRAINING   SQUADS   MP ARMORY   PERKS   KILLSTREAKS   **MP MAPS**   MP GAME MODES   SAFEGUARD   EXTINCTION   CLASSIFIED   ACHIEVEMENTS & TROPHIES

259

TREMOR

A mazy, urban battleground, Tremor takes place in the ruinous aftermath of wide-scale devastation around the city. On top of the cracks and rubble, the level periodically shakes, bouncing your view off target—it's named Tremor for a reason!

Tremor features narrow alley fights mixed with inner building CQB battles. Bring a strong CQB setup, or be sure to post up in buildings that cover approaches, with either teammates or equipment guarding your back. Getting jumped from behind in a building is guaranteed to be fatal.

Many of the buildings have multiple floors, and a lot of windows and ledges provide high ground over enemies on the streets below. Check these windows for targets when you're rounding corners—a quick corner lean can give you an early warning. Hugging walls as you move around the map is good practice to protect you from hostiles above who can't see you directly below.

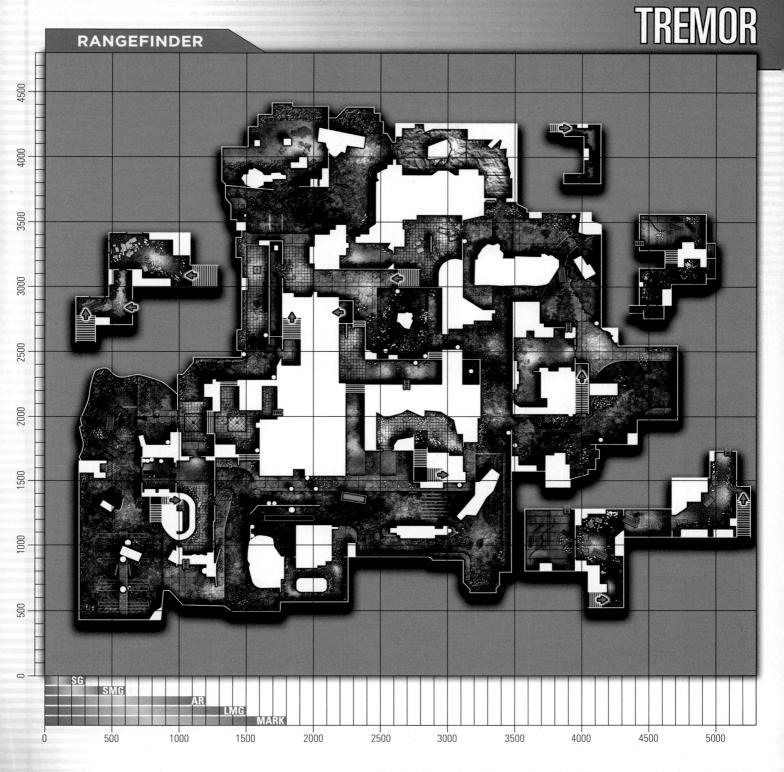

The colored bars marked with weapon class abbreviations serve as a quick-reference tool to judge the *average* effective range for each of the following weapon classes:

SG = Shotgun   **AR** = Assault Rifle   **MARK** = Marksman Rifle

SMG = Submachine Gun   **LMG** = Light Machinegun

SPECIALIZED TRAINING   THE CAMPAIGN   MP INTRO & BASIC TRAINING   SQUADS   MP ARMORY   PERKS   KILLSTREAKS   MP MAPS   MP GAME MODES   SAFEGUARD   EXTINCTION   CLASSIFIED   ACHIEVEMENTS & TROPHIES

263

TREMOR

	DYNAMIC ELEMENT		SPAWN POINT		WINDOW		BOMB
	OVER/UNDERPASS		BLITZ GOAL		LADDER		CONNECT TO SAME-COLORED ARROWS ON MULTI-LEVEL AREAS
	CAPTURE POINT		PLANT SITE		BANK		

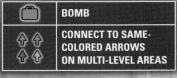

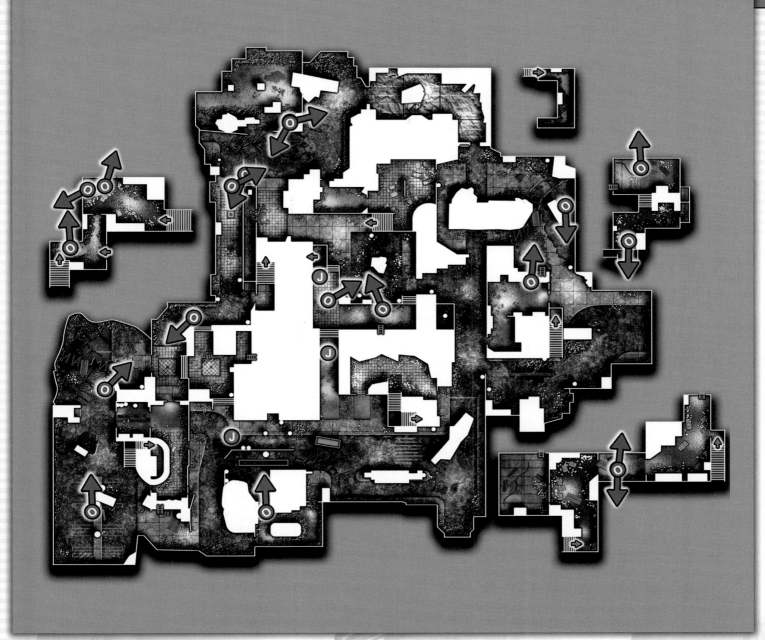

TREMOR

TACTICAL

J	JUMP SPOT
⊙→	OVERWATCH VANTAGE POINT
⇧⇧⇧⇧	CONNECT TO SAME-COLORED ARROWS ON MULTI-LEVEL AREAS

SPECIALIZED TRAINING   THE CAMPAIGN   MP INTRO & BASIC TRAINING   SQUADS   MP ARMORY   PERKS   KILLSTREAKS   **MP MAPS**   MP GAME MODES   SAFEGUARD   EXTINCTION   CLASSIFIED   ACHIEVEMENTS & TROPHIES

265

WARHAWK

Warhawk takes place in and around a small town's main street. It encourages a mix of open fights in the center streets and back lots behind the buildings. Multiple buildings have several floors, many of which provide good line of sight over the map center. As a general rule, unless an objective forces you there, stay out of the middle. It's a kill zone with too many points of contact to cover while you move through it.

Despite the map's mixed urban nature, midrange combat is easier to carry out here than it is on Tremor, for example. There are more lines of sight, both behind the buildings and across the center street.

You can function here with CQB builds or midrange fighting. Just pay attention to where and how you approach enemy positions.

On top of a few breachable and/or destroyable paths, there is a major Field Orders reward. Acquire this special mission award, and you can call down an artillery barrage on the entire map!

If you get this reward, take cover immediately. You don't want to die to your own barrage! If an enemy calls it in, take cover, because... well, that should be obvious.

[[sector.3.◇.4.sector]]

RANGEFINDER

The colored bars marked with weapon class abbreviations serve as a quick-reference tool to judge the *average* effective range for each of the following weapon classes:

SG = Shotgun **AR** = Assault Rifle **MARK** = Marksman Rifle

SMG = Submachine Gun **LMG** = Light Machinegun

SPECIALIZED TRAINING · THE CAMPAIGN · MP INTRO & BASIC TRAINING · SQUADS · MP ARMORY · PERKS · KILLSTREAKS · **MP MAPS** · MP GAME MODES · SAFEGUARD · EXTINCTION · CLASSIFIED · ACHIEVEMENTS & TROPHIES

269

	DYNAMIC ELEMENT		SPAWN POINT		WINDOW		BOMB
	OVER/UNDERPASS		BLITZ GOAL		LADDER		CONNECT TO SAME-COLORED ARROWS ON MULTI-LEVEL AREAS
Ⓐ	CAPTURE POINT	Ⓐ	PLANT SITE	Ⓐ	BANK		

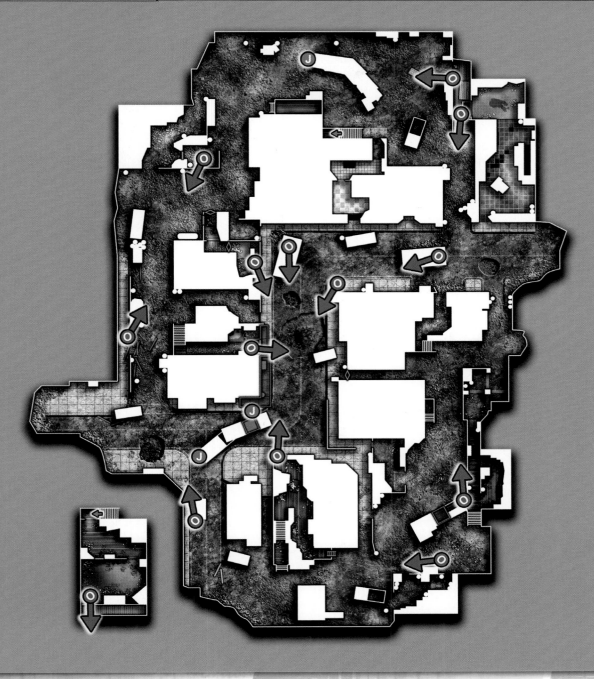

SPECIALIZED TRAINING   THE CAMPAIGN   MP INTRO & BASIC TRAINING   SQUADS   MP ARMORY   PERKS   KILLSTREAKS   **MP MAPS**   MP GAME MODES   SAFEGUARD   EXTINCTION   CLASSIFIED   ACHIEVEMENTS & TROPHIES

271

J JUMP SPOT

O→ OVERWATCH VANTAGE POINT

⇧⇧ ⇧⇧ CONNECT TO SAME-COLORED ARROWS ON MULTI-LEVEL AREAS

WHITEOUT

Whiteout is a large, snowy wilderness map. Mixed engagements take place in and around winter cabins and houses. Open-field fighting occurs over frozen water and amongst tumbled rocks. Whiteout has a wide range of combat areas, from a cave passing through the middle to a forested area riddled with miniature canyons through the rocks below.

Almost any type of build can fare well here, though mid- and long-range setups are preferable to CQB builds, simply because of the map's size and the distances involved. You can get into close range with some effort, but it's definitely easier to pick off targets from a distance.

In objective-based game modes, beware of the cave in the middle. It can rapidly become a massive killing ground. We recommend defensive perks and equipment if you plan to tackle it head-on.

Finally, Whiteout has the last of the special Field Orders care packages. Acquiring and triggering this map-specific reward causes a satellite crash. The satellite plummets down over the center of the map and crash lands in the forested area. Make sure you aren't nearby when it hits!

The satellite itself emits an EMP-like effect to nearby players, but it also gives level-1 SATCOM coverage for the rest of the match to the team that calls it down! If your opposition gains this reward, it can be a crippling disadvantage to your team. In such a case, either switch to a build that uses Off the Grid, or keep in mind that even a single enemy SATCOM usage to initiate satellite sweeps will easily reveal your position.

⟦sector.1.◇.2.sector⟧

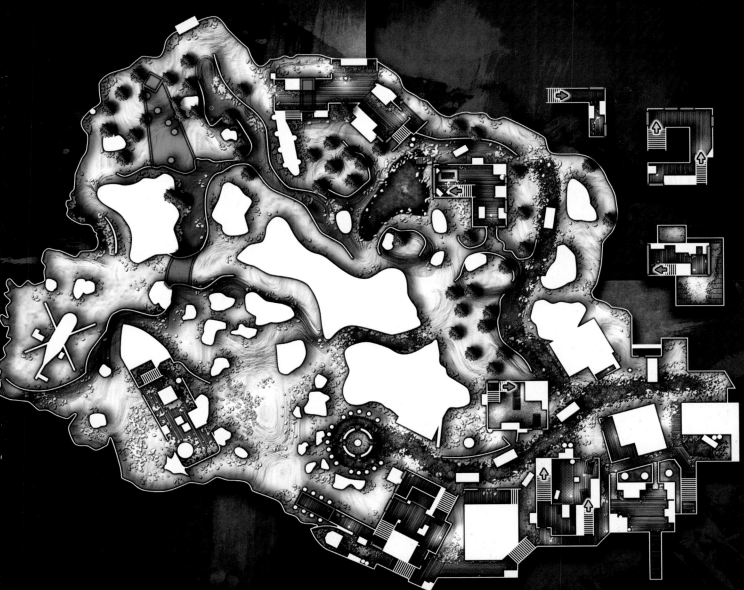

⟦sector.3.◇.4.sector⟧

273

RANGEFINDER

The colored bars marked with weapon class abbreviations serve as a quick-reference tool to judge the *average* effective range for each of the following weapon classes:

SG = Shotgun   **AR** = Assault Rifle   **MARK** = Marksman Rifle

SMG = Submachine Gun   **LMG** = Light Machinegun

SPECIALIZED TRAINING   THE CAMPAIGN   MP INTRO & BASIC TRAINING   SQUADS   MP ARMORY   PERKS   KILLSTREAKS   MP MAPS   MP GAME MODES   SAFEGUARD   EXTINCTION   CLASSIFIED   ACHIEVEMENTS & TROPHIES

275

	DYNAMIC ELEMENT			SPAWN POINT			WINDOW			BOMB
	OVER/UNDERPASS			BLITZ GOAL			LADDER			CONNECT TO SAME-COLORED ARROWS ON MULTI-LEVEL AREAS
	CAPTURE POINT			PLANT SITE			BANK			

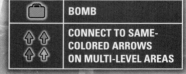

WHITEOUT

(J)	**JUMP SPOT**
(O→)	**OVERWATCH VANTAGE POINT**
⇧ ⇧ ⇧ ⇧	**CONNECT TO SAME-COLORED ARROWS ON MULTI-LEVEL AREAS**

MP GAME MODES

Call of Duty: Ghosts multiplayer matches are played in a variety of game modes. From the straightforward deathmatch modes to the intense single round Search and Destroy or grinding wars of control in Domination, there are many ways to engage your fellow players online.

Game modes in *Call of Duty* are grouped into a variety of playlists. You can use these to find like-minded players for Squad battles against AI, clan battles against organized groups, or your regular evening matches with a friend or two against another random lobby of players.

> ### Party Time!
>
> In addition to the modes that are included in the game at launch time, Infinity Ward can add and tweak new playlists for special events and in response to community requests.
>
> On top of that, you are always free to create a private lobby and customize a whole host of options if you want to take a base game mode and tune it to the preferences of you and your friends.

DEATHMATCH MODES

Deathmatch modes are the most basic multiplayer modes, focusing on killing other players and racking up a high kill count above almost any other concern.

Unlike objective modes, where focus on the objective takes priority over self-preservation to score a win, deathmatch modes have a strong focus on your personal performance. Killing more frequently than you die is paramount in deathmatch modes.

FREE FOR ALL (FFA)

Every woman for herself. First player to the score target wins.

Free for All is won by earning kills at the fastest possible rate. You can suffer a lot more deaths in an FFA match than you can get away with in a Team Deathmatch (TDM) or Kill Confirmed (KC) match.

One viable tactic for pulling off FFA wins (and racking up streaks while doing so) is to pick a defensible area of the map as "yours." Then, simply patrol it, pick off any players who spawn nearby, and take out anyone who comes back for a revenge kill.

This technique removes a lot of the danger of having hostile players spawning around or behind you if you are patrolling the map, and it gives you a good chance to rack up a streak.

Another option is to patrol the edges of the map, moving around in a clockwise or counter-clockwise fashion and clearing out enemies as you move. By avoiding the center, you minimize your exposure, and by staying on the move, you are at slightly less risk from opponents spawning behind you.

Stealthy builds are highly recommended in FFA, as showing up on the minimap can be a death sentence with so many hostile players gunning for you.

TEAM DEATHMATCH (TDM)

The team-oriented version of basic deathmatch, where the first team to the score target wins.

TDM has much more of an ebb and flow to it than basic FFA, with the two teams forming firing lines as they meet.

This opens the possibility of powerful flanking attacks if you can push past the front line and attack the enemy from behind.

Be aware that spawns tend to shift throughout a TDM match. When your team pushes into or through an enemy position, the opposing team is likely to respawn in an entirely different part of the map, possibly even where you started the match.

Paying careful attention to your position relative to your teammates and where adversaries are appearing is a vital skill to master in TDM. If you can predict where the enemy is likely to spawn, you can be in position and ready to engage them instead of being surprised when they show up behind you!

KILL CONFIRMED (KC)

Kill Confirmed is basic TDM with a twist: every time a player dies, they drop a dog tag. An enemy can pick it up to score a point, while a teammate can pick it up to save a point.

The first team to reach the dog tag score limit wins. Oh, and your dog can pick up dog tags. Of course.

KC is almost identical to TDM in terms of combat flow, with one very important exception: because players have to expose themselves to pick up enemy tags in the open, KC tends to be a more aggressive mode than TDM.

While it is possible to sit back at long range and pick off targets in KC, you won't be scoring any points doing so. This can be helpful if your teammates are quick to pick up dropped tags, but in general, fast and aggressive builds work best here for scoring well.

SPECIALIZED TRAINING   THE CAMPAIGN   MP INTRO & BASIC TRAINING   SQUADS   MP ARMORY   PERKS   KILLSTREAKS   MP MAPS   **MP GAME MODES**   SAFEGUARD   EXTINCTION   CLASSIFIED   ACHIEVEMENTS & TROPHIES

279

CRANKED

Cranked is a TDM mode that amps up the intensity of conflict past even than of KC.

Once you score a kill in Cranked, you have 30 seconds to get another kill, or you explode!

This turns Cranked matches into frantic run-and-gun affairs, as players race to locate each other to avoid dying from the timer.

Get Cranked!

When you kill an adversary and get Cranked, you automatically earn a host of perks. Don't use these on your builds unless you don't mind the "waste" of getting them again.

| Sleight of Hand
| Quickdraw
| Reflex
| Ready Up
| Marathon
| Stalker

INFECTED

BRAAAAAINNNSSS…

One zombie armed with a pistol and a Tactical Insertion begins looking for live foes to consume.

Human players are armed with a shotgun, a Claymore, and a 9-Bang grenade. Whenever a human player falls, they join the zombie team. How long can you survive?

Old Friends

Tactical Insertions are an old piece of equipment from previous *Call of Duty* titles. When placed, they allow you to set your own spawn point. In this case, it lets the zombies set their spawn points near their prey and keep up a relentless onslaught!

Claymores are an old proximity explosive, but unlike the improvised explosive device (IED), they can only be placed on the ground, and they only detonate in one direction.

Use them to defend yourself from the undead hordes… temporarily, at least.

HUNTED

Hunted is a unique gameplay mode, as you do *not* have your normal builds in Hunted.

Instead, you spawn with two throwing knives, a 9-Bang, and a lot of care package choppers flying inbound.

These choppers drop special weapon crates, each containing a random weapon with one magazine!

Hunted is a constant nonstop scramble to pick up new weapons and steal weapons from other players.

You can only carry one weapon at a time, and picking up an enemy weapon just gives you any ammo remaining in the chamber. Get good with your knives, and covet high-damage weapons with low ammo consumption or LMGs.

DEMOLITION MODES

As classic no respawn modes, these two target demolition modes are played in a series of rounds.

The offense is given a bomb to take to one of two key targets on the level and destroy it. In each round, all players on the team have one and only one life.

The defense needs to defuse the explosive to win. Either team can win a round by eliminating all players on the other team.

Bomb Placement

One important tip for the offense: the location where you place the bomb on the target is important. The enemy can only defuse it from the same location in which you planted it.

If you're planting and then covering the bomb, put it in the most awkward and exposed position for the opposition to defuse. Choose an area that gives you the most cover and lines of sight to fire on any defuse attempt.

Stealth perks like Dead Silence are particularly useful in these modes, as surviving to sneak in a plant, defuse a bomb, or ambush enemy players are all crucial goals in these limited respawn modes.

Leaning is a significant change for demolition modes, as it is now possible to cover an area while exposing less of your body. Leaning naturally affects all modes in the game, but with no respawns, the stakes are higher in demo modes. Get used to hunting for enemy heads and shoulders hiding around corners!

SEARCH AND DESTROY (S&D)

Search and Destroy has two target bomb locations, A and B.

The offense spawns near a single bomb case—one player must pick up the bomb and deliver it to a bomb site, where it must be armed and then detonated after a countdown.

On defense, the team spawns near the bomb sites and has a slight time advantage to get into position and set up before the offense arrives.

Because there are no respawns in a round of S&D, playing sloppily and carelessly on offense or defense is a really bad idea. Throwing away your life can severely damage your team's chances of victory, as each player down costs the team manpower and intelligence.

Planting the bomb takes time and is a noisy process. When on offense, either be sure a teammate has your back, or only go for the plant if you think it is your sole chance of victory. Once you've planted the bomb, you can set up shop nearby and take down any enemy who tries to disarm it.

For defenders, if you hear the "bomb planted" warning, you can expect that the offense is in the process of setting up around the bomb site. Depending on your positioning, you should either rush to engage immediately before they can get set up, or approach more cautiously if you know you can't arrive before they get into position.

Psychic Players

S&D and Search and Rescue (S&R) greatly reward knowledge of map flow.

Players tend to take certain routes through maps more often than others. Once you know these routes, you can throw explosives in their path and set up shop in good defensive terrain with line of sight to their common approaches (on defense) or camping spots (on offense).

This can result in getting shot through a wall or sniped the instant you run around a corner—not a good feeling.

If you're new to the demolition modes, follow behind other experienced players until you start to get a feel for where (and why) players move throughout the level.

SEARCH AND RESCUE (S&R)

Search and Destroy with a twist—when a player dies, they drop a dog tag, similar to Kill Confirmed.

If a teammate picks up this tag, the friendly player respawns instantly. If an enemy picks up the tag, they are out for the round.

S&R's simple tweak to the core gameplay of S&D has a lot of ramifications for play—for one, this is no longer a one-life mode. It is possible to get a few respawns in any given round with some luck and good teammates.

This also means that moving in groups is often a good idea. If you engage at long range with a buddy watching your back, retrieving your tags becomes much easier.

This is important for both defense and offense, but defense can take advantage of the respawning slightly more easily simply because they can set up in pairs at a distance. Meanwhile, the offense naturally has to expose themselves to advance and plant the bomb or eliminate defenders.

CONTROL POINT MODES

All three of these modes focus on key hotspot objective areas scattered around the map. Because these modes have known target areas, expect more explosive Lethal and Tactical usage here than in other modes, and more players camping out around objective areas hoping to rack up big killstreaks.

The fixed nature of the objectives in these modes is shared with S&D and S&R, but unlike those modes, respawning is not restricted at all. Basically, victory in control point modes can come down to the team that works better together, even if they suffer more deaths to secure objective points.

Unlike the deathmatch modes, your personal kill score is *not* the most important factor for winning matches. Still, don't let that encourage excessively suicidal play; you don't want to give away free streaks to the enemy team. Reckless play can aid the enemy team greatly.

DOMINATION (DOM)

The most classic of all *Call of Duty* objective modes, Domination is a tug of war over three control points scattered around the map: A, B, and C.

Standing on a point long enough captures it for your team. Holding points increases your team's score over time, and the first team to the score limit wins.

Typically oriented in a straight line or a triangle, A and C are usually located very near each team's initial spawn points, while B is either somewhere in the middle of the map or off on an edge forming a triangle.

B is naturally the most hotly contested of the three points when the points are set up in a straight line, as the action gets focused in the middle of the map. However, on a triangular setup, the action can continuously shift around the level as points are taken and lost.

Half Capping

New to *Call of Duty: Ghosts* is the ability to uncap a Domination point.

If you stay on a point long enough, you can return a point to a neutral uncontrolled status. While not as good as capping it fully, this can stop the bleeding if your team is down 2-1 (or even 3-0!).

This makes the struggle over control points particularly intense. Even a momentary lapse in attention by defenders can cause a point to be reset to neutral.

Like TDM and KC, it pays to carefully monitor the spawns in Domination. When your team controls two points, the enemy team typically spawns near the third. This can let you lock the enemy team into their spawn point and seal a victory.

If this happens to you, make an effort to push out and capture the other team's rear point. This can cause your team's spawn point to shift around, breaking a lock on your original spawn location.

Sneaky Caps

A classic Domination trick: wait for a friendly to touch a flag, and when you hear the audio cue, immediately step onto a second flag.

Your second capture won't trip an announcer audio cue, and unless an enemy player notices the Domination flag flashing on their HUD, you can sneak a flag without attracting any attention.

This tactic is particularly effective if you coordinate and have one player tag B while you steal either A or C. Even if the player who touches B dies instantly, their sacrifice can swing the game by giving you a rear cap.

GRIND

A new team- and objective-based variant of Kill Confirmed, Grind challenges you to collect dog tags and deliver them to one of two points on the map (A and B). If you are killed, you lose a single dog tag.

You can carry any number of dog tags with you, but the number of tags you are carrying shows up over your head, making you a very appealing target if you have a lot of tags. You can only deposit one tag on a point every two seconds.

The first tag you deliver is instant when you touch a point, so if you are concerned about nearby enemies, you can sprint past a point to drop a tag, then seek cover nearby to see if any adversaries investigate the delivery.

Capturing Tags

Whenever any player is delivering dog tags to one of the control points, your HUD is updated, showing if a point has a hostile player delivering tags to it.

Use these visual updates to identify enemy movements and engage as appropriate.

Be very careful when delivering tags—opponents can and will lurk nearby to assassinate any player who goes for a delivery without securing the area.

BLITZ

Blitz is a new game mode and a spiritual replacement for the classic Capture the Flag mode. In Blitz, each team has a single control point at their base. When you reach the enemy control point and touch it by running into it, your team scores a point, and you are teleported back to your side of the map.

Blitz is a very offense-focused mode because it is extremely difficult to completely lock an enemy team out from scoring when all they have to do is touch your control point.

That said, much like Capture the Flag in the past, a strong defense can win the match by simply delaying the opposing team from scoring. If your offense can pull ahead because your defense is stalling the enemy pushes, you can cruise to an easy victory.

It's important to understand that you don't need to stop every enemy player from scoring when playing defense; you just need to stop enough opposing players to give your team an edge.

On offense, speed is paramount. Bring your fastest builds. Every second longer it takes you to cross the map and reach the goal means fewer points for your team.

If the enemy team is actively defending, you may need to switch your weapons around to suit the map and pick off the defenders once you know where they are likely to be hiding. In general, though, a fast-moving build that can engage rapidly in CQB to mid-range fighting is what you want.

When halftime is reached, teams switch sides and play until the score or time limit is hit.

One viable tactic is to save up your hard-hitting killstreaks for the second round and bombard the enemy team. Though this is typically more useful to cement a victory, you can use this technique to come back from behind if you can disrupt the opposing team enough to score some extra points while you delay their offense.

SPECIALIZED TRAINING   THE CAMPAIGN   MP INTRO & BASIC TRAINING   SQUADS   MP ARMORY   PERKS   KILLSTREAKS   MP MAPS   **MP GAME MODES**   SAFEGUARD   EXTINCTION   CLASSIFIED   ACHIEVEMENTS & TROPHIES

283

CUSTOM CLASSES

Following is a list of class templates for various game modes.

Rather than simply mimicking them point for point (though you can certainly do so!), look at the intent behind the builds presented here. You can use the basic concepts here as a basis to build your own custom classes.

Much like the perk builds, these custom classes are intended to show you examples of cohesive builds that use a combination of weapons, equipment, perks, and killstreaks to create a powerful and effective class suited for different game modes and playstyles.

Similarly, when putting together killstreak packages, customize them to suit your personal playstyle and the specific mode you are playing.

There is no "one size fits all" build in *Call of Duty: Ghosts*, and part of the fun is experimenting. The Squad system lets you build up a roster of soldiers with different gear, and you can organize your soldiers by game mode, each with a set of custom classes specifically tailored to that mode.

When assembling your own classes from scratch, use the advice in the Armory, Perks, and Killstreaks sections, and build with a specific purpose in mind.

Your primary weapon determines your preferred engagement range, your secondary weapon can give you backup, your equipment aids your role on the battlefield, and your perks enhance your performance in specific aspects of combat.

Finally, use your killstreaks to complete the class, aiding you or your team in a way that most suits your personal taste and the mode you are playing.

FFA, TDM, KC, CRANKED

Deathmatch Classes

Almost any sort of build can work effectively in deathmatch modes.

Because they have no fixed objective points, combat tends to flow around the map, though there are usually hotspots where many routes join together, particularly around the center of the map.

That being the case, the most important factor in deathmatch classes is comfort. You want classes that you can play well with, no matter the situation or the map involved.

Short or long range makes no real difference, as you can fight effectively at any range (map permitting).

If any mode encourages CQB over the others, it's Kill Confirmed. But even there, you can play a ranged fighter if your teammates are aggressive about picking up the tags you generate at a distance.

ROAMER

A combat supremacy setup, use your edge in gunfights to rack up the kills. Try to keep your engagement ranges to medium distance, and abuse your perk edge to take down targets.

Use your under-barrel shotgun or quick swap to your pistols when entering CQB environments, and use them to eliminate targets at close range quickly.

If you expect multiple rapid engagements, take Sleight of Hand. If the map is larger or speed is a priority, take Marathon or Agility.

If you run Specialist, swap the position of Scavenger and Incog depending on which weapon you choose. If your ammo consumption is low, you can delay acquiring Scavenger.

SPEED

Choose your favored submachine gun (SMG) with a silencer. Abuse your Scavenger ammo with Steady Aim, and mow down targets from the hip while you move swiftly around the map.

It is possible to run this setup with a shotgun, but shotguns (especially when silenced) are even more restricted in their range than an SMG, and they rely on picking up a longer range weapon on the field to be fully effective.

That said, on certain maps, a shotgun can be even more effective than an SMG if you can keep to knife fight distance for the reliable one-shot kills.

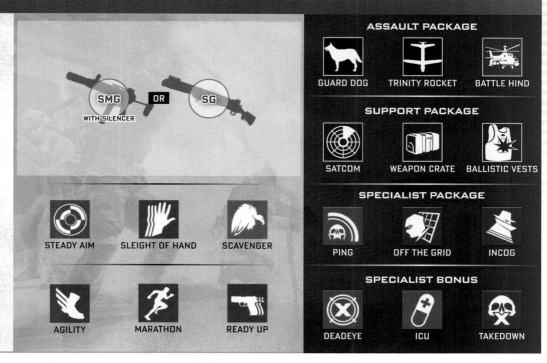

SMG OR SG
WITH SILENCER

STEADY AIM   SLEIGHT OF HAND   SCAVENGER

AGILITY   MARATHON   READY UP

ASSAULT PACKAGE

GUARD DOG   TRINITY ROCKET   BATTLE HIND

SUPPORT PACKAGE

SATCOM   WEAPON CRATE   BALLISTIC VESTS

SPECIALIST PACKAGE

PING   OFF THE GRID   INCOG

SPECIALIST BONUS

DEADEYE   ICU   TAKEDOWN

HEAVY GUNNER

The Chain SAW light machine gun (LMG) is particularly well-suited for this setup, and the K7 or CBJ-MS with their integrated silencer or armor-piercing ammo also work quite well. Most importantly, choose the gun you are most comfortable with.

No subtlety whatsoever to this build. Use your high rate of fire and the Deadeye perk to mow down enemies anywhere from close- to close-medium range with your tricked-out weapon.

This build is well-suited to Specialist, using the consecutive kills to power up Deadeye and unlock more perks.

If you are running Specialist with the SMG, you may want to swap Sleight of Hand with Quickdraw to pick it up earlier on account of the much more frequent reloads than the LMG setup. If you're running it with an LMG, swap the order of Quickdraw and Stalker.

LMG OR SMG
WITH RAPID FIRE   WITH RAPID FIRE

DEADEYE

EXTRA ATTACHMENT

ASSAULT PACKAGE

SATCOM   GUARD DOG

SUPPORT PACKAGE

SATCOM   WEAPON CRATE   BALLISTIC VESTS

SPECIALIST PACKAGE

SCAVENGER   QUICKDRAW   STALKER

SPECIALIST BONUS

MARATHON   AGILITY

SLEIGHT OF HAND   GAMBLER   READY UP

SPECIALIZED TRAINING   THE CAMPAIGN   MP INTRO & BASIC TRAINING   SQUADS   MP ARMORY   PERKS   KILLSTREAKS   MP MAPS   **MP GAME MODES**   SAFEGUARD   EXTINCTION   CLASSIFIED   ACHIEVEMENTS & TROPHIES

285

ALL-PURPOSE

Overkill and Extra Attachment together give you your pick of the perfect long- and close-range setup.

Customize your two favorite long- and close-range weapons to their fullest. Reflex removes most of the speed danger from swapping between two primary weapons.

It is very important to switch weapons frequently. Otherwise, you're not getting full value out of the points spent on Overkill and Extra Attachment, and you should run a different build.

Specialist gives you the extra punch to compete with builds running gun combat perks. Scavenger ensures that your custom weapons stay loaded, but you can get away with using the Weapon Crate, as well.

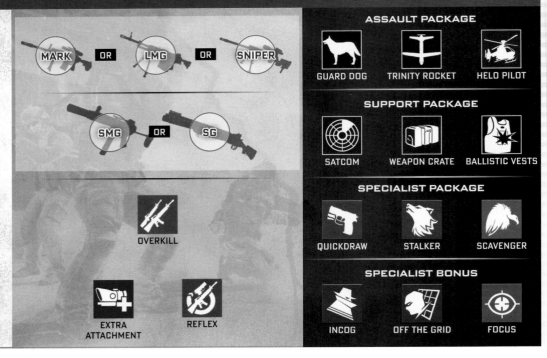

S&D AND S&R

Demolition Classes

S&R and (especially) S&D require a different mindset than the other modes. While S&R has some respawning, S&D has none, and both modes tend to be filled with short, high-intensity, and high-fatality rounds.

Consequently, high streaks are generally inadvisable, and you want builds on offense or defense that give you an edge for stalking enemies, hiding from them, planting the bomb, or granting extra mobility to hunt down planters.

OFFENSE

Choose your primary weapon based on map size and expected engagement range. Use your silenced pistol if you completely get the drop on a defender to stay off the radar.

Use Smoke grenades to cover (or fake) a plant.

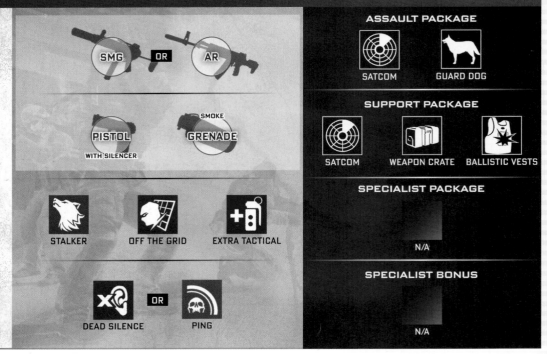

DEFENSE

Set up your explosives near expected approach routes by the offense, then settle in to pick off any players who make it through safely. Depending on the map size, a marksman rifle or even sniper rifle may also be effective, though mobility can be a problem for the heavier snipers if you need to relocate in a hurry.

If you're using an SMG, you may want to swap out Incog for Marathon or Agility to aid your mobility. Doing so also opens up the option to drop Ready Up for another two-point perk.

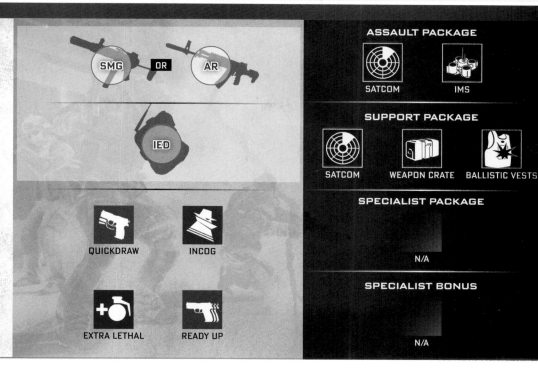

SMG **OR** AR

IED

QUICKDRAW

INCOG

EXTRA LETHAL

READY UP

ASSAULT PACKAGE

SATCOM

IMS

SUPPORT PACKAGE

SATCOM

WEAPON CRATE

BALLISTIC VESTS

SPECIALIST PACKAGE

N/A

SPECIALIST BONUS

N/A

DOMINATION, GRIND, BLITZ

Control Point Classes

Generalist classes can do quite well in Domination and Grind. Blitz tends to call for more focused offensive or defensive setups, though you can still play either in a pinch with an all-purpose build.

Domination is also very friendly to classes built for either breaking points or defending them. (You might uncharitably say camping them.) Either way, it is effective for racking up streaks.

CAPPER

Particularly effective in Domination for securing impossible points. Use your Trophies or Smoke grenades alongside your Riot Shield and perks to force uncap or fully cap a point.

With any team backup at all, it's extremely difficult to stop this build from taking a point.

RIOT SHIELD

PISTOL

BLAST SHIELD

TROPHY SYSTEM **OR** SMOKE GRENADE

ICU

TAC RESIST

MARATHON

EXTRA TACTICAL

ASSAULT PACKAGE

SATCOM

IMS

SENTRY GUN

SUPPORT PACKAGE

BALLISTIC VESTS

NIGHT OWL

GROUND JAMMER

SPECIALIST PACKAGE

N/A

SPECIALIST BONUS

N/A

SPECIALIZED TRAINING   THE CAMPAIGN   MP INTRO & BASIC TRAINING   SQUADS   MP ARMORY   PERKS   KILLSTREAKS   MP MAPS   **MP GAME MODES**   SAFEGUARD   EXTINCTION   CLASSIFIED   ACHIEVEMENTS & TROPHIES

287

SIEGE

The other brute force approach to clearing any point or any defense. Use your explosives to lay waste to enemies guarding an area. Use the large blast radius from your Thermobarics to light up opponents with Recon, then finish them with your Lethals, your launcher, or your underbarrel grenade launcher.

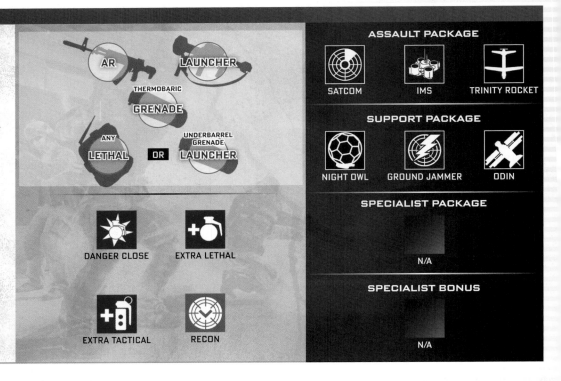

AR   LAUNCHER

THERMOBARIC
GRENADE

ANY
LETHAL   OR   UNDERBARREL
GRENADE
LAUNCHER

DANGER CLOSE   EXTRA LETHAL

EXTRA TACTICAL   RECON

ASSAULT PACKAGE
SATCOM   IMS   TRINITY ROCKET

SUPPORT PACKAGE
NIGHT OWL   GROUND JAMMER   ODIN

SPECIALIST PACKAGE
N/A

SPECIALIST BONUS
N/A

DEFENSE

Set up shop a good distance away from any point you want to guard. Gun down anyone who gets anywhere near it from long range. Shift position to make yourself difficult to spot, and don't let anyone get to grips with you.

If you irritate enemies enough that they start skipping the objective and coming after you, you're doing your job. If you're comfortable without extra protection from the Trophy System or Motion Sensor, you can swap the equipment and Extra Tactical out for another two-point perk.

Another option if you take the Assault Package: determined point defense can rack up very long streaks, so you could take Trinity Rocket, Battle Hind, and any one of Gryphon, Juggernaut, Helo Pilot, or Loki.

LMG   OR   MARK   OR   SNIPER

PISTOL

TROPHY
SYSTEM   OR   MOTION
SENSOR

QUICKDRAW   INCOG

FOCUS   EXTRA TACTICAL

ASSAULT PACKAGE
IMS   SENTRY GUN   VULTURE

SUPPORT PACKAGE
BALLISTIC VEST   GROUND JAMMER   ORACLE

SPECIALIST PACKAGE
BLAST SHIELD   BLIND EYE   TAC RESIST

SPECIALIST BONUS
DEADEYE   ICU   READY UP

RUNNER

Particularly useful for Blitz, but it can also be used to run rear flags in Domination.

Take a shotgun or SMG. If you go Specialist, aim to pick up a second mid- to long-range weapon from the battlefield once you've expended your launcher ammo.

SMG OR SG

LAUNCHER

MARATHON AGILITY

STEADY AIM OFF THE GRID READY UP

ASSAULT PACKAGE

SATCOM GUARD DOG VULTURE

SUPPORT PACKAGE

SATCOM NIGHT OWL ORACLE

SPECIALIST PACKAGE

SLEIGHT OF HAND SCAVENGER REFLEX

SPECIALIST BONUS

DEADEYE INCOG

TEAM SUPPORT

Continuously deploy cheap SATCOMs on the battlefield with Hardline looping, giving your team powerful situational awareness. Use your other awareness perks to keep tabs on the opposing team's movements even when they are running Off the Grid.

Locate enemy equipment (and nearby enemies) with SitRep, hear nearby foes with Amplify, and boost your already strong satellite coverage even further with Wiretap.

And on top of all that, every enemy you kill generates a mini radar sweep and gets you one step closer to yet another SATCOM.

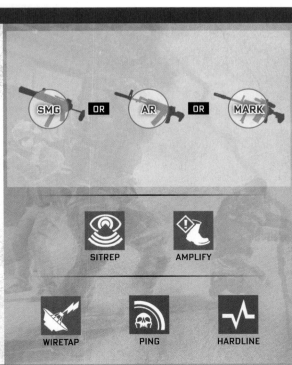

SMG OR AR OR MARK

SITREP AMPLIFY

WIRETAP PING HARDLINE

ASSAULT PACKAGE

SATCOM

SUPPORT PACKAGE

SATCOM

SPECIALIST PACKAGE

N/A

SPECIALIST BONUS

N/A

SPECIALIZED TRAINING   THE CAMPAIGN   MP INTRO & BASIC TRAINING   SQUADS   MP ARMORY   PERKS   KILLSTREAKS   MP MAPS   **MP GAME MODES**   SAFEGUARD   EXTINCTION   CLASSIFIED   ACHIEVEMENTS & TROPHIES

289

SAFEGUARD

Safeguard is a cooperative game mode that pits you and up to three other players against waves of increasingly difficult bots. The Safeguard maps are all from the Multiplayer game. Additionally, experience and Squad Points earned in online Safeguard carry over into the main Multiplayer game.

SAFEGUARD TYPES

There are three types of Safeguard games that contain different Leaderboards.

- **Safeguard** lasts for 20 rounds.
- **Safeguard Extended** lasts for 40 rounds.
- **Safeguard Infinite** continues until your squad is defeated.

Select the game type based on how much time you have to play. Safeguard Extended and Infinite games can take over 45 minutes, depending on how well your team does.

OBTAINING WEAPONS AND PERKS

You earn Support Drops by killing enemies. Your Support Drop bar is just below your Weapon bar in the screen's upper-left corner. As your team kills more and more enemies, this bar increases. When filled up, a helicopter arrives and drops Support Crates. You get two crates, plus one for each additional player in the game.

Support Crates can contain weapons as well as Perks. The only way to obtain new weapons is via Support Crates; you cannot loot enemy corpses for munitions.

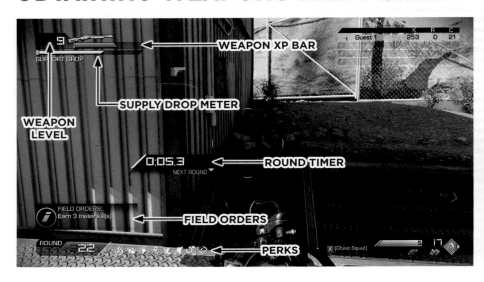

LOOT ROUNDS

The first round in Safeguard is a Loot Round. Every five rounds after that (Round 6, 11, 16, etc.) is also a Loot Round. During a Loot Round, you have 20 seconds to grab as many Killstreak bonuses as possible. You can hold up to three Killstreaks, and you can obtain multiple Killstreaks of the same type.

KILLSTREAKS

In Safeguard, you can carry up to three Killstreaks. There aren't as many Killstreaks available as in Multiplayer, but the ones that are available function identically to the ones in the MP game.

IMS: Plant this device on the ground and it lobs grenades at enemies that come into range. Good for covering streets, alleys, or corridors.

Sentry Gun: Set this weapon up, and it mows down enemies that come too close for a limited time. You can use it to cover entranceways.

Trinity Rocket: This Killstreak gives you a rocket that fires down on surrounding enemies. It's rare that enemies get bunched together, but if they do, the Trinity Rocket is ideal.

Vulture: The Vulture is an automated Drone that follows wherever you go. It kills nearby enemies and is very effective in wide-open spaces. It lasts for about sixty seconds.

Helo Scout: Activate the Helo Scout to enter a helicopter with a sniper rifle. From the helicopter, you are safe from enemy attacks and free to snipe any visible enemies. Use this to escape a hairy situation.

Battle Hind: This is an automatic attack chopper that arrives and blows away enemies. It can target for about sixty seconds.

GHOSTS

Your most potent deployable asset is a Ghost. The Ghost is a powerful bot that can resurrect you. They do a pretty good job of killing enemies too. In solo mode, you get one Ghost to deploy every 20 rounds; in multiplayer, you only get one to use. You cannot stack multiple Ghosts.

Ghost squad members last as long as you can keep them alive. Try not to run off without your Ghost when lots of enemies are around. This usually ends with a dead Ghost.

The Ghost can take a lot of damage, but as soon as he's overwhelmed, he can get killed. Therefore, your top priority is to keep enemies off the Ghost while he's alive. If you can keep enemies back, the Ghost can survive many rounds, keeping you both alive much longer.

The Ghost is particularly vulnerable to the Striker enemies. Use stun grenades if one gets too close.

PERKS

Perks work the same as they do in the Multiplayer game. They provide a powerful edge against your enemies, allowing you to reload faster, sprint longer, or inflict more damage.

The following is a complete list of Perks available in Safeguard. For in-depth coverage of these Perks, please refer to the Multiplayer chapter:

Agility: Move Faster.

Sleight of Hand: Reload your weapon twice as fast.

Quickdraw: Halves time to ADS.

Marathon: Unlimited sprint.

Reflex: Quickly swap weapons.

Steady Aim: Reduces hipfire spread.

Ready Up: Brings weapon up more quickly after a sprint.

Blast Shield: Provides damage resistance against explosives.

Stalker: ADS does not slow you down.

Focus: Reduces flinching in combat; reduces weapon sway.

ICU: Increases health regeneration speed.

On the Go: Can reload while sprinting.

Trigger Happy: This is the only Perk unique to Safeguard. Whenever you get a kill, your gun auto-reloads, provided you have the ammo stock. This is an amazing Perk that pretty much eliminates the need to ever reload your gun.

SPECIALIZED TRAINING   THE CAMPAIGN   MP INTRO & BASIC TRAINING   SQUADS   MP ARMORY   PERKS   KILLSTREAKS   MP MAPS   MP GAME MODES   **SAFEGUARD**   EXTINCTION   CLASSIFIED   ACHIEVEMENTS & TROPHIES

291

WEAPONS

You always start a Safeguard session with a meager pistol. But as Supply Drops are earned, you get better and better guns. You start off receiving SMGs and shotguns, but as you get to further rounds, you can find more powerful weapons like assault rifles and LMGs.

In Safeguard, you can always carry two weapons. If you pick up a new weapon, your old weapon disappears forever; it can't be picked up again.

Generally speaking, you should stick to long-range weapons. This gives you an edge on the enemies with medium- or short-range weapons (the exception is the final enemy type). Looting a crate for a weapon that you currently have equipped provides two benefits. First, your weapon gets a free level (see Upgrading Your Weapon section); second, you get a full stock of ammo for the weapon.

Here is a list of all the weapons that can be found in crates:

MP-443 Grach (Pistol): Starting weapon; armor piercing.

MTS-255 (Shotgun): Equipped with Muzzle Brake and Red Dot Sight.

FP6 (Shotgun): Equipped with Muzzle Brake and Red Dot Sight.

Vepr (SMG): Equipped with Grip.

MTAR-X (SMG): Equipped with Holographic Sight.

AK-12 (Assault Rifle): Equipped with Flash Suppressor and Grip.

ARX-160 (Assault Rifle): Equipped with Flash Suppressor and VMR Scope.

M27-IAR (LMG): Equipped with Flash Suppressor and VMR Scope.

Chain SAW (LMG): Equipped with Flash Suppressor.

USR (Sniper Rifle): Equipped with Variable Lens Scope and Extended Mags.

Throwing Knife

Wild Widow: A rare weapon that has extra-high damage (one hit kills) and extra-high penetration

UPGRADING YOUR WEAPON

> ### Sniper Rifles
> Sniper rifles level up more than twice as fast as normal weapons.

While using each of your weapons for kills, the weapon increases in level. The higher your weapon's level, the more damage it does. This is important because the enemies' health slowly increases as the waves increase. You need to pick your primary weapon within the first 2-10 waves; this gives you time to level it before the enemies get too difficult.

GETTING DOWNED

In Safeguard, when in Last Stand mode, you receive unlimited ammunition for your weapons. Just because you're down, doesn't mean you're helpless! Once in Last Stand, you have 30 seconds to be revived. When downed, you can still activate your Ghost (provided you haven't yet), and he will come and try to revive you.

In multiplayer, either the Ghost or a teammate can revive you. If you revive another player, you are rewarded with a Flak Jacket, which can absorb some damage. Also in multiplayer, if you die in Last Stand, you return at the start of the next wave.

When downed, you slowly lose the Perks you've earned. It's very important that your team revives each other as quickly as possible.

POWER-UPS

As you kill enemies, they have a chance of dropping one of two power-up types.

WEAPON LEVEL-UP

The sheriff's badge icon grants a free weapon level on your currently equipped weapon. Your weapon level jumps to the next level's start, so if your current weapon is about to level up, consider sharing it with a teammate or switching to an alternate weapon before grabbing it.

AMMO REFILL

You can also find much-needed Ammo Refills on enemies. These look like a rotating line of assault rifle rounds. Grabbing one of these power-ups refills your entire team's ammo stocks. As an added bonus, it also refills your entire team's health. It can be a viable strategy to charge through enemies to grab an Ammo Refill since it instantly heals you. Be sure to let your team know before grabbing one.

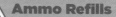

> **Ammo Refills**
> Only one Ammo Refill can be present on the map at a time.

GRENADES

You're equipped with IEDs for your Lethal grenade, and Flashbangs for your Tactical grenade. These grenades are refilled whenever you find an Ammo Refill power-up.

You can only have two IEDs deployed on the map at once. If you throw out a third, the first explodes.

ENEMIES

RAVAGER
FIRST APPEARS: ROUND 1

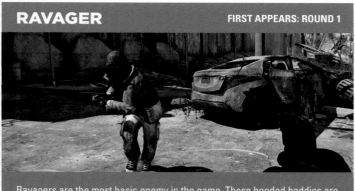

Ravagers are the most basic enemy in the game. These hooded baddies are armed with shotguns. Solo, they aren't much of a threat. If your character is surrounded in close quarters, they can down you in moments.

ENFORCER
FIRST APPEARS: ROUND 5

Enforcers are lightly armored troops with SMGs. The SMGs have slightly longer range than the shotguns, but they are still easy to pick off before they get too close. Up close, they can inflict a lot of damage quickly, as they have excellent accuracy. Go for headshots for quicker kills.

TOWER
FIRST APPEARS: ROUND 4

Tower is a crazed German Shepherd who charges your position and attempts to bite you. They are best taken down with short-range weapons. The dogs have low health and inflict low damage.

STRIKER
FIRST APPEARS: ROUND 9

A Striker is a Ravager with a Riot Shield. These enemies don't try to fire on you; instead, they charge with shield raised and try to get a melee hit. Try to get behind them (best done with a teammate) to take them down. They are also vulnerable to I.E.D.s. If you flashbang them, they are stunned and run blindly forward, giving you an opportunity to knife them from behind.

SPECIALIZED TRAINING   THE CAMPAIGN   MP INTRO & BASIC TRAINING   SQUADS   MP ARMORY   PERKS   KILLSTREAKS   MP MAPS   MP GAME MODES   **SAFEGUARD**   EXTINCTION   CLASSIFIED   ACHIEVEMENTS & TROPHIES

293

DESTRUCTOR

FIRST APPEARS: ROUND 13

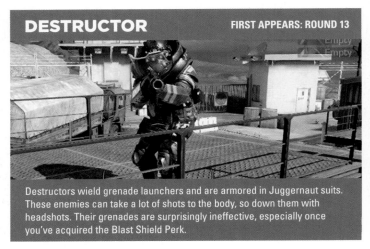

Destructors wield grenade launchers and are armored in Juggernaut suits. These enemies can take a lot of shots to the body, so down them with headshots. Their grenades are surprisingly ineffective, especially once you've acquired the Blast Shield Perk.

HAMMER

FIRST APPEARS: ROUND 24

The Hammer looks very much like the Enforcer, but it's armed with an LMG. These are the longest-range enemies in the game, and they can hit you from afar. When these guys start showing up, your team better find some good cover. Hammers are highly vulnerable to melee attacks.

TEAM FIELD ORDERS

In round 4, you receive special Field Orders. These can be things like get 10 Headshots, or get 10 Melee Kills. When your team reaches this target, everyone receives a Death Machine minigun with explosive ammo for 60 seconds. This essentially makes your team invincible for the duration, so try not to waste it by completing a challenge at the end of a round.

After round 4, every fourth round presents a chance for new Field Orders. But you first need to complete the previous orders.

GENERAL STRATEGY

MULTIPLAYER

Safeguard is a game best played with friends. The number of enemies that appear can be very difficult to defend against solo. Plus, the chance to be revived multiple times by your teammates gives you a huge edge.

When playing with friends, search the map for a room that has one or two entrances and can easily be defended. This way, you and your teammates can all stay near each other in case someone is downed. Wait to go for supply crates between rounds to ensure no one gets caught in the open.

Getting downed is the worst thing that can happen in the game. Not only could it mean the beginning of the end for your team, but it also means you might lose some of your hard-earned Perks.

SOLO

Solo play in Safeguard is an extreme challenge. You only get one Ghost every 20 rounds, so you need to save him for when you really need it. Unlike in multiplayer, holing up in a room is not the best strategy since it means the enemies will eventually be able to overwhelm you. The enemies always know your position, and even if you kill the first four enemies, the fifth might get you when your clip clicks empty.

The best strategy is to find a room or hallway that has a good escape route. A one-way escape route like a hole in a floor is perfect since you can be sure enemies won't be coming up that way. As soon as you start taking damage, evade through the hole. Then come back around to surprise the enemies from behind with a fully-reloaded weapon.

Eventually, you're going to get downed. When you do, pull out your Ghost. Your Ghost has excellent range, accuracy, and health. When you've summoned your Ghost, your strategy should change slightly. Both you and your Ghost have superior range over your enemies. Try to find a long corridor or street that only allows enemies to approach from one direction. Use your superior range to wipe out the enemies before they get close enough to you. Stay near your Ghost, and keep him alive. Once he goes down, the game gets much, much harder. Good luck!

TIPS

When only a few enemies are left to kill in a round, they are highlighted with an orange outline. This makes them easier to spot and kill.

If you're hit by an enemy, they are outlined on your HUD, making it easy to see who is targeting you.

Knifing an enemy grants experience for your currently-equipped weapon.

All enemies are one-hit melee kills except for the Destructors.

Points are rewarded for each bullet hit. Weapons that fire more rapidly, but do less damage, result in more Support Drops. Conversely, weapons that do major damage, like Wild Widow and the USR, are not as good at calling in Support Drops.

Completing a round auto-revives any downed players.

Players take slightly less damage while they are reviving a team member.

Crates won't disappear while you are looting them. As long as you start the looting action before the end of the Loot Round, you still get the Killstreak (provided you don't cancel before the progress bar finishes).

Support Drops stay on the map until another Support Drop is called in. There's no rush to get them; don't endanger your strategy just to score an extra Perk.

Be sure to use your Killstreaks on the level before the Loot Round (Round 10, 15, 20, etc.). You can only carry three Killstreaks, so those you don't get are wasted.

If everyone on your team goes for melee kills the first round, you can score an early Support Drop before the round is over.

With the Death Machine equipped, you can still switch to other weapons. This is handy if you find a weapon level-up. It's better to level up a regularly-used weapon than the Death Machine.

SPECIALIZED TRAINING   THE CAMPAIGN   MP INTRO & BASIC TRAINING   SQUADS   MP ARMORY   PERKS   KILLSTREAKS   MP MAPS   MP GAME MODES   **SAFEGUARD**   EXTINCTION   CLASSIFIED   ACHIEVEMENTS & TROPHIES

295

EXTINCTION MODE

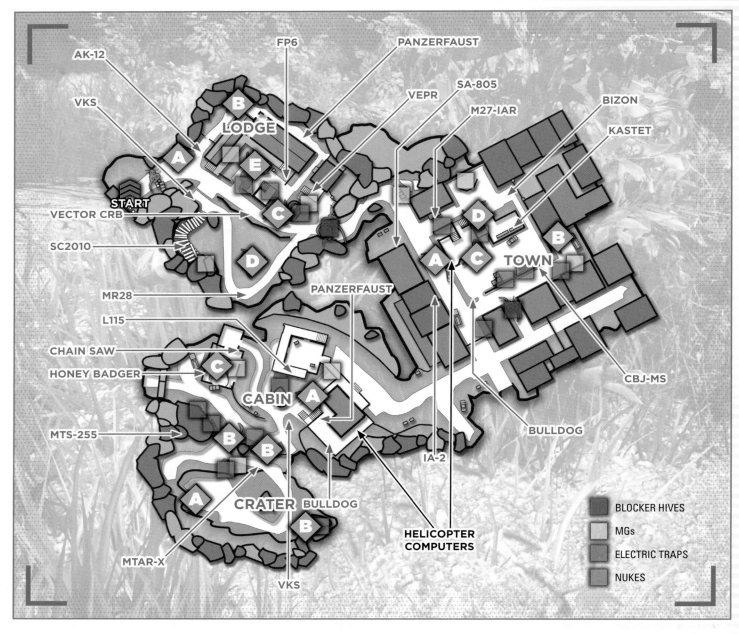

AK-12
FP6
PANZERFAUST
VEPR
SA-805
M27-IAR
BIZON
KASTET
VKS
B
LODGE
E
A
START
C
D
A
TOWN
VECTOR CRB
SC2010
D
D
C
B
MR28
PANZERFAUST
L115
CHAIN SAW
C
HONEY BADGER
A
CBJ-MS
CABIN
MTS-255
B
B
BULLDOG
A
CRATER **BULLDOG**
IA-2
B
MTAR-X
HELICOPTER COMPUTERS
VKS

BLOCKER HIVES
MGs
ELECTRIC TRAPS
NUKES

Call of Duty: Ghosts includes an entirely new type of cooperative gameplay mode. You and your friends will be pitted against a tremendous horde of aliens as you work to nuke the aliens and send them back to wherever they came from.

You unlock Extinction mode by hitting rank 5 in MP or Squad mode and completing the first chapter of the Ghosts campaign.

Achievements

If you are looking for Extinction Achievements, those are marked secret; you can read about them in this guide's Achievements chapter.

EXTINCTION BASICS

Your goal in Extinction is to destroy 14 hives, activate a nuke, and evac to the drop zone without getting killed. You can play with 1-4 people. If you are playing at home, you can play split-screen with a friend.

Completing Extinction is possible with any number of players, but if you are playing with more than one player, it requires great teamwork, a solid understanding of the gameplay fundamentals, and lots and lots of practice.

PURCHASING WEAPONS

Among all three maps, there are purchasable weapons scattered on the ground. To acquire a weapon, move near it to see how much it costs. Hold down the *Interact* button to purchase the weapon and equip it.

Unlike other game modes, in Extinction, you can only have one primary attack weapon (although there is a pistol skill tree upgrade that allows you to carry a second one).

In order to replace your primary attack weapon, you must equip it and purchase the new weapon. If you have already purchased one weapon and then try to purchase a second with your pistol out, the game informs you that you can't do that.

DESTROYING HIVES

There are two types of hive encounters in Extinction: drillable hives and helicopter hives.

Drillable Hives

Drillable hives require a team member to place a drill in a marked sensitive hive zone. Once the drill has been placed, a special HUD element appears on the left side of the screen.

The vertical bar shows how close the drill is to destroying the hive. The percentage shows how much health the drill has. As enemies attack the drill, this percentage goes down.

Once the drill is below 75% armor, you can repair the drill by hitting the *Interact* button. Repairing a hive restores it to the full 100% no matter how much damage it's taken.

All damage to the drill is repaired automatically when you successfully destroy a hive.

As you progress through the game, the aliens inflict more damage more quickly. If the drill ever decreases to 0% health, you lose the mission, so protect that drill!

Blocker Hives

Some hives are too big for your drill, and you need helicopter support. When you reach one of these hives, a helicopter flies on the scene for support. Your job is to protect the helicopter from taking damage from the Scorpion alien type.

If the helicopter takes too much damage, it evades and temporarily won't be able to attack the hive. The longer it takes for the helicopter to down the hive, the tougher the enemies get. Keeping fire off your helicopter must be your top priority.

If you find an opening in the aliens' attack, you can help speed up the Helicopter's damage by attacking with incendiary weapons and propane tanks.

LAST STAND

If you are playing single player, you get one automatic revive. If you are downed, you automatically get back up in a few seconds. You get a new revive as you break through to each new area (after each blocker hive). Multiple revives (Last Stands) stack up to two.

When playing cooperatively, you need to have a teammate revive you. When you are first downed, you enter last stand mode and can attack with your pistol. You now have 30 seconds until you bleed out, and your teammates can come to revive you.

If the 30 seconds expire, you are moved to spectator mode, and a set of dog tags drops on the ground where you died. Your teammates can still revive when they have an opening but it takes longer than when you're in Last Stand.

Whenever you are downed, you automatically lose $500.

TRAPS

You can find traps in all areas of the map. When deployed, traps damage enemies when they move through them.

Fire and electric traps work the same way; just start the trap up, and it will inflict damage when an adversary runs over it.

SPECIALIZED TRAINING   THE CAMPAIGN   MP INTRO & BASIC TRAINING   SQUADS   MP ARMORY   PERKS   KILLSTREAKS   MP MAPS   MP GAME MODES   SAFEGUARD   **EXTINCTION**   CLASSIFIED   ACHIEVEMENTS & TROPHIES

297

Traps vary in cost from $300-$700. It's almost always worth activating a trap if it is near a drill you are defending. Remember, any aliens you don't have to kill are saved ammunition refill costs.

The Engineer class has a special ability that makes traps cheaper, deadlier, and last longer.

There are special traps in the Town and Cabin sections (see the map).

In Town, there is a laptop located on the second floor of the middle building (see the map). Put $3,000 (or $6,000 in MP) into this laptop, and the helicopter gunship arrives to help you defend the drill. This cannot be done while attacking a blocker hive.

In the Cabin area, look for the cabin in a basement that opens after you destroy the first hive. (The hive covers the entrance to this basement.) The cost is the same, but the helicopter does not do a good job of covering the Crater area (the area that opens up after you clear Cabin).

ALIENS

Scouts

Scouts are the first type of creature you encounter in Extinction mode. These little guys move fast and have fierce melee attacks. They also have moderate armor on their heads and backs.

They aren't a major threat to your drill, but you should do your best to keep them off. Traps work very well against them.

Scorpions

These ranged attackers fire acidic mini-bombs at your team. If one hits you, you take ongoing poison damage, and it becomes harder to see. These are the primary attackers of your helicopter during the helicopter siege objectives.

Scorpions prefer to attack from buildings. Once they show up (starting at the first helicopter event), keep your eyes on the top of structures in the surrounding area. You need a long-range weapon to attack them effectively.

Scorpions attack with gas clouds. Unless you are a Medic, you continue taking damage from the cloud if you stand in it. Always move out of the way whenever a Scorpion hits you; that ongoing damage can really add up.

Keep a careful eye on the ground for yellow pools of acids, as stepping in these causes severe damage.

Scorpions begin appearing during the first helicopter barrier event.

Hunters

Hunters are heavily armored, larger versions of Scouts. Hunters deal massive damage to the drill, and their good amount of health and armor makes them difficult to kill quickly.

If a Hunter is on you, quickly switch to your pistol, and sprint to get some distance. Once they are in melee range, they can take down your entire health bar in no time.

Hunters begin appearing when you reach the Town area.

Seekers

When meteors fall from the sky, these nasty little explosive buggers come out and attack your drill and your team. They don't take many hits to kill, but if they are too close, their explosion still hurts you.

Seekers begin appearing when you start the second drill in the Town.

Rhinos

Rhinos are the ultimate alien defense. These massive, armored creatures emerge from the ground and have a charge attack that does major damage and is difficult to evade.

Their thick armor can absorb massive damage. When they appear, they are always a significant threat. Taking them down needs to be a top priority.

Try to get to higher ground and use buildings to evade them. Armor-piercing weapons are the best type of attack to use.

Rhinos first appear when you reach the Cabin area.

SCAVENGE LOCATIONS

You can search random hot spots called *scavenge locations* throughout the campaign. These appear in different places each time you play through Extinction mode. Sometimes they appear as ammo crates, sometimes as garbage heaps.

These scavenge locations will provide a random item.

The item is never bad, and the worst thing you can get is a semi-useless item like an ammo clip. Therefore, it's always worth taking a few seconds to search a scavenge location when you find them.

Cash: You can earn $50 to $500 cash from searching.

Ammo Clip: An extra clip of ammo for your currently equipped weapon.

Specialized Ammo: This can be one clip of armor-piercing, incendiary, stun, or explosive ammunition.

Rapid Fire Upgrade: This weapon attachment can only be used on non-pistol weapons. It increases the speed the weapon fires.

Burst Fire Attachment: Allows a semi-automatic weapon to fire in bursts (rifles only).

Muzzle Brake Attachment: Improves weapon accuracy.

Grip: Reduces weapon recoil.

Red Dot Sight: Equips a medium-range scope on your weapon.

Holographic Scope: Equips a medium- to long-range scope on your weapon.

ACOG Scope: Equips a long-range scope on your weapon.

Thermal Hybrid Scope: Adds a special scope to your currently equipped weapon. Allows you to switch between Thermal and regular scoped vision.

Explosives: Canister Bomb, Bouncing Betty, Claymore, or Semtex grenade. You can also acquire these explosives with the explosives skill tree. Press the *Frag Grenade* button to deploy these explosives.

Flare: The flare distracts any aliens caught in its light. The aliens are then frozen and make for easy targets. Press the *Tactical Grenade* button to deploy.

Hypno Knife: If you hit an alien with this knife, it will fight on your side against other aliens for three minutes. (This does not work on Rhinos.) Press the *Tactical Grenade* button to deploy.

Trophy System: The Trophy System can be set up to deflect incoming Scorpion acid blasts. Set it up near your defensive position to neutralize the Scorpion threat. Press the *Tactical Grenade* button to deploy.

SOFLAM: A special weapon that fires massive grenades from the sky that decimate any aliens unfortunate enough to be nearby. Focus on targeting the ground rather than an individual enemy. It takes a couple of seconds for the explosives to hit. The SOFLAM is very effective against armored adversaries. The SOFLAM acts as an extra weapon, and you switch to it with the regular *Switch Weapon* button.

SPECIALIZED TRAINING   THE CAMPAIGN   MP INTRO & BASIC TRAINING   SQUADS   MP ARMORY   PERKS   KILLSTREAKS   MP MAPS   MP GAME MODES   SAFEGUARD   **EXTINCTION**   CLASSIFIED   ACHIEVEMENTS & TROPHIES

299

LEVELING UP AND LOADOUTS

Extinction features its own leveling system separate from the Multiplayer game. As you play Extinction sessions, you gain access to new skill trees that you can use as you play the game.

After each session, the game shows you what levels and abilities you've earned.

There are six skill slots that you can customize. Each skill slot has four possible skill trees that you can choose from, but you won't have access to any skill trees except the first one until you rank up in Extinction.

As you rank up each skill, effects that are for the same skill do not stack. For example, the Tank class gives bonus health. The maximum health bonus is 100%, not 250%.

CLASS

Weapon Specialist
LEVEL REQUIRED: 1

BASE ABILITY	20% MORE BULLET DAMAGE.	COST TO UPGRADE
+1	Swap weapons faster. Move faster while aiming down sight (ADS). Faster offhand use.	1 skill point
+2	Faster ADS.	1 skill point
+3	Faster reloading.	2 skill points
+4	50% more bullet damage + less spread.	3 skill points

The Weapon Specialist skill tree dramatically increases your lethality when utilizing regular weapons. No matter how much you focus on secondary abilities, you still use your weapons as your primary means of attack.

Other skills like the Ammo trees can provide additional damage to your enemies, and it's smart to stack this with a high-end Ammo upgrade.

The biggest disadvantage to the Weapon Specialist is what you don't get. If you are the Weapon Specialist, you'll be more vulnerable to attacks since you don't get the extra health from Tank or the regen from Medic. Additionally, you won't get the drill bonuses that Engineer receives, meaning that protecting the drill is even more important.

Stick to Weapon Specialist only when you are playing on a team where the Engineer and Medic roles are already filled (or when you are low level).

Tank
LEVEL REQUIRED: 3

BASE ABILITY	25% MORE HEALTH.	COST TO UPGRADE
+1	Melee attacks do 25% more damage.	1 skill Point
+2	50% more health.	1 skill point
+3	75% more health + 50% more melee damage.	2 skill points
+4	100% more health + 100% more melee damage.	3 skill points

Like the Weapon Specialist, the Tank increases your abilities to perform as an individual. The melee damage bonuses are not very helpful, but the health bonus can be huge, particularly when you're paired on a team with a Medic. A well-armored Tank working side by side with a Medic can make for a formidable force.

The first melee upgrade allows you to one-shot Scout enemies.

Engineer
LEVEL REQUIRED: 5

BASE ABILITY	PROVIDE ARMOR FOR THE DRILL AND EARN MORE CASH PER HIVE BONUS.	COST TO UPGRADE
+1	Repair the drill faster.	1 skill point
+2	Traps earn cash back.	1 skill point
+3	Increased protection while repairing the drill. Traps last longer.	2 skill points
+4	Increased trap and explosive damage, and a larger wallet to hold more cash (up to $8,000).	3 skill points

The Engineer not only provides a few great bonuses to the drill, but it also makes better use of the traps. Plan on spending a lot of your money on traps since these provide your team with the most bang for your buck. Additionally, the Engineer should always plant the drill so that it gets the 25% bonus to armor.

Medic
LEVEL REQUIRED: 10

BASE ABILITY	REVIVE ALLIES MORE QUICKLY.	COST TO UPGRADE
+1	Move faster. Increased protection while reviving others.	1 skill point
+2	Longer sprint. Teammates near you regenerate health faster.	1 skill point
+3	Ignore ongoing damage from gas clouds.	2 skill points
+4	Very fast movement. Provide health regeneration to your team no matter how far away they are.	3 skill points

The Medic requires the highest level to unlock, but Medics are the most vital part of any team. Resurrecting players and getting them back into action is much easier, and the Medic can actively regenerate everyone's health.

The class' benefits are not all team-oriented. The extra speed and invulnerability to the nasty Scorpion gas clouds can make a huge difference.

PISTOL TYPE

P226	.44 MAGNUM	M9A1	MP-443 GRACH

Long range, med damage, large clip size	High caliber six-shooter	Three round burst-fire pistol	Fully automatic close-range pistol
LEVEL REQUIRED: **1**	LEVEL REQUIRED: **7**	LEVEL REQUIRED: **13**	LEVEL REQUIRED: **16**

Upgrade Tree

ALL PISTOLS SHARE THE SAME UPGRADE TREE.

UPGRADE	DESCRIPTION	COST TO UPGRADE
+1	Increased damage at long range. Faster movement when the pistol is equipped.	1 skill point
+2	50% more ammo in each magazine.	1 skill point
+3	Carry your pistol, plus two primary weapons.	2 skill points
+4	Hip-fire two pistols for twice the firepower, and twice the ammo capacity.	3 skill points

It's easy to overlook the pistol tree since you can so quickly move on to better weapons in the game. However, the +3 upgrade allows you to carry a third weapon, which is a stellar improvement. Keep in mind that not only do you have a third weapon, but you also get a full allotment of ammo for that weapon whenever you grab an ammo chest.

The Akimbo (+4 upgrade) is too expensive. It's unlikely you will be seriously using pistols once you reach the Town and can afford it. Additionally, Akimbo makes it so you can't use ADS with your pistols, dramatically shortening their range.

AMMO TYPE

Ammo

LEVEL REQUIRED: **1**

COST TO DEPLOY: **$1250**

BASE ABILITY	REFILL BULLET WEAPONS TO 40% OF MAX AMMO.	COST TO UPGRADE
+1	Refill bullet weapons to 70% of max ammo.	1 skill point
+2	Fills the team's weapons ammo stock to the maximum.	1 skill point
+3	Fills the current clip before adding max ammo.	1 skill point
+4	Ammo regenerates for all players within a 20-foot radius of the deployed ammo box.	1 skill point

The base Ammo upgrade isn't too shabby, and an argument can be made that it's more efficient than the enhanced ammunition since it only takes two upgrade points to completely refill your team's ammo with each pack.

However, the aliens gain more hit points and armor as you progress through the game, and eventually, you need as much bonus damage as you can get in order to efficiently kill the aliens. As such, the base Ammo upgrade does quickly become obsolete.

If you do outfit with the Ammo upgrade, you should hold off on the +3 and +4 upgrades. While they provide some benefit, they aren't worth the high cost of upgrade points.

SPECIALIZED TRAINING   THE CAMPAIGN   MP INTRO & BASIC TRAINING   SQUADS   MP ARMORY   PERKS   KILLSTREAKS   MP MAPS   MP GAME MODES   SAFEGUARD   **EXTINCTION**   CLASSIFIED   ACHIEVEMENTS & TROPHIES

301

Stun Ammo

LEVEL REQUIRED: **2**

COST TO DEPLOY: **$1000**

BASE ABILITY	GIVES 30% MAX STOCK STUN AMMO TO ALL WEAPONS.	COST TO UPGRADE
+1	Gives 40% max stock stun ammo to all weapons.	1 skill point
+2	Gives 50% max stock stun ammo to all weapons.	1 skill point
+3	Gives 60% max stock stun ammo to all weapons.	1 skill point
+4	Gives 70% max stock stun ammo to all weapons.	1 skill point

Stun ammunition temporarily shocks any enemy it hits, doing a small amount of bonus damage. If the enemy is vulnerable, it also stuns them for a moment.

Incendiary Ammo

LEVEL REQUIRED: **12**

COST TO DEPLOY: **$1200**

BASE ABILITY	GIVES 30% MAX STOCK INCENDIARY AMMO TO ALL WEAPONS.	COST TO UPGRADE
+1	Gives 40% max stock incendiary ammo to all weapons.	1 skill point
+2	Gives 50% max stock incendiary ammo to all weapons.	1 skill point
+3	Gives 60% max stock incendiary ammo to all weapons.	1 skill point
+4	Gives 70% max stock incendiary ammo to all weapons.	1 skill point

Incendiary ammo lights an enemy on fire, inflicting a small amount of ongoing damage to the creature. It also can be used to help attack Barrier Hives.

Explosive Ammo

LEVEL REQUIRED: **20**

COST TO DEPLOY: **$1250**

BASE ABILITY	GIVES 30% MAX STOCK EXPLOSIVE AMMO TO ALL WEAPONS.	COST TO UPGRADE
+1	Gives 40% max stock explosive ammo to all weapons.	1 skill point
+2	Gives 50% max stock explosive ammo to all weapons.	1 skill point
+3	Gives 60% max stock explosive ammo to all weapons.	1 skill point
+4	Gives 70% max stock explosive ammo to all weapons.	1 skill point

Explosive ammo deals a lot of damage, inflicting small explosions on each enemy it hits. In addition, it can cause minimal splash damage if you fire into groups of opponents. This splash damage can also set off explosive items like propane tanks.

Armor-Piercing Ammo

LEVEL REQUIRED: **25**

COST TO DEPLOY: **$1000**

BASE ABILITY	GIVES 30% MAX STOCK ARMOR-PIERCING AMMO TO ALL WEAPONS.	COST TO UPGRADE
+1	Gives 40% max stock armor-piercing ammo to all weapons.	1 skill point
+2	Gives 50% max stock armor-piercing ammo to all weapons.	1 skill point
+3	Gives 60% max stock armor-piercing ammo to all weapons.	1 skill point
+4	Gives 70% max stock armor-piercing ammo to all weapons.	1 skill point

Armor-piercing ammo is vital against Hunters and particularly the Rhinos later in the game. Without the armor-piercing rounds, it can take many clips to down a Rhino.

TEAM SUPPORT

Team Explosives

LEVEL REQUIRED: **1**

COST TO DEPLOY: **$800**

BASE ABILITY	GIVES 2 SEMTEX GRENADES + 1 AMMO FOR EXPLOSIVES LAUNCHERS.	COST TO UPGRADE
+1	Gives 2 Canister Bombs + 2 ammo for explosives launchers.	1 skill point
+2	Gives 2 Bouncing Betties + 3 ammo for explosives launchers.	1 skill point
+3	Gives 4 Claymores + 4 ammo for explosives launchers.	1 skill point
+4	Gives 4 Bouncing Betties + 5 ammo for explosives launchers.	1 skill point

Generally speaking, Team Explosives is not a vital stat to invest in. If you really like the Panzerfaust weapon, then it might be worth it, since you get a significant amount of extra ammunition for it. Bouncing Betties are decent defense, but the weapons in the Strike Package are much more effective. This skill is only recommended if you are on a team of four and your teammates have already invested in Armor.

Feral Instincts

LEVEL REQUIRED: **4**

COST TO DEPLOY: **$800**

BASE ABILITY	BOOSTS TEAM'S VISION AND HEARING. YOUR TEAM CAN ALSO SEE ALIENS THROUGH THE WALLS.	COST TO UPGRADE
+1	Move 20% faster while boosted.	1 skill point
+2	Regenerate health faster.	1 skill point
+3	Increases the booster's duration by 2x.	1 skill point
+4	Increases the booster's duration by 3x and adds increased sprint endurance.	1 skill point

Due to its low cost, it becomes easy to constantly keep Feral Instincts up later in the game. Not only does it provide better health regen and faster speed, but it allows your team to see through walls. This is an incredibly useful ability when you are fighting Scorpions that are hard to track. It also makes fighting a chaotic swarm of enemies much easier, as it's much harder for the aliens to sneak up on you. If you have a team of two or more, Feral Instincts is recommended on the guy who is not upgrading Armor.

Armor

LEVEL REQUIRED: 8

COST TO DEPLOY: **$1000**

BASE ABILITY	DEPLOY ARMOR TO ALL TEAM MEMBERS.	COST TO UPGRADE
+1	Light armor with double the effectiveness.	1 skill point
+2	Medium armor, capable of withstanding tremendous force.	1 skill point
+3	Maximum armor for the team.	1 skill point
+4	Extra reserve armor provides additional protection for the team.	1 skill point

Armor acts as a buffer when you take damage. Whenever an enemy hits you, your armor absorbs the vast majority of the damage. Armor is vital to a team's end-game survival. One caveat, however, is that it can be more difficult to notice that enemies are hitting you when you have armor up. Keep your eye on your armor level if you are in a place where you can get hit from behind.

Team Booster

LEVEL REQUIRED: 14

COST TO DEPLOY: **$700**

BASE ABILITY	TEAM BOOSTER SPEEDS UP WEAPON HANDLING FOR 15 SECONDS.	COST TO UPGRADE
+1	Faster weapon handling for 30 seconds.	1 skill point
+2	Faster weapon handling and drill repair for 30 seconds.	1 skill point
+3	Faster weapon handling and drill repair for 45 seconds.	1 skill point
+4	Faster weapon handling and drill repair for 60 seconds.	1 skill point

The Team Booster is an excellent upgrade, particularly in Solo play. "Weapon handling" includes reloading, which is vitally important when using a light machinegun (LMG) since the reload times are so long. Since the booster is cheap, keeping it active all the time in the Cabin area isn't too difficult.

Additionally, you get a bonus for repairing the drill, letting you repair it at double speed. This can be a huge benefit in the late game.

Random Supplies

LEVEL REQUIRED: 17

COST TO DEPLOY: **$900**

BASE ABILITY	DEPLOY RANDOM SUPPLIES FOR THE TEAM.	COST TO UPGRADE
+1	A random mix of +1 level support items, as well as a variety of rare items.	1 skill point
+2	A random mix of +2 level support items, as well as a variety of rare items.	1 skill point
+3	A random mix of +3 level support items, as well as a variety of other items.	1 skill point
+4	A random mix of +4 level support items. Rare items are more common.	1 skill point

Random Supplies gives you one random item, which could be anything from a random loot item, to armor, to a particular type of ammunition. While you do get better items as you level it up, the unpredictability of the items makes this ability too much of a money sink to recommend.

STRIKE PACKAGE

IMS

LEVEL REQUIRED: 1

COST TO DEPLOY: **$1250**

BASE ABILITY	THE INTELLIGENT MUNITIONS SYSTEM (IMS) DETECTS AND ELIMINATES ENEMY COMBATANTS.	COST TO UPGRADE
+1	Four explosives each, with a wider radial blast.	1 skill point
+2	An enhanced targeting mechanism for quicker firing of explosives.	1 skill point
+3	Improved explosives for a large-scale damage increase.	2 skill points
+4	Increased capacity allows the IMS to contain six explosive canisters.	3 skill points

Deploy IMS, and it automatically fires an airborne grenade at any enemy that comes within range. These grenades are powerful and can inflict significant damage. The major drawback to the IMS is that it only has four canisters, so it quickly runs out when you use it to defend the drill. The upgrade to six canisters is a major improvement.

A great thing about the IMS is that it's effective against the Rhino. Drop it near the Rhino, and run it back and forth near the IMS for some easy explosive damage.

Mortar Strike

LEVEL REQUIRED: 9

COST TO DEPLOY: **$1300**

BASE ABILITY	THREE MORTARS STRIKE WITH MEDIUM DAMAGE, SMALL RADIUS.	COST TO UPGRADE
+1	Four mortars strike with medium damage, small radius.	1 skill point
+2	Four mortars strike with high damage, medium radius.	1 skill point
+3	Five mortars strike with high damage, large radius.	2 skill points
+4	Six mortars strike with high damage, large radius.	3 skill points

The Mortar Strike is a difficult attack to use effectively. It's best to use against large groups of enemies. The damage inflicted by the mortars is moderate, and it's very hard to aim precisely. If you can score a direct hit with a Mortar, it can hurt a Rhino. Two mortar strikes can kill it outright. However, scoring a direct hit can be costly and difficult due to the difficulty of aiming them.

Mortar Strikes can also be used to aid taking down Barrier Hives.

SPECIALIZED TRAINING   THE CAMPAIGN   MP INTRO & BASIC TRAINING   SQUADS   MP ARMORY   PERKS   KILLSTREAKS   MP MAPS   MP GAME MODES   SAFEGUARD   **EXTINCTION**   CLASSIFIED   ACHIEVEMENTS & TROPHIES

303

Trinity Rocket

LEVEL REQUIRED: **18**

COST TO DEPLOY: $1800

BASE ABILITY	A REMOTE-CONTROLLED MISSILE SYSTEM WITH CONTROLLABLE THRUST.	COST TO UPGRADE
+1	Improved targeting outlines the enemies.	1 skill point
+2	Fire a smart drone projectile while controlling the Trinity Missile.	1 skill point
+3	Fire two high-velocity smart drone projectiles.	2 skill points
+4	Fire four high-velocity smart drone projectiles.	3 skill points

When you activate the Trinity Rocket, you will pull out a laptop that you can activate and control the rockets as they fire down around you. When you receive the smart drone upgrades, you can hit the Fire button repeatedly to fire smaller rockets before the main rocket ejects to hit the ground.

While you are firing the rocket, you remain vulnerable to incoming attacks, so be sure you activate it in a safe area.

The Trinity Rocket is not very effective against Rhinos, but it works well against an overwhelmed drill defense.

Trinity Rockets are great at completing the "Kill the Leper" challenge since it can often be difficult to find the Leper in time, and it avoids the player.

Sentry Gun

LEVEL REQUIRED: **22**

COST TO DEPLOY: $2000

BASE ABILITY	PLACE AN AUTOMATED SENTRY GUN.	COST TO UPGRADE
+1	Upgraded with improved targeting, a wider firing arc, and double the range.	1 skill point
+2	Dramatically increases the firing rate of the Sentry Gun.	1 skill point
+3	Armor-piercing ammo is effective against the Rhinos, plus 30% more ammo.	2 skill points
+4	Place two turrets at once with less chance of either of them overheating.	3 skill points

The Sentry Gun is the closest thing you can have to a second player in a Solo game (well, until you unlock the Vulture). These aren't the wimpy Sentry Guns from the Multiplayer game; these are devilishly engineered machines of alien destruction.

Don't worry about deploying the Sentry Gun early in the game. It's overkill, and it doesn't really hit its stride until you have at least level +3. Once you start regularly encountering Hunters and Rhinos, the Sentry Gun becomes your best friend. The weapon can cut through enemy armor, and when deployed in a drill defense, it pays back its costs in enemy kills alone.

Hunters are good at sneaking up behind your Sentry Gun and ripping it in half. As such, always be sure to remain in view of the gun, and keep an eye on it while you are defending a drill. If a Hunter or Rhino gets on it, unload on them to distract or kill them before they can deal too much damage.

Vulture

LEVEL REQUIRED: **28**

COST TO DEPLOY: $2200

BASE ABILITY	A COMPANION DRONE THAT PROTECTS YOUR SIX.	COST TO UPGRADE
+1	The Vulture's turret delivers increased damage to enemy targets.	1 skill point
+2	Enhanced detectors increase the tracking range of the Vulture's turret.	1 skill point
+3	Longer operating time.	2 skill points
+4	Fires an occasional incendiary rocket.	3 skill points

The Vulture is the closest thing to having an extra teammate on your team. When you launch it, it flies closely behind you, targeting and firing on any nearby enemies.

There are two big drawbacks to the Vulture: its short duration and the high cost. While you can upgrade the duration, the fact that it only lasts about 60 seconds makes it a cost-prohibitive option until the very end game. However, if you have a fully upgrade Vulture, it can make the final couple of hives much easier.

EQUALIZER

Portable Minigun Turret

LEVEL REQUIRED: **1**

COST TO DEPLOY: $1100

BASE ABILITY	A PLACEABLE TURRET, CAPABLE OF DELIVERING BLISTERING FIREPOWER.	COST TO UPGRADE
+1	Larger ammo capacity, and a much faster spin-up time.	1 skill point
+2	Maximum damage at all distances, and a slightly larger ammo capacity.	1 skill point
+3	Armor-piercing ammo rips through the headplates of Hunters.	2 skill points
+4	Maximum ammo capacity and explosive bullets.	3 skill points

The really nice thing about the minigun turret is that you can put it in a corner of the level and not have to worry about any aliens getting behind you. One problem with the turret is that if an Scorpion targets you, it can hit you with a gas attack. If you are hit by a gas attack while on the turret, quickly get off the turret, and wait for the acid to dissipate before you get back on it.

All of the upgrades for the minigun are fantastic and are well worth the cost if you decide you like the turret and want to focus on it.

Grenade Turret

LEVEL REQUIRED: **6**

COST TO DEPLOY: **$1000**

BASE ABILITY	MANNED TURRET WITH 10 GRENADES.	COST TO UPGRADE
+1	Fire faster grenades, and utilize a larger grenade capacity.	1 skill point
+2	Significantly increased explosive radius and more damage for the turret.	1 skill point
+3	A larger ammo capacity provides more firepower per dollar.	2 skill points
+4	Equipped with incendiary rockets that burn their targets after impact.	3 skill points

The grenade turret starts off very weak, but as you upgrade it, it gets better and better. The grenade turret isn't something you should use much early on, but it becomes more useful when you hit the seventh hive. Use it to take down powerful enemies like Scorpions and Hunters.

The turret has a blast guard that means you won't take damage if you fire a grenade too close.

With both manned turrets, the major disadvantage is that you must remain stationary while on it. This can work well in the early sections of the game, but it can be very difficult to use effectively once you reach the Town because enemies come from so many different directions.

Crowd Control

LEVEL REQUIRED: **15**

COST TO DEPLOY: **$700**

BASE ABILITY	RIOT SHIELD WITH 10 SHIELD HEALTH.	COST TO UPGRADE
+1	Riot Shield with medium speed and 15 shield health.	1 skill point
+2	Riot Shield with fast speed and 15 shield health.	1 skill point
+3	Fast Riot Shield melee with 20 shield health.	2 skill points
+4	Fire melee with 25 shield health.	3 skill points

Crowd Control gives you a Riot Shield. The Riot Shield itself is so-so in combat against the enemy. Where it really becomes a benefit is when you switch it out for your primary weapon. When the shield is on your back, it absorbs damage whenever enemies hit you from behind. This is a great pairing with Armor, which makes it hard to tell when you are hit from the back.

As long as the shield icon is above your health bar, your shield remains active. Each time your shield takes a hit, it loses some health. Be sure to replenish your shield when it runs out.

Upgrading the shield can be low priority, as the shield gives you quite a bit of protection even at 10 shield health.

MK32 Launcher

LEVEL REQUIRED: **23**

COST TO DEPLOY: **$1500**

BASE ABILITY	POWERFUL SIX-ROUND GRENADE LAUNCHER.	COST TO UPGRADE
+1	Blast shield prohibits grenades from damaging the player.	1 skill point
+2	Faster movement, and explosions have a larger radius.	1 skill point
+3	Fire grenades deal increased damage.	2 skill points
+4	Doubles the grenade count to 12.	3 skill points

The MK32 is an excellent grenade launcher. It has extremely high damage and supreme accuracy (use ADS to increase precision).

The grenades are powerful enough to kill two hunters, and one volley of six grenades can inflict serious damage on a Rhino. It won't deal quite enough to kill one outright, but it'll provide enough softening for you to down it with your primary weapon.

The MK32 Launcher is a good choice, especially when enemies heavily surround you.

Death Machine

LEVEL REQUIRED: **29**

COST TO DEPLOY: **$2000**

BASE ABILITY	PORTABLE MINIGUN WITH 100 ROUNDS.	COST TO UPGRADE
+1	Recoil is dampened.	1 skill point
+2	Movement speed is increased, and ammo can piece the headplates of Hunters.	1 skill point
+3	Fire rounds inflict increased damage.	2 skill points
+4	Doubles the ammo count to 200.	3 skill points

The Death Machine is a gigantic minigun that cuts through enemies like butter. The Death Machine never overheats and has great damage at long, medium, and short range. Best of all, you never have to reload it.

The disadvantage of the Death Machine is that it is extremely expensive, and you only get 100 rounds per activation (200 once you hit +4.) One hundred rounds won't last very long if you spray and pray. Instead, you should fire your ammunition in short bursts. Once you get the +1 upgrade for the Death Machine, it's highly accurate when you use ADS.

One fantastic use for the Death Machine is as an emergency alternative to your primary weapon. If you are ever surrounded by enemies and must reload, consider activating the Death Machine instead to avoid getting killed. Remember, a down costs you $500 (and potentially a game over!), so the $2,000 cost is not as severe when you consider the full ramifications.

An Upgraded Death Machine can cut down a Rhino. A +3 Death Machine can kill a Rhino with about 100 rounds.

SPECIALIZED TRAINING   THE CAMPAIGN   MP INTRO & BASIC TRAINING   SQUADS   MP ARMORY   PERKS   KILLSTREAKS   MP MAPS   MP GAME MODES   SAFEGUARD   **EXTINCTION**   CLASSIFIED   ACHIEVEMENTS & TROPHIES

305

CHALLENGES

Whenever you start a drill objective, you receive a bonus challenge. If you can complete the challenge, you earn a bonus Skill Point.

The challenges you earn are random, but you only get a challenge if it is possible to complete on your current drill session. For instance, killing 25 enemies with shotguns is not possible on the first drill objective, so you won't receive that challenge there.

Use only melee attacks to damage aliens until you destroy the hive. If this challenge appears, it is always on the first hive. Just don't shoot the aliens, melee them instead.

Don't take any damage from aliens before the hive is destroyed. This is one of the challenges for the very first hive. Have your team back all the way against the cliff (as far away from the drill as possible). Then, fire at the aliens from a long distance to ensure no one takes damage.

Kill 15-25 aliens with shotguns before the drill completes. All of these 15-25 challenges are dependent on the number of players in the game. With one player, the requirement is 15; with four, the requirement is 25.

Kill 15-25 aliens using pistols before the hive is destroyed.

Kill 15-25 aliens using an SMG before the hive is destroyed.

Kill 15-25 aliens using LMGs before the hive is destroyed.

Kill 15-25 aliens using sniper rifles before the hive is destroyed.

Kill 15-25 aliens while prone.

Kill 5-10 aliens with propane tanks before the hive is destroyed. These 5-10 challenges change depending on the number of players in the game. One player requires five kills, whereas four players require 10.

Kill 5-10 aliens with traps before the hive is destroyed.

Kill 5-10 aliens with turrets before the hive is destroyed.

Kill 5-10 aliens while in the air before the hive is destroyed. You must catch an enemy while it is jumping. Scorpions are the best bet for this since they frequently jump between aerial positions.

Keep shot accuracy at 50-75% or above until the hive is destroyed. Like all challenges, this one is shared with your teammates. What makes this more challenging is that everyone really needs to ensure their attacks hit to keep the percentage high. If this is an early challenge, you can easily master this one by scoring one hit on an alien, then having your team switch to melee attacks for the rest of the drill. Melee attacks are probably not strong enough for this to be possible after the third drill. In that case, it's advisable that your team primarily use shotguns and avoid fully automatic weapons to avoid missing the aliens as much as possible.

You can also use manned turrets to defend the drill. The shots you fire with the turrets do not count against your shot accuracy.

Do not go into last stand before the hive is destroyed. Last stand is what happens when you have 0 health and are "downed" by an alien.

Do not bleed out before the hive is destroyed. "Bleeding out" is what happens if your teammates don't revive you before your revive timer runs out. If you bleed out in a single-player game, the game is over, so you don't have to worry about this challenge.

Don't let the drill health get below 50%.

Don't reload your weapon for one to two minutes. Since the game automatically reloads when you reach zero bullets, you must be extra careful not to fire when you only have one or two bullets left in your weapon. Stick to melee and special attacks until the timer expires.

Find and kill the Leper in less than 30 seconds. The Leper is a special enemy that spawns in and runs from you instead of trying to attack your squad. Search the outskirts of the area for it. You can distinguish the Leper from its regular alien counterparts by its bright red glow.

Don't use any abilities for 90 seconds. This one should be easy as long as everyone's paying attention. Just don't use any of your special Tactical abilities for the first 90 seconds of the drill (ammo, armor, Deployable MG, and so on).

Do not take any damage from the Seeker aliens until the hive is destroyed. Seekers are the aliens that arrive in the spikey meteors. They love to attack players more than drills, so avoiding damage from them can be difficult. If one lands, try to get in a position so you can see the Seekers coming at you from a good distance away.

Spend $XX before the hive is destroyed. The amount you have to spend increases based on the number of the players in the game.

Don't spend any money for two minutes. This mission tends to pop up in the second section of the game. For this reason, it's best to buy any ammo before you activate a drill hive in the Town area.

Kill five Scouts with melee damage before the hive is destroyed.

Kill a Scorpion with melee damage before the hive is destroyed.

Protect Player X from entering last stand. This is only applicable in multiplayer games. The player you have to protect is chosen randomly.

TEAM STRATEGY

Your goal in Extinction is to make it to the 14th hive, set the nuke, and extract before the bomb goes off.

You won't be able to play all the way through Extinction mode the first time you play. Most likely, you won't be able to complete the Point of Contact map the 20th time you play. The strategy provided here can get you in and out in a Solo game, but only once you've sufficiently mastered the ins and outs of Extinction mode. The best way to get better is to practice.

Jump online into some public games, and communicate with the other players. The more you communicate, the more you can learn from others.

Team Roles

Once you have leveled up a bit, you will have many choices about which classes and abilities you can use in the game. You need to coordinate with your team members to determine who will play what role on your team. There are several vital roles to your survival:

ESSENTIAL ROLE: ENGINEER

Engineers are in charge of placing the drill (the drill receives bonus health). Additionally, Engineers are the best at repairing the drill, as well as deploying environmental traps. The Engineer is always responsible for dropping the drill and setting off environmental traps. You only need one Engineer on your team.

ESSENTIAL ROLE: MEDIC

Reviving a player normally takes a lot of time, during which you are open to attack from enemies. The Medic class excels at quickly reviving allies, and a Medic rapidly earns the power to regenerate their entire team's health. Having a fully leveled Medic is essential once you make it past the first area. Quickly getting players back in the game is key to surviving in the harder areas. If you already have an Engineer, you should consider having multiple Medics on your team.

VITAL ROLE: AMMO GUY

Whoever is the highest level should be chosen as the ammo guy. Ammo guys should equip the highest ammo they have access to and focus on upgrading it as quickly as possible. If you complete the challenges, you can max out your ammo after the second drill. The ammo guy's responsibility is to regularly spend money to deploy ammo and refill their team's munitions. Ammo guys need to prioritize spending money on ammo over upgrading weapons or deploying extra attacks like Equalizers or Strike Packages.

VITAL ROLE: ARMOR GUY

The importance of armor to your team's long-term survival cannot be overstated. You need to have a player dedicated to upgrading their Armor support ability and regularly deploying it to the field. Deploying armor can be expensive, but it's worth it. Armor absorbs almost all the damage from attacks and keeps your team alive much longer than they would live without it.

While your team can survive without the vital roles, it's recommended that one player focus on the roles because spending upgrade points in those skills makes them significantly better for everyone on the team.

If you are playing with fewer than four players, you need to double up on some of the roles. This is easy to do, since only Medic and Engineer are in the same tree.

SOLO STRATEGY

Yes, Extinction can be conquered in Solo mode. You don't even have to get to the max level to stand a good chance of winning. More important than the upgrades is map memorization, practice with fighting the aliens, and knowledge of how each ability works. Luckily, this guide covered all that earlier in this chapter.

The following strategy is designed for experienced players who can use their ammo and money efficiently and nail most of the challenges. You don't need to play perfectly, but being smart about when to reload and when to buy things goes a long way.

This strategy requires that you have unlocked the Sentry Gun, which you do not acquire until Level 22. Getting to Level 22, you will learn a lot about the game, and you can use the strategy up until the Cabin area. It's still possible to beat the game without the Sentry Gun in Solo mode, but you'll have to be crafty, as all of the good abilities to kill the Rhinos don't start unlocking until the 20s.

THE LOADOUT

The recommended loadout is:

Class: Medic (for quicker health regen, reduced Scorpion damage, and faster run speed and sprinting).

Pistol: Player's choice (whichever you prefer. The M9A1 is quite good, but this choice is relatively unimportant.).

Ammo: Explosive (armor-piercing is better, but not required).

Team Support: Team Booster (speeds up drill repair, eliminating the need for an Engineer. Speeds up reload times, making the LMGs more viable in the end game.).

Strike Package: Sentry Gun (late-game offensive powerhouse).

Equalizer: Crowd Control (for cheap back armor).

SKILL UPGRADE PATH

Here's a recommended skill upgrade. Since the speed at which you receive the skill points depends on how many challenges you complete, exactly when you can purchase each upgrade depends on how well the Extinction session is going for you.

1 Explosive Ammo +1	6 Medic +2	12 Team Booster +2
2 Explosive Ammo +2	7 & 8 Medic +3	13 Team Booster +3
3 Explosive Ammo +3	9 Sentry Gun +1	14 Team Booster +4
4 Explosive Ammo +4	10 Sentry Gun +2	15 & 16 Sentry Gun +3
5 Medic +1	11 Team Booster +1	17, 18, & 19 Sentry Gun +4

No further skills are required for this strategy. If you earn skill points beyond 19, feel free to use them to finish off Medic (which gives you more speed, making the evac easier) or Crowd Control (which improves the durability of your back shield).

PLAYTHROUGH: LODGE

For the first drill, you receive one of two challenges. The melee Challenge is preferable, since it requires you to waste less ammo and is easier. If you get the "Don't Take Damage" challenge, hang all the way to the back and to the left of the area, and let the enemies attack the drill (they can't hurt it significantly). Be ready in case you attract the attention of any Scouts.

Put the points into Explosive Ammo to ensure you get the most ammo for your buck when you eventually run out. If you have any trouble surviving these first few hives, feel free to put the points into Medic instead. The extra health regen makes meleeing the Scouts much easier.

When you reach the main area, you get a random selection of hives to destroy. Destroy the hives in this priority order:

You want to save the parking lot of the lodge for last since there are traps to make the attack easier. You should attack the harder hives first since the waves increase in difficulty as you play.

Don't buy any weapons before you place a drill. It's common to get the "Destroy 15 enemies with shotguns" or the SMG or assault rifle variants for challenges. If you do score one of those challenges, grab the appropriate weapon (see the Extinction map) for an easy challenge complete.

If you don't get any of those challenges, just get your favorite weapon at some point before the barrier hive. A recommendation is the AK-12, located immediately at the beginning of the area.

Be sure to use both traps at E to make it easier.

PLAYTHROUGH: THE FIRST BARRIER HIVE

At the end of Outskirts, hopefully you've completed at least two of the challenges, which means you have unlocked Medic +2 for the barrier hive. The Scorpions appear there, and they can pile on the damage.

It's not worth lighting the fire trap here, as it just doesn't hit enough enemies to be worth it. Instead, spend the money on your first Crowd Control purchase. Select the shield, then hit the **Fire** button to purchase it. Now, switch back to your main weapon. The shield protects your back as long as it still has health. Keep your eye on the shield icon in the bottom-left corner of the screen.

If you are stuck with the shotgun, you need to switch it out for a longer-range weapon so you can effectively attack the Scorpions. Don't worry about spending money here; you receive a bonus for clearing the hive as well as a bonus for getting into the Town area, and a ton of money from killing the enemies. It's easy to hit the money cap after you complete this hive.

The Scorpions attack from the house on the right, the billboard, and the cliffs on the left. Fire on them whenever you see them, but also be aware of the Scouts that attack from the ground level.

PLAYTHROUGH: THE TOWN

Once the barrier hive is down, the road to the Town is clear. The Town section is a much harder version of the Outskirts. You now have to contend with Seekers and Hunters.

Grab the reward money near the hive, and bring the drill into the Town. Drop the drill, and move left into the Town. You want to purchase the M27 LMG. It's located up a ladder in a raised area at the Town entrance. (Refer to the map for its specific location.) This gun remains your weapon until the end of the game, and it's well worth the $3,000.

Yes, it's possible you'll get a challenge requiring a weapon other than the M27. If you do, it's best to just fail the challenge. Buying another weapon and then rebuying the M27 is a tremendous money sink and not worth the one skill point.

Now that you have a gun, it's time to tackle the hives in the recommended order:

As above, you should work on the harder-to-defend drills first to ensure that you have plenty of traps for the harder waves.

For the C hive, be sure to activate all three electrical fences. The front fences are particularly helpful.

For the D hive, be sure to activate the nearby electrical puddle, as well as the fire trap. It is not recommended that you spend the money on a Sentry Gun yet. You should save the money to ensure you have it to use a Sentry Gun on the second barrier hive.

When you get to your third hive, before you drop the drill, run up to the helicopter laptop (see the map), and put $3K in it to get some air support. The third hive can be very difficult, so you need all the help you can get.

PLAYTHROUGH: THE SECOND BARRIER HIVE

The second barrier hive is much more difficult than the first. It's essential that you keep all four traps in the area active, and that you are familiar with the patterns of the Scorpions' movements.

There are two electrical traps directly in front of the barrier. These are crucial to keep live, as they can kill Scorpions, keep Scouts off of you, and inflict heavy damage to Hunters. Additionally, there are a third electrical fence and a fire trap. With your back to the barrier hive, you can find the third electrical fence to the left and the fire trap to the right.

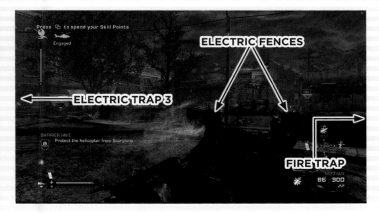

When you have all the traps activated, it's time to set up your first Sentry Gun. Set it up directly in front of the hive, as close as possible. Even if you don't have the turret maxed out, it can still help a lot in the defense.

PLAYTHROUGH: THE CABIN

After breaking through the barrier hive, the path leads to the Cabin area. Before you get to the Cabin, you encounter your first Rhino. If you leave the Rhino alone, it runs away. However, it's not a terrible idea to practice downing a Rhino for the upcoming drill events.

Fire on the Rhino to lure it to attack you. With +4 Sentry Gun, you can place two Sentry Guns. Use the reward money to purchase another Sentry Gun, and place it in the open. Activate your Team Booster to decrease the reload times of your LMG.

Now, unload on the Rhino with the MG. You can take a couple of hits from the Rhino, but do your best to evade its charges. Ideally, the turret will distract it. If this happens, immediately reload the LMG, and unload on the Rhino at point-blank range. This should kill it before it has a chance to turn its attention back to you.

With the Rhino down, it's time to move on to the Cabin area. While a drill is active, you want to keep two things up at all times: the Team Booster and the Sentry Gun. Losing a Sentry Gun can happen, but it's not the end of the world. Try to keep the Sentry Gun with a good view of the drill, but backed into a corner so it's harder for Hunters to get behind it.

Always keep moving. Whenever you have a moment between waves of enemies, reload your LMG. Luckily, the Team Boost makes reloading your LMG much easier. Remember, you can go up and down ladders while reloading the weapon.

Whenever a drill drops below 75 health, heal it between any waves of opponents. With the Team Booster, repairing the drill takes much less time.

For the **Cabin A** hive, you should put the Sentry Gun on the wooden stairs. If a Rhino arrives, try to run it in front of the Sentry Gun to inflict extra damage. Evade the Rhino by moving up and down the wooden walkway. The Rhino spawns when drill completion is around 50%.

Cabin B hive can be in one of two different locations. It's also the toughest because it's more in the open than the others. There are some traps you can activate in the area, but they don't help much. Position the turret on the right side of the hive. This way, the electric fence defends its rear.

Cabin C hive is in a barn and is fairly easy to defend since you have so much cover. Place the Sentry Gun near the drill, and hide out on the porch area (facing the drill, this is the porch on the right). Fire on the aliens safely from here, and duck into the barn if the drill starts taking damage. Toward the end of this drill, another Rhino shows up. Run it in front of your Sentry Gun to inflict damage, and keep moving up and down the barn ladders, unloading with your LMG when you get a clear shot. The Rhino spawns when drill completion is around 75%.

PLAYTHROUGH: THE CRATER

With the Cabin hives down, an area opens up near the **Cabin B** hive that leads to a Crater area. This Crater area has the last two hives.

Again, you should do these hives in the alphabetical order as they are marked.

Crater A hive is on a cliff. Set up the Sentry Gun near the hive so it can look out on the upper cliff area. Keep moving along the upper and cliff areas to pick off the Scorpions and Hunters as they arrive. (There won't be too many Scouts at this point.)

SPECIALIZED TRAINING THE CAMPAIGN MP INTRO & BASIC TRAINING SQUADS MP ARMORY PERKS KILLSTREAKS MP MAPS MP GAME MODES SAFEGUARD **EXTINCTION** CLASSIFIED ACHIEVEMENTS & TROPHIES

309

If you make it past **Crater A**, you only have one hive left to clear! Set up the Sentry Gun next to the **Crater B** hive, and then look around for the downed telephone pole in the upper area to activate the electrical trap. Once you've activated the telephone pole, place the drill, and get ready for the best the aliens have got! The Rhino spawns when drill completion is around 50%.

The keys to success here are to have a fully upgraded Sentry Gun and to keep the enemies off the Sentry Gun. If a Rhino or Hunter attacks the Sentry Gun, be ready to quickly replace it (money is no longer an obstacle at this point).

You can also get a *little* help by calling the helicopter from the basement laptop (see the map). Just don't do that once you start the drill. The Hunters can down the drill before you can make it to the laptop and back.

PLAYTHROUGH: THE NUKE

If you survive the last hive, you can now arm the Nuke. The Nuke is activated via a laptop right near the **Crater B** hive. Once you **Interact** with it, you will have five minutes to get back to the evac zone.

Luckily, if you are following the recommended skill tree, you are playing the Medic, the fastest class in the game. Switch to your pistol, and sprint back through the way you came. When you reach the passage back to the Town, you encounter a meteor blocking your exit. Don't panic! The meteor persists for about 30 seconds depending on how quickly you arrive at the stop point. Just turn back around, and fire at incoming enemies. If a Rhino gets to you, just evade it. No point in fighting one now.

Now, sprint back through the Town. When you reach the first barrier hive, another meteor blocks your exit out. Switch back to your LMG, and hold off the aliens until the meteor crumbles. As soon as it does, switch back to the pistol, and sprint to the evac zone to complete the mission!

TIPS

» Don't put down team items like ammo or armor until after you spend points upgrading them. The cost does not increase, and you will give more of the resources to everyone.

» When running from aliens, switch to the pistol, as you can evade much more effectively.

» Never ever turn and run from an enemy while carrying a heavy weapon, as they'll just hit your vulnerable back. Instead, back away while you're reloading, and fire as soon as your weapon is ready.

» Traps don't just hurt the aliens: they can also hurt you. Be careful when running through fire and electric traps.

» The strategies you employ should vary based on the number of players in the game. Solo players will have very different leveling strategies than four-player games. Additionally, teams of two need to employ different tactics than teams of four.

» The damage, health, and quantity of aliens drastically changes depending on how many players are in the game.

» If you like sniper weapons, consider upgrading your pistol tree early. This ensures that you are not defenseless when you need a reload or an enemy makes it to short range. Melee attacks quickly become ineffective as you progress through the game.

» Skill Points are almost always more important than money. If you have to waste some money to earn a challenge (for instance, buy a shotgun for a challenge), it's almost always worth it. Money is plentiful, but stat points are very limited, and you need as many as you can get before you get to the really difficult areas.

» Don't wait too long before moving the drill. Fierce waves of enemies spawn in if you wait too long.

» Listen for audio clues. Your team members will shout out warnings like "Scorpions!" These warn you of imminent threats and should give you a bit of time to prepare for incoming enemies.

» Watch out for post-drill waves. After the drill is destroyed, the aliens make you their primary target. It's during this period that you are at the greatest risk of enemies overwhelming you. Keep an eye on the drill progress, and reload your weapons before it finishes.

» There is a money cap of only $6,000. This means that any money you earn past that is lost. Use your abilities regularly to make sure you never lose money because of the cap.

» You can buy more ammo for a weapon by going to the weapon's spawn point on the map. Unfortunately, the ammo costs as much as buying a new weapon, so it's generally not worth it. It's better to spend the money on ammo crates.

» No need to carry the drill up to the helicopter events. After you defeat the barrier hive, the drill automatically teleports up.

» You can search while you are reloading. It's not a bad idea to start a reload before you start searching a trash pile, particularly once you get to some of the harder defenses. You can also search while you are firing!

» You get more money per alien kill if you score a head shot to kill it. This scores a 33% bonus to the money earned.

» If you can prevent the drill from getting damaged at all, you receive a big score bonus, and in turn, more money.

» Riot Shields on your back protect you from attacks from behind, so you can reload while running from an enemy without worrying about taking damage.

» Whenever you use one of the level turrets, always ask another player to back you up. The aliens are good at getting behind the turrets and hitting you from behind. But if you have a teammate watching your back, you can open up on the attackers.

» A sneaky tactic to use for the helicopter sequences is to lure the aliens back to the beginning area of the zone. Since you can't outright fail the barrier hive missions, it's no problem to abandon the hive completely. Eventually, the enemies start spawning in near the starting zone, well away from the barrier hive. While the strategy works, this tactic is time-consuming, and the barrier hive events are generally not as hard as the drillable hive events. As such, it's usually not worth the effort.

» If you want to generate a lot of money in the beginning, you can avoid putting down the second drill. Eventually, an endless wave of Scouts arrives, which you should be able to handle. You can use this wave to purchase some upgrades and ammo. However, because the money cap is so low, it's generally not worth wasting the time saving up money in this manner. If you use the outlined Solo strategy, you should have plenty of extra money by the end of the first section without having to waste any time.

» In co-op mode, prevent your teammates from getting downed and bleeding out to maximize your team bonus score.

» Spend cash and use your abilities during a drill event to get bonuses to your Personal Skill score at the end of the drill round.

» Completing hive challenges doesn't just give you a skill point. It also rewards you with a major post-drill score bonus, which translates into bonus cash to spend.

» Use propane tanks to help speed the demise of a Barrier Hive.

SECRETS

When you reach the max rank of Extinction (30), you go to Prestige, reverting you to Level 1 (don't worry, you get to keep all your unlocked loadouts), and giving you special Prestige Relics you can use in-game. These Prestige Relics make the game harder in different ways.

Relic 1: Take More Damage — Aliens deal more damage to you.

Relic 2: Pistols Only — You can only use pistols in-game.

Relic 3: Smaller Wallet — Your money cap is decreased and aliens give out less money per kill.

Relic 4: Mortal — No class selection is available.

Relic 5: Do Less Damage — You inflict less damage against aliens.

You receive more points for completing a drill with these Prestige Relics enabled. Additionally, there is an Achievement that requires you to beat a session of Extinction with a Prestige Relic enabled.

SPECIALIZED TRAINING THE CAMPAIGN MP INTRO & BASIC TRAINING SQUADS MP ARMORY PERKS KILLSTREAKS MP MAPS MP GAME MODES SAFEGUARD **EXTINCTION** CLASSIFIED ACHIEVEMENTS & TROPHIES

311

CLANS AND CLAN WARS

Clans can be formed with up to 100 players, allowing you to create a larger organized group to play *Call of Duty: Ghosts* together as a bigger team.

Clans have 25 unlockable levels, and on each level, you can acquire a variety of new rewards: camouflage, reticles, character customization, wallpapers, backgrounds for your player card, and other goodies.

Clan XP is earned for your clan any time you are playing in a match with a clan mate.

Gaining enough levels as a clan also allows you to unlock special colored clan tags for your clan only.

CLAN WARS

Clan Wars is a territory "metagame" overlaid on the regular playlist experience. You battle it out against a small group of similarly ranked clans.

Compete in two-week cycles to control virtual territory by playing specific game modes with your clan. Every two weeks, a new conflict zone on the global map becomes the focus of online matches.

The way Clan Wars works is simple: you can claim each territory on the Clan Wars map by winning matches within a certain game mode. Win enough matches, and you seize that territory.

Once you hold a territory, every other clan begins to count their wins against yours, so while you can hold a territory a bit longer by continuing to focus on that game mode, holding it against the dedicated force of several other clans is impossible in the long term. Why all the struggle over turf? Sweet, sweet XP. While you hold territory, your entire clan gains XP boosts for playing in that game mode. Rank up your Squad that much faster!

The best part: Clan Wars is totally automatic. You don't even have to pay any attention to the Clan Wars map if you don't want to. Simply playing matches online together is enough. If you win enough matches, sooner or later, you're going to earn turf and bonus XP in your favorite modes.

If you want to get more involved in the Clan Wars metagame, there are "supply drops" and other special abilities you can use as a clan to bolster your position on the bi-weekly Clan Wars map. You can even send out notices to your entire clan to let them know to focus on a specific game mode.

If you manage to win a two-week cycle of Clan Wars (or even accomplish certain Achievements for holding and claiming territory), you can unlock special cosmetic rewards, player card artwork, and other items. Additionally, you can access Clan Wars from anywhere: you can check it out in-game, or look up your battles on the web, your PC, or your phone.

PROGRESSION

The progression system in *Call of Duty: Ghosts* has been revamped and improved significantly from past *Call of Duty* titles. Rather than having a single character whom you would level and Prestige repeatedly, you are now given control of a Squad of trained soldiers.

Each soldier in your Squad can be leveled, outfitted, and equipped individually. On top of that, your entire Squad carries over between cooperative Squad match play and online play. You can bounce seamlessly between matches against bots and online multiplayer matches, always earning XP, always with the same Squad.

Whenever you are playing any Squad mode or online mode, you are earning XP that goes toward earning **Squad points**. You can spend these **SP** to unlock new Squad members (until you reach your full roster size of 10) and unlock new equipment for your Squad members. This is how you unlock new weapons, attachments, equipment, killstreaks, and so on.

The system is very freeform. You can choose to focus on a single Squad member just like the classic *Call of Duty* leveling until you unlock everything, or you can spread your focus around, unlocking stuff and customizing several different Squad members. One other cool thing about this setup: each Squad member can have their own set of custom classes.

With this enhanced flexibility, you can set up one Squad member for a specific game mode and have all of their classes configured appropriately for just that particular mode.

No more swearing about forgetting your Smoke grenades or Trophy System when you're trying to play a serious objective match on a TDM class!

You also unlock new customization options for your Squad. You can modify their gender, body type, armor type, helmets, face paints, hair color, and many other choices. Make your Squad the way you want it!

OPERATIONS

Operations is the name of the *Call of Duty: Ghosts* challenge system.

Every day (and every few hours), new challenges pop up on the Operations menu.

You can select one challenge from each different Operations category. Completing that challenge earns you bonus XP (and potentially straight SP, too).

Note that while the available Operations change from day to day, you never need to worry about losing progress. Once you select a challenge, it stays selected until you complete it or drop it.

If you want to work on a tough, high-reward challenge, go for it; it's not going to time out on you or waste your time and progress.

Alternately, you can focus on a bunch of easier challenges and earn bonus XP for completing multiple challenges quickly.

The Operations system is a flexible bonus system on top of your normal match play XP. Be sure to set your Operations after every match if you're knocking them out quickly to boost your rate of progression.

ACHIEVEMENTS & TROPHIES

SINGLE-PLAYER CAMPAIGN

CAMPAIGN ACHIEVEMENTS

You can't miss these Achievements; you obtain them for simply playing through the campaign on any difficulty.

 GHOST STORIES
ESCAPE
Complete "Ghost Stories" on any difficulty.

 THE HUNTED
MAKE IT OUT ALIVE
Complete "The Hunted" on any difficulty.

 ALL OR NOTHING
GATHER THE TROOPS
Complete "All or Nothing" on any difficulty.

 BRAVE NEW WORLD
RENDEZVOUS IN FORT SANTA MONICA
Complete "Brave New World" on any difficulty.

 CLOCKWORK
HACK THE SYSTEM
Complete "Clockwork" on any difficulty.

 SEVERED TIES
DESTROY THE FEDERATION'S SATELLITE ARRAY
Complete "Severed Ties" on any difficulty.

 NO MAN'S LAND
MAKE IT TO SAN DIEGO
Complete "No Man's Land" on any difficulty.

 ATLAS FALLS
DISTRACT THE FEDERATION FLEET
Complete "Atlas Falls" on any difficulty.

 LOKI
COMMANDEER THE ENEMY SPACE STATION
Complete "Loki" on any difficulty.

 STRUCK DOWN
FIND AJAX
Complete "Struck Down" on any difficulty.

 INTO THE DEEP
DESTROY THE ENEMY SHIP
Complete "Into the Deep" on any difficulty.

 THE GHOST KILLER
CONFRONT RORKE
Complete "The Ghost Killer" on any difficulty.

 HOMECOMING
DEFEND LA
Complete "Homecoming" on any difficulty.

 END OF THE LINE
STORM THE FACTORY
Complete "End of the Line" on any difficulty.

 LEGENDS NEVER DIE
HUNT DOWN ALMAGRO
Complete "Legends Never Die" on any difficulty.

 SIN CITY
PLAN YOUR NEXT MOVE
Complete "Sin City" on any difficulty.

 FEDERATION DAY
GATHER INTEL ON RORKE
Complete "Federation Day" on any difficulty.

BIRDS OF PREY
CAPTURE RORKE
Complete "Birds of Prey" on any difficulty.

SPECIAL SP ACHIEVEMENTS

You earn the following Achievements by performing special actions throughout the campaign. All levels have a special Achievement you can earn, and some have more than one.

This section provides some basic coverage about each Achievement, but if you want even more info, check out the descriptions in the individual walkthrough chapters.

SPATIAL AWARENESS

KILL YOUR FIRST ENEMY IN THE *CALL OF DUTY: GHOSTS* CAMPAIGN

▌**Mission:** Ghost Stories

You earn this during the second part of the campaign's first mission.

SLEEPING BEAUTY

KILL SLEEPING ENEMY IN FACE-DOWN RAPPEL SECTION

▌**Mission:** Federation Day

This snoozing soldier is located a floor below the first balcony populated with enemies as you rappel down the side of the skyscraper.

LIBERTY WALL

TAKE DOWN BOTH ATTACK HELICOPTERS IN "BRAVE NEW WORLD"

▌**Mission:** Brave New World

You earn this by killing both of the attack choppers at the end of "Brave New World" with the missile launcher.

CARBON FACEPRINT

CATCH THE PHOTOCOPIER WITH YOUR FACE

▌**Mission:** Federation Day

When you blow the power to capture your target in "Federation Day," you find yourself rappelling down the skyscraper, with debris falling above your head. One of those pieces of debris is a giant photocopier. Just hit the photocopier for the Achievement.

BLIMEY O'RILEY

POUNCE ON 10 ENEMIES WHILE CONTROLLING RILEY

▌**Mission:** No Man's Land

You need to kill a few extra soldiers with Riley during Mission 3. Your opportunity to do this occurs the second time you control Riley. Kill some of the pairs of soldiers instead of just walking by them.

BURN BABY BURN

DESTROY 80 FUEL CONTAINERS

▌**Mission:** Birds of Prey

There are a ton of fuel containers to destroy on this level (much more than 80); just look for the gas-filled cylinders spread out near the buildings in the area.

WASTE NOT

EVERY SHOT WITH THE REMOTE SNIPER KILLS A PERSON OR VEHICLE

▌**Mission:** Struck Down

You operate a remote sniper robot four times during Mission 4. Line up every shot, and only fire when you have an enemy in your sights. Don't worry: every shot with the weapon is already a one-hit kill.

JUNGLE GHOSTS

FINISH THE MISSION WITHOUT BREAKING STEALTH

▌**Mission:** The Hunted

"Breaking stealth" means alerting the guards to your presence. If you make a mistake and alert the guards, just use the Last Checkpoint feature in the Pause menu.

GO UGLY EARLY

A-10 STRAFE 50 ENEMIES

▌**Mission:** Homecoming

When you control the A-10 early in Mission 5, instead of aiming for the big targets, focus on the small soldier targets. The kills you score add up quickly.

DEEP FREEZE

DROP EIGHT VEHICLES INTO ICE HOLES

▌**Mission:** Clockwork

While escaping in "Clockwork," you operate a grenade launcher while your team drives a Jeep over ice. Instead of using the grenade launcher to hit vehicles directly, blast holes in the ice, forcing them to drive straight to their peril.

IT CAME FROM BELOW!

KILL SIX ENEMIES WITH THE KNIFE WHILE UNDERWATER IN "LEGENDS NEVER DIE"

▌**Mission:** Legends Never Die

After the city floods in "Legends Never Die," you have a few sequences where you engage enemies in waste-high waters. Crouch under the water, and sneak up on the foes to score melee kills. This is best done on Recruit difficulty.

PIECE OF CAKE

STORM THE COMMON ROOM, AND KILL EVERYONE WITHOUT TAKING DAMAGE ON VETERAN

▌**Mission:** Atlas Falls

This is the hardest Achievement in the campaign because it requires Veteran. It's best if you hang back to the left of the common room door, tossing in Flashbangs and grenades. If you are patient, your team will actually kill much of the resistance inside.

SPECIALIZED TRAINING   THE CAMPAIGN   MP INTRO & BASIC TRAINING   SQUADS   MP ARMORY   PERKS   KILLSTREAKS   MP MAPS   MP GAME MODES   SAFEGUARD   EXTINCTION   CLASSIFIED   **ACHIEVEMENTS & TROPHIES**

315

GRINDIN'

BLOW THE PRESSURE VALVES ON YOUR FIRST ATTEMPT

Mission: Atlas Falls

"Atlas Falls" ends with a special mini-game. Simply pass it on the first try to earn this Achievement.

DAVID & GOLIATH

TAKE DOWN THE LCS ON THE FIRST GO

Mission: Into the Deep

"LCS" stands for littoral combat ship, which is the ship you are asked to destroy with the scuba torpedo halfway through the mission. If you miss, you must restart the level, so be very careful with your aim!

COG IN THE MACHINE

KILL FIVE ENEMIES WITHOUT BEING DETECTED BEFORE INFILTRATING BLACK ZONE

Mission: End of the Line

You kill three enemies just by following the story. The fourth and fifth can be the two with their backs turned to you when the big cargo doors open into Black Zone.

JACK-POT

DESTROY 21 SLOT MACHINES

Mission: Sin City

There are 20 slot machines on the main casino floor, with five more on a balcony across from the curving escalators a little later in the level. The slot machines in question are the tall standing ones with the breakable screens.

END OF YOUR ROPE

CUT A GRAPPLING HOOK ROPE WITH AN ENEMY ON IT

Mission: All or Nothing

In "All or Nothing," you are tasked with defending the railing of an aircraft carrier from Federation raiders. These raiders toss ropes up the side of the ship. Use a melee attack to cut the rope.

FLY-BY-WIRE

DESTROY THREE OUT OF THREE HELICOPTERS WITH THE REMOTE MISSILE

Mission: Severed Ties

Very close to the start of the mission, three helicopters attack your tank. Switch to the tank's heat-seeking missile, and quickly down all three. If you take too long, the other tanks in your battalion may down one of the helicopters.

THEY LOOK LIKE ANTS

DESTROY ALL ENEMY GROUND TARGETS, AND KILL NO ALLIES WITH THE RODS

Mission: Loki

This is a very difficult task since it's at the very end of Loki, and if you fail the last section, you must restart the level. Just carefully target any ground Xs, and stay away from the blue Xs. Don't try to hit the flying Federation targets, as they don't count toward this Achievement.

TICKETS PLEASE

SHOOT THE GRAPPLE GUYS OFF THE SIDE OF THE TRAIN

Mission: The Ghost Killer

After two attack choppers engage you on the train, the next car features some enemies trying to grapple up the side of it. Shoot them before they can get on board.

AUDIOPHILE

COLLECT ALL 18 RORKE FILES

There is one Rorke File located in every level. For specific details on where to find a Rorke File, refer to that chapter. For your convenience, you can use the checklist here to keep track of which files you've discover as you play through, as well as read hints about where to find the file.

MISSION	HINT	FOUND
Ghost Stories	During 3rd Sequence, don't follow Hesh too closely; explore the houses.	
Brave New World	Near Elias.	
No Man's Land	In the first base area, inside on a desk.	
Struck Down	In a locker.	
Homecoming	On the first floor of the main operations room.	
Legends Never Die	In a sunny room.	
Federation Day	In a dark side room near the first hacking job.	
Birds of Prey	In Rorke's room.	
The Hunted	In the jungle, near a stream, before you reunite with the Ghosts.	
Clockwork	In a computer room after the lights go dark.	
Atlas Falls	Near the pressure regulators.	
Into the Deep	Near a wreck, and before the coral doorway.	
End of the Line	Near the underground satellite.	
Sin City	After the casino (before the spiral escalators).	
All or Nothing	In a bunk.	
Severed Ties	After you find out Rorke is on a train.	
Loki	Floating in space after the explosion.	
The Ghost Killer	Immediately at the level start.	

YOU'VE EARNED IT

EARN THE MASK. FINISH THE CAMPAIGN ON VETERAN

Veteran is the hardest difficulty mode. Beating the game on Veteran isn't easy, but it shouldn't be very difficult for *Call of Duty* veterans. If this is your first *Call of Duty* game, consider playing on Hardened or Regular on your first playthrough to warm up and to better learn the game.

SAFEGUARD

SAFEGUARD

REACH LEVEL 20 ON SAFEGUARD

Reaching Level 20 on Safeguard is challenging, but not unobtainable. To get there, refer to the chapter on Safeguard, and play online until you find a solid team. You'll be at Level 20 in no time.

Alternatively, you can do this offline in Solo mode. There, you can change the settings so you have more health that regens faster. If you are set on doing this alone, that's your best chance.

You must beat Level 20 to earn the Achievement.

EXTINCTION

Extinction Achievements are all secret! No one wanted to reveal the secret game mode too early.

CITY DWELLER

MADE IT TO THE TOWN

The Town is the second area of Extinction.

CABIN FEVER

MADE IT TO THE CABIN AREA

The Cabin is the third area of Extinction.

MADE IT OUT ALIVE

ESCAPE THE FIRST TIME

You earn this the first time you complete Extinction mode. This guide features complete coverage of how to beat Extinction mode alone in the Extinction chapter.

COMPLETIONIST

COMPLETE ALL CHALLENGES, AND ESCAPE

Challenges pop up whenever you plant a drill. Getting this Achievement means scoring all 14 challenges as you play through the mode, then making it to the exit — a serious challenge! For tips on how to complete the specific challenges, refer to the Extinction chapter.

SPRINTER

ESCAPE IN UNDER THREE MINUTES

The easiest way to earn this is to play a Medic, who gets a big bonus to his speed. However, any class can make it out. You just need to focus on sprinting to the escape as quickly as possible. The meteors do get in your way, but just wait patiently for them to dissolve to clear the path.

ANY MEANS NECESSARY

KILL 50 ENEMIES WITH ELECTRIC FENCE AND FIRE TRAPS

For this Achievement, you want to play as an Engineer. As an Engineer, traps last longer and are cheaper to deploy. Refer to the map in the Extinction chapter for the locations of all the traps. Whenever you are near a hive that has traps, keep them active the entire time you are fighting.

TRASH PICKER

SCAVENGE 40 ITEMS

When you are playing Extinction, you can find randomly placed scavenge locations, which can be trash bags, mounds of dirt, or ammo boxes. Search these to find items.

THROTTLED ESCAPE

ESCAPE USING A PRESTIGE RELIC

Once you reach the Extinction level cap (30), you automatically Prestige and flip back to Level 1. When you do, it unlocks the ability to activate Prestige Relics. Prestige Relics make the game harder in different ways. For more information on Prestige Relics, refer to the Extinction chapter.

SPECIALIZED TRAINING   THE CAMPAIGN   MP INTRO & BASIC TRAINING   SQUADS   MP ARMORY   PERKS   KILLSTREAKS   MP MAPS   MP GAME MODES   SAFEGUARD   EXTINCTION   CLASSIFIED   **ACHIEVEMENTS & TROPHIES**

317

BE THE GHOST THE COMPETITION FEARS
CALL OF DUTY GHOSTS
TURTLE BEACH
EAR FORCE PHANTOM
EAR FORCE SPECTRE
EAR FORCE SHADOW
WWW.TURTLEBEACH.COM/GHOSTS
infinity ward
ACTIVISION

CALL OF DUTY GHOSTS

OFFICIAL MULTIPLAYER MAP APP

Get the perfect digital companion for *Call of Duty®: Ghosts*. This official multiplayer map app provides detailed, top-down views of the MP maps. Get the drop on your opponents with this easy-to-use map reference and learn the layout of all the levels inside and out! Use it to memorize the locations of all the key items and take your online experience to the next level.

Plus, check out the all-new weapon range markers! Utilize these interactive indicators to determine the optimal firing range for Shotguns, Submachine Guns, Assault Rifles, Light Machine Guns and Marksman Rifles. Drag the markers all around the map to see the effective damage ranges for these weapons.

- All 14 multiplayer maps rendered in incredible detail
- Quickly toggle between the various gameplay modes
- Callouts and key locations identified for each gameplay mode
- Interactive weapon range markers!

ONLY $2.99

AVAILABLE FOR APPLE AND ANDROID DEVICES

BRADYGAMES

 ACTIVISION®

www.bradygames.com   www.infinityward.com   www.activision.com

CALL OF DUTY GHOSTS

PRESTIGE EDITION STRATEGY GUIDE

Written by Phillip Marcus, Thom Denick, Jason Fox, Michael Creque, Trevor Martin, Arthur Davis, Jon Toney, Daniel Herrera, and Jamison Carroll

Maps illustrated by Rich Hunsinger and Darren Strecker

DK/BradyGames, a division of Penguin Group (USA) Inc.
800 East 96th Street, 3rd Floor
Indianapolis, IN 46240

ISBN: 978-0-7440-1518-8

Printing Code: The rightmost double-digit number is the year of the book's printing; the rightmost single-digit number is the number of the book's printing. For example, 13-1 shows that the first printing of the book occurred in 2013.

16   15   14   13   4   3   2   1

Printed in the USA.

CREDITS

Title Manager
Tim Fitzpatrick

Manuscript Editor
Matt Buchanan

Copy Editor
Angie Lawler

Book Designers
Tim Amrhein
Dan Caparo

Production Designer
Tracy Wehmeyer

BRADYGAMES STAFF

Global Strategy Guide Publisher
Mike Degler

Editor-In-Chief
H. Leigh Davis

Licensing Manager
Christian Sumner

Marketing Manager
Katie Hemlock

Digital Publishing Manager
Tim Cox

Operations Manager
Stacey Beheler

ACKNOWLEDGMENTS

BratdyGAMES sincerely thanks everyone at Activision, Infinity Ward, and Neversoft for their expert support throughout this project, and for their gracious hospitality hosting our authors. Very special thanks to Alex Gomez, Pete Blumel, Yale Miller, Alicia Mandeville, Charnjit Bansi, David Rose, Lee Ross, and Thomas Szakolczay—without your generous assistance, this guide would not be possible. Thank you very much!

Phillip Marcus: IW is awesome. Pete, Joe, Jordan, Eric, Dave, Aaron, Wallace, thank you. Jason, Mike, Trevor, the SS crew, and Tim, well done.

As ever, Evilgamer fans, you rock.

And my last and most important thanks to my wife, for keeping me happy and healthy through long nights of writing. Love you!

I'll see you *CoD* fans online…

Thom Denick: Dedicated to my loving wife, Ji Young. For general help at Infinity Ward, Pete Blumel. For build help, Steve Myers. For the maps, Darren Strecker. For Sabotage mode tips, Eric Su, Amos Hodge. Extinction and Sabotage partners, Arthur Davis (SS Grunt), Jon Toney (SS Wally), and Jamison Carrol (SS Hobo).

Jason Fox: First I'd like to thank Phil for bringing me along for another *Call of Duty* guide. Thanks to Mike Creque for his coding assistance and the Savory Strawberries for providing knife and drop shot targets the entire week. Thanks to Infinity Ward for their hospitality during our week on site, and a huge yet still unavoidably understated thanks to Joe Cecot for his help with the intricacies of *Ghosts* weapon mechanics. Lastly, as always, a huge thanks to Lindsey, Jake, and Ellie for being so supportive. I love you guys with all my heart.

Rich Hunsinger: Thanks to BradyGames' Leigh Davis and Tim Fitzpatrick for giving us the opportunity to work on this project. Thanks to Infinity Ward for their incredible hospitality, especially Pete, Kate, Sean, Bill, Simon, Kyle, DJ, and Tabari. Thanks for everything you did to make our trip awesome! Thanks to my wife Kate for just about everything—I love you!

Trevor Martin: I'd like to thank Leigh Davis and Tim Fitzpatrick for the opportunity to work on this project. Thanks to Phil, Jason, Darren, and Rich and his crew for all the good times and laughs. Big thanks to Infinity Ward for all the hospitality and for keeping my belly full during those long gaming sessions. Finally, thanks to my Mom, my girlfriend Haley, and all of my YouTube subscribers for supporting me on all of my crazy adventures!

Arthur "Tony" Davis: First, I would like to thank BradyGames and Infinity Ward for the great experience I had during this project. You ladies and gentlemen made my dream come true. I would like to say thank you to my family, Marques, Khyree, and, most of all, my princess that was in the hospital during our trip, Khyra. Dad loves you all. Last but not least, I'd like to thank the Sea Snipers and Rator for also including me in this. This is family—Semper Fi and Fratres!

Jon "Wally" Toney: I would like to thank my family for their support. Some of these trips couldn't happen without their help, and it is never taken for granted. Thanks to BradyGames and Activision for the opportunity to give gamers the information they crave. Also, a big thank you to Infinity Ward and their amazing staff for the hospitality, interest, and respect you show for what we do. We appreciate it.

Daniel Herrera: I would like to thank the men and women at BradyGames and Infinity Ward for this great opportunity. I'd like to thank my friends and family for all of the support. An especially important thank you goes out to my brother Sebastian; if anyone could encourage me to be better and reach my goals, it's him.

Jamison Carroll: I'd like to thank Leigh Davis and Tim Fitzpatrick at BradyGames for allowing me the opportunity to be a member of the team for this project. Thanks to all the members of our on-site guide team for some great memories. Thanks to all staff at Infinity Ward for the hospitality. Thanks to all of my family and friends for your support. And special thanks to Brooke—you are truly amazing and I love you.